THE LIFE OF
LOU REED

ALSO BY
Howard Sounes

Amy, 27
Fab: An Intimate Life of Paul McCartney
Heist
Seventies
The Wicked Game
Down the Highway: The Life of Bob Dylan
Bukowski in Pictures
Charles Bukowski: Locked in the Arms of a Crazy Life
Fred & Rose

For more information about Howard Sounes
and his books, visit his
website at www.howardsounes.com.

THE LIFE OF
LOU REED

NOTES FROM THE
VELVET
UNDERGROUND

Howard Sounes

DIVERSION
BOOKS

Diversion Books
A division of Diversion Publishing Corp.
443 Park Avenue South, suite 1004
New York, NY 10016
www.diversionbooks.com

For more information, email info@diversionbooks.com

First Diversion Books edition September 2019
Hardcover ISBN: 978-1-63576-638-7
eBook ISBN: 978-1-63576-641-7

First published in the United Kingdom by Transworld Publishers.

Printed in The United States of America

1 3 5 7 9 10 8 6 4 2
Library of Congress cataloging-in-publication data is available on file.

CONTENTS

I

CONEY ISLAND BABY

• 1942–59 •

ISTEN. **LOU REED HAS** fallen silent. That black-clad curmud-
geon, the rock 'n' roll poet they called the King of New York,
co-founder of the Velvet Underground band, master of the wry,
observational lyric, author of "Walk on the Wild Side," "Heroin"
and "Sweet Jane," among hundreds of extraordinary and some quite
ordinary songs, is dead. Lou lived so fast, he drank so much and he
took so many drugs that few expected him to live to seventy-one.
But now he has sung his last song. What was he really like?

ONE QUICK STORY SERVES as a paradigm. In the autumn of 1963,
when Lou was twenty-one, he drove to St. Lawrence University in
upstate New York with his college band to perform at a fraternity
weekend. The terms of the engagement were that LA and the Eldorados would play at a student dance on Friday night, then for
an hour on a pleasure boat on the St. Lawrence River on Saturday
afternoon, before performing at a fraternity party in the evening.

"I'm not playing on the boat," Lou announced when they arrived, having decided that this was beneath his dignity. The others looked at their band mate in exasperation. Lou was a slim young man of 140 pounds, five foot ten, with simian features, short, stubby fingers, bushy brown hair and clever brown eyes. The left eye was lazy, giving him a sly appearance. He spoke in a whiny, theatrical voice and gave the general impression of being trouble. "He was just a prick," says band mate Richard Mishkin, using a word that many friends chose to describe Lou over the years. Yet he was the heart and soul of LA and the Eldorados, their lead singer and guitarist, and they couldn't go on without him.

"You don't have a choice," Richard told him. "You are going to play on the boat and be happy. . . . They are paying us a lot of money, and you have to do it."

That was not the way to speak to Lou, ever. "Mishkin, fuck you!" he retorted, thrusting his right hand through a glass door. Lou laughed as he looked at the injury he had done to himself, blood streaming down his arm as he held his hand up.

"Because he doesn't have to play now," explains Richard, who took Lou to the hospital for stitches. "He's won!"

As he would show time and again during his long career, Lou would rather harm himself than be coerced into doing anything he didn't believe in. Such integrity is a mark of a true artist. It also helps explain why Lou never achieved as much success as he craved, or deserved.

THIS TALENTED, DIFFICULT MAN was born Lewis Alan Reed at Beth-El Hospital in Brooklyn, New York, on Monday, March 2, 1942. A story later emerged that his real name was Louis Firbank, and this name is still cited in books and articles; it is completely erroneous. Some friends called him by his given name of Lewis, which he didn't object to, though he disliked his middle name, but to most people he would always be Lou. "Lewis was his name, [but] it wasn't him," says his brother-in-law, Harold Weiner. "He was Lou."

The temperature fell below freezing the night Lou was born, bringing snow to the five boroughs of New York City, of which Brooklyn is the second largest and most populous: eighty-one square miles of tightly packed houses, tenements, shops and factories, bisected by pot-holed highways, tram lines and rust-brown elevated train tracks; the teeming borough separated from its more glamorous neighbor Manhattan by the East River, spanned by the majestic Brooklyn Bridge. It was wartime and the newspapers were full of stories of America's struggle with "the Japs," as well as the wider world war against the Hitler Axis. The mood at home was patriotic but jittery, with fears of attacks on the mainland. The day after Lou was born, to everyone's dismay, the *Brooklyn Eagle* reported the sinking of a US destroyer by a German U-boat off the coast of New Jersey. The paper also warned its readers that the lights would shine as usual at Brooklyn's fun fair, Coney Island, that summer, "but at the sound of an alert signal the entire amusement area will be blacked out." In a time that has passed into history, men and women hurrying home from work in the snow were formally dressed, nearly everybody wore a hat and an overcoat and most adults smoked cigarettes. New releases at the cinema included *Woman of the Year*, with Spencer Tracy and Katharine Hepburn; while Eddie Cantor promised to "keep you laughing" in black face in a Broadway show called *Banjo Eyes*, a production that would now be considered outrageously racist. Lou was capable of casual racism himself in later life.

There was a substantial African-American community in Brooklyn, part of the borough's heterogeneous mix of races and creeds, enlarged and diversified by waves of immigrants. Lou's family was part of that classic American story. His father, Sidney Joseph Rabinowitz, was born in New York in 1913, the son of Russian Jews who had immigrated to America to escape persecution. Sid's father,

Mendel, was a printer who went bankrupt during the Depression, so Sid had known hard times. At the outbreak of the Second World War, the family was living in a tenement in Borough Park.

"I know what it is like to be on the outside. I know what it's like to have an unhappy childhood," Lou said in 1992, going to the root of his formative experiences. His principal problem was with his father. Lou's sister concedes that dad had his faults. Sid was "controlling and rigid" and, like his son, "[he] could be a verbal bully." At the end of his life Lou told his friend the artist Julian Schnabel a story about how he had once reached out to his father, only for Sid to hit him. "He put his hand near his father, and his father kind of smacked him. He never got over that," reports Schnabel. "He felt the cruelty of that." Father and son may have been too alike. Sid had a quick wit, he enjoyed music and had ambitions to become an author. His mother persuaded him to study to become an accountant instead, a steady job that enabled him to join the middle class, but not work in which he could express himself. He was, perhaps, a frustrated man.

Radical politics thrived in blue-collar Brooklyn in the forties. Sid's cousin Shulamit "Shirley" Rabinowitz caused such a stir in the garment industry, agitating for better pay, that the local newspapers nicknamed her Red Shirley. Sid was also active in the labor unions, "which was considered leftist and the FBI was investigating, so he changed [his name] to protect his father, ostensibly," explains Lou's sister. So Sid Rabinowitz became Sid Reed. Soon after adopting his new name, Sid met Toby Futterman, who would become Lou's mother, when they were working together at a court service company. Toby's background was almost identical to Sid's in that her parents were European Jewish immigrants. She was born in 1920, making her seven years his junior. Although her father died when she was young, putting a financial strain on the family, the Futtermans were better off than the Rabinowitzes, owning their house in a more salubrious part of Brooklyn. Judith Futterman, one of Lou's cousins on his mother's side, became a professional singer who performed with the

Metropolitan Opera. Toby was vivacious and attractive, crowned Queen of the Stenographers in a 1939 office beauty contest, but she lacked confidence. "An anxious individual throughout her life, she took a traditional role with my father, always subservient to him," notes their daughter.

Toby married Sid not long after they met, and Lou was their first child. He was always closer to his mother

1620 Avenue V, Brooklyn.

than his father, taking after Toby in looks, as well as inheriting her chronic anxiety, something he learned to hide in public. Their first family home was a small house on Avenue V in the Sheepshead Bay area of Brooklyn. Shortly after the end of the war (Sid was registered for service, but not called up), they moved to a larger house in leafy Midwood. The Reeds were living there in 1947 when Lou's sister was born. There has been some confusion over the years regarding the size and makeup of Lou's family, with one author writing since Lou's death that he had a younger brother. He did not. His sister, his only sibling, was named Margaret Ellen, but soon acquired the endearing nickname of Bunny. In adult life she became a psychotherapist and assumed the name Merrill, thinking Bunny too silly for work, but Lou always called her Bunny. The siblings were alike: dark, good-looking, sharp-tongued, with the same strong New York accent, both somewhat controlling; and they were close. One of Bunny's earliest memories of Lou was waiting at the window for him to come home from school. "And when he came home, I was so happy, and that never changed. I always adored him."

These were the innocent early years of childhood when Lou discovered the pleasure of drinking egg cream milkshakes made with soda in the milk bars on Kings Highway, which he sang about nostalgically in his 1996 song "Egg Cream." In the humid New York summer, Lou would have been taken to the swimming pool at Brownsville and to Coney Island. He was part of an extended Jewish immigrant family with numerous relatives who spoke with East European accents. He began his education at a local redbrick elementary public school, where he played stick ball and stoop ball in the playground, as he describes in "My Old Man" on the album *Growing Up in Public*, a song that refers to a bullying father who beat his wife. Lou said he wrote the song for his father, but denied that Sid hit Toby. Throughout his career he was at pains to explain that he saw himself as a writer who created characters, in the way a novelist does, a position that allowed him to write from different points of view, to invent things, and to distance himself from his material. "I see myself as a writer. Whether I'm a nice guy, whether I'm a liar, whether I'm immoral, should have nothing to do with it."

The family left Brooklyn in 1951 for suburban Nassau County, Long Island; "the armpit of the world," Lou called it. Topographically, Long Island is the flat, narrow strip of land that extends east from New York City. Long Island Sound laps the ritzy *Great Gatsby* communities of the North Shore. The utilitarian South Shore faces the Atlantic Ocean. Long Island becomes less populated and more expensive the farther east one travels on Route 27, until the dwindling highway reaches the millionaire homes of the Hamptons.

The Reeds bought a new ranch-style house at 35 Oakfield Avenue in Freeport, an expanding middle-class community on the South Shore. The house was a three-bedroom, single-story brick building on a street of identical homes, separated by driveways and lawns: the classic 1950s American abode. These were the unremarkable environs of Lou's early life. It was evidently too dull a backstory for Lou, who sometimes gave the impression that he was from a

35 Oakfield Avenue, Freeport.

wealthy Long Island family. "My parents were self-made million-aires. On paper they were very rich," he told Melody Maker in 1976. This was fiction. Sid Reed was a Certified Public Accountant (CPA) who worked as the treasurer of a Long Island packaging company. Lou was no more the son of a millionaire than he was a child of the streets, though he also adopted that image. "[Later] he decided to portray himself as a guy who had grown up on the mean streets of New York City, when in fact he grew up in middle-class Freeport," notes Allan Hyman, who lived around the corner and went through school and college with Lou. Even before Freeport, the Reeds had lived in nice areas of Brooklyn. Still, Lou struggled at first in the city's public-school system. "The reason they moved out of Brooklyn to Long Island is that Lou was getting beat up on the way to school," says his first wife, Bettye Kronstad.

Lou started school in Freeport in fifth grade, when he was nine years old. He walked to school each morning, past the elevated train track that carried commuters into Manhattan, past the water tower and the United Methodist Church, all of which were landmarks of a suburb with the atmosphere of a small town. He was an honor-roll student in middle school, and was assessed as having a relatively high IQ of 132. Although his family was not particularly religious, Lou celebrated his bar mitzvah and took time off for Jewish holy days. "We were Jewish, but my father was rather opposed to organized religion," says Bunny. "He was a cultural Jew, I think you might say." The children were indulged. Sid acquired a piano so they could take music lessons. Home movies show Lou as an apparently happy, toothy little kid frolicking in the yard with his sister and playing at the beach. One summer he worked as an attendant at Jones Beach, which entailed wearing a sailor's suit and cap—an early echo of the lyrics of "Heroin"—as he collected litter with a stick pin, an episode he alludes to on the album *Take No Prisoners*.

There were problems, though. Lou was bullied again at junior high in Freeport, according to Bunny, who says he was "beaten up routinely after school," and he began to suffer panic attacks. "It was obvious that Lou was becoming increasingly anxious and avoidant and resistant to most socializing unless it was on his terms," she states, in the jargon of psychotherapy. "He was possessed with a fragile temperament. His hyper-focus on things he liked led him to music, and it was there that he found himself. Self-taught, he began playing the guitar, absorbing every musical influence he could."

Music came to Lou initially through AM radio, and he developed Catholic tastes, enjoying doo-wop, rock 'n' roll, modern jazz and gospel. A keen reader, words were equally important to him. Ian Fleming's James Bond stories were among his favorite books as a child. As a teenager, Jack Kerouac's *On the Road* made an impression. "He was a very big fan of Jack Kerouac. I remember when he read *On the Road*. That was a big deal, and he wanted to talk to me about it, and I couldn't get that whole existential concept," says Allan Hyman. While other boys snickered over *Playboy*, precocious Lou read the erotic French novel *The Story of O*.

Yet in many respects he remained a conventional middle-class teen. He was smartly turned out, remaining a neat, organized person throughout his life. He enjoyed basketball and tennis, and joined the track and field team at Freeport High. In his song "Coney Island Baby," Lou sang about a boy who yearned to play football for his school coach. Was this autobiographical? Lou had a friend on the team, running back Jerome Jackson, one of the few African-American students at Freeport High. He doesn't recall Lou expressing any interest in trying out for Bill Ashley, who coached the Freeport High Red Devils, and says that Lou was one of the quieter kids in school. As with many writers, he was someone who lived much of his life in his imagination. He wasn't a jock, nor was he much of a mixer. "Lou wasn't that popular. He was very friendly, but you had to be in his circle for him to warm up to you." Their friendship was based on music. Jerome sang with the Valets, one of several high-school bands Lou was involved in. Another band, the oddly named Tretoads, performed "Mickey Mouse Rock" at a school variety show, while the most significant of Lou's school bands was the Shades.

Composed of Lou and two older schoolboys, Phil Harris and Al Walters, the Shades performed at the 1958 Freeport High variety show in sunglasses, hence the name. Lou and Phil wrote a couple of songs together, "So Blue" and "Leave Her for Me." "I wrote all of 'So Blue' and helped Lou out with 'Leave Her for Me,'" Harris recalled. "Lou played all of the music, but we both sort of kicked around some chords during the writing phase." Remarkably, they recorded these songs in New York City with a professional sax player, King Curtis, Phil singing lead vocals while Lou played guitar and added backup vocals. The music was generic, the lyrics formulaic, but the recording was good enough to be released as a single on the Time label in 1958 under the band name of the Jades (it turned out that there was another group called the Shades). Although the disc made no impression on the national charts, in a year of novelty hits like

"The Purple People Eater" and "The Chipmunk Song," many kids in Freeport bought Lou's first record.

Adventures of this kind brought Lou into conflict with his father, who fretted about his son getting involved in the music business. This was the start of their problems. Lou complained about Sid to friends, telling Allan that his dad was one of the biggest assholes in the world. Allan was surprised. He liked Lou's parents. "For whatever reason, Lou had a whole number going with [Sid]—always—and I don't know why," he says. "I remember that he was always upset with him for one reason or another." There was an increasingly bad atmosphere at home. "The stage was set. Anxious, controlling parents, limited communication, a society that valued secrecy, underlying mental-health issues," comments Bunny. "Verbal fights between Lou and my parents erupted—about going into the city, about the dangers he might confront. My parents were frightened, angry, bewildered." There was a lot of yelling. After a period of crisis, however, things calmed down again. "Remarkably, during Lou's senior year in high school, there were moments of normalcy at home," adds Bunny. "Family dinners could be enjoyable. Lou and my father were both extremely witty, with erudite, dry senses of humor and remarkable literary sensibilities. I enjoyed their verbal jousting, as did they."

By the time he was seventeen, Lou had started to write in earnest: song lyrics, poems and stories in which he began to express aspects of his sexuality. Allan Hyman was shocked by what he read. "He would write poems and he would write short stories that had a gay theme about them." There was violence in these stories, with characters punished for their sexuality. Sex and violence would be themes in Lou's adult writing, often linked. "In some of the stories the hero would end up beating up the [other] person, catching somebody having sex in a public bathroom and having the hero of the story beat them up." Allan further claims Lou told him that a man paid him to watch him masturbate in a local park. He thought this "kind of odd," but didn't draw conclusions. "The idea of being gay was not something I had even heard of. I knew a couple of kids in school who appeared to be, you know, gay, but nobody called them gay. [We] just thought they were sissies." He didn't think of Lou as a sissy. Rather, his stories seemed to be part of his emerging rebelliousness, and who knew how much of what he said and wrote was true? Lou's sexuality remained enigmatic throughout his life, a conundrum to many friends and, one suspects, himself. Was he gay or straight? As the facts emerge, we see that his sexuality was mutable and not easily defined. If a label must be applied, Lou was bisexual, though he never used that word himself and didn't seem to welcome categorization. Nevertheless, importantly, his sexuality set him apart from society from an early age.

Even by the standards of teenage boys, Lou's behavior with girls at high school was gauche and crude, probably because he was un-sure of himself. When a girl in Gene's candy store asked Lou one day if he'd had his hair cut, for example, he snapped, "Oh, fuck you, Carol!" at a time when middle-class American boys simply didn't talk to girls that way. This was the wholesome era of Pat Boone, *I Love Lucy* and the hula-hoop craze. His friends were shocked. Then there was dating. "Lou never had girlfriends," says school-friend Richard Sigal, meaning that Lou didn't have a steady high-school girlfriend like Richard and Allan did. "Lou had one-night stands. Lou had dirty girls." Before the contraceptive pill, fumbling around in the back seats at the Freeport Theater, getting a hand job in a parked car or "dry humping" (rubbing against your sweetheart with your clothes on) were the early sexual experiences for their generation, but Lou was quick to boast that he had gone "all the way." He'd met an older girl named Bonnie who, he said, allowed him special favors. She had also introduced Lou, an avid cigarette smoker since fourteen, to marijuana, which was seemingly his en-tree into the world of stimulants. Bonnie was evidently quite a char-acter, and she must have left a strong impression. One wonders if

Lou had her in mind when he wrote "Sweet Bonnie Brown" for the Velvet Underground. Drug use of any kind was highly unusual in fifties Freeport. "[When the rest of us] were drinking beer, Lou was rolling joints, which was unheard of," says Richard, while Lou's sister confirms that he got into drugs as a schoolboy. "I do not know how much of the drug use was apparent to my parents."

Allan and Richard sometimes tried to fix Lou up with a girl so they could double-date, now that they were old enough to borrow their parents' cars, but double-dating with Lou rarely turned out well. One weekend Allan persuaded Lou to accompany him to New Jersey, where he knew a girl named Susan who had offered to invite a friend for Lou. Susan came to the door to greet the boys, her eight-year-old sister simultaneously sliding down the bannister to welcome them. Lou asked the child: "Do you always masturbate on the bannister?"

"Get out!" Susan shouted. It was the end of the date.

There was an equally disastrous double-date with Richard Sigal. One night when Richard's parents were away, he invited Lou over for an evening with himself and his girlfriend, who had brought a friend for Lou. He showed up late, apparently drunk or high, and asked for a Scotch, which Richard gave him, in one of his father's crystal tumblers. Lou then nonchalantly mentioned that he had another girl outside, passed out in his parents' car. He went to check on her. "She's OK," he said, when he came back. "But I dropped the glass." Richard looked outside to see his father's expensive tumbler smashed on the drive. Then he looked at the poor girl who had come to the house to meet Lou. He felt like hitting him. "To this day I can't tell you why I didn't—he deserved it." The evening was ruined.

When Lou performed at the annual variety show at Freeport High in his senior year, he did so as part of a number of student groups, including a foursome made up of himself, Johnny Dekam, Richard Sigal and Judy Titus, one of the most popular girls in school. Lou had them perform under the name CHDs, later explaining to Judy that the letters were a rearrangement of DHC, for Dry-Hump Club. "They

Lou and the CHDs, Freeport High, 1959. Richard Sigal on left.

totally embarrassed me," says Judy. The senior prom was a couple of months later. Allan, who chauffeured his girlfriend and Lou and his date around town for the evening, recalls that Lou made a move in the back seat while he and his girlfriend were in front. "He's in the back seat banging this girl, and my date is getting angrier and angrier. It's like they don't care that we were in the front seat." Allan's girlfriend complained that what the others were doing was disgusting.

"Fuck you," replied Lou. "Don't look if you don't like it."

This was typical of his behavior, and part of his emerging persona as a *provocateur*. His friends found it entertaining initially but

Lou's high school yearbook photo.

He listed "basketball," "music," and "girls" as his interests.

later came to think of Lou as a selfish person. "Lou felt there was no one else in the world other than him. And he was nasty. He was a person who could [not] care less how you felt," says Allan.

Despite such juvenile and boorish behavior, despite the dope smoking and conflicts with his father, Lou was far from a high-school dropout. When he graduated in June 1959, he was ranked eighty-fourth out of the 312 students in his year, and appeared to be as clean-cut as any of his contemporaries. In light of the fact that he went on to become associated with a life of dissipation, the caption under his yearbook photo seems comically guileless: "Tall, dark-haired Lou likes basketball, music and, naturally, girls. He was a valuable participant on the track team. He is one of Freeport's great contributors to the recording world. As for the immediate future, Lou has no plans, but will take life as it comes."

IN FACT, THE PLAN was for Lou to pursue his education at Syracuse University in upstate New York, almost three hundred miles northwest of Freeport, where Allan was also bound. The boys took a trip to look at the campus together. Then Lou changed his mind, deciding he would rather go to New York University in Manhattan, where he had also been offered a place. He felt that Syracuse was too provincial and middle class and he wanted to be in the city. "I feel it will be better for my writing," he told his friend.

He moved into a dormitory on the University Heights campus of New York University, in the Bronx, in September 1959. Living alone in Manhattan, away from his family and friends for the first time, Lou became anxious and depressed, to the extent that he suffered a breakdown. Bunny recalls the dramatic events that took place that autumn. "Sometime during his freshman year at NYU, when I was twelve, my parents went into the city and returned with Lou, limp and unresponsive. I was terrified and uncomprehending. They said he had a 'nervous breakdown.' The family secret was tightly kept and the entire matter was concealed, from relatives, from friends. It was our private and unspoken burden. . . .

"My parents finally sought professional help for Lou. I heard only the superficial pieces of what was going on. My mother came into my room and told me that they thought he might have schizophrenia. She said that the doctors told her it was because she had not picked him up enough as an infant but had let him cry in his room." Toby sobbed as she explained herself to her daughter: "The pediatrician told me to do that! He said that's how you teach a baby to go to sleep." A psychiatrist wrote, in a letter that Lou later had framed, that he suffered from delusions and hallucinations and reported seeing spiders crawling on the walls. "Lou was not able to function at that time. He was depressed, anxious and socially avoidant. If people came into our home, he hid in his room." He also hid under a desk. "He might sit with us, but he looked deadeyed, noncommunicative. I remember one evening when all of us were sitting in our den, watching television together. Out of nowhere, Lou began laughing maniacally. We all sat frozen in place. My parents did nothing, said nothing, and ignored it, as if it was not taking place."

All this happened in the short space of time between Lou enrolling at NYU in September 1959 and the Thanksgiving holiday in November. When Allan visited his friend at home during the break, Lou told him the story. "I think I'm having a nervous breakdown," he said.

"Why do you think that?"

"I'm very depressed and I'm having a lot of problems, and I'm taking some [medication]. I feel like crap." Looking back, Allan says Lou often seemed to be depressed. "He was always looking on the dark side of things, rather than having a positive view."

When Lou didn't improve, a psychiatrist referred him to Creedmoor Psychiatric Center near Freeport, a forbidding mental hospital, in the plain language of the day, with the grim appearance and high security of a prison. It was here that he received electroconvulsive therapy (ECT), a controversial form of shock treatment used to treat severe depression. "I don't know which psychiatrist recommended the Electro Shock Therapy [sic]," comments Bunny. "I assume that Lou could not have been in any shape to really understand the treatment or the side effects. It may well be that he was fearful that he would be committed to a psychiatric hospital and not allowed home if he did not agree to the treatment. . . . Was he suicidal? Impaired by drugs? Schizophrenic? Or a victim of psychiatric incompetence and misdiagnosis?" These are questions his sister poses but cannot answer. The precise nature and cause of his breakdown was seemingly a mystery to the family in 1959, and it remained a mystery because they never discussed it. Something shameful had happened, which they were unable to confront.

ECT was given as a course of treatment: twenty-four shocks over several weeks, in Lou's case. He was required to fast before being strapped to a gurney. Muscle-relaxant drugs and an anaesthetic were administered. A gag was placed in his mouth to stop him from biting his tongue. Electrodes were then attached to the sides of his head, and an alternating current passed briefly through his brain. This was the radical, frightening part of the treatment. Patients lost consciousness instantly. The body went into seizure. Although insensible, Lou grimaced, looking as if he was in pain, his fists clenching and his legs trying to kick, his whole body trembling briefly before going limp. The treatment had first come into use in Europe in the late thirties after it was observed that schizophrenics felt better after a fit. The electric shock is meant to induce a fit artificially. It is not clearly understood why this should be beneficial, but some patients say they feel less depressed after ECT, and the treatment is still used. There are, however, side effects.

"Our family was wrenched apart the day they began those wretched treatments," laments Bunny. "I watched my brother as my parents assisted him coming back into our home afterwards, unable to walk, stupor-like. It damaged his short-term memory horribly and throughout his life he struggled with memory retention, probably directly as a result of those treatments." She further claims that Lou's breakdown, and the therapy, "set in motion the dissolution of my family." Lou came to blame his parents for subjecting him to ECT, mostly Sid, against whom he developed what Bunny terms "incredible rage." The closest he came to expressing this was in his song "Kill Your Sons," singing that he was told he would be able to live at home if he accepted the treatment, rather than being confined to a hospital, but his memory was so bad after the shocks that he couldn't even concentrate to read a book.

Years later Lou gave an interview in which he suggested that ECT was administered because he had homosexual inclinations. "That's what was recommended in Rockland County then to discourage homosexual feelings," he told *Creem* magazine in 1979. Victor Bockris suggested in his 1994 biography of Reed that ECT was administered because his parents wanted to "cure" his homosexuality. While Lou was given ECT at a time when homosexuality was classified as a mental illness in the United States,[1] and ECT was sometimes used as a "treatment" for homosexuality, his sister

---

1   The American Psychiatric Association classified homosexuality as a mental illness until 1973.

rejects the theory "that ECT was undertaken because Lou had confessed bisexual urges." She believes her parents simply wanted to
help Lou at a time when he was suffering a full-blown breakdown
(not merely being wayward and showing mood swings, as Bockris
writes), and they followed the advice they were given. "My father,
controlling and rigid, was attempting to solve a situation that was
beyond him. My mother was terrified and certain of her own im-
plicit guilt since they had told her this was due to poor mothering,"
comments Bunny. "It has been suggested by some authors that ECT
was undertaken because Lou had confessed to bisexual urges. How
simplistic and unrealistic. He was depressed, weird, anxious, avoidant. My parents were many things—anxious, controlling—but they
were blazing liberals. Homophobic they were not. They were caught
in a bewildering web, of guilt, fear and poor psychiatric care. Did
they make a mistake in not challenging the doctor's recommendation for ECT? Absolutely. I have no doubt that they regretted it
every day until the day they died."

It is an unhappy story. Bunny believes that the accusations Lou
later made against his father, or implied in songs, stem from this period. "His accusations, of violence, a lack of love, seemed rooted in
that time. The stories he related—of being hit, of being treated like
an inanimate object—seemed total fantasy to me. I must say I never
saw my father raise a hand to anyone, certainly not us. Nor did I
see a lack of love for his son during our childhood." Yet the anger
and bitterness Lou developed were real, and vital to his art. Bunny
poses the essential rhetorical question: "Would Lou have become
the artist he became without the furious anger that the treatments
engendered?" Anger was one of the motifs of his songwriting, the
anger of an outsider who specialized in writing about damaged,
neurotic people like himself.

II

ON TO THE
DARKENED SEA

• 1960–64 •

LOU WAS UNABLE TO resume his studies at New York University. His name was removed from the register in May 1960, by which time he was eighteen years old and deeply unhappy. "I was miserable when I was young," he later said. "I wouldn't want to be eighteen again."

Following treatments at Creedmoor hospital and the Payne Whitney Psychiatric Clinic in New York, he recuperated at home in Freeport, looked after by his mother. He later spoke tenderly of Toby Reed nursing him back to health. By contrast, he remained furious with his father, though Sid probably felt awful about what had happened. The Reeds tiptoed around their son, frightened to do or say anything that might upset him, and Lou learned to exploit their guilt; this became their unhealthy relationship. And he remained emotionally fragile. Bunny reveals that even after he recovered from his breakdown, her brother "suffered from anxiety and panic attacks throughout his life."

It was several months before he felt well enough to make another attempt at college. In September 1960, he enrolled at Syracuse University, where he had originally intended to go. Allan Hyman was now beginning his sophomore year, and he was having a wonderful time. He tried to take Lou under his wing when he arrived on campus, introducing him to his fraternity brothers with a view to Lou becoming a fraternity member, which was, he says, "a huge mistake." Lou was more rebellious than ever, projecting the image of a tortured intellectual musician-writer, part beatnik, part folk singer, part James Dean from *Rebel without a Cause*, a film that had a major impact on more than one budding rock star.

Although Allan asked Lou to dress smartly for the fraternity party, he arrived in his scruffiest clothes. "How could you wear that?" Allan asked him. While they were talking, a senior member of the fraternity came over. "Mike, I'd like you to meet Lou Reed," said Allan, making the introduction.

The senior looked the newcomer up and down. "There's no way you will become a member of this fraternity," he told him.

"You fucking asshole," replied Lou. "Do you think I would join this fraternity as long as you are a member? You are the biggest asshole I have ever met in my entire life. You should simply kill yourself."

Despite this inauspicious beginning, Lou and Allan remained friends, and they formed a college band, the aforementioned LA and the Eldorados, the "L" and the "A" standing for Lou and Allan (who played drums). A changing cast of musicians included Richard Mishkin on piano and bass, and Nelson Slater, a Canadian art student, who sang and played guitar.

Sometimes they used the name Pasha and the Prophets, while Lou also played with another college band called the All-night Workers. The Eldorados were a dance band, essentially, with a regular Friday-night gig at a local golf club, as well as performing at college dances and fraternity parties all over the state. They wore matching velvet jackets onstage and drove to gigs in Richard's Chrysler, which had the band name painted across the trunk. Although Lou was a limited singer and a rudimentary guitarist, he was their front man and leader, singing most of the songs and choosing the set list, which typically included covers of Ray Charles and Jimmy Reed tunes, and pop hits of the day like "Angel Baby." Moody and unpredictable, he would refuse to play at all if he got out of bed on the wrong side, and he liked to shock audiences by performing a composition of his own called "Fuck Around Blues," which sometimes got the Eldorados fired. "He was definitely crazy, like, 'Man, he's nuts!'—that kind of crazy," says Richard Mishkin, adding that Lou told the band about the shock treatment he had received. He was angry about it, but he also used it as part of his image. As Richard got to know Lou better, he came to a more precise diagnosis of his personality. "In some ways he was kind of a borderline-personality type, in terms of narcissism [and] compulsive behavior. He had visions of who [he was] and what he wanted to do that didn't necessarily coincide with anything else. Lou just didn't give a shit about people, in general. If he stepped on you, it didn't matter. . . . It was about advancing himself."

There was music in the air at Syracuse in the early 1960s. Several contemporaries went on to have professional careers in music, including Lou's friend Garland Jeffreys, a singer-songwriter who supported him in concert in the 1970s. His college band mate Nelson Slater later made an album for RCA, though neither he nor Garland rivaled Lou in terms of success. Nelson says that Lou learned guitar phrases from him, and claims to hear these guitar licks in "Vicious" and "Walk on the Wild Side." "I showed him the chords and changes that I thought were great, and Lou was very good at picking up things and utilizing them." Nelson was impressed by Lou, whom he recalls as one of the big characters at Syracuse, but not everybody saw him that way. "I remember a very quiet, introverted type of person who would hang around the arty-type places in town," says another contemporary, Felix Cavaliere, who went on to have a

Lou performed at Syracuse with LA and the Eldorados. Richard Mishkin is seen playing bass (left).

notable career in music as a member of the Young Rascals. "Unless you really got to know him, you couldn't penetrate that [façade]."

One of Lou's most significant college friends was Lincoln Swados, an awkward, gawky boy who shared his interests in music and literature and had a similar history of mental-health issues. After Lincoln started complaining of hearing voices, his parents sent him to a psychiatric hospital, where, like Lou, he underwent ECT. They roomed together for a while, sharing a cluttered, unsanitary student pit with a piece of pizza stuck to the ceiling. "There wasn't even a space to sit down," says Richard Sigal, recalling a visit he made to see Lou. Richard couldn't find his friend at first in the gloomy room when he let himself in. "I was looking at the bed, and in the dark I saw a hand and wrist sticking out from the sheets, so I kicked the bed and the sheet comes off and it's Lou—rubbing sleep out of his eyes."

"What are you doing? It's five o'clock in the afternoon."

Lou, a lifelong insomniac, explained that he was in the habit of staying up all night writing. "The sheet was gray from use," says Richard. "Then I looked closer and there were scribblings all over the sheets, so I guess when he had a thought in his head he'd write it on the sheet."

Although he kept irregular hours, Lou was a busy and active student who took a wide range of classes at Syracuse, including journalism, theology, drama, creative writing and botany. In Film Appreciation, he directed a short, silent film featuring fellow student Peter Maloney, later a stage and screen actor, whom he cast as a clown, "[just] me, a clown, putting makeup on. . . . It was fun." He also directed at least one play and was an amateur deejay with his own campus radio show, *Excursion on a Wobbly Rail*, named after a piece of cool modern jazz by the Cecil Taylor Quartet. As well as jazz, Lou played folk music, the blues, doo-wop and rock 'n' roll on air, and he was always looking for new discs to spin. Late one night he heard music coming from the floor below him in the dormitory and traced the sound to the room of student Jim Tucker, who grew up not far from Lou on Long Island. Jim's high-school friend Holmes Sterling Morrison was staying over. Known as Sterling or Sterl, Morrison was a loquacious, lanky youth of six foot three who liked to drink beer, chase girls and play guitar. He was also from Long Island, born the same year as Lou in nearby East Meadow. His widow Martha shades in the background: "Blue collar. His mother was a cocktail waitress. His stepfather was a cop." Having begun his college education at the University of Illinois, studying physics, Sterling was thinking of transferring to Syracuse. He never actually enrolled; he just hung around the dorm for a while. He and Jim were playing Lightnin' Hopkins records when there was a knock at the door. "We thought it was the person in charge of the dormitory coming down to complain," Sterling recalled. "Instead it was the guy upstairs, who turned out to be Lou, and he needed records because he had a campus radio show and was running out of blues and that sort of thing."

One day soon after this encounter, a brass band struck up outside the dormitory as the Reserve Officers' Training Corps (ROTC, a form of military training) began band practice in the yard. Lou claimed to have been dismissed from ROTC in his freshman year at Syracuse after he pointed a gun at his commanding officer, a story he made part of his official biography when he became a solo artist. It sounds like something he either invented or exaggerated. None of his contemporaries remember it happening, though they remember Lou saying it did. Sterling was listening to the ROTC band when, as if in opposition to the martial music, an electric guitar rang out from Lou's room.

"Then I knew that Lou was a guitar player, too. And we just went from there." Sterling and Lou jammed together at Syracuse, forming the basis of a friendship that developed significantly when they met up again in New York City in 1965.

IN SEPTEMBER 1961, FRESHMAN student Shelley Albin was getting a lift across campus when the guy who was driving her pointed to a student walking by the side of the road. "This is Lou Reed," he said, slowing to offer him a ride. "He's really evil."

Shelley was intrigued by the young man who got into the car. He didn't look evil. In his beatnik/folkie phase, Lou was dressed in black corduroy trousers, a shirt and jacket, his hair just long enough to touch his collar. "He was cute," says Shelley. "His mouth would curl up. He had good skin. Slightly built. Five ten maybe, skinny . . . a small, lightweight guy, and not at all muscly. . . . He had the build of a twelve-year-old, [and] a lot of curly hair." She watched Lou in the rearview mirror and saw that he was looking at her. She turned to meet his gaze. He was trying to make an impression. "When we looked at each other in the eye in the car it was kind of funny:

I know what you are up to here, it's an act. He was only in the car two minutes, [but] when he got out I knew I was going to hear from him, and I did within an hour."

This was the start of Lou's first significant love affair, one that inspired several important songs, including "Pale Blue Eyes," in which Lou quoted Shelley telling him off. "I [told him], 'Down for you is up. You like to be depressed. . . . Just don't work it [out] on me.'" She says that another Velvet Underground classic, "I'll Be Your Mirror," was also based on a discussion they had. "Those are words that I said to him . . . but it's always attributed to Nico." Girlfriends of songwriters often believe that they know the "real" story behind famous songs, and songwriters have been known to flatter girls by leading them to think that they inspired certain songs, whereas inspiration often comes from sundry sources. Although Shelley was certainly an important muse, she is unlikely to have been Lou's only source of inspiration. His literary influences should never be overlooked. "Pale Blue Eyes" is a phrase in William Burroughs's *Junky*: "He looked at me with his pale blue eyes that seemed to have no depth at all." He may likewise have borrowed inspiration for "I'll Be Your Mirror" from another favorite book, John Rechy's *City of Night*, in which the masochist Neil says: "Youll [sic] exist in My Eyes! I'll be a mirror!"

More specifically, Lou mentioned Shelley by name in the original version of "I Can't Stand It," while other songs, including "New Age," may include references to their relationship. Shelley was the kind of attractive, intelligent, friendly girl who could inspire a boy to write songs. She was Jewish, from Illinois, majoring in art history. When she arrived on campus, she dressed conventionally in long skirts and cardigans, but like Lou she had a bohemian streak and soon began to wear more informal clothes. She was intrigued by Lou from the start. "I knew from the second I met him this wasn't an ordinary person." One of the first things he told her was the story of his ECT. "That was like his introductory bit. 'This horrible

Shelley Albin.

thing happened to me . . . I'm tortured, and I don't have any memory, and I'm this and I'm that, and I'm a little weird for today's college kid, and just a little dangerous.'"

"You just don't scare me," she said.

They started to date. "Look," Lou told a friend proudly, "you couldn't do better."

The fact that Lou now had a regular girlfriend was significant. It wasn't until the late 1970s that he identified himself in public as gay, having previously danced around the subject. In one interview, he reflected on his youth and suggested that he had been acting straight with girls at college when he felt attracted to male students. He had a crush on one boy in particular, but never did anything about it, and spoke of the torment he went through. "I remember that time in college, sitting around, trying to get myself together so I could 'do it right'—and I resent it. It was a very big drag," he said, suggesting plausibly that this embittered him. Bitterness was one of his characteristics. "If the forbidden thing is love, then you spend most of your time playing with hate." He added that his lack of interest in women attracted girls, perversely. "Being gay, I have found that so many women—deluded creatures that they are—are attracted to you because you're not interested in them . . . it came across as the ultimate cool."

While this rings true, it isn't the whole story. Lou had an active heterosexual life in college and afterwards, so much so that girlfriends like Shelley struggle to see him as gay. "I never thought of him as being gay at all, or even bisexual." Rather, it seemed to Shelley, and women who came after her, that Lou flirted with homosexuality to create an image and get a reaction. "He always walked in a very effeminate way, but that was a very studied thing," she says. He admired handsome men, but she says that this was like a joke. "There was a guy that we both liked very much [who] was in a lot of my classes . . . Lou said, 'I really like him, I'm going to get him.' [I] said, 'No, no, he's for me.' Neither one of us did anything about it. Maybe he did . . . I doubt it."

Shelley gained a deeper understanding of her boyfriend at Christmas when he invited her home. Lou had recently acquired a dog named Seymour, the first of several dogs he owned over the years, but he seemed incapable of looking after Seymour at college. Part of the reason for the trip home was to give the dog to his mother. Shelley hadn't been at Oakfield Avenue long before she concluded that Lou was spoiled by Toby Reed. "Lou was, in his way, very dependent on his mother and very close to his mother, very much a mother's boy [and] a Jewish Prince. . . . Lou could manipulate his parents very easily at home. I saw him do that." He seemed to delight in annoying his father. Shelley noticed Lou exaggerating his effeminate side in front of Sid. "I could see that [Sid] was frustrated with Lou being effeminate, and [Lou] would act super-effeminate in his presence. He would flip his hands and wiggle his ass." Despite what Lou told her about his father, Shelley liked Sid. She was learning not to believe everything Lou said. "When you looked at this man, he had a twinkle in his eye and a ready, warm smile." Many of Lou's friends agree that Lou misrepresented his father. "He gave off to me an aura of being absolutely warm, absolutely one hundred percent concerned about Lou as a parent [and] mystified by Lou's behavior."

Sid was evidently pleased that Lou had brought Shelley home. He increased his allowance so Lou could take her out, and offered the couple the use of the family car. Lou drove Shelley to the Hayloft, a nightclub in nearby Baldwin. "I don't remember if he told me ahead of time we were going to a gay bar." Although Lou's straight Long Island friends avoided the Hayloft assiduously, Lou was a regular at

the club, where he also worked briefly. When Richard Sigal questioned Lou about his part-time job, Lou said that the male customers sometimes touched him. "What do you do about it?"

"I just laugh."

"Lou was an experimenter," concludes Richard, a sociologist in
adult life who lectured on what he calls "deviant behavior." "I think
he probably experimented with everything at one time or another.
I've always looked at his sexual adventures that way, because as a
kid I had a feeling that Lou was attracted to boys, [yet] he ended up
being married three times. So he obviously liked women."

It was at the Hayloft that Lou probably first encountered drag
queens and transgender people, for whom he developed a fascination. Candy Darling, whom Lou wrote about in "Candy Says"
and "Walk on the Wild Side," was the alter ego of James Slattery
from nearby Massapequa, Long Island, and Shelley believes that
Lou may have known him initially at the Hayloft, getting to know
him better later in New York City. Shelley took her visit to the gay
club in stride, enjoying a dance with a woman. "He thought it was
wonderful that I was dancing with a woman . . . and he was trying
to get me to go home, or out in the parking lot with the girl I was
dancing with, which was not at all what I was interested in, but he
was always setting up a scenario."

During the Christmas break, Lou also drove Shelley into Manhattan—to buy drugs in Harlem. Surprisingly, the thirty-mile ride
into the city was the scariest part of the expedition. With his poor
eyesight and limited concentration, Lou was a bad driver. "I remember thinking, *Oh my God, this is horrible, he's just the worst driver
in the world!* I was much more frightened of his driving than going to Harlem." Then, as now, drugs were available at the corner
of Lexington Avenue and 125th Street, the junction Lou invoked
in the first verse of "I'm Waiting for the Man"; also from connections in the nearby brownstone apartments. "My memory is that
[he said], 'We have to pick up some drugs,' and that it was heroin."

They went into a brownstone, where they met a guy Lou seemed to know, sat around talking for ten minutes, then left to hear some jazz in Greenwich Village. "I got the impression he liked to shock me by taking me to Harlem. He knew we shouldn't be there and now he's taking this—as he used to call me—'little flower from the Midwest' into the evil [city]. He liked that, [and] he liked to scare himself."

Although Shelley can't be sure that Lou bought heroin on this visit to Harlem, it is clear that he first used heroin during his college years. Drugs had been part of his life since high school, illicit drugs and the prescription medication doctors gave him (pills he inevitably misused). Drugs were also part of his imaginative life. Lou read about junkies before he became one, and he associated drugs with the underground culture he felt drawn to. People he admired took drugs: the jazz musicians he listened to smoked grass and used smack; William Burroughs was a junkie; so was the comic Lenny Bruce, whose work Lou adored. As noted, Lou started smoking pot at high school, and he continued to smoke at college. Indeed, he became a dealer. One night he went to see fellow student James Gorney with some marijuana he needed to hide. "Clearly, he was drug dealing. He was drug dealing in a substantial quantity," says James, who took care of the drugs in return for as much as he could smoke. "If he had been caught, that would not have gone well with him." James's girlfriend Paula Swarzman, later his wife, corroborates the story, but thinks the amount involved was smaller than the "large suitcase" James talks about. "It was buy a little stuff for my friends," she qualifies. "It was dealing, but no capital 'D.'"

Shelley confirms that Lou sold marijuana on campus, and says he dealt other drugs, too, up to and including heroin. "He was selling it [heroin] to another fraternity group," she says. Lou would give Shelley bags of marijuana to store in her dorm. "I was stupid. I said OK. I didn't even think about it. And he'd call up, 'I need so much of it, give it to somebody and get the money.' . . . What he was really doing was keeping himself out of trouble at the expense of this girl." When he bought peyote from a supplier in Arizona, he had the drugs posted to Shelley's address. "That's not nice. You don't do that to your girlfriend. . . . He could be a prick in that way. He took care of himself first, even with someone he loved madly. And he did, and I was crazy about him."

Drugs got Lou into trouble, initially in an unexpected way. Karl Stoecker was an art-student friend who lived off campus with his young wife. "We both liked Karl," says Shelley. "He was cute." Lou invited Karl home to Freeport a couple of times. During one of these trips, he drove into a toll booth on the parkway. "Rather than go through the aisle where you are supposed to pay the toll on the highway, he ran right through the middle of the thing," laughs Karl. The accident resulted in Lou losing his license. He didn't drive again for many years. His sister remembers the accident and says that he was probably "high on drugs."

Karl was one of a number of friends who helped Lou publish a literary magazine on campus in 1962. *Lonely Woman Quarterly* was named after a tune by the saxophonist and free-jazz pioneer Ornette Coleman, who abandoned the harmonic conventions of mainstream jazz in the 1950s, creating strange, semi-abstract soundscapes. Some people hated this radical new music; others, like Lou, were enthralled by what was true outsider art. Free jazz became a passion for a man who was always attracted to the difficult and the outre, and would remain so long after he became a rock 'n' roll star. Indeed, Lou's musical career can be interpreted as a clash of experimentation and conventional melody, the tide ebbing and flowing from project to project. Jazz ideas can be heard on almost all his records. "I liked Ornette Coleman a lot, and [his trumpet player] Don Cherry a *whole* lot. I used to always go to see 'em at clubs [in New York], the original Ornette Coleman Quartet."

Shelley and Karl created the illustrations for *Lonely Woman Quarterly*, while the writers included Lou, Peter Maloney and Jim Tucker. They assembled the first issue at the Savoy Restaurant on

Marshall Street, a student hangout where the owner let them use his mimeograph machine. The magazine—neatly typed by Lou—contained the first substantial examples of his writing, and while much of what he wrote was verbose and jejune, a recognizable voice emerged. The first issue featured a short story about incest, which, together with other articles, showed Lou to have been reading Freud more than anything more sinister. Curiously, he wrote these pieces under the name Luis [sic] Reed.

In the second issue he published a character assassination of a fellow student named Michael Kogan, the leader of the right-wing Young Americans for Freedom organization on campus, and an aspiring rabbi. Lou and Michael were in the same theology class, taught by Professor Gabriel Vahanian. They attended a party at the professor's house one night, memorable for the fact that Lou sang an outrageous song casting aspersions on the professor's sexuality. "Vahanian threw us all out," says Kogan, who doesn't recall speaking to Lou directly before he saw himself ridiculed in the *Lonely Woman Quarterly*. He was shocked by the spiteful tone of the article, which he showed to his lawyer father, who complained to the chancellor of the university, who told Lou to apologize, which he did. "He didn't mean it—he hated me," says Kogan. "It was a forced apology." Looking back, he believes that he presented an easy target. "He was a Jew who was at war with his Judaism and I was very active in the Jewish student groups, so it was as religious as it was political. I represented to him everything he hated, from wearing a tie and jacket to school to being a conservative Republican [and] an active member of the Jewish community." The antipathy was mutual. "I detested Lou Reed. I found him a loathsome person."

Lou reserved his best writing for the third and final issue of *Lonely Woman Quarterly*. In his short story "And What, Little Boy, Will You Trade for Your Horse?" he wrote about a young man who tours the pornographic bookshops, diners, pinball arcades and sex cinemas around Times Square in New York, watching the street hustlers and "mincing and giggling" boys, before going to a bar, where he is picked up by a man in drag, "a regular queen." Here was the landscape and subject matter of many Lou Reed songs, and the story rang true, as if drawn from experience.

Yet he was still with Shelley. When summer came and she went home to Illinois for the vacation, Lou missed her. He wrote to her regularly, telling her about his trips to the Hayloft, and sending her a macabre short story, reminiscent of the work of Edgar Allan Poe, about a boy named Waldo who mailed himself to his girlfriend, Marsha, only to perish when she plunged a blade into the box to open it. The Velvet Underground later set this darkly comic story to music, creating "The Gift." "He used to call himself Waldo and he used to call me Marsha," explains Shelley, who was delighted to receive the story in the mail. Lou then elaborated on the joke by sending her a large toy animal in a box. "It was the story come to life. . . . He was fun when he wanted to be."

Later that summer Lou flew to Illinois to see Shelley. Typically, he attempted to create discord in the Albin household by espousing right-wing political ideas to annoy Shelley's liberal parents. Nevertheless, the Albins lent him their car. "He crashes the car into a ditch," sighs Shelley, who compares Lou to a wayward kindergarten child. "If he was a kid, you'd say this is one you've got to keep your eye on, or he'll go and put someone else's hand under the paper cutter, and get the other kid to feel responsible. He required watching." The Albins were glad to see the back of Lou when he went home, and told Shelley she could only return to Syracuse if she promised never to see him again. Shelley agreed, but continued the relationship. "[My mother], to this day, if you mention Lou Reed, [will say], 'What a horrible, disgusting person!'"

DELMORE SCHWARTZ ARRIVED AT Syracuse for the academic year starting in September 1962, Lou's junior year. Schwartz was hailed in his youth as a brilliant new writer, the author of an outstanding short story, "In Dreams Begin Responsibilities." But his work didn't sell, and he suffered with mental illness. Manic and paranoid, he fell out with friends and colleagues, drank to excess and took drugs, to the extent that he was repeatedly admitted to the hospital. By the time he came to Syracuse to teach, aged forty-eight, he was a physical and emotional wreck, but nevertheless he was an inspiring figure. Saul Bellow used Schwartz as the model for the character Von Humboldt Fleisher in his novel *Humboldt's Gift*, "a wonderful talker, a hectic non-stop monologist" who elevated his students to "a state of great exultation about literature." Lou was such a student.

"By the time we encountered him, Schwartz was [taking] a lethal combination of speed to get him going, and barbiturates to slow him down, probably mixed with alcohol," says James Gorney, who was also in Schwartz's creative-writing class. "He was disheveled, looked like he had rolled out of bed. Often the socks did not match, the shoes did not match. Looked kind of crazed. But none of that mattered." Schwartz lectured his students on the work of T. S. Eliot, James Joyce and W. B. Yeats, teaching them to appreciate the music in the language, which surely helped Lou become the writer he did. The lectures on *Ulysses* were the highlight of the course. "It was really a course in teaching you how to read *Ulysses*," explains James. "One time he said, 'When you first read a paragraph, and you don't understand it, read it aloud and listen to the music and you'll probably understand it.'" If they still didn't get it, he said that they should have a few drinks, because Joyce wrote much of the book under the influence. Lou took this advice to heart. A lot of his own writing was done when he was drunk or stoned.

One day Schwartz brought his copy of *Finnegans Wake* into class. The book was in ruins, the binding broken, the pages loose, the volume strapped together with shoelaces. He beckoned his students to gather around as he opened the book, explaining how he had been studying the text for years. He had filled virtually every blank space with notes, in various colored inks. He said that Joyce had referred to a particular edition of the *Encyclopaedia Britannica* while writing the book, so he had read every volume of that edition in an attempt to decode it. The magnitude of this task was almost beyond the comprehension of the students. The classroom windows were open as Schwartz told his mad story, and a gust of wind caught the pages and blew them about the room. Lou and others dashed to save them. The scene left a deep impression. "I remember Lou and I talking about this a lot," says James. "Very poignant. It touched us both very much."

The teacher bonded with his students, meeting them for drinks in the Orange bar (orange being the Syracuse color), where he told stories about famous writers he had known, and attempted to conduct informal lessons. Lou made a particular connection with his tutor: a fellow Jew from Brooklyn who was old enough to be his father but seemed to understand him better than his own father, who wanted him to take up a conventional career after college. Lou didn't want to become a fucking accountant like Sid. He wanted to write and make music. Schwartz urged him to follow his instinct, warning him never to compromise his talent. "Once, drunk in a Syracuse bar, he said, 'If you sell out, Lou, I'm gonna get ya.'" Delmore Schwartz became Lou's first mentor, a beloved and heroic figure in his eyes.

As Lou began his intellectual love affair with Delmore, his temporal affair with Shelley came to an end. Things hadn't been going well for a while by the time they attended a fraternity party at Syracuse in January 1963. Lou took another girl into one of the rooms at the party. Shelley was invited to watch. She walked out in disgust. Lincoln Swados gallantly escorted her home through the snow. A fourteen-month romance was over. Shelley loved Lou, but he was manipulative and sometimes nasty. "He did some shitty things to me. He wasn't happy until he got somebody to call him a prick." That word again. "That's what he was after."

Yet Lou remained infatuated with Shelley, never seeming to understand why she left him. As late as the 1980s, when he was middle-aged and famous, he was still calling her, trying to win her back. The couple did get together again briefly, at Syracuse and afterwards, but she chose not to take things further. "He couldn't understand why we couldn't just pick up again—for the next twenty years. He was really pissed at me for twenty years." She had decided that Lou was not the man she wanted to spend her life with, marry or have children with. Lou never had children, and Shelley thinks that was wise. The issue had come up. "He liked the idea of [having children]," she says, but she decided that someone who couldn't even look after a dog was not the man for her. "I had an innate sense, *This is not someone you want to have kids with.*" Yet Lou could easily have become a father at this stage in life. Prior to the widespread use of the contraceptive pill, it was common for college girls in the early 1960s to become pregnant, and many had illegal abortions. Shelley reveals that Lou got girls pregnant on no less than three occasions at Syracuse, but says that all three pregnancies were aborted. "There were people he made pregnant, through his own lack of responsibility. They didn't . . . choose to have his children."

THERE WERE NEW ROMANCES and new influences for Lou in his final college year, starting in September 1963. At the start of the first term, he pinned a poster to his bedroom wall, a black-and-white image of a solitary man standing under the lights of Times Square. This was the cover of John Rechy's groundbreaking gay novel *City of Night,* which documented the life of an itinerant hustler in bold, poetic language that foreshadowed Lou's mature songwriting.

Despite his evident fascination with gay life, Lou's relationships were still primarily, possibly exclusively, with girls. Soon after he broke up with Shelley he started to see her friend Erin Clermont, a likeable, waifish girl with an infectious sense of fun who was also in

Schwartz's class. They were to have an unusually long relationship, lasting until the 1990s. "From the day I met him I accepted him as this complicated, different guy [who] had something to offer. It wasn't music at that point. It was his head, and what he was into, and we shared these interests," says Erin, who told Shelley as soon as she had slept with Lou, so there wouldn't be bad blood between them. The girls remained friends, often discussing Lou, who fascinated them both. Although Shelley knew him first, Erin maintained the longest relationship. "I lasted all those years because I was eternally interested in him, not in love with him, although we did love each other. We said that."

Although Erin and Lou shared what she calls an "intense interest in sex," theirs was more a friendship, allowing her to make a cool study of Lou over the years. Like Shelley, she considered him to be predominantly heterosexual but, unlike Shelley, she ultimately concluded that he was bisexual. She says he was highly sexed in his youth. He slept around, and was pursued by at least one jealous boyfriend at Syracuse as a result. Never a particularly brave man, Lou ran and hid. Erin describes Lou as a "coward," adding that "he was always horny." Lou boasted to male friends of all sorts of sexual adventures, including having sex with a girl in a cemetery and taking part in a threesome with two women in New York. Some of this may well have been fantasy. Such a level of sexual activity certainly wasn't a constant in his life. There were long periods later when he gave the impression of having little or no interest in sex.

He possessed an insistent, nagging personality that could be irritating to some people but which Erin found amusing. "He was so probing. He wouldn't let go of things. He would just go on and on and on until he got his way, talked you into it. There was a great deal of neediness, too. . . . He was extraordinary in that sense: how he could get you in his mindset, convince you to come out at three o'clock in the morning—'No! I have to go to work tomorrow!'—and just keep at it [until you gave in]. 'All right! All right!'" He had characteristic poses, mannerisms and phrases. Erin noted his theatrical walk and sardonic tone of voice. He was critical by nature, reluctant to give praise, and would laugh mirthlessly, sarcastically, if somebody made a joke that didn't quite work. It was a challenge to get him to laugh properly, and a pleasure when he did so. "If I said something really funny, he would be suspicious," she recalls. "'Where did you get that?'" It was indicative of his grudging disposition that his favorite phrases included, "Don't make fun" and "Lucky you," said in a laid-back tone of voice, "flat, very flat—but amusing in its own way if you knew him. . . . 'Be nice' was in the same category as 'Don't make fun,' [also] said in his flat, sardonic style."

LIKE MANY MUSICIANS OF his generation, Lou was influenced by the folk music revival of the early 1960s, so much so that Nelson Slater says that when Lou first came to Syracuse he was "presenting himself as a folk singer." The biggest star of the folk movement by 1963 was Bob Dylan, whom Lou saw perform at the Regent Theater in Syracuse in November. Then twenty-two, Dylan was only ten months older than Lou, but he was already established as a major international figure. His second album, *The Freewheelin' Bob Dylan*, released that year to great acclaim, contained sophisticated songs that articulated the mood of the young and inspired a generation of songwriters, including Lennon and McCartney, to be more ambitious in their work. Lou was one of many budding songwriters who fell under Dylan's spell, learning his songs and performing them in his style, to the extent that he took briefly to playing a rack harmonica. "We would sit and listen to Bob Dylan [records] and we learned the chords to everything he played," says Richard Mishkin, who says that Lou was "blown away" by Dylan. "[But he] would never admit that he was impressed as he was, and would never admit then that that's who he wanted to be." Nevertheless, Dylan's influence helped Lou make a leap forward in his songwriting.

Drugs were also a factor in his development as an artist. Although they were no longer an item, Lou and Shelley remained in touch, and she says that he "really got heavy into heroin" in his last year at college, around the spring of 1964. "I can handle heroin," he told her. "I'm not gonna [get addicted]. I just do it to get the experience. But I'm in control." Lou needed experiences to write about something beyond the lightweight pop he had so far created. Six months before he met Delmore Schwartz, before he had heard *The Freewheelin' Bob Dylan,* he recorded two of his compositions for the same New York producer who had recorded his high-school band, the Jades. This time Lou also sang lead vocals. The songs, "Your Love" and "Merry Go Round," were trite. Delmore Schwartz had little regard for this sort of pop music. There was one magical evening at the Orange bar in early 1964 when Lou and James Gorney were drinking with their teacher and the Beatles' number one "I Want to Hold Your Hand" came on the jukebox. Delmore, James and Lou played the song repeatedly, as they got drunker and drunker, and left the bar arm in arm singing the lyric. This was, however, a rare example of Schwartz enjoying pop. He expected Lou to do more serious work. "I remember [Schwartz] lecturing me about how it was my job to make sure that Lou went to a proper graduate school, like Harvard or Princeton, and become 'a real writer,' as he would put it, not a crappy rock 'n' roll writer," says Shelley. It is surely no coincidence that Lou started to write more ambitious songs after falling under the twin influences of Schwartz and Dylan, and that his creative breakthrough came with a song about a subject he understood.

In his final months at Syracuse, Lou wrote "Heroin," describing what it feels like to inject and get high on heroin in language that is convincing, thrilling and scary. He later gave a colorful, maybe embellished, account of how he came to write this remarkable song: "I had recently been introduced to drugs at this time by a mashed-in-faced Negro whose features were in two sections (like a split-level house) named Jaw." It is astonishing that he wrote such an accomplished song so soon after "Your Love," but Lou insisted that this was the case, and Richard Mishkin remembers accompanying Lou while he worked up the tune. "I used to sit around with him. We'd smoke pot and I'd play the bass, and he'd play the guitar, and he wrote the words [while] I fudged around with the bass line."

Part of the reason Reed is an important artist is the fact that he became one of the first singer-songwriters of the 1960s to combine poetic, literary language with rock 'n' roll, also addressing subjects that hadn't been tackled before in popular song. He was much more literary than most of his contemporaries, someone for whom the work of writers including Raymond Chandler, Dostoyevsky, Edgar Allan Poe, Hubert Selby Jr. and Delmore Schwartz were as big an influence as any musician. One can compare him best in this sense to Leonard Cohen. Throughout his career, Lou wrote poetry, short stories and nonfiction essays as well as songs, and he long aspired to write a novel. Some of his prose and poetry was published, and he won a poetry prize in the 1970s. Although he never managed to finish his literary novel, Lou often said that he hoped his songs would be seen in aggregate as the equivalent of the Great American Novel, and he began that ambitious work with "Heroin." Some of the lyrics put one in mind of what Dylan was already doing. The references to the "clipper ship" sailing on "darkened seas" in the third verse, and "the politicians making crazy sounds" in the fourth, have a Dylanesque quality, but the subject matter was Lou's own. Nobody else working in popular song in the early 1960s, Dylan included, was writing explicitly and realistically about using hard drugs. Rather, Lou took his lead from authors like William Burroughs, who had covered this ground in prose. Eschewing euphemism, he used authentic jargon to describe shooting up, and he didn't spare his listeners the unpleasant details, describing for example a junky method of attaching an eye-dropper to a hypodermic needle. When the needle pierces the vein, a little blood "shoots up the dropper's neck." He didn't moralize but presented drug use frankly, as the way his character dealt with his problems "in the big city." For Lou, life was always more intense in the city.

> I have made a big decision
> I'm gonna try to nullify my life . . .

In shooting up, the character flirted with death but didn't care about the consequences. One minute he wanted to die, the next he was in a state of bliss. He brushed away well-meaning people who tried to help him, telling them to "go take a walk." This sneering wise-guy line was classic Lou, the cocky nihilist character he created and sold to the public over almost fifty years, attractive in the way that a book like *Junky* is appealing to people of a certain disposition, especially so perhaps to those for whom addiction is merely an exotic spectacle. The song also acknowledged that drugs might not be the answer; Lou's character seemed bewildered about what he was doing to himself.

"Heroin" was a major breakthrough, though it may be that Lou worked on the song over several months before he perfected the lyric. In any event, his college career was over. He received his BA in Liberal Arts in June 1964, during the first summer of the so-called British invasion of the American pop charts, headed by the Beatles with "Love Me Do" and "A Hard Day's Night." Lou was as big a fan as anyone. In recent months, he had become increasingly unpopular with the local police, who disliked his disrespectful manner and knew that he was involved with drugs. They threatened to rough him up unless he left town as soon as possible, "because of various clandestine operations I was alleged to have been involved in," as Lou later wrote, making the matter as mysterious as possible. "They knew who he was and they didn't like him," says Shelley, more directly. Nevertheless, Lou hung around campus for a couple more weeks, staying with Shelley. They'd recently had one of their reunions and she wasn't feeling well.

When Lou returned to Freeport he, too, fell sick. A yellow tinge appeared in the whites of his eyes, an early sign of jaundice that is itself the result of liver damage. Lou's doctor diagnosed viral hepatitis, which Lou blamed on his heroin connection and a dirty needle. "Jaw gave me hepatitis . . . which is pathetic and laughable at once, considering I wrote a famous amplified version of the experience in a song ["Heroin"]." He telephoned Shelley, who was home in Illinois, advising her to see a doctor, because hepatitis can be transmitted through intercourse. "That was the first time he had hepatitis," she says. It was the start of a lifetime of lifestyle-related health problems for Lou, who had cast off on to the darkened sea.

III

HONEYBUN, BLACK JACK, STERL AND MOESY

• 1964–65 •

OWARD THE END OF his time at Syracuse, Lou was approached after a gig by Terry Philips, a representative of Pickwick City Records of New York, who explained that he was looking to sign songwriting talent and had driven up to Syracuse to hear Lou on a recommendation. "I heard him play and I really liked him," recalls Terry, who says that one of the songs he sang that night was "Cycle Annie," a faux-surf song about a Californian girl who bicycled in the nude, a very different proposition to "Heroin." In fact, Lou would always have the capacity to create comic songs. "He couldn't sing, and he couldn't play, but he had a sound and he had a point of view, and beyond some of the poppy songs he wrote he was very smart. He wanted to be a writer." Terry was a songwriter himself. He had been a staff writer for Leiber and Stoller, which is how he came to know Phil Spector. Terry and Phil wrote together before Spector went on to bigger things. Terry was proud of these connections, and Lou must have been impressed by his CV because, when Terry offered him a songwriting contract, he signed.

Sid Reed was concerned to hear that his son had blithely put his name to a Tin Pan Alley deal, and contacted Philips to discuss it. Terry agreed to come over to Freeport on a day when Lou was out of the house so they could talk privately. It was at this stage that he discovered how worried the Reeds were about their son, beyond his choice of career. "[Sid] also wanted to make sure, as I later found out, that his son, who had a pill problem, was not getting in with somebody who would get him further into trouble." Although Lou had been using heroin and other substances at college, Terry insists that he was now "popping pills like crazy." This probably refers to his misuse of Placidyl, which had been prescribed as a sedative, though he may have been abusing other pills as well. His parents were aware of the situation, and they were worried. "The mother used to sit there and cry," says Terry, who spoke to Sid and Toby several times over the following months, developing sympathy for the couple. "The father was a good guy. Lou beat the shit out of him [emotionally]. He cursed him, and he did all kinds of stuff, but he was a good father."

Lou started work at Pickwick after he got over his hepatitis, catching the Long Island Railroad each morning from Freeport to Long Island City in Queens. At the end of a street of industrial buildings leading down to the East River was a warehouse where Terry worked in a corner office with two other songwriters, Jimmie Sims and Jerry Vance, writing pastiches of the pop hits of the day, in various genres, which they recorded under fictitious band names on the office reel-to-reel tape machine for the cheap exploitation albums Pickwick purveyed. The warehouse was full of boxes of records awaiting shipment. Lou later dismissed his Pickwick job as "hack shit" but conceded that it was a useful experience. "I had this horrifying job writing songs on command, like a songwriter machine. But that job taught me about the studio, and how to write really quickly. They'd just say, 'Give me ten surf songs.'" Blessed with natural writing ability, and a love of rock 'n' roll, Lou found that he enjoyed the challenge of writing to order. He wrote songs for films in later years. In 1981, he even wrote for the rock band Kiss, a stretch for a serious artist.

Lou usually turned up for work on time, but not necessarily in a fit state to work. "There were days that he could hardly stand up," says Terry. Lou was so stoned that he bumped into furniture and once passed out in the office. "We had to call an ambulance . . . we thought he'd died." He was also a handful when he was compos mentis. He groused about his job and gave the impression that he looked down on Terry, which didn't endear him to his boss, who considered himself to be a sophisticated, switched-on music business insider. "I didn't have to have long hair in order to be a cool person," says Terry. "I liked his talent, but I didn't like him. He was obnoxious, he was pedantic. He was a punk. A guy with a big mouth who would always be a wise guy, be obnoxious, and would have me threatening to bust him one in the chops if he didn't shut up . . . I would grab him and say, 'Stop this crap!' Or he would come in so whacked out I would get him coffee and I would spend half the time lecturing him. . . . He kept bullshitting that he wanted to write and be a writer. I said, 'So be a writer. I'm not telling you not to come in and work on a book idea, if you have it. I'm just saying, see if the idea leads to songs. That's why we are here. These people are giving us the money, and we are giving you the money.'"

During his time at Pickwick, Lou wrote a string of songs, all pastiches of chart hits of the early 1960s, including "You're Driving Me Insane" (by the Roughnecks) and "Put a Tiger in Your Tank" (by the Intimates). The lyrics of his most notable composition, "The Ostrich," instructed kids how to perform an impossible new dance that required stepping on their own heads. It is amazing that the author of "Heroin" wrote such nonsense. One explanation is that Lou was stoned. Terry says he was high on pills when he wrote "The Ostrich," as he was when they recorded the song on the office Ampex. Lou shrieked the lyric like a maniac while Terry and others (it is unclear who played all the instruments) accompanied him and yelled like banshees in the background. "It made no sense. It was stupid. He was on pills, and I had a bottle of Old Bushmills, and we were feeling good." None of this would be of much import save for the fact that Terry decided to release "The Ostrich" as a single. "I had to fight [with the company] to get them to release this record. . . . Even Lou thought I was nuts."

In order to promote "The Ostrich," Terry needed personable young musicians to pretend to be the band that cut the record. He was at a party in New York when he was introduced to a graduate mathematician named Tony Conrad, who played fiddle in his spare time, and his friend John Cale, a tall, slim Welshman with a solemn face and floppy, dark hair. Terry invited them over to the office. They brought a friend, an artist named Walter De Maria, who played drums. Lou was in the music room when the visitors arrived. Cale said, "My first impressions of Lou were of a highly strung, intelligent, fragile college kid in a polo-neck sweater, rumpled jeans and loafers," describing the meeting in his memoir, *What's Welsh for Zen*. He added that Lou struck him as being "bruised, trembling, quiet and insecure." Lou played them "The Ostrich." Then he and John sat down to talk over coffee.

They discovered that they were the same age, born one week apart in 1942, making them twenty-two. John was from South Wales, where his father was a coal miner. He had studied piano from the age of seven, taking up viola at grammar school, at which point he also started to compose music. Like Lou, he was an intelligent, gifted, but fragile person who suffered a nervous breakdown in his teens. At eighteen, he won a scholarship to Goldsmiths College in London, where he began to mix with the leading figures in avant-garde music. An interest in *musique concrete* led to a correspondence with the American modernists John Cage and Aaron Copland. John had come to the United States in 1963 to study at the Berkshire Music Center at Tanglewood, Massachusetts, on a

Leonard Bernstein scholarship. One of his teachers was another leading modernist composer, Iannis Xenakis. It was a stellar start to a career.

Although prodigiously gifted, John suffered a lack of self-confidence that made it possible for others to dominate him. He also admits to "a crackpot side" that made him a natural outsider. John loved to shock. He achieved this at Tanglewood in the summer of 1963 by taking an axe to a table during a conceptual performance. In September he moved to New York City, where he became involved in the downtown music scene, taking part in a marathon recital of Erik Satie's *Vexations*, organized by John Cage, that lasted nineteen hours. He also met La Monte Young, a philosopher-musician who led recitals at his loft apartment under the title of the Theater of Eternal Music, performing strange compositions that featured sustained notes sounding like the buzz of a machine or the drone of an insect. The "drone" was one of the big ideas of the minimalist movement, of which Young was a pioneer. Musicians who collaborated with Young and Cale in these experiments included Tony Conrad and Tony's buddy Henry Flynt, another Harvard-educated mathematician who played violin; also Billy Linich, aka Billy Name, a photographer friend of the pop artist Andy Warhol, who sang; and Angus MacLise, a proto-hippie who played hand drums. "We created a kind of music that nobody else in the world was making and that nobody had ever heard before," Cale wrote. One of his achievements was to bring these new ideas to a wider audience.

Radical politics and drug use were part of this scene. Angus MacLise would sometimes be found unconscious on the street. Cale admits to dealing drugs at the time to supplement his income. He was arrested during a deal in 1964 and spent a night in jail. "The problem was that I had a nickel bag on me. But when they analyzed it, it was nothing, so they let me out the next day." After this incident he moved in with Tony Conrad, sharing a fifth-floor walk-up at 56 Ludlow Street on the Lower East Side, then largely populated by poor immigrant families and therefore affordable for bohemian musicians. Angus lived next door. This was Cale's domestic setup when he met Lou.

Like the Ancient Mariner, Lou felt compelled at this stage in his life to tell everybody he met about his past, and so he told Cale almost immediately about the ECT. "I think I'm crazy," he said. John didn't think Lou was insane. On the contrary, he was impressed to discover that he had detuned his Gretsch guitar to one note to create the drone sound on "The Ostrich." It was the same technique Cale used with La Monte Young. He was even more impressed when Lou played him his serious songs. Lou responded warmly, as he usually did with people who liked his work, no doubt recognizing someone who could be useful to him. Lou was not as accomplished a musician as John Cale. "Lou, to say he was just an average player, is giving him more credit than he deserved. He was a crappy player," says Terry Philips, a little harshly. Apart from having a technical knowledge of music theory and composition, John could play a variety of instruments to a high standard, and he sang beautifully. By contrast, Lou merely strummed guitar, and he struggled to sing in tune. He would be able to make much more interesting music with his new British friend than he could alone.

Meanwhile, Terry had work for them to do. He put Lou together with Cale, Tony Conrad and Walter De Maria to form a band called the Primitives. Featuring two future members of the Velvet Underground, a Harvard mathematician and, in De Maria, someone who became a leading conceptual artist, the Primitives was one of the more unusual acts in the history of pop music. Terry drove them around the New York area doing promotion for "The Ostrich." They did radio spots, a high-school gig, a supermarket opening and a show at the Riverside Plaza Hotel on December 3, 1964, around the date of the single's release. Lou soon started acting up, to the extent that Terry lost his patience one day in the car. "The woman who was going to be my wife was in the car and Lou started his [crap].

He was a little high. He was cursing and stuff, and I smacked him in the face. . . . Everybody was afraid of Lou, because he could get so nasty that most people didn't want to confront him. For me it was a joke. He was no fighter." Unsurprisingly, "The Ostrich" didn't do any business, which was the end of the Primitives. But Lou and John continued to work together on their own.

Although John was impressed by the words to Lou's serious songs, he wasn't keen on the way he was performing them, in the folk style, at a time when Joan Baez, the Byrds and Peter, Paul and Mary were enjoying great success with pop versions of folk songs and Dylan was at the peak of his early success. Folk music was very trendy in New York in the early 1960s, but John didn't think highly of the genre. As they jammed together at the Ludlow Street apartment, he helped Lou develop more original and appropriate arrangements informed by his knowledge of minimalism. This was the start of one of the great songwriting partnerships of the 1960s, comparable to Lennon and McCartney in that Cale and Reed created a catalogue of peerless work in a short space of time, becoming as close as brothers in the process, though, unlike Lennon and McCartney, one partner, Lou, wrote all the words. However, he did allow John to edit him, which was vital. "When I first met Lou, we were interested in the same things. He had a certain expertise in songwriting that I thought was absolutely amazing. We both needed a vehicle. Lou needed one to carry out his lyrical ideas, and I needed one to carry out my musical ideas. . . . I was going off into Never Never Land with classical notions of music [at the time]," Cale explained the collaboration. "Lou was exorcising a lot of devils back then, and maybe I was using him to exorcise some of mine. So when we first started working together it was on the basis that we were both interested in the same things. That's why the Velvet Underground was put together."

Lou continued to live at home for the time being, and to work for Pickwick, in a period of transition. He took his Selective Ser-

vice medical on February 4, 1965, to see if he was fit enough to
be drafted into the armed forces, when the Vietnam War was escalating alarmingly. That February, President Johnson ordered an
intensive bombing campaign against North Vietnam, and the de-
ployment of US troops increased substantially during the year. Lou's
mental-health record, and the fact he was on medication, was to his
advantage. He was classified 1-Y, meaning he was to be drafted only
in an emergency. With this problem solved, he had more freedom to
plan his future. When Tony Conrad moved out of the Ludlow Street
apartment, Lou moved in to share with John.

It was exciting to be living in the heart of the city after years in
the boondocks, and Lou soon developed a profound love of Manhattan. It became his place, as if he had grown up there, defining
him as a man and an artist. Apart from his job at Pickwick, Lou
gave guitar lessons to help keep himself afloat in the city. "I would
say he was a very good teacher," says Henry Flynt, who paid Lou
ten dollars an hour for lessons. "The thing that was striking about
his personality was that he was a very tightly organized person in a
very middle-class way on some level, and very disciplined." When
Henry asked Lou for his contact details, he gave his parents' address
and phone number in Freeport, and when he mailed a demo tape to
himself on May 11, 1965, to establish copyright of his new songs, he
posted the package to Freeport, showing that he still remained tied
to and to some extent dependent on his family. It may well be that
Sid and Toby also helped support him financially in the city.

Drugs were part of the scene on the Lower East Side. "Do you
take heroin?" John asked Henry one day when he was visiting the
apartment.

"No."

"What are you, chicken?"

Prior to meeting Lou, John had used a variety of drugs. Now
he and Lou started doing heroin together. John had never injected
before and he was squeamish about needles. "Lou took care of that

by shooting me up for the first time. It was an intimate experience, not least because my first reaction was to vomit." When they formed a band, they initially called themselves the Falling Spikes, "spike" being drug slang for a hypodermic needle, a term Lou used in "Heroin." Now he drew on these experiences to write another important song.

While "Heroin" was a song about what it felt like to use smack, "I'm Waiting for the Man" concerned the business of buying drugs. The first verse was one of the best Lou ever wrote, grabbing the listener's attention and setting the scene with a few carefully chosen words that conveyed a wealth of information.

> I'm waiting for my man
> Twenty-six dollars in my hand
> Up to Lexington 1-2-5
> Feeling sick and dirty more dead than alive . . .

One of Lou's songwriting maxims was "to be terrific, be specific," and the opening verse of "I'm Waiting for the Man" demonstrates the wisdom of this phrase. By citing a real place where drugs were scored (the junction of Lexington Avenue and 125th Street in Harlem) and specifying how much the buyer took with him to make the deal ($26), Lou created an immediate sense of realism. The words also conveyed tension. Buying drugs on the street was risky. What would happen? Lou proceeded to introduce the dealer, a creep in a floppy hat and "PR" (Puerto Rican fence-climber) shoes, who inevitably showed up late. The frustration of waiting for the connection was at the heart of the song, and this, too, was realistic. The deal went down in a nearby brownstone apartment where the buyer borrowed the dealer's needle so he could get high at once. Then bliss.

These were among the most succinct and evocative lyrics Lou ever wrote, but not everything he was writing was in this spare, almost journalistic style. "Black Angel's Death Song" was a surrealistic poem, which John helped Lou work up. Instead of describing something real in the manner of a reporter, Lou presented a series of vivid images.

Cut mouth bleeding razors forget in the pain
Antiseptic remains cool goodbye So you fly
To the cozy brown snow of the east

The reference to razors cutting the face is disturbing, reminiscent of the infamous scene in Luis Bunuel's 1929 film, *Un Chien Andalou,* in which a woman's eye appears to be slashed with a razor; a picture Lou may well have seen screened at this time. The following line emphasized the feeling of being trapped in a nightmare, while "the cozy brown snow of the east" is a wonderful phrase, evoking New York winters when snow is swept into dirty brown heaps on the sidewalk, or imported brown heroin powder, or both.

Not long after the last of that winter's snow had melted, Lou and John went busking in the city, performing "I'm Waiting for the Man" *in situ* at 125th Street. During one of these uptown expeditions they met a girl named Elektrah Lobel, who briefly joined the Falling Spikes. They played coffeehouses as a trio. Then they met another girl, Daryl, with whom Lou and John both had an affair. That didn't stop Lou making passes at John, who realized that his new friend was bisexual and declined his overtures. One night Lou picked up a gay black preacher and went to bed with him in a hotel in Harlem, while John pretended to sleep in the same room. "I wasn't going to go all the way downtown in the freezing cold."

Another important song from this period was "Venus in Furs," inspired by the nineteenth-century novel by Leopold von Sacher-Masoch, after whom the term "masochism" is named. The novel documented the relationship between a nobleman named Severin and a dominatrix, Wanda, who mocked, cuckolded and whiplashed her lover, often when she was dressed in fur, which was exquisite stimulation to them both. Lou borrowed the characters for a song of the same name, creating a work that has itself become synonymous with S&M. Oddly, he and John played "Venus in Furs" initially in the style of an English folk song reminiscent of "Scarborough Fair." It would change radically.

We might imagine Lou and John in the spring of 1965 as two pale, shabby, half-starved young men trudging the streets of New York, like the down-and-outs in *Midnight Cowboy*. They filled their bellies with porridge, which was the cheapest and simplest meal they could cook at home. To earn a few bucks they sold their blood at donation centers and posed for pictures in tabloid magazines, which depicted them as criminals in lurid "true crime" stories. "And when my picture came out, it said I was a sex-maniac killer and that I had killed fourteen children," Lou recalled. "And when John's picture came out in the paper it said he had killed his lover because his lover was going to marry his sister." They were on the subway one day during this lean period when they ran into Sterling Morrison, the guitarist Lou had met at Syracuse. Sterling, a perennial student, was living with his girlfriend's brother while he studied at the City College of New York. They invited him back to Ludlow Street to jam. It was so cold in the apartment that they broke up crates to make a fire, huddling around the blaze with blankets over their shoulders while they played. Angus MacLise wandered in from next door and joined them, on hand drums. This was the start of the Velvet Underground, though at this stage it was only friends making music together in an apartment.

Their other drummer friend, Walter De Maria, was still on the scene, later talking of how he "joined the Velvet Underground" around this time. "It was a great band," De Maria said after he became established as an artist. "But then I said, 'Do I want to go to rehearsal every day and every night, you know, take all these drugs? Do I really just keep playing these rhythms, is that going to be enough?' That was a really painful decision. I said, 'No, put it down.'" In truth, neither De Maria nor MacLise were committed to the group. De Maria disliked the discipline of band practice and, at twenty-nine, he already felt too old to become a rock 'n' roll drummer. "You see, being a musician is something like being an athlete to some extent; you really have to be young and strong to do it." The same was probably true of MacLise, who turned twenty-seven in 1965, and who had other interests. MacLise kept his thoughts on the subject to himself, dying in obscurity in India in 1979.

As well as changes of personnel, changes of name are often part of the evolution of a group. The Falling Spikes became the Warlocks for a while, appearing under that name with Angus at the Film-maker's Cinémathèque, an event organized by the underground filmmaker Piero Heliczer. They played behind a screen on to which films were projected, which was the start of the band being drawn into New York's visual arts scene. Lou didn't give himself over to the bohemian life just yet. He maintained his involvement with Pickwick Records, which brought in some income. "We worked there and were songwriters on occasion," said Sterling. "At one time they called us the Beachnuts." Under this name Lou recorded his absurd tale of the nude bicyclist, "Cycle Annie," breaking up with laughter halfway through the session. The song appeared on a Pickwick album entitled *Soundsville!* Lou sang on one other track and probably wrote, or co-wrote, most of the tunes.

The Warlocks evolved into the Velvet Underground after their friend Tony Conrad brought a book of that name to the apartment, a pseudo-academic study of "the sexual corruption of our age" by Michael Leigh, published in paperback with an S&M-theme cover. "It will shock and amaze you," promised the blurb. It was, in fact, a trashy work, its only strength the title, which evoked an urban netherworld of illicit and deviant behavior. "The Velvet Underground" also had a double meaning for the musicians at the time. "We thought it was a good name because it had 'underground' in it, and we were playing for underground films," explained Sterling. "We considered ourselves part of the underground film community."

Lou, John and Sterling recorded their practice sessions at Ludlow Street. One surviving tape from July 1965 captured the boys rehearsing six songs, including "Heroin" and "I'm Waiting for the Man," without a drummer, demonstrating the peripheral status of De Maria and MacLise, though the latter was on hand for band pictures that summer. Lou had perfected his lyrics, but the arrangements were still fluid. Sung by John to acoustic guitar, "Venus in Furs" still sounded like "Scarborough Fair." "Prominent Men," co-written by Lou and John, was a rip-off of a Bob Dylan protest song that would remain an obscurity. "Heroin," however, was already the song the public would come to know, the dramatic, escalating arrangement complemented by John's manic viola. "All Tomorrow's Parties" also sounded as it would when it was released, while "I'm Waiting for the Man" had a curious hillbilly arrangement. They made several attempts at the songs on the tape. Lou and John shared lead vocals while Sterling played guitar, sang backing vocals and kept time by tapping a sarinda. "Too fast," complained Lou, as Sterling started another song, "Wrap Your Troubles in Dreams."

"Well, that's what . . ." his friend defended himself, the rest of his argument inaudible on the tape, which captured the sound of traffic on the street outside.

"Well, that doesn't prove it's right!" Lou scoffed. "What the fuck's wrong with you?"

"OK."

Lou started laughing. "All right. Jesus Christ!"

It wasn't a serious disagreement, but it is early evidence of Lou's sharp tongue and lack of patience.

Toward the end of the year the Velvets came to the attention of Al Aronowitz, a journalist for the *Saturday Evening Post* who had the distinction of having introduced Bob Dylan to the Beatles while also being friends with the Rolling Stones. Aronowitz harbored ambitions to move into music management and had one band under contract. His friend the filmmaker Barbara Rubin told him about the Velvet Underground, whom she had encountered on the underground film scene, telling him that they were looking for representation. "Barbara gets me a tape. I listen to the tape. Awful! A piece of shit!" Aronowitz later wrote, possibly referring to the tape described above. Nevertheless, he made the effort to meet them. Lou boasted to him of being an ace guitarist, and seemed to think the Velvets were destined to become the new Beatles. "I can't promise that," said Al. "I can get you exposure." He offered them a gig opening for his band, the Myddle Class, at a high-school dance in New Jersey. The job paid $75, split between four—Lou, John, Sterling and a drummer. But Angus refused to play, explaining that he didn't want to turn professional. Lou was furious. They needed a replacement fast. Sterling mentioned that Jim Tucker's sister Maureen played drums. Sterling's girlfriend, Martha, later his wife (and hereafter referred to as Martha Morrison), drove Lou out to Long Island to hear her. "I used to do a lot of the driving with Lou," Martha explains, "because he lost his license somewhere along the way [when] he drove into a toll booth." This was the aforementioned incident when Lou was driving home from Syracuse, with a college friend, stoned.

Maureen Tucker, known as Moe, was two years younger than Lou, John and Sterling, having been born in 1944. Dad was an alcoholic house painter who died when she was nineteen, leaving the Tuckers in straitened circumstances. She was a small, homely, churchgoing Roman Catholic who became interested in drumming at high school, enthused by a school visit from the great Nigerian drummer Babatunde Olatunji ("Oh my God, it was stunning!") and by listening to the Beatles, Bo Diddley and the Rolling Stones. Moe was one of millions of American kids who were transfixed by the Beatles' first appearance on the *Ed Sullivan Show* in 1964. "I started not to be satisfied just to listen. I wanted to participate somehow. So I bought a snare drum." She began to play along to pop records with her drum in her bedroom. "I wasn't thinking, 'I'll be a drummer.' I was just having fun." Then her mother gave her a cheap drum kit. "It had an old beat-up cymbal, like a truck ran over it." Teaching herself to play, she developed a weird style of her own, which included playing the bass facedown on the floor like an African tribal drum. "So Lou came to my house to see if I could actually keep a beat, I guess." She passed the audition. "It was supposed to be just that one show, the New Jersey show." They rehearsed together at Ludlow Street, "just to show me the songs so I'd know when to stop!" Moe was shocked to see where Lou and John were living. "This was a real bad place, and a scary area." And she was surprised by their songs. "When they started to play 'Heroin,' I thought, 'This is really different, and good-different.' I liked the music right away. I was impressed, like, *Holy mackerel! What is this?*"

There were three acts on the bill at Summit High School on December 11, 1965, with the Myddle Class headlining. "When the curtain went up, nobody could believe their eyes!" student Rob Norris recalled. "There stood the Velvet Underground—all tall and dressed mostly in black; two of them wearing sunglasses. One of the guys [John] with the shades had *very* long hair and was wearing silver jewelry. He was holding a large violin [actually a viola]. The drummer had a Beatle haircut and was standing at a small, oddly arranged drum kit. Was it a boy or a girl? Before we could take it all in, everyone was hit by a screeching surge of sound, with a pounding beat louder than anything we had ever heard." The song was "Heroin." Fascinated, Rob edged forward. Others turned away. The band played two more songs, "Venus in Furs" and "I'm Waiting for the Man." Moe's kit almost fell apart during the short set. By the end, many of the students had left the auditorium. "I was sitting at the back feeling sorry for the band," says Martha Morrison. "They really wanted people to like them." In fact, the Velvets were elated. They had played their first gig, and it had been fun. They went back to Al Aronowitz's house for a celebratory spaghetti dinner, asking their manager where they were going to play next.

Al booked them into the Cafe Bizarre, a Greenwich Village club catering to the tourists who streamed into the Village in the evening to see young comics and musicians. There was a debate about whether they needed Moe. The experience of having Elektrah and Daryl in the Falling Spikes, and the complications caused by Lou and John getting romantically involved with the girls, had put John off female band members. "No chicks," he told Lou and Sterling. Nevertheless, Moe was with them when they began their two-week residency in December. The classic lineup of the Velvet Underground band was thereby established.

The original four Velvets each had a distinct and different character. Lou was a writer first and foremost, fascinated with the outré but also in love with good-time rock 'n' roll. He was highly egocentric, with an aggression to succeed, dominating his friend and songwriting partner John Cale, who was different in the sense that he was British but also because he came from a musically academic background and was steeped in avant-garde composition. The fact that he played amplified viola onstage helped give the band a unique look and sound, and he didn't bring any pop-music clichés to the mix, as Sterling Morrison observed astutely. By contrast, Sterling was a sociable, jovial journeyman guitarist without ambition. Yet he was also intelligent, bookish and witty. Moe was perhaps the most unusual band member. The fact of her gender was remarkable. Moe knew that it was highly unusual for a girl to play rock 'n' roll drums; as far as she knew, she was the only girl in America doing so in 1965. She also had a unique style. She played drums like a kid hitting pots and pans. She didn't know how to play properly. "I can't play a roll. A drummer, you can't play a roll? But if I could have, it would have been Ginger Baker playing 'Heroin.' Can you imagine what that would have been like? It would have sucked. Not because he sucks. . . . Anyone is a better drummer than me. But I just thought about it differently, or something."

Moe and Sterling didn't take the band as seriously as Lou and John. They enjoyed making music but didn't see it as their career and held down day jobs for a long time. Moe worked in data entry. Sterling did various jobs, including working as a cook in a fish restaurant and delivering air-conditioning units. Moe took little interest in business decisions. She avoided disputes and didn't get involved in relationships with her band mates. "That wasn't my style." Paradoxically, for a band associated with drug culture and deviant sex, their drummer was also a rather unworldly person, with conservative, almost puritanical, views about certain behavior, including bad language. She enjoyed a beer but didn't touch drugs and turned a blind eye to what the guys did in that respect. What really upset her was their swearing. "The mouths on them! Oh my God!" Moe was one of the few people Lou never fell out with and always listened to. They roomed together on the road and were friends until the end of his life, whereas there were long periods when Lou, John and Sterling didn't speak to each other. It is indicative of the warmth between Lou and Moe that she called him Honeybun, which gives a glimpse of Lou's softer side, and he called her Moesy. Sterling was Sterl, while John was usually referred to within the band by his surname, or as Black Jack, because he liked to wear black.

As it turned out, the manager of the Café Bizarre didn't want Moe playing drums, because the patrons wouldn't be able to hear themselves talk in the small club, so she was merely required to shake a tambourine during the shows. The band performed short sets throughout the evening, while customers sat at tables a few feet away, drinking and talking. The audience more or less ignored them, save one young fellow who got up and danced—with a whip. "I grabbed some girl that I didn't know sitting down at a table. She was pretty and I asked her to dance," he recalled. "No one was dancing to the Velvets' music, it almost seemed like it was undanceable music. So I started dancing, and I had a whip at the time. I actually bought the whip at an umbrella shop in the West Forties as a mere decoration [and] I started using the whip as a prop." As there was no stage, this strange couple was dancing directly in front of the group.

"Who is this lunatic?" Sterling asked himself.

The dancer was Gerard Malanga. He had come to the Café Bizarre at the behest of his friend, the ubiquitous Barbara Rubin, who continued to advocate for the Velvets. Having got Al Aronowitz to manage them, she wanted Gerard to film them, knowing that photography and filmmaking were among his interests. More importantly, Gerard worked for Andy Warhol, one of the city's newest and brightest celebrities, who had the uncanny ability of making his friends famous, too. Warhol had achieved fame in 1962 with a gallery show of radical new pictures of everyday objects, including soup cans and Coke bottles, as well as silkscreen portraits of celebrities like Elvis and Marilyn Monroe. From that point on he was constantly in the papers, associated with a vogue for manufactured, commercial art that seemed to many people to be a put-on, as well as being a familiar face on the party scene. He was also ambitious to branch out into the film business, and music.

Next day at work Gerard told Andy and his business manager, Paul Morrissey, about the strange band he had seen at the Café Bizarre, suggesting that Paul come back to the club to check them out. Paul was looking for a band to present under Andy's name at a new discotheque on Long Island, one of several business propositions they were considering. They needed a band loud enough to fill a large venue and, just as importantly, a band with a distinctive look. So Paul went with Gerard to the Café Bizarre. "I thought they were peculiar and unusual," he recalls his first impression, intrigued by the fact that Cale played viola and the percussionist was a girl. "Do you have a manager?" he asked them. "No," they said, apparently forgetting Al Aronowitz, who exits the story at this stage, feeling ill used by the Velvets, despite the fact that he never had any empathy for their music.

It was decided that Paul would bring Andy to the club. Moe recalls how thrilled they were about this. "That was exciting—to see a famous person." Warhol arrived the following night with Paul,

Gerard and other friends who trooped about Manhattan with the artist in the evening, looking just like he did in the newspapers: a slightly built man of thirty-seven, with fine, silvery hair and pale, spotty skin. He wore shades and spoke softly like a child, yet commanded attention and respect. It was said that Warhol had "a whim of iron." After the band played a set, he came over and told them in his fey voice that they were great, his expression both innocent and mischievous. Never much of a talker, he habitually said everything was great. "We liked the idea that their drummer was a girl, that was unusual," he enlarged slightly in his autobiography, *POPism*. "And Lou looked good and pubescent then—Paul thought the kids out on [Long] Island would identify with that."

It is frequently debated whether talent or ambition is most important in a successful career, but this is to forget that luck, or timing, usually plays a part. The Velvets were fortunate to run into Andy at the right time. They were fired from the Café Bizarre almost immediately after they met, for playing the disturbing "Black Angel's Death Song" once too often, so were out of work when they came to his studio loft for a second meeting around Christmas 1965. The artist worked in an industrial building on East 47th Street, near the United Nations. A freight elevator took them up to the fourth floor, where they entered a large silver room. Andy's friend Billy Name, who lived in the studio, had sprayed the whole place with silver paint at Andy's request, including the toilet and the telephone, and had wrapped the water pipes and pillars in foil. As a result, the studio was known as the Silver Factory. It shone in the sunlight. Andy lived uptown with his mother, arriving each morning at around eleven o'clock to work in front of the windows, where the light was best. Gerard came in at about two in the afternoon to assist him. Artwork, including silk-screened Brillo-pad boxes, portraits of Jackie Kennedy and Liz Taylor, and life-size silver silkscreens of Elvis, were created on a production-line basis, then stacked against the walls for collection by Andy's dealer. The pictures were already valuable. This was only part of what went on at the factory. Film cameras were arranged around a couch where Warhol shot his "screen tests" and strange, unsettling art films, many with a sexual theme. The red couch was "as dirty as the gutter," recalls Factory habituée Mary Woronov, a mannish girl with cat eyes and a filthy laugh. It was not uncommon to find actors walking about in the nude between scenes. Opera would often be playing on the hi-fi.

The Velvets agreed to be managed by Andy and Paul Morrissey, on the basis that the duo would help support the band until they started to earn money. The initial idea was to present the group at the Long Island disco they were thinking of calling Andy Warhol's Up. Beyond this, Andy and Paul were ambitious to get into the music business, as they also wanted to become seriously involved in the film business; they were highly ambitious and businesslike in their own eccentric way. There was an initial problem with Lou when he refused to sign a contract, perhaps in light of the fact that he had signed too readily with Pickwick City, a contract that Terry Philips says he chose not to enforce. "[It] was eight or nine months, or more, before they signed a contract. Lou Reed was not going to do anything for anybody," complains Paul Morrissey, who came to loathe Lou. "Do you think people want to read about the life of Lou Reed?" he asked waspishly, in an interview for this book. "You need a good title like *The Hateful Bitch* [or] *The Worst Person Who Ever Lived*. Something that says this isn't a biography of a great human being, because he was not. . . . He was a stupid, disgusting, awful human being."

The Velvets started to hang out at the Silver Factory, becoming part of an extraordinary creative and social scene. They discovered that the factory ran on drugs, principally various forms of amphetamine known generically as speed. Andy took Obetrol, an amphetamine that gave him "that wild happy, go-go-go feeling" that made him "want to work-work-work." Billy Name used methamphetamine daily. Many of their friends were also A-men (amphetamine users): flamboyant, highly strung young men known by enigmatic nicknames such as Ondine, Rotten Rita, Won-Ton and the Turtle. Most were gay. They liked speed partly because it kept them thin. Some of their behavior was alarming. Ondine was known to inject his eyes. When Factory A-man and dancer Freddy Herko went off his head in 1964, he danced out of a window to his death. Lou felt a kinship with these extreme characters. Methamphetamine became his drug of choice, not heroin, which he only dabbled with. Meth made him feel like Superman. He told Nelson Slater that he was going to take meth every day for the rest of his life. For years, he did.

Friends gathered at the Silver Factory each evening prior to going out on the town with Andy as his entourage, filling the studio with their cigarette smoke, excited, speed-fueled chatter and exaggerated laughter. The Factory crowd was a decadent, narcissistic bunch of clever, attractive people who vied for Andy's attention and were quick to put each other down. There were women in the group as well as men, some of them beautiful, some from wealthy or socially prominent families, all unusual. The queen of the scene when Lou arrived was the model and actress Edie Sedgwick, a dissipated rich kid with a history of mental illness who appeared in Warhol films with stark one-word titles like *Bitch, Restaurant* and *Vinyl*. Edie had become almost as famous as Andy himself by 1965, having her hair cut short and dyed to look like his twin. Barbara Rubin was another regular. "She [was] indecent," recalls Moe, shocked to hear a woman use words like "cunt." Then there was Brigid Berlin, the obese and wayward daughter of the chairman of the Hearst publishing empire, who walked around the factory topless, occasionally applying paint to her breasts to make "tit paintings." She was another speed freak, giving rise to her nickname Brigid Polk, a labored pun on the fact that she was forever poking needles in her bum.

Celebrating New Year's Eve with this hedonistic bunch was fun.

The Velvets had recently taken part in an underground film shot by their pal Piero Heliczer. They had performed in a crowded apart-

The Velvets being filmed by Piero Heliczer, late 1965. Lou and Sterling Morrison on guitars, John Cale on viola.

ment building, Lou, John and Sterling stripped to the waist and decorated with body paint, with Angus MacLise and Moe Tucker both playing percussion, Moe in a veil. CBS Television sent a crew to cover the happening, as an example of the crazy things the downtown kids were doing. The item was to be broadcast as part of the evening news on December 31, 1965. That night, the band went out with their new friends from the Factory, including Andy, Edie and Gerard, going uptown in Edie's limousine to see James Brown at the Apollo Theater. High on speed, they then raced back downtown to watch themselves on flickering black-and-white TV, before partying into the small hours. So began 1966, the seminal year of Lou's career.

IV

THE EXPLODING
PLASTIC INEVITABLE

• 1966 •

N THE MIDDLE OF the roast-beef course at the annual New York Society for Clinical Psychiatrists' dinner at the Hotel Delmonico, on January 13, 1966, the Velvet Underground began to play "Heroin" as loudly as possible. As Lou sang about mainlining drugs, Barbara Rubin and her filmmaker colleague Jonas Mekas ran into the ballroom and fired outrageous questions at the shrinks and their wives, all of whom were in evening dress. "What does her vagina feel like?" Barbara asked the women on camera.

"Is his penis big enough?"

"Do you eat her out? Why are you getting embarrassed? You're a psychiatrist; you're not supposed to get embarrassed."

Andy Warhol simultaneously projected a film of a man being tortured. Diners stared at the shocking images, and at the outlandish musicians. Still dressing like a hobo, Lou wore his brown winter jacket and favorite flat-sole cowboy boots. Cale was dressed in black, with a diamanté torque around his neck. He was playing his viola as though he meant to break it. Edie Sedgwick, pretty in a red skirt and black top, was dancing with Gerard Malanga, who was wielding his whip. They were grinning at each other, evidently enjoying their audience's surprise. A second woman, handsome and solemn, stood at a microphone. When Lou finished "Heroin," she intoned another strange song in a German accent.

Although the Velvet Underground were a surprise to most of the 350 guests at the dinner, Andy and his troupe had been invited to the event, and the artist had warned the organizers that he was going to stage a "happening." While many of the guests took this in good spirit, indulging the young people who were evidently having so much fun, others felt that their dignity had been offended. "I suppose you could call this gathering a spontaneous eruption of the id," Dr Alfred Lilienthal huffed. Dr Marcel Helman said he felt like being sick. "Why are they exposing us to these nuts?" a third shrink asked a reporter from the *New York Times*.

The stunt was reported prominently in the *Times* and the *Herald Tribune* the following day, January 14, 1966, as a good joke at the expense of the head doctors. It was light relief from the grim daily news from Vietnam. This was the first significant press coverage the Velvets had received, and it established a tone. While Andy Warhol was expert at garnering publicity for himself and his friends, the mainstream press treated the Velvet Underground as a mere sideshow to his pranks. Their music was mocked as a "din," comparable to a fire alarm going off, in the opinion of the *Herald*. There was no mention of Lou Reed, let alone any serious appraisal of his songs.

Nico, the solemn blonde who sang with the Velvets at the Hotel Delmonico, had recently been imposed on the band by Andy's right-hand man, Paul Morrissey, to Lou's fury. "Boy, did he hate that!" Paul didn't think Lou had sufficient charisma to hold an audience's attention. While Nico couldn't carry a tune, partly because she was deaf in one ear, she had the benefit of being glamorous. So he decided that she was going to be the band's chanteuse. "John Cale was all for that. Lou wasn't. He wanted to sing all the songs. Oh

God! He had no voice at all. He dominated John Cale. He tried to dominate me, [but] he couldn't." Nico became a kind of guest star, who wandered onstage to sing a couple of songs with the Velvets, then wandered off again as if she had another engagement to go to. One could almost hear Lou's teeth grinding.

The tension eased briefly after they slept together. "I fell in love with him. He was so beauuu-tu-full, and very tuff . . . tuff like a stat-tuu," was how Nico explained her feelings for Lou. Fluent in four languages, she spoke English ponderously, with a heavy accent, elongating her vowels. The relationship fascinated their friends. "I thought Lou was in love with her," says Richard Mishkin. Maybe he was for a short time; Nico was a beauty. "Lou was just completely stunned [by] her, and could never quite figure it out—what was going on," John Cale says, adding that Lou and Nico had "very much a love-hate relationship." Mary Woronov, who joined the Factory scene around this time, suggests that Lou slept with Nico to keep control of the act. "I seriously think he fucked her because she was part of the band and it was a way of controlling her, or finding out about her, at least. He used her as an instrument, so why not fiddle with it?" For her part, Nico may well have thought that by sleeping with Lou she was neutralizing her enemy.

Nico was an extraordinary person. Born illegitimately as Christa Paffgen in Cologne in 1938, she grew up as an only child after her father died in the Second World War. She claimed to have been raped by a soldier when she was thirteen, which may or may not have been true; Nico was a fabulist. By the time she left school, she was a tall, big-boned girl with a gloomy demeanor, a deep voice and long ash-blonde hair. She adopted the name Nico as a model, working in Paris and New York. Small film roles followed. She played herself in Fellini's *La Dolce Vita* and had an affair with the actor Alain Delon, the first of a series of famous lovers. Nico subsequently gave birth to a son, Christian, known as Ari, who most people believed to be Delon's, though he denied paternity. By 1965, she was in

London, where she was romantically linked with both Brian Jones and Bob Dylan, inspiring Dylan to write "I'll Keep It with Mine," which she sang as if it were her own. She came to the Silver Factory in November 1965, shortly after which Paul Morrissey put her together with the Velvets.

Once Lou got over the shock of having to work with a chanteuse, he gave Nico three of his best songs to sing. Despite what Lou's college girlfriend Shelley Albin says, Nico always maintained that *Loouu*, as she called him in her deep, doomy voice, wrote the limpid "I'll Be Your Mirror" for her after she told him precisely that, in the sense of being his muse. As further evidence of how complex such matters are, another girlfriend has yet another explanation. "I know for a fact that 'I'll Be Your Mirror' is about Pisces," asserts Barbara Hodes, who met Lou a little later in 1966. She says that Lou, who was a Pisces and took an interest in astrology, told her so. "It's not about any one person, it's about the astrological sign Pisces." Edie Sedgwick was almost certainly the inspiration for "Femme Fatale," which Nico also sang. The third song Lou gave her was "All Tomorrow's Parties," which evoked the hedonistic scene at the Silver Factory. Nico sang these three songs in a way that was much mocked within their circle at the time. "We used to imitate her a lot, like 'vat a cloooun,'" giggles Martha Morrison, imitating her foreign pronunciation. "We always made fun of Nico, and she was probably a poor lost soul who could have used a good girlfriend . . . poor Nico."

Despite the fact that Nico was sleeping with Lou and had a child by a former lover, a rumor swept the factory that she was a lesbian, which spooked Martha and Moe. "It's so stupid, but we were very young and unsophisticated," says Martha. "Nico was too much for us." There was indeed plenty to shock a conventional Long Islander at the Silver Factory. The drug use, nudity and profanity was startling. "They were degenerates, that's all, of all kinds," says Martha, still shocked. Lou had no difficulty fitting in, though, quickly becoming one of Andy's favorites. He had found his second mentor, after Delmore Schwartz.

"Lou was sort of like Andy's Mickey Mouse," says Billy Name, who knew both men well. "He was his animated puppet." The artist made little films of Lou, and whispered to him about his career. Lou listened to what he said, learning from Andy, as he had from Schwartz. The artist taught him all sorts of things, including giving tips on how to deal with the media. He said, for example, that it wasn't necessary to tell journalists the truth. Most importantly, perhaps, he urged Lou to work hard. Despite all the crazy things that happened at the Factory, Andy worked assiduously at his art and the business of art, and he encouraged Lou to be equally industrious, often asking him how many songs he had written that day. Although Lou was writing prolifically, whatever number he cited wasn't enough for Andy, who said he should have written more. It was a lesson Lou never forgot, and often referred to. "Andy works very hard," he said in 1971. "One of the things you can learn from being in the Factory is if you want to do whatever you do, then you should work very hard, very hard all the time, and if you don't work hard all the time, well then, nothing will happen." He took his advice to heart. Lou worked hard for the rest of his life, writing hundreds of songs, recording dozens of albums, performing countless shows and getting involved in numerous side projects. He was ultimately as busy as his mentor.

The happening at the psychiatrists' dinner was the prototype for a mixed-media show, called *Andy Warhol, Up-tight*, first staged at the Cinematheque in New York in February. Once again, the Velvets performed with Gerard and Edie dancing, while Andy and his helpers projected still images and Factory films on to them, and screens behind them. The band started to wear black onstage so they stood out against the projections, while they adopted sunglasses partly in order to protect their eyes from the light. Lou, who up until now had dressed in the scruffy style of a folk singer, made black leather and dark glasses his image for most of the rest of his career, with the result that he is sometimes credited for originating the look. Of course, he didn't. Roy Orbison beat him to it, as did Bob Dylan, to name only two. Lou and Nico bickered at the Cinematheque about how many songs she could sing with the group. "Lou wanted to sing everything," she complained. She wanted to sing "I'm Waiting for the Man," but he wouldn't let her, jealous of one of his very best songs. "We quarreled a lot," she told her biographer, Richard Witts. "But he could be nice to me."

Andy then took the show on the road, starting with a gig at Rutgers University in New Jersey on March 9, 1966. Approximately a dozen people made up the touring version of *Up-tight*. In addition to Andy and his lieutenant, Paul Morrissey, there were the four Velvets and Nico; roadie Dave Faison and lighting man Danny Williams (who later vanished, believed to have taken his own life); Gerard Malanga, whose whip dance was integral to the show; filmmaker Barbara Rubin; photographer Nat Finkelstein; Factory A-man Ondine; and Ingrid Superstar, a sexy blonde who had taken Edie Sedgwick's place in the entourage after Edie upset Andy by telling him that people were laughing at their films, and drifted away from the scene. (The rest of her life was not happy. She met a drug-related death at the age of twenty-eight in 1971.) There were so many people in the party that Paul had to hire a minibus. When they arrived at Rutgers, Andy led everybody into the university cafeteria, where they deliberately created a scene. Ingrid flirted with the male students, eating off their plates, while Barbara filmed them and asked provocative questions, as she had at the psychiatrists' dinner, and Nat Finkelstein took pictures. When a staff member objected to the intrusion, there was a scuffle and the police were called. Although less than 20 percent of the tickets had been sold in advance of the two evening shows, this incident ensured that the auditorium was full when the first show began at eight o'clock.

It started with a screening of Andy's film *Lupe*, which featured Edie puking into a toilet. "Down with Andy Warhol, up with art!"

shouted an excited student. Then the Velvets came onstage, dressed
in white on this occasion, so that when Andy projected his films, including films of Lou on to Lou and Nico on to Nico, they appeared
to dissolve. The projections became increasingly complicated as the
show progressed, image layered upon image, the auditorium strafed
with light. Students and members of the revue danced, ran and
played in the light beams like children. It was joyous. Not everyone
was satisfied, of course. Nico was heckled.

"Speak English, if you can," shouted a xenophobe.

The next day, they drove to Ann Arbor to perform at the University of Michigan Film Festival. Nico was behind the wheel. She
liked to drive and was one of the few people on board who had a
license, though she was a truly terrible driver. As Nico sped across
the country, clipping curbs and ignoring stop signs, the Velvets attempted to rehearse in the back of the vehicle. When Lou lay down
to rest, Andy fondled his crotch. Lou didn't object. Nat Finkelstein
took their picture.

There was a party in Ann Arbor. A local teenager named Jim
Osterberg, later better known as Iggy Pop, was among the guests.
Friends flew in from New York to join the fun, including Danny
Fields, editor of the teen magazine *Datebook* and an early devotee
of the Velvet Underground. "I put a picture of the Velvets and Nico
in *Datebook* magazine, which would have been the first picture of
the Velvet Underground ever in a national magazine, because I had
a column where I would throw in everything I liked," says Danny,
who had a major crush on Lou. They became good friends. "He was
the cutest guy in town, he was the sexiest boy, and everyone was
in love with Lou. He was so hot . . . I became a groupie of theirs,
following them around."

The bus broke down on the way home. They rolled to a stop at
an isolated gas station in Ohio. Paul Morrissey went for help as the
others peered hopelessly under the hood. Andy remarked that his
next superstar would have to be a mechanic. The unusual appear-

ance and behavior of the troupe soon attracted attention in this isolated spot. "And before we knew it there were three cop cars, with six or eight cops surrounding the bus, because the person in the garage saw Paul, who looked like trouble, and they called the police, and they wanted to search the bus. 'Everybody out!'" recalls Moe. "And then we were told we needed to be across the state line by noon the next day. . . . That was totally on account of our looks."

FOR LOU AND THE Velvets, April 1966 was the best month they spent with Andy Warhol. In many ways, 1966 was their greatest year. When plans for the Long Island disco fell through, Andy and Paul Morrissey became concerned about the amount of money the Velvet Underground was costing them and decided to find a venue in New York where they could put on a show quickly to make some cash. They settled on a scruffy Polish club on St. Mark's Place, on the Lower East Side, called Polski Dom Narodowy, better known as the Dom. Paul hired the main room for the month of April. Trying to think of an exciting name for the event, he came up with the Erupting Plastic Inevitable, which appeared in an advertisement in the *Village Voice* the day before opening night, Friday, April 1. They couldn't get access to the Dom before 3 p.m. on the Friday, at which point Gerard started to whitewash the back wall to create a projection screen, refreshing the musty club with the clean smell of emulsion, and Andy got busy installing his projectors and lights on the balcony. He also hung a vintage mirror ball over the dance floor. They opened at eight o'clock, having decided at the last minute to rename the show the Exploding Plastic Inevitable: a month of live music, dancing and film projections, for an entrance fee of two dollars. A hand-printed banner was draped from the fire escape: ANDY WARHOL. LIVE. THE VELVET UNDERGROUND. LIVE DANCING. FILMS. PARTY EVENT *now*.

The scene outside the Dom, April 1966.

Andy's name was enough to draw a crowd of over seven hundred people. "It was packed," says Paul. "It was an enormous success from its very first night."

TO ENTER THE DOM in April 1966 was to step into a world of wonder. The Velvets had been involved in mixed-media shows before, with Andy, and before they met him, while rock concerts were being enhanced with psychedelic effects in San Francisco, where bands like the Grateful Dead were becoming established, their use of music and lights linked to the taking of LSD—but there had never been anything quite like the Exploding Plastic Inevitable. Directed by the preeminent pop artist of the day, the show was an authentic and innovative art happening and, more importantly, it was fun. Thousands of people flocked to the Dom over the following four weeks—ordinary New Yorkers, tourists, fashionistas and celebrities—to dance to the music of the Velvet Underground and Nico under a barrage of strobe lights, colored gel projections and black-and-white movies. The mirror ball spun overhead, its facets casting myriad dots of light on their happy faces.

Andy stayed up in the balcony most of the evening, operating his cameras, although almost anyone was welcome to lend a hand with the equipment. There was a bar downstairs selling beer, Coke and sandwiches to the public, and little tables covered with gingham cloths where people sat in semi-darkness waiting for the show to begin. When the Velvets sauntered onstage and started to play, casually, as if they didn't care who was watching, sometimes with their backs to the room, the lights came on and everybody got up and danced. "It was exciting for all of us, but it was really weird in that we had the place mostly all dark, and then when the band would start we would flash images on projectors and we would be showing films on the walls, films of the Velvet Underground that we had taken, and we were now showing on them while they were performing," says Billy Name. "It wasn't an announced thing. It wasn't a presented, with literature, thing. It was just a *happening* thing, and it was happening and happening and happening. And people came in and started dancing. It was a great time."

Among the films that were shown was footage of a drag queen named Mario Montez, his head enlarged in close-up to gigantic size, eyes blinking massively, mouth opening like a cavern. "Dwarfed by Mario Montez's lipstick-stained teeth and looking like insects that had just crawled out of his mouth, the Velvet Underground played in their wrap-around shades," wrote Mary Woronov in her Factory memoir, *Swimming Underground*. Mary was Gerard's new dance partner. "He bought me a whip, and then he bought me leather pants, and a leather bracelet and everything. I was perfect." They devised dance routines for Velvet Underground songs. Speed gave Mary energy, so she lifted weights during "I'm Waiting for the Man." Gerard mimed mainlining with a prop syringe during "Heroin," and they did a whip dance for "Venus in Furs." "Gerard was the victim always, and I was the dominatrix," she says. It was an act, of course. Mary didn't even like sex. "The S&M was a pose, definitely."

Ingrid Superstar tried to dance with the couple, who were in many ways the stars of the show, but Mary didn't want a threesome. "Ingrid, you can't dance up here, you're fucking everything up," she told her rival, whom she thought common and stupid.

"Yes, I can," protested Ingrid. "Andy said it was okay. And I'm sure it's cool with Gerard."

"No, it's not okay. I'm dancing with Gerard, you skull fucker, not you, me."

"Let go of my arm, you're hurting me . . ."

Others were having more innocent fun out on the dance floor. Grooving under the twinkly mirror ball to the music of her boyfriend's band, Martha Morrison told herself that she was having the time of her life. Absolutely the best time ever. Stamina was an issue.

Some of the band's songs lasted fifteen minutes or more. High on speed, Lou could play his guitar almost indefinitely, which became tiring to dance to. One night Martha's friend Ellie became so exhausted she fell asleep with her head on a speaker.

Nico took an excessive amount of time to get ready for her brief guest spot, her elaborate backstage ritual involving lighting candles. "Lou had very little time for women and their accoutrements, and this ritual would really irritate him," recalls John Cale. "The comic thing was that she'd do all this to help her performance, and then she'd start off singing on the wrong beat!" When Nico glanced around at the band as if *they* were at fault, Lou would say cuttingly, "We know what *we're* doing, Nico." Once she had sung her three songs, she stood aside and banged a tambourine for a while, out of time, then walked off.

Between sets, Gerard went around the hall with a hand-held Bell & Howell film projector, which he shone on the audience. A deejay named Norman Dolph played records to keep people dancing until the Velvets came back on. Norman was a twenty-seven-year-old sales executive for CBS who collected art and ran a mobile disco in his spare time. One night Andy told him that he wanted to make a recording of the band to try to get them a record deal. Norman offered to make the arrangements at his own expense in return for a Warhol painting. "[Andy] said, 'Just do it.' I said, 'OK, I'll do it for a painting.' The conversation took no longer than [that]." Norman hired a studio at Broadway and West 54th Street from a small company called Scepter Records. The Velvets arrived on April 18 to begin recording what became their debut album, *The Velvet Underground & Nico*, also known as the Banana Album because of the banana artwork on the cover.

The band would spend two days in the studio making their demonstration record, working office hours so they could still perform at the Dom in the evening. Another couple of days were set aside for mixing the sound. Andy came with them on the first morning, and gave Lou some advice. "Whatever you do," he told him, "keep all the dirty words." There were no curse words in Lou's lyrics, but his use of drug jargon and fetishistic language about mainlining smack, whiplash sex and such was risqué. Andy knew that this gave the songs authenticity, and that had to be maintained. There was limited time and tape was expensive so they worked fast in the small, beige studio, a piano in one corner and a clock overhead to remind them of the time. Although Andy was the nominal producer, he soon left them to their own devices. Norman Dolph oversaw the sessions, with the help of engineer John Licata.

"There was not two minutes wasted," says Norman, who recalls that Lou and John were intensely focused during the sessions, and Lou wasn't friendly. "Lou projected a sort of hostility, whereas John Cale projected intensity." This was Lou's chance to make a professional recording of the best of the songs he had written since Syracuse, a body of work developed with John, Sterling and Moe and practiced nightly at the Dom. As a result, the band was tight. The songs were lyrically sophisticated, dealing with unusual and difficult subject matter, such as drug use, as well as the complexities of the heart and mind. "Heroin" and "I'm Waiting for the Man" were the jewels in the collection, and there was an extra intensity when Lou sang them. "You did have the feeling it was being sung from the vein, as it were," says Norman. "That's what made it so freezing to listen to. Is this true? And if it is true, how can a person with the talent to make a song out of it not have succumbed to it? You didn't have the feeling Lou Reed had fantasized any of this. You had the feeling he was speaking firsthand."

Arrangements had developed since Lou met Cale. "Basically, Lou would write these poppy little songs and my job was to slow them down, make them 'slow 'n' sexy,'" said Cale, explaining how he helped create the stern and sometimes chilling music. "Everything was deeper, too. A song written in E would be played in D. Maureen didn't use cymbals. I had a viola, and Lou had this big drone guitar we called an 'Ostrich' guitar [used on the Pickwick song 'The Ostrich']. It made a horrendous noise, and that's the sound on 'All Tomorrow's Parties,' for instance. In addition, Lou and Nico both had deep voices. All of this made the record entirely unique." The sounds and ideas of the avant-garde were heard, including the use of drone, but never to the extent that the music became academic. "European Son" was a guitar jam that sped up after the sound of a chair being scraped and a glass broken, sounds John introduced as *musique concrete* to punctuate the composition. It worked. A radical new arrangement of "Venus in Furs" turned what had sounded like a folk song into a sexy, sinister dirge. Drug references and influences were pervasive. Speed energy propelled "Run Run Run," in the course of which Lou referred to his characters scoring drugs on Union Square.

Lou's love of pop music was also part of the recipe, lightening the tone at times. He borrowed a riff from Marvin Gaye's "Hitchhike" to create "There She Goes Again," a catchy little song with a misogynistic lyric that opens up an issue with Lou's songwriting. It was the first of many songs he wrote over the years in which women were physically abused. Lou argued that such songs were not an expression of his personal point of view. Rather, he was putting himself in the shoes of characters who were violent and misogynistic. "It's about a guy whose girlfriend is giving him a bad time. She's split and he thinks she's making it with all his friends," he said of "There She Goes Again." "The line I always liked is 'Well, you'd better hit her.' I thought no one would ever notice. But they did . . . for me it's just a song, attitude. It's got nothing to do with me. Look, I write songs I don't agree with 'cause I don't have a real viewpoint. It has to do with a movie I saw, or a character who was a certain way. Or somebody I read about in the papers or met at a party. I put him in a song and act him out." Yet many people who knew Lou describe him as a misogynist, and there are examples of him hitting women. One will serve for now. One evening, Lou and a date went to see his school friend

Allan Hyman and his young wife. During the evening Lou repeatedly slapped his girlfriend. "She would say something. He'd get pissed off at what she said and smash her around the back of the head," says Allan. "[My wife said,] 'Lou, if you continue to hit her, you have to leave.' And then he smacks her in the back of the head [again]. So she said, 'Get out!'" As we shall see, this was not an isolated case.

Lou's relationships rarely ran smoothly. By the time the Velvets came to record the Banana Album, he and Nico were finished. She dumped him, announcing the split to the band with the words: "I cannot make love to Jews anymore." As a result, Lou was not nice to her at Scepter Records, and the other musicians took their lead from Lou. "We reduced her to tears in the studio, because we wanted her to sing in a soft voice rather than in a hard Germanic voice," said Sterling. Yet Nico's voice was integral to the character of the album, while her name alone would feature on the sleeve as part of the title.

At the end of the sessions, Norman Dolph made an acetate disc of nine songs, which he sent to colleagues at Columbia Records, hoping that they would sign the band. He received a swift reply saying that they weren't in the least bit interested. Andy made good on his promise, nevertheless, rewarding Norman with a silk-screen picture, which he later sold for $17,000. Andy and Paul Morrissey were not fazed by CBS's rejection. They were taking in several thousand dollars a week at the Dom, out of which they paid the Velvets only five dollars a day each, so they had easily covered their investment in the band, and another record company was showing interest in the group. The record division of Metro-Goldwyn-Mayer (MGM) wanted to make a deal. A trip to Los Angeles was arranged to sign the contract and present some West Coast shows.

ANDY, PAUL, THE VELVETS and Nico, together with key members of the Exploding Plastic Inevitable, arrived in Los Angeles on May 1, 1966. Andy, the Velvets (including Lou), Nico and Mary Woronov stayed at the Castle, a mansion in the Hollywood Hills owned by the actor John Phillip Law, while the rest of the party checked into the Tropicana Motel.

The following day, the Velvets signed with MGM for a $3,000 advance against royalties. Although this was a break, Lou was unhappy about the fact he was also required to sign a management agreement with Andy's company, Warvel, whereby MGM payments would be made to Warvel, which would deduct 25 percent commission, before paying the net to the group. Lou had so far refused to sign anything. "He wouldn't sign a contract after Andy supported him for months and months and months," groans Paul, who lost his patience. "I said, 'Well, then there's no record.'" When he said that, Lou gave in. "Finally he did [sign], with hate and hate and hate . . . Lou [always] wanted more money. He wanted this. He wanted that. He was in agony." Lou still wasn't satisfied. Two months later the band sent MGM a letter, signed by all four members plus Nico, to the effect that payments should be made directly to them in future. Moreover, money should be paid in the first instance to Lou.

The day after they signed with MGM, the Exploding Plastic Inevitable opened at the Trip, a trendy nightclub in West Hollywood where they were booked for a two-week residency supported by Frank Zappa's Mothers of Invention, another way-out MGM band. The two groups had the same in-house producer, Tom Wilson. The Velvets took an instant dislike to the Mothers, having formed a prejudice against West Coast bands in general, and seeing Zappa, a talented and articulate musician, as a rival. Opening night, Tuesday, May 3, began inauspiciously, when Nico drove them down from the Castle for the show. "Before we even got out of the driveway she had scraped the car on the gates and pulled the chrome off the rental. Oh my God!" recalls Moe, who feared for her life as Nico negotiated the winding road down from the hills. "And when we got to the place, she hit a parking sign." Celebrity guests at the opening included the actors Dennis Hopper and Ryan O'Neal, and Sonny and Cher, who left early—telling journalists how unimpressed they were. "We were a flop," wails Mary Woronov. "Cher looked in and then said the Velvets should go back underground." Once again, journalists evinced more interest in Andy and his "superstars" than in the Velvet Underground, none of whom was mentioned by name in the reviews. Rather, the musicians were mocked for their androgynous appearance, with one local journalist writing, "Their drummer is a girl who looks like a boy." "They were very depressed that they weren't received in a better way," says Patti Elam, who was also staying at the Castle with her husband, the singer Barry McGuire, who had just had his huge hit, "Eve of Destruction." "They were all very down about it." If so, Mary Woronov maintains that the depression didn't last. "It's hard to feel down when you've got so much fucking amphetamine."

Two days later, the Trip closed, due to an unrelated legal dispute, leaving them in limbo in Los Angeles. With time on their hands, the Velvets went into TTG Studios, a big old building off Sunset Boulevard, to rerecord some songs for Tom Wilson. He wanted new cuts of "Heroin," "I'm Waiting for the Man" and "Venus in Furs." On these LA recordings, the versions heard on *The Velvet Underground & Nico*, Lou didn't sing so much as speak the lyrics, enunciating his words slowly and carefully, which was an effective approach for an artist with a limited voice. Indeed, he never sounded more authoritative than when he intoned the opening verse of "I'm Waiting for the Man." The listener was transfixed.

There was still time to kill before the band's next engagement in San Francisco, and they were bored at the Castle. Although the views from the house were spectacular, most of the band members couldn't drive, and they felt stranded in the hills without a car. Andy paid for Moe to take a taxi to church on Sunday, which briefly got her out of the house. To entertain the others, a trip was organized to Venice Beach. But when they arrived, they sat in the car scowling at the people sunbathing on the sand. "A tan? Uh! We were horrified," snorts Mary, who concedes that this studied anti-Californianism was a pose. It bolstered their self-image as sophisticated New Yorkers to look down on the frivolous Californians, with their suntans and happy pop music. "Monday, Monday" by the Mamas & the Papas was playing almost constantly on the radio in LA at the time. They professed to loathe it.

This East-West culture clash became marked when the show transferred to Bill Graham's Fillmore Auditorium in San Francisco, the epicenter of the West Coast music scene and hippie culture, at the end of the month. Graham tried to relate to Andy and Paul Morrissey when they met at the venue as he would to the managers of hip Bay Area bands, bullshitting them that he couldn't pay them much bread, man, but he believed in the same things they did, and the show was going to be far out. The New Yorkers—who disdained hippie patois—could barely conceal their contempt. As they talked to the promoter, Paul ate a tangerine, carelessly dropping the peelings on the floor of Bill's theater, which annoyed him. Then the conversation turned to drugs. Paul posited the theory that musicians performed better on heroin than on LSD, suggesting outrageously that heroin might be healthy. If he meant to antagonize Graham, he succeeded. "You disgusting germs from New York!" the promoter exploded. "Here we are, trying to clean up everything, and you come here with your disgusting minds . . . and whips!"

As the Velvets went onstage that night, he hissed: "I hope you fuckers bomb."

They did. The San Francisco audience didn't like the show at all, and reviews were scathing. Ralph Gleason mocked the Velvets in the *San Francisco Chronicle* as the Velvet Underpants, writing that, "It was all very campy and very Greenwich Village sick." Gleason went on to co-found *Rolling Stone*, which quickly became the preeminent journal of popular music. The magazine ignored the Velvet Underground at first, and seemed suspicious of Lou for many years. Part of the problem was that the Velvets were out of step with the prevailing love-and-peace culture, of which the magazine was part. "Let's say we were a little bit sarcastic about the love thing, which we were right about, because look what happened," Lou said. "They thought acid was going to solve everything. You take acid and you'll solve the problems of the universe. And we just said, 'Bullshit, you people are fucked. That's not the way it is and you're kidding yourselves.' And they hated us."

At the end of what had been a fairly disastrous West Coast expedition, Lou fell ill with hepatitis after injecting speed. He was admitted to the hospital when he returned to New York. He was still there on July 14 when he read in the *New York Times* that Delmore Schwartz had died of a heart attack in a hotel near Times Square at the age of fifty-two. His body lay in the morgue for two days before it was identified. Lou had tried to see his teacher a short time before, but Schwartz had turned him away. He had become even crazier, believing that his students were conspiring against him. "He had a theory that Nelson Rockefeller was paying everyone at Syracuse to spy on him," says Erin Clermont, who was one of the last of the Syracuse gang to see the writer. Lou left the hospital to attend the funeral. He mourned for Delmore, and never forgot him. "O Delmore how I miss you," he wrote toward the end of his own life. "You inspired me to write. You were the greatest man I ever met." After the funeral he went home to Freeport to recuperate. "He came home when he had hepatitis, and my parents cared for him," says his sister, Bunny. "They shipped me out of the house on a teen tour. Yet another family secret." Then Lou found himself a new apartment in the city.

LOU MAINTAINED A HOME in Manhattan for almost fifty years. He moved frequently during this time, living at more than twenty addresses, mostly within a few favorite areas. In the early years, he lived predominantly on the cheap Lower East Side and in bohemian

Greenwich Village, at a time when it was still possible to find an apartment in the city for little money. Even Lou, with the modest income he made with the Velvets, could afford a place in 1966, especially if he shared the rent. After Ludlow Street, he shared with John Cale for a while at 450 Grand Street, a decrepit Lower East Side walk-up. While the band was playing at the Dom one night, a thief got in and stole Lou's record collection, leaving sneaker prints on his bed. This became known as the Great Sneaker Robbery. In the summer of 1966, Lou moved to the Village for the first time, living initially at 86 West 3rd Street, one block from Washington Square. The apartment consisted of one large room lined with mirrors. There was an elaborate furnace in the form of a golden dragon and, strangely, a coffin. Andy, Ondine, Rotten Rita and Ingrid Superstar were among friends who partied here with Lou. Another friend, Stanley Amos, lived next door. Stanley was an art critic renowned for his parties. He gave his guests bags of glitter, which they would toss in the air when they were high on LSD, so the glitter fell on them in showers while they tripped. But Lou's main drug interest was speed. Obtaining, trading and using methamphetamine occupied an increasing amount of his time. He had become an amateur pharmacologist, reading up on drugs, learning their various names and properties, applying the same attention to detail to his habit as he did to his music. "Lou and Ondine would have furious fights over trading Desoxyn for Obetrols," Warhol recalled in his autobiography, Desoxyn being a pharmaceutical form of methamphetamine and Lou's favorite pill. "And Rotten Rita used to come in with his homemade speed that everyone knew was the worst in the world."

"That's why he's rotten," said Lou, who called another drug connection the Turtle because he was always late.

Meth is an aphrodisiac, and A-men took a carnal interest in Lou as a handsome young man of ambivalent sexuality, but despite his flirtatious manner he didn't seem interested in having sex with any of them. "He wanted to be wanted, and to be desirable, [but] it was mysterious. Who was he sleeping with?" asks Danny Fields. Lou's fling with Nico aside, he seemed to be into drag queens and trans people at this stage in his life, people like Candy Darling, who inspired one of his most tender songs, "Candy Says," a sympathetic ballad written during this period about a young man who had come to hate his body, as Lou's friend James Slattery (aka Candy) had. He called his penis his flaw. Lou was also close to a drag queen known as Brandy Alexander. "There were a bunch of them," says Danny. "When we [first] knew him, his girlfriends were boys—drag queens. . . . We assumed they were sexual relationships. [Guys said,] 'Forget it, you'll never get Lou unless you are a drag queen,' because although he was said to be gay we never knew any guy in our world he had sex with, except drag queens [supposedly]."

Lou had allowed himself to be more effeminate since he joined the camp circus of the Silver Factory. Cale recalls that Lou was "very full of himself and faggy in those days," which is how he acquired the nickname Lulu. "He wanted to be the queen bitch and spit out the sharpest rebukes of anyone around." It wasn't just a pose. In the evening he toured the gay and after-hours bars of the city with Billy Name, looking for action. "I loved after-hours bars. It's where I first saw someone beaten to death," Lou once said. The bars were a good place to get material for songs, and meet lovers. "We were never lovers," says Billy. "We played together, though. We used to go to the after-hours bars, after your regular bars closed at 4 a.m. I remember we went into one, and Lou and I separated, and I looked over and on the stage area René Ricard was giving Lou a blow-job. It sort of surprised me." René was an ostentatious, witty aesthete, a poet and art critic, who appeared in several Warhol movies, including his then most recent picture, *The Chelsea Girls*. "So that was Lou with René. But then Lou would be with Nico. He was bisexual."

While he was evidently attracted to men, Lou maintained concurrent heterosexual relationships. He still saw Erin Clermont, who had moved to the city after leaving Syracuse. He also kept in touch with Shelley, becoming quite upset when she got married in December 1965, as if he still had a claim on her. Lou tried to persuade her to leave her husband, saying he was lonely. Shelley felt sorry for Lou, and comforted him. "I did feel bad for him, because Lou was so lonely." But she stayed with her husband. After an attempt to win Shelley back, he wrote "Pale Blue Eyes," one of his two greatest love songs, the other being "Perfect Day." Confusingly, Shelley's eyes are hazel, but she and Lou agreed that "Pale Blue Eyes" was about her. Lou started the song by singing that sometimes he was happy, sometimes sad, while there was someone who made him mad. "I'm making him mad, because I won't leave my husband, [and] I'm the 'mountain top,'" explains Shelley, referring to the next verse. It was the final verse, in which Lou sang about his beloved being married, making their love a sin, that caused her embarrassment when the song was recorded. "Thanks a lot, Lou." She assiduously avoided listening to it.

Although Lou complained of being lonely, there was yet another girlfriend in his life. One day, Andy and René came by the apartment on West 3rd Street with a young woman who'd been living there previously. She had left some belongings behind, including her bed, which Lou was using. "I want my bed back," she told him. It was the start of a relationship. The girl's name was Barbara Hodes. She was still only a teenager, having just left school in upstate New York to attend college in the city. A fashionable, middle-class, well-connected young woman who became a clothes designer in adult life, she mixed in the same circles as Lou. She attended the opening of Betsey Johnson's boutique, Paraphernalia, in March, for example, an event at which the Velvets performed. Lou had been at Syracuse with Betsey, who later married John Cale. Barbara also went to the Dom when the Velvets were performing. She had taken a shine to Lou after watching him at a distance, and now they began to date. "Lou was my first boyfriend," she says. "We were together, on and off, for over [ten] years."

When Barbara moved to West 15th Street in Chelsea that summer, Lou moved in with her. The relationship was serious enough for Lou to telephone her parents to tell them that he was seeing their daughter, asking them not to be alarmed, considering the fact that she was underage. Lou's solicitude impressed Barbara, or Babs, as he called her. Lou was a rebel, but a middle-class rebel with a conventional side. He was protective of her, wrote her soppy letters and called to say he missed her when they were apart. But she also knew a darker side to Lou and, like Shelley, never entertained the idea that they would marry. "There were so many different sides to Lou. He could be really sweet—with his sister he was very sweet— then he could turn around and be a complete prick." Lou seemed to relish that reputation. He was funny, clever, talented, quirky, all those things, "sometimes very nice, sometimes maudlin," she says, "and sometimes he was a prick."

While he was at the heart of the art-music scene in New York, Barbara recalls that Lou had surprisingly conventional tastes in many respects. He subsisted on junk food, being particularly fond of hot dogs, though he also went through phases of eating macrobiotic and other faddish food. He was prone to fads. He loved Top Forty pop music. For a long time, his favorite record was *You've Lost That Lovin' Feeling* by the Righteous Brothers. He liked to watch TV, and became an early fan of *Star Trek*. Lou and Barbara would go to a friend's apartment to follow Captain Kirk's adventures. Less attractively, Lou was tight with money, leaving Barbara to pay the rent and rarely buying her gifts. He used drugs, and he was vain. "Lou had glasses and a lazy eye and he would never wear his glasses. He would never talk about it." He was also highly unpredictable, loving and caring one minute and spiteful the next. "He was just nasty. There was a part of Lou that was this nurturing, loving, extremely tender person. I have love notes that [are] mushy. There was a whole mushy side to him. . . . Then six hours later a wall would come down," says Barbara. "He would do these outrageous [things]. He was self-destructive."

Lou's sexuality was as enigmatic to girlfriends as it was to his gay male friends. "Did Lou have sex with men? Yeah," says Barbara, but she never knew the details. "What kind was it? I don't know. I didn't ask. He didn't offer." On this basis, they were an item, on and off, into the mid-1970s. Still, they didn't stay together at West 15th Street for long. Within a few months Lou had moved back to the Lower East Side, renting a walk-up on East 10th Street. Lou lived in a succession of small Manhattan apartments of this type, which was all he could afford for many years. He didn't seem to give much thought to where he lived. Although neat and tidy, he was remarkably careless in some aspects of life. Barbara recalls that Andy Warhol gave Lou a gift of his cow wallpaper, which was already collectible and valuable. Most people framed it as art. Lou actually stuck the paper on the wall of his rental, leaving it for the next tenant when he moved out a few months later.

ANDY'S MOVIE *THE CHELSEA GIRLS* was a surprise commercial success when it was released in September 1966, at which point Warhol became more focused on films than on the Velvet Underground. The fact that Lou had been difficult about contracts had also put strain on the relationship. Yet they continued to work together for the time being.

The plan had been to bring the Exploding Plastic Inevitable back to the Dom after California, but when they returned to New York they discovered that the main room had been hired out to rival pro-motors and was now operating as a club called the Balloon Farm. Unable to secure the lease, Andy's troupe reluctantly agreed to stage their show at the Balloon Farm two nights a week as guest artists, but it wasn't the same and reviews were lukewarm at best. The *Village Voice* likened the evening to "zombie night at a Polish casino." Like anything trendy, the Exploding Plastic Inevitable had quickly become passe. When Cale fell sick, Richard Mishkin and Henry

Flynt took turns sitting in with the Velvets. Lou and Richard had stayed in touch since college, despite the disapproval of Richard's mother. "When I was living at home, my mother found a hypodermic needle in my drawer. 'What's this?' I said, 'It's Lewis's.' 'Lewis the Creep!' That's what she called him." The stand-ins found the songs easy to play. Lou told them the chords, how many minutes each song should last, "then we would just start jamming," recalls Henry, who notes that Lou had enough spare energy to get up and dance between sets. No doubt this was speed energy. "I think he was the greatest disco dancer I ever saw."

The show ran until October at the Balloon Farm, at which point Nico decided that she wanted to continue performing as a solo act downstairs in the basement bar. She had a child to support, after all. She needed somebody to accompany her on guitar. Paul Morrissey asked Lou if he would do it. He refused, and discouraged John and Sterling from playing with Nico, arguing that it would be bad for the band's image. Morrissey thought this was very cruel. Finally, Lou and John made a tape for Nico, which she tried to sing along to onstage, becoming so befuddled that she burst into tears. It was a pathetic scene and perhaps deliberately humiliating. If Lou had ever loved Nico, he seemed to hate her now. "So she photographs great!" he yelled one day. "I'm not playing with her anymore."

Their producer, Tom Wilson, had other ideas. He wanted Lou to write a fourth song for Nico for the album, a record that would, after all, bear her name. Paul Morrissey goes so far as to claim that MGM signed the band primarily because of Nico. "Then Tom said, 'Listen, the only thing I don't like about the record is there's not enough Nico. You've got to get another song [for] Nico. And there's nothing here we can use on the radio, so why don't you get Nico to sing another song that would be right for the radio?'" So Lou wrote "Sunday Morning." Inspiration came when he was returning from a party with Sterling and John in the early hours of a Sunday morning. They completed the song at the apartment of Lou's college friend Rosalind Stevenson, who had the presence of mind to film them in the act. "When I did that footage it was in the spirit of someone who was a filmmaker, i.e., me, just for fun, turning my camera on my friends," she explains. This short piece of silent film is often seen in documentaries about the band, with the finished song dubbed on to it. Although one of the prettiest Velvet Underground tunes, the lyric conveyed the drug-fueled paranoia of the Factory scene, as expressed in the line "Watch out the world's behind you." "Sunday Morning" was written for Nico, but when the band went into the studio to record it, Lou insisted on singing it himself. Paul Morrissey was outraged. "He sang it! The little creep. He said, 'I wanna sing it 'cause it's gonna be the single.'"

Relations with Nico deteriorated further when the Exploding Plastic Inevitable toured Massachusetts, Michigan, Ohio and West Virginia that autumn and winter, with an excursion across the border to Hamilton, Ontario (Canada being the only foreign country the Velvets visited prior to their 1993 reunion). The troupe traveled by station wagon, the mirror ball strapped to the roof. Andy didn't attend every show. He was less interested in them now, and less keen on covering their expenses. "I'd chase Andy around if I didn't have money for gas to get home," recalls Moe. Andy would pretend he had no cash, fluttering away.

"Come back here, damn it, and give me some money!" she would yell, running after him.

Lou refused to let Nico sing with them in Columbus. Gerard Malanga noted in his diary that Lou and John were both "drug sick" at the time, the yellow in Lou's eyes indicating that he had hepatitis again. Andy joined them in Detroit for the World's First Mod Wedding at the Michigan State Fairgrounds, during which a couple actually got married. After the usual mixed-media show, spiced up on this occasion by a cast member attacking a car with sledgehammer, Andy gave the bride, Randy Rossi, away to her fiancé, Gary Norris. The wedding ceremony was followed by a "Carnaby Street Fun Festival." This tacky event fell well short of the artistic heights of the Exploding Plastic Inevitable, reinforcing the image of the Velvets as publicity-seeking charlatans rather than major artists. Hardly anybody outside their circle appreciated that the opposite was true. The hope was that things would change when they released some records.

There had already been an attempt to put out a single. "All Tomorrow's Parties" was released on MGM's Verve label in July with "I'll Be Your Mirror" on the B side. For reasons that remain obscure, the record was not widely distributed, and it made no impression on the charts. A second single followed in December. "Sunday Morning" was the A side, sung by Lou, with "Femme Fatale" on the reverse, sung by Nico. The fact that Nico featured on three of the four sides released indicated that MGM saw her as the main attraction. But once again little effort was put into promoting the single, which suffered the same fate as the first. It looked as if MGM had lost confidence in the band. The company had signed them for little money on the strength of Warhol's celebrity and Nico's film-star looks. Their trip to Los Angeles, where MGM executives would have seen them play live, had gone badly, as had their visit to San Francisco. The press didn't take them seriously, their music was not on-trend in terms of "love and peace," and the public didn't seem at all interested. There may have been a feeling within MGM that the company had made a mistake and there was little point putting much effort into promoting the band. There was still no release date for their album.

The Velvets finished the year with two shows in Philadelphia. The full mixed-media show was staged at the YMHA (Young Men's Hebrew Association) in the city in December 1966, with lights, films, dancers, and the Velvets playing. Andy was present. A large crowd came for "Philadelphia's first happening," up to two thousand people on opening night. "They came in droves," noted Judy Altman in the *Philadelphia Daily News*. She added that many walked out during the show and that objects were thrown at the band. "This is a great town. People curse at you and throw things. Great town," the reporter quoted an unhappy band member. A year that had begun with such promise, a year of enormous creativity onstage and in the studio, ended with a sense of anti-climax for Lou. He had written and recorded some of the most radical songs of the 1960s, yet he remained almost completely unknown.

V

LIGHT AND DARK

• 1967–68 •

T WAS A THRILLING moment for Lou and his band mates when their debut album finally reached the shops in the spring of 1967. Moe was so excited to see the LP in her local record store on Long Island that she bought a copy. "That was cool." The album was cool; few albums in the history of rock 'n' roll have been cooler than *The Velvet Underground & Nico*. Above and beyond the extraordinary songs, the cover was a significant work of pop art, designed by one of the foremost artists of the second half of the twentieth century. The LP was issued in a white gatefold sleeve adorned with a stick-on picture of a banana, with Andy Warhol's name and the instruction "Peel *slowly and see*." The yellow sticker came away to reveal the meat of the fruit, suggestively tinted pink. Neither the band name nor the album title appeared on the front; that information was printed on the spine and back. "We thought it would seem better with his name on it," explained Lou with uncharacteristic modesty (his own name was listed first on the credits inside). "Produced by Andy Warhol. It was like being on a soup can."

The back cover featured a color photo of the band onstage during the Exploding Plastic Inevitable, with Gerard dancing under a barrage of projections. One of these images was of a dancer named Eric Emerson who had featured in a couple of Andy's films. An extrovert of unusual habits—he wore hot pants and taught yodeling—Emerson created a major problem for the band immediately by demanding $500,000 compensation for unauthorized use of his picture. MGM withdrew the LP while it altered the artwork to remove his image, which damaged sales at the critical moment. "It had started to go up [the charts] and then MGM pulled it, said, 'No, until this lawsuit is settled we're pulling it off the shelves,' and that busted the rise of the album," laments Billy Name, who took most of the photographs inside the gatefold. "When somebody does something like that from within your troupe, it's really a pisser."

Although MGM spared no expense on the production of the album sleeve, sanctioning a complex printing process to create the peelable banana, the publicity campaign was crude. It also traded heavily on Warhol's name. "What happens when the daddy of Pop Art goes Pop Music?" asked print ads. "The most underground album of all!" Even worse, there was an implied apology. "Sorry, no home movies. But the album does feature Andy's Velvet Underground (they play funny instruments). Plus this year's Pop Girl, Nico (she sings groovy)." The mainstream press ignored an album that was presented almost as a joke. The few reviews it received, mostly in small magazines and in the underground press, were mixed. "The Velvets are an important group, and this album has some major work," Richard Goldstein wrote cautiously in New York's *Village Voice*, one of their most positive reviews, but while he praised "Heroin" he dismissed "Black Angel's Death Song" and "European Son" as pretentious.

The album crept up to 171st place on the *Billboard* chart of America's Top 200 albums, only to slip into oblivion when it was briefly withdrawn from sale due to the Emerson problem. This was as high as the Velvets charted in the USA in the 1960s. In sales terms, they were a total failure. "There was no audience for them," crows Paul Morrissey, who had little regard for the music. "Nobody bought their albums." This was not literally true. From the beginning, the band had a small, discerning audience who not only bought their music but were profoundly affected by it. Brian Eno later observed that while only a few thousand people bought *The Velvet Underground & Nico*, it seemed as if every one of them started a band, and it is true that a remarkable number of people who became significant in the art-rock scene in the 1970s were influenced by the Banana Album.

Not least among these was nineteen-year-old David Bowie, who heard an advance copy of the record in suburban London, where he was beginning his career. It was a revelation. "This music was so savagely indifferent to my feelings. It didn't care if I liked it or not. It could [not] give a fuck. It was completely preoccupied with a world unseen by my suburban eyes," was how he described the experience of hearing *The Velvet Underground & Nico* for the first time. "One after another, tracks squirmed and slid their tentacles around my mind. Evil and sexual, the violin [*sic*] of 'Venus in Furs,' like some pre-Christian pagan-revival music. The distant, icy, 'Fuck me if you want, I really don't give a damn' voice of Nico's 'Femme Fatale.' What an extraordinary one-two knockout punch this affair was. By the time 'European Son' was done, I was so excited I couldn't move. It was late in the evening and I couldn't think of anyone to call, so I played it again and again and again." Bowie soon began to perform "I'm Waiting for the Man" as part of his set.

There were several such acolytes in the USA. The Velvets were appearing at a venue known as the Gymnasium in New York in the spring of 1967 when their support act canceled. A teenager named Chris Stein filled in at short notice with his band. "So we got on the subway with our guitars and went up to [the] Gymnasium. It actually was an old gymnasium. . . . The place was big and echoey, and kind of dark. The Velvets used the ambience of the room to their advantage." Chris and his buddies were "totally taken aback" by the band's music, at the Gymnasium gig and on the record. "My friends and I were really amused by the Velvets' record when it came out among all the love and peace." By way of context, the Beatles were just about to release *Sgt. Pepper's Lonely Hearts Club Band.* "The darkness of it in the midst of that was quite a contrast. . . . To this day, the first record sounds so modern in its weird fuzziness." Stein later found fame with his girlfriend Debbie Harry as Blondie, one of several bands to emerge in the 1970s that were inspired by the Velvets. Others include Roxy Music (featuring Brian Eno), Talking Heads and U2.

The fact that the Velvets had caught the attention of a select number of smart young people who would build on their ideas, often with far greater commercial success, was unknowable in 1967, and probably of little comfort to Lou had he been able to see into the future. Having had their record released at last, the band was immediately frustrated not to hear their songs on the radio, and dismayed to discover that the album, and their subsequent releases, were not well distributed. "We were disappointed," admits Moe. "Verve didn't know what to do with us. We'd go play in St. Louis or something and people [would tell us,] 'We can't find your record.'" Lou began to wonder if their association with Warhol was holding them back.

Andy had been an important mentor, showing more interest in him than most of the kids who hung around the Silver Factory. He took the trouble to give Lou advice, in a way he rarely did, and the younger man heeded what he said, which was just as unusual. "He and Lou would talk. Lou would ask him, 'Do you like this, or that?' That's the only time I heard him say things like that," says Mary Woronov. Now Lou began to resent Andy's proprietorial position. "Lou didn't like the fact of Andy owning the Velvets, and Lou thought Andy was selfish," says mutual friend Brigid Berlin, who notes that it was around this time that Lou began to call Andy by the nickname Drella, a portmanteau of Dracula and Cinderella that some friends thought insulting. Andy himself didn't like the name. "He was the one person that called Andy 'Drella,'" adds Brigid. "He didn't like the fact it was Andy Warhol's Velvet Underground. He wanted to be on his own."

Artist and pupil had a frank talk about the future. "Do you want to keep just playing museums from now on and the art festivals?" Andy asked, referring to a show they had just done at the Chrysler Art Museum in Massachusetts. "Or do you want to start moving into other areas?" Andy generally encouraged his protégés to move on and do their own thing, but he surely didn't expect Lou to fire him, which is what Lou claimed happened. The day he fired Andy as their manager, and Andy was so shocked that he called him a rat ("It was the worst thing he could think of"), became one of Lou's favorite stories, one he told many times in interviews and wove into the lyrics of "Work" on *Songs for Drella*. Andy said that it wasn't as dramatic as Lou made out, while Paul Morrissey maintains that *he* let the Velvets go. "I said, 'The management is over, do what you want.' It was done legally. He always wanted to be in charge with John Cale [under his thumb]. He was, I think, the worst person I ever got involved with . . . he was not nice. It was difficult dealing with him." The band continued to appear under Andy's name for the time being, but henceforth they were increasingly independent. And they were actively looking for new management.

In May 1967, they played two nights at the Boston Tea Party, a hip new club on Berkeley Street in Boston. "It was just a big open thing, no seats," says Moe of a venue where they played more frequently than anywhere over the next few years. Nico showed up for the second night with Andy, direct from the Cannes Film Festival, where they had been promoting *The Chelsea Girls*. She had recently recorded four of Lou's songs for her solo album *Chelsea Girl*, including the track "Chelsea Girls," in which Lou name-checked Factory friends, including Brigid, Ondine, Ingrid Superstar and Mary Woronov. He also played guitar on the album. But when Nico asked to join the Velvets onstage in Boston, Lou refused. Nico was no longer their chanteuse, and wouldn't appear on their next record. To make it official, the original four members signed a new agreement with MGM, "the 1967 agreement," cutting her out of the deal.

The Boston gig was arranged by a businessman named Steve Sesnick, who had an interest in the club and ambitions to manage the band. Sesnick was only a few months older than Lou, but he had the manner and appearance of a more mature person. He was thickset, dressed conservatively and liked to smoke cigars, all of which lent him what Moe describes as an air of "false pomposity." She liked him nonetheless. "He was fun . . . he had grand plans [for us], which was cool." Cale was less keen. Indeed, he came to blame Sesnick for creating a fatal rift between Lou and himself. "Suddenly Lou was calling us his band while Sesnick was trying to get him to go solo."

In June, the Velvets performed at a garden party at the country estate of the architect Philip Johnson in New Canaan, Connecticut. They played in front of Johnson's Glass House. Andy was among the guests at the party, which was a benefit for the choreographer Merce Cunningham. It was a sophisticated, enjoyable evening. Afterwards, the band was chauffeur-driven back to New York at Johnson's expense. During the long drive they discussed their future and made the fateful decision to hire Sesnick as their manager. It was what Lou wanted at the time, though he would come to regret it bitterly.

THAT SUMMER, LOU MOVED west again. His new home was a loft apartment in the fur district of New York, at Seventh Avenue and West 28th Street. The smell of hides was pungent, while tufts of fur got everywhere, including the cracks in the floor. But when the furriers went home at night, he could play his guitar as loud as he pleased. "You have to hear this," he told his girlfriend Barbara Hodes, when she came over to hang handmade curtains in the loft to make the place more homely for Lou. "It was all feedback," she says of the loud, discordant music. These were songs for the second Velvet Underground album, *White Light/White Heat*, which the band recorded at Mayfair Sound on Times Square in September 1967.

It could be argued that Lou had two principal songwriting styles. In the first place he liked to tell stories with named characters like a novelist. Such songs were often inspired by things he had seen, done or heard about. Sometimes he used the names of real people he knew, as in "Candy Says." His second style was more impressionistic. Songs didn't tell a story but relied upon the artful juxtaposition of phrases to create images to evoke feelings. "White Light/White Heat," the title track on the second album, was such a song, open to a range of interpretation. Like most songwriters, Lou frequently repeated words. In this case "white" alternated with "light" and "heat" created two phrases, repeated over a two-chord guitar progression (G5/D5). Played loudly in a style that would become known as heavy metal, the song achieved considerable binary power. One of the simplest tunes Lou ever wrote, "White Light/White Heat" was also one of his strongest and most enduring compositions. Amphetamine use was an obvious influence. "White heat" was then a slang term for a speed rush, and Lou made reference to speed freaks in his hyper vocal.

Song ideas were precious. Lou noted them down and hoarded them if he didn't have an immediate use in mind, sometimes returning to an idea years later. For the Velvets' second album, he reached back to college for the story he wrote for Shelley when they were exchanging letters in their summer holidays, about the boy who mailed himself to his girlfriend. Lou now gave the story of Marsha and Waldo to John Cale to narrate. He did so over a grinding backbeat with squeals of feedback guitar, creating "The Gift," an unusual and funny highlight of the album. "Lady Godiva's Operation" was another short story set to music, partly inspired by Lou's ECT experience, but less successful than "The Gift." The story—told by Cale, with help from Lou—was unclear, and the music meandered tediously to its conclusion. In contrast to these long, wordy recordings, "Here She Comes Now" was brief, insistent and sexy. Another short song, "I Heard Her Call My Name," was truly manic, Moe maintaining a frantic beat as Lou delivered a speed rap ending with a mind-splitting guitar solo.

The magnum opus was "Sister Ray," a droning jam named after a drag queen of Lou's acquaintance that had become a staple of their act. The lyric introduced a cast of weird characters, including Duck, Sally and Miss Rayon (Lou was good at names), as well as an anonymous sailor. The lyric blended his two basic songwriting styles: a semi-abstract story with use of repetition and drug slang, also playing with the sounds of words, stuttering and jamming words together. Some of it sounded like nonsense, but a murky story of drug use and murder emerged, reminiscent of Tralala's tale in Hubert Selby's *Last Exit to Brooklyn* and the Mardi Gras chapter in *City of Night,* favorite books whose influence ran throughout Lou's songwriting. Guitars created a dense musical backdrop to the words, through which the bright notes of Cale's electric organ broke after several minutes. Sterling and Lou turned up their amps to try to drown John out in what became an epic battle of musical power, while Moe struggled to keep the beat. "'Sister Ray' could have turned into just noise. It's very easy to make noise," she says. "Lou goes flying off, and Cale is going crazy, but there is a beat going on [and] when Lou has stopped fooling around, here is something to come back to. Not only to come back to, but while the audience is listening to this cacophony they are [still] hearing a beat. If music doesn't have a beat it's not music—it's noise."

Lou introduced a new character in the third verse, Cecil, who shoots the sailor. Lou objected to the crime in a whiny voice, saying Cecil shouldn't have done that and asking for a dollar, which led to a rare explicit sexual reference, "sucking on my ding-dong." Lou had a talent for inventing slang terms like "ding-dong" that sounded right and had the benefit of not dating. After a quarter of an hour of churning music, the band let the volume drop and Lou reprised the lyric in the lull. Moe picked up the beat, and all four thrashed their way to the end. The whole song lasted seventeen minutes. They recorded it once. Mortified by what he heard, the studio engineer walked out.

"Sister Ray" was one of the most extreme and powerful tracks Lou ever created, but in the mixing stage he discovered that the recording of this, and other songs on the album, was distorted because the band had played too loudly in the studio. It was often hard to make out the words. "I wrote the lyric—I think—while we were riding to and from a gig," Lou said of "Sister Ray." "It has such an attitude and feel to it, even if you don't understand a word of it. It sounds sleazy. . . . It's just a parade of New York night denizens. But of course it's hard to understand a word of it. Which is a shame . . ." With limited studio time at their disposal, they were unable to fix the problem. Lou remained unhappy with the result, but the distorted nature of the recording became part of the essential character of what is one of his most iconic and important records. It is also true to say that "Sister Ray" worked just as well in concert.

"White Light/White Heat" was another muddy recording. Released as a most unlikely single in November 1967, at a time when the Monkees were topping the charts with "Daydream Believer," it flopped. The eponymous album followed in January 1968. To illustrate the record, Lou chose the image of a skull tattoo from Andy Warhol's film *Bike Boy*, which Billy Name enlarged for the cover. "It was black and white, and we did it black on black," says Billy. "That was the original black tattoo on the black album cover." This was a dark, difficult album in every sense, the antithesis of a commercial record, and it managed 199th place on the *Billboard* Top 200, an even lower position than their debut. There was virtually no airplay, and reviews were sparse. Many publications, including the new *Rolling Stone,* ignored it. Other publications slated it, while a precious few critics recognized that the Velvets were doing unusual and interesting work. "Probably the most blatant injustice perpetrated by the media on the contemporary music scene has been the virtual black-out coverage of the Velvet Underground," Wayne McGuire wrote in *Crawdaddy,* praising *White Light/White Heat* as genuinely original and subversive, unlike the music of more popular posturers, such as the Doors, predicting that the Velvets would be vindicated in time. "Put simply, the Velvet Underground is the most vital and significant group in the world today." McGuire was proved right.

In the long term, the first two Velvet Underground albums were recognized as being among the most innovative rock records of the 1960s, and although initial sales were poor, they have been selling for decades. *The Velvet Underground & Nico* had sold nearly 3 million copies worldwide by the time of Lou's death in 2013, making it the most successful Velvet Underground album. *White Light/White Heat,* a more challenging listen, sold over half a million copies in that time, putting it in second place in the league table of VU sales.[2] And as Chris Stein of Blondie notes above, the music, like all great art, has retained an extraordinarily modern quality through the years.

While Lou and John enjoyed their foray into extreme experimentation, the music of *White Light/White Heat* was John's forte more than Lou's, and now the band turned away from sonic excess. When they returned to the studio in February 1968, they recorded more melodic songs, though the lyrics were just as sophisticated. These numbers included "Stephanie Says," a pretty song about a girl suffering with depression. Lou used the "she says" conceit several

---

2   Excluding compilations. Worldwide sales of the third Velvet Underground studio album are roughly equal with *White Light/White Heat.*

more times over the years, also creating "Lisa Says" and "Caroline Says." Cale recalls that "there was heroin involved" in the session for "Stephanie Says," which has an anaesthetized sound. In contrast, "Temptation Inside Your Heart" was a lively, happy sort of song, punctuated with laughter and doo-wop harmonies. It would be almost twenty years before these recordings were officially released, but this was the way forward for the band.

Under Steve Sesnick's management, the Velvets were making an effort to be more accessible and thereby, hopefully, more popular. As well as recording less confrontational music, they began to play more shows, though not in New York. They focused instead on cities like Boston, Philadelphia and San Francisco, where they began to build a student following. There was also a change of image. Eschewing austere black clothing and shades, Lou started to dress in the foppish fashions of 1968, wearing paisley shirts with bell-bottom trousers and wide belts. He let his hair grow, looking like a member of any mainstream band of the day. John remained a more radical dresser, appearing as unorthodox as he sounded in publicity photos for the second album, for which he wore a white shirt with a huge collar and elaborate cuffs that ended in bows. This was partly the influence of fashion designer Betsey Johnson, whom he married in April 1968.

Lou seemed to resent the fact that Betsey was ambitious for her new husband, pushing John forward in the band. A few days after the wedding, the men almost came to blows onstage. Both had started to drink heavily. Lou liked Scotch whisky, preferably Cutty Sark or Johnny Walker. On top of speed, the booze made him aggressive. He and John were struggling for control of the group. "They played brilliantly together, and they worked brilliantly together, but in a management-type situation Lou and John were always head to head, wanting to manage the situation. They both wanted to be the lead," comments Billy Name. "They couldn't agree." Brigid Berlin's sympathies were with John. "You know, Lou was a strange person.

I had a lot of fun with him, but he had a side to him. He was very cranky, and he could be mean," she says. "John was a much nicer person than Lou was. Lou was a troublemaker. Lou had an *act* going all the time."

LOU HAD STAYED IN touch with Lincoln Swados since they had shared a room together at Syracuse. While he was busy with his music, Lincoln's life had become increasingly troubled. Around the time the Banana Album was released, he attempted suicide by stepping in front of a subway train in New York. He survived, with the calamitous loss of his right arm and right leg, after which he took to living in an old storefront on the Lower East Side and singing on street corners. He also had a job in the box office at La MaMa, a theater on East 9th Street where his sister was beginning a successful career as a composer. Elizabeth Swados had a difficult relationship with her brother. "I began to wince at the strange little songs he sang in the box office and the sometimes nasty manner in which he treated the foreign directors and actors," she wrote in a book about their family. "He didn't wash and I was embarrassed by his body odor."

Lincoln was back in the hospital in the spring of 1968, on suicide watch at Bellevue, when Lou paid him a visit, bumping into a friend of Lincoln's at the lift. Bettye Kronstad was nineteen years old, pale and slim with wavy brown hair, full lips and the look of a girl who might be about to cry. Bettye always felt emotional after seeing Lincoln, whom she knew from La MaMa. She was a sensitive person in any case, affected by a difficult and disrupted childhood. After her parents broke up acrimoniously, and fought over her, she was raised with the help of her grandparents in Pennsylvania, coming to New York in 1967 when she was eighteen. Good looks got her modeling assignments and an audition to be a Bunny girl, but she was currently doing secretarial work at Columbia University, where she was also studying English. Lou may have timed his visit to see Lincoln in the hope of meeting her. "I'm a friend of Lincoln Swados. My name's Lou Reed," he introduced himself at the hospital lift, as if his name should mean something to her. Bettye nodded, stepped into the lift and pushed the down button. Lou held the doors open. "So you'll tell Lincoln you met me?" When Bettye agreed, he let her go. She made a mental note of his appearance as the doors closed. "I actually didn't really like him at first, because he's not my type. He had the whole rock 'n' roll star thing going on, with the blue-white snap pearl buttons, shirt open almost to his navel, couple of chains, hair coiffed, blue bell-bottoms, puddling out just perfectly."

The next time she visited Lincoln, he asked, "So you met my roommate—what do you think?"

"He's the rock star, right? The Velvet Underground?"

"Yeah."

"Oh, come on, Lincoln, you know he's not my type."

"He's actually really not like that at all," said Lincoln, evidently aware of the fact that Lou could make a bad impression. "He isn't the arrogant person he's coming off as. He is actually a nice guy. . . . He's a good writer." An interest in writing was something all three of them had in common. Lincoln and Lou had evidently discussed Bettye. "He wants your phone number. May I give him your phone number?" he asked, like a teenager enquiring on behalf of a shy friend (Lou was twenty-six at the time). Bettye was reluctant. "Oh come on, Bettye, give the guy a shot. He likes you and he'd like to see you. Would you at least [let him] give you a call?"

Bettye was living in student accommodation near Columbia. Lou telephoned her several times over the next few days. He was at his parents' house in Freeport. She got the impression that he was living on Long Island. He asked if he could come into the city and take her out. They agreed to meet at the West End, a bar near the university. "I met him there and all he basically did was rave about John Cale, [and] he drank a lot. He was talking about how the album [hadn't] gone right, and nobody was listening to him. And it was just about Cale, Cale, Cale." Lou said John was a madman who never listened to him. They fought constantly and John was trying to take the band away from him. "I'm the leader!" he exclaimed, as he drank Scotch. "They are not listening to me in the studio." It became repetitive. "John is doing his thing, and we don't want [him] droning on and on and on . . ."

It was a typically disastrous Lou date. By the end of the evening Bettye was bored and Lou was drunk. He insisted on walking her home. "I think I walked *him* home. . . . He opened the door to me at my old apartment building, which was at the corner of Riverside Drive and 116th Street, down the hill. I seriously wondered how he was going to get back up the hill to the subway station at 116th and Broadway. But he was very polite. He thanked me." He said they should meet again.

Columbia shut early that year because of student demonstrations on campus, culminating in a sit-in. The whole country seemed to be in an uproar, over civil rights and the war in Vietnam. In recent months there had been a major race riot in Detroit and a standoff between peace protestors and police at the Pentagon. Then Dr. Martin Luther King Jr. was assassinated in Memphis on April 4, 1968, causing national outrage. The young Laurie Anderson, studying art history at Barnard College in New York, was among the students who occupied the campus of Columbia University that spring, protesting about race relations and other matters. Unusual for someone of his generation and education, Lou remained uninterested in such issues, showing little or no engagement with politics until much later in life. "I worked in the anti-war movement. I worked for mobilization against the war in Vietnam," says his friend Erin Clermont. "I never told Lou I was working there. It seemed completely irrelevant to his life. I never heard him say *a word* about Vietnam."

With Columbia shutting early, Bettye decided to go to Europe for the summer with friends. Lou wanted to see her again before she left, pestering her with calls up until her last night in New York. She told him that it was impossible to meet in the circumstances, and thought his behavior odd. As she would discover, neediness was a trait in Lou's personality. "I didn't mean to blow him off, but there were other people I wanted to see the night before I left the country than a person I had only met [twice]." Lou asked her to let Lincoln know when she got back. It was several weeks before Bettye had cause to think of Lou again. She was in Paris, at a cafe on the Left Bank, when she opened a US newspaper and saw an article about the Velvet Underground. "I read the newspaper article and put it down. So that's Lou. Hmm. So that actually interested me. That's how I began to think of him pretty seriously."

EVEN THOUGH THEY WEREN'T in business together anymore, Lou continued to socialize with Andy Warhol, who had recently moved his studio downtown to 33 Union Square West. A short walk across the square was Max's Kansas City, a restaurant that became a club-house for the artist and his friends.

Max's Kansas City (named for a cut of steak) was long and thin, with a bar and booths in front and a mezzanine where bands played. The Warhol crowd congregated in the downstairs back room, around a circular table within the glow of a light sculpture. "We went to Max's every night [and] sat at a big round table at the back with a Dan Flavin big red light installation—everyone looked really good in that lighting. Red is really good for the face," recalls David Croland, a model who had recently joined the Factory crowd. Mary Woronov observes more tartly that the Flavin made everyone look like they were broiling in an oven. "There was always a spill-over table," adds Croland. "Sometimes it was like twenty of us, on one side of the room, and the whole rest of the room was staring at us." The gang could be as outrageous as they liked in the back room. "My younger brother, for his twelfth birthday, I took him to the city to see [a movie]. Then we went to Max's. Brigid came and sat down, and all of a sudden she pulled out her needle and pulls down her pants"—Moe Tucker cites an example of the open drug use—"'Brigid, my brother! He's twelve years old!'" There was exhibitionism of all kinds. Factory loon Andrea "Whips" Feldman regularly did a striptease on the table while singing "Everything's Coming Up Roses." Andy kept an open tab, which he settled by giving artwork to the owner, Mickey Ruskin, so all his friends ate for free, Lou included. Lou spent a lot of time at Max's over the next couple of years. One night he bumped into Erin and a girlfriend at the restaurant and tried to talk them into a threesome. "Didn't happen, [but] it was sort of a cool night. Max's was incredible," giggles Erin. "Anything could happen there, it was just crazy."

Andy's new studio, on the sixth floor of the nearby Decker Building, was split into two parts. There was a dark back area painted black for developing film, where Billy Name resided, and a white front office for business. The new studio was not as informal as the Silver Factory, but crazy people still floated in and out. Few were nuttier than Valerie Solanas, founder of the Society for Cutting Up Men (SCUM). That summer she presented Andy with a film script, *Up Your Ass*. It was so obscene that he suspected she might be an undercover cop trying to entrap him. The artist was on the telephone at the office on the afternoon of Monday, June 3, 1968, a warm day, when he heard a bang, turned and saw Solanas pointing a gun at him. "Valerie, don't do it!" Andy cried out, feeling like a character in a B-movie speaking movie dialogue. She fired nonetheless. "I felt a horrible, horrible pain, like a cherry bomb exploding in me."

Billy opened the dark-room door to see his friend lying in a pool of blood in the white office. He picked him up, asking what had happened.

"Don't, Billy, don't make me laugh, it hurts too much."

Far from trying to make Andy laugh, Billy was in tears, "wondering what was going on . . . then I looked around and there was [art critic] Mario Amaya, who was also shot in the back, and other people just standing around frozen. Everybody was traumatized. And then somebody told me Valerie Solanas had come and shot Andy and then she'd run out. I was there holding him in my arms, crying."

The news flashed around the world. ANDY WARHOL FIGHTS FOR LIFE. The pop artist had been shot repeatedly, the bullets piercing his stomach, liver, spleen and lungs, and was in a critical condition in a New York hospital.

Lou was with the band on the West Coast, staying at the Beverly Wilshire. He was coming down in the lift the next morning with Steve Sesnick when he saw the headlines. "In that particular hotel, they put the morning papers on the floor of the elevator," Sesnick recalled. "We were both extremely shocked and startled when we looked down and saw the headlines."

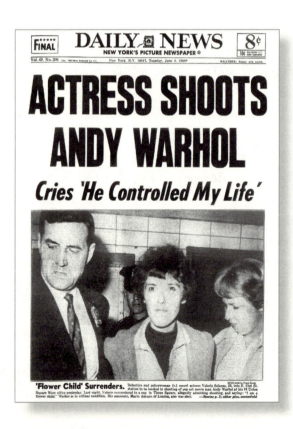

Andy narrowly survived the shooting, spending the next seven weeks in the hospital. He was left heavily scarred, and his health was permanently impaired. Lou was slow to call, let alone visit. "Why didn't you visit me? Where were you?" the artist asked when he finally got in touch. Instead of hurrying to the bedside, Lou acted as if *he* were at the center of the drama. Shelley Albin agreed to meet Lou at Max's when he got back from the coast. "He was scared," she says. Lou explained that he had recently told Valerie Solanas that women were inferior to men. "Lou, if he had the right audience, would say women are inferior. They're not as smart, they're not as capable. He would say whatever he had to [in order] to piss off who he was talking to." Now he was paranoid that Solanas wanted to shoot him, too. He had little real cause for concern. Solanas was arrested within hours of shooting Andy and held in a psychiatric hospital. Hearts quickened at Christmas, when she was unexpectedly granted bail, but she was soon returned to custody, ultimately receiving a three-year prison sentence. That Lou had twisted Andy's shooting into a drama in which *his* life was at risk revealed his egocentricity. The two men nevertheless remained friends.

ANDY RETURNED TO WORK in September, the same month that Lou decided to settle his issues with John Cale. He invited Sterling and Moe to meet him at the Riviera Café in Greenwich Village, where he staged a coup d'état. He told them that Cale was out of the band. "You mean out for today, or for this week?" asked Sterling. When Lou made it clear that John was out for good, Sterling became angry.

"You don't go for it?" asked Lou. "All right, the band is dissolved."

To his lasting regret, Sterling decided that the continuation of the band was more important than loyalty to John, and acquiesced. Moe also went along with it. It was the second example, after the dismissal of Andy as their manager, of what became a pattern in Lou's career. At some stage he turned against almost everybody who worked with him, even if this was to his detriment. He had to be in control.

Steve Sesnick hired Cale's replacement. "I really don't know that Sesnick consulted anyone before calling me down to New York City. The offer was made over the phone and it was without any qualifications or conditions," says Doug Yule, who was at home in Boston when Sesnick called to offer him a job as bass guitarist in the Velvet Underground. He was needed immediately. Doug accepted and asked a friend to drive him to the city. Although it was a journey of over two hundred miles, he met Lou and Steve at Max's that evening. As they sat down to talk in the back room, Doug looked around at the other strange people in the glow of the Flavin light sculpture: Factory freaks and sundry eccentrics, including the obese drag queen Divine. He had entered an almost infernal scene.

Sesnick explained that the band had a gig in Cleveland on Friday, October 4. "Think you can learn all the songs in two days?" Doug said he thought he could. He was a bright young man of twenty-one, born and raised on Long Island. He could have passed for Lou's younger brother: they were both slim with curly brown hair. Doug was the more able musician. He could read and write music and play a variety of instruments, including guitar and keyboards. He sang, too, in a high voice. He had been in a couple of small bands in Boston, including the Glass Menagerie, which played the Boston Tea Party, and had seen the Velvets perform. Although he had never played bass, he didn't doubt that he could turn his hand to the instrument.

"You can stay at my loft," said Lou. "It'll give us time to practice."

Sterling wandered over to say "Hi," a beer in hand. There was a hint of suspicion, perhaps, in the way he addressed the new boy archly as Douglas. Oddly, there was no explanation as to why Doug in particular had been chosen to replace Cale. "Sterling [must] have been told ahead of time as well as Lou, but I don't know how Sesnick presented it to them," he reflects. "Maureen was living on

[Long] Island, so she didn't come. I don't know much more about the process. I always assumed I was the first choice, driven by the astrological fit (Pisces/Virgo/Pisces/Virgo) and time constraints (a gig in two days)." By the "astrological fit," he means he was a Pisces, like John and Lou. "Sesnick and Lou seemed to think, at the time, that it was important."

It was late. Sesnick hailed a cab, dropping Lou and Doug at Lou's loft in the fur district, where Lou spent the next forty-eight hours teaching Doug the repertoire. "The next two days were a blur of music and agreement with whatever Lou said. He had a very forceful personality and it was clear to me that he wanted what he said agreed with, so that's what I did." Apart from being a talented, available musician known to Sesnick, Doug's amenable nature was undoubtedly part of the reason he was hired.

It was only at this late stage that John Cale discovered that he was out of the band. "We were supposed to be going to Cleveland for a gig and Sterling showed up at my apartment and effectively told me that I was no longer in the band," he says. "Lou always got other people to do his dirty work for him. I don't think I'm blameless about what happened, but Lou never confronted me, saying, 'I don't want you around anymore.' It was all done by sleight of hand." Lou had destroyed the original, classic lineup of the Velvet Underground. But in doing so he discovered a melodious new sound for his songs.

VI

A NEW VU

• 1968–70 •

WHEN THE VELVET UNDERGROUND appeared at La Cave in Cleveland, a tiny club where the stage was only inches off the floor, on October 4, 1968, it was the first time that Doug Yule had played with the whole group. "The sound was pretty good for no rehearsal, but then the music was straightforward, without any serious complications," he recalled. "I made the usual mistakes that plague a newcomer trying to fit into an established group . . . I missed a lot of cues, got caught hanging over endings and had to keep asking, 'What key?' But the audience seemed to love it . . ." Indeed, the new Velvet Underground swung. By replacing one member, they became a more conventional, accessible band purveying the kind of melodic rock 'n' roll Lou had always loved. "It made a huge difference," confirms Moe.

Doug enjoyed flirting with girls backstage after the show, though he noted that Lou didn't join in. Lou was unusual as a touring rock musician in that he rarely got involved with people on the road, of either sex, though he occasionally disappeared with someone. He contracted a venereal disease in California in this way. Still, such behavior was sufficiently unusual to be noteworthy. For long periods he didn't seem interested in casual sex, or any kind of sex. He was a voyeur. "Lou watched it all across his psychological moat, remaining somewhat detached," Doug observed. He was also intensely focused on the music. Later that night Lou called Doug into his motel room to discuss the show. He was still talking when the sun rose.

The following month the band flew to Los Angeles to make their third album, simply titled *The Velvet Underground*, as if they had returned to Year Zero following the Riviera Café coup. They were recording again at TTG, staying nearby at the Chateau Marmont, and doing a few gigs at the Whisky a Go Go to help pay the bills while they were in town. The main studio at TTG was large enough to accommodate an orchestra. The Velvets huddled together in a corner of the big room as they created their most intimate and subtle album.

On the first track, "Candy Says," Lou showed considerable empathy for his friend James Slattery, aka Candy Darling, a man so confused about his sexuality that he asked women friends for tampons. Lou asked Doug to sing it, knowing that his high voice, with a vulnerable quality, would suit the tender lyric better than his own. This wistful recording wouldn't be bettered until Antony Hegarty performed "Candy Says" on tour with Lou in the twenty-first century.

The next track in sequence, "What Goes On," was, by contrast, a simple rocker that had become a mainstay of the band's act. Then came Lou's most erotic song, "Some Kinda Love," a seductive conversation between characters named Tom and Marguerita. Lou delivered the sexy lyric in a breathy vocal, over a simple, metronomic beat, making it plain that the couple had something other than the missionary position in mind, singing, "Let us do what you fear most." His ability to twist a subject to imply something sinister was one of his characteristics as a songwriter.

This intriguing song was followed by a true masterpiece. "Pale Blue Eyes" had been part of the band's repertoire since the early days. Now they recorded it andante, to the stately beat of Moe's tambourine, Lou's voice quavering (struggling to hold a note but giving the impression that he was feeling emotional) as he sang about his first love, Shelley, who remained a major figure in his imagination. Sterling's ravishing guitar solo may be his single most important contribution to the Velvet Underground canon. Bettye Kronstad, who started to date Lou properly after returning from Europe, believes that the rapturous language of "Pale Blue Eyes," describing Shelley as the best thing that ever happened to Lou, the peak of his existence, contained some make-believe. The fact that Shelley was effectively out of his life enabled him to indulge in the fantasy of a perfect love, whereas in reality he drove her away with his behavior; and the fact that she was married to someone else meant he could idolize her without having to deal with her. "I think there was a certain type of girl that I might have fallen in with, that were the unobtainables, and then when he got them he kind of didn't know what to do with them anyway," suggests Bettye, another very attractive girl whom Lou pursued ardently, only to neglect her when he caught her. There was a sense that, while he set his cap at such women, perhaps to prove his virility, his heart wasn't in it. "[We were] his perception of a trophy girlfriend." Lou set Bettye on a pedestal, calling her his Princess, but she doesn't believe that he even liked women. "He was a misogynist," she asserts. "I was his Princess in a certain sense, [but] as much as you idolize someone you might resent [them, too], because they are not real to you."

Lou's insistence that he wasn't necessarily writing about himself in his songs but from the perspective of his characters allowed him to adopt some unlikely positions. It enabled him to sing a song like "Jesus" on the new album, a secular hymn written by a Jew who showed no interest in religion until he turned to Tibetan Buddhism late in life. That didn't detract from the power of "Jesus," which was reaffirmed years later when he performed it with the Blind Boys of Alabama on David Letterman's *Late Show.*

The theme of revelation continued with "Beginning to See the Light," one of the strongest songs on the album, and "I'm Set Free"; while a gnomic remark by Billy Name about his own life and "the difference between wrong and right" provided the title and lyric for "That's the Story of My Life." "I would have said something like that. . . . He paid attention to things I said, because I was sort of a prophet. I had a way of saying things in those days that was very Zen-like," explains Billy, who is one of a handful of Lou's friends to be name-checked in more than one song, the others being "Slip Away" and "A Dream" on *Songs for Drella* (1990). An unusual man in many ways, Billy withdrew to live as a hermit in the dark room of Andy Warhol's studio at this time, hiding himself in the room for two whole years. Lou was one of the few people admitted to talk to him. He reported back to Andy that Billy had been reading Alice Bailey's books about astrology and white magic, which Lou had introduced him to; it seemed the literature had turned his head. One day, Andy came to work and found the door to the dark room open. Billy had gone. He wasn't seen again for seven years.

"The Murder Mystery" was the most experimental track on the album, an audio cut-up in a style pioneered in prose by William Burroughs and Brion Gysin, whereby the band recited scripts that were overdubbed in the hope of creating interesting verbal juxtapositions. Unfortunately, the result sounded like babble. "It was supposed to be fun with words, fun with rhymes and sounds," Lou commented, disappointed to find his ideas compromised by a lack of technical knowledge in the studio. It was frustrations like this that made him obsessive about sound recording in later years.

The last song was, by contrast, a work of perfect lucidity. Lou persuaded Moe to sing "After Hours," thinking that her childlike personality ("Moe was an undeveloped person," observes Mary Woronov) would suit the lyric about a timid person watching others having fun and wishing they could join in. "I couldn't sing that song. Maureen could sing it and believe it, and feel much more. Because it's about loneliness," Lou remarked. Despite her shyness, Moe proved the ideal choice for "After Hours," which became a minor Velvet Underground classic. "I was scared to death to get up and sing it."

Presented in this sequence, the ten songs that made up the third Velvet Underground album formed a story in Lou's mind, though this wasn't immediately apparent to most listeners. "It's not just arbitrary. They're all supposed to complement the preceding song," he explained. "'Candy Says' had this person asking all these questions, and then 'What Goes On' kind of asked like one specific one, and then 'Some Kinda Love' and 'Pale Blue Eyes' explicated some of it. It just went on and on . . ." More importantly, six of the ten songs were among the best he ever wrote, with "Pale Blue Eyes" becoming a staple of his show for the rest of his career.

In suggesting that Moe was better suited to singing about loneliness than himself, Lou was being less than honest. He often complained about loneliness. He had recently moved to an apartment at East 60th Street, a slightly better apartment than his band mates could afford on the modest income they earned from record advances and live shows reflecting his status as their leader, but nevertheless a bare, cheerless place. "Why don't you come shopping with me and help me buy some furniture?" he asked Shelley, who found her ex in a pathetic state in his new bachelor quarters. "He was depressed from being lonely . . . I did feel bad for him."

With Shelley ultimately unavailable, Lou turned increasingly to Bettye for support. Indeed, he asked her to marry him. "He actually asked me to marry him about a year after I met him . . . I think he wanted me around him as much as possible, because he trusted me, he trusted me like no one else." Bettye didn't accept Lou's initial proposal. She had reservations about her boyfriend, including concerns about his use of alcohol and drugs, which may be why he attempted to curb some of his bad habits at this time. There is evidence that he was relatively clean in 1969–70. "I never saw him take anything except alcohol and the occasional joint in all the years I knew him," says Doug Yule. When fan Rob Norris went backstage at the Boston Tea Party, Lou surprised him with "a brief lecture on the evils of drugs." However, like many users, what Lou said and what he did were often two different things.

Before the release of *The Velvet Underground*, Lou went back into the studio and remixed the recordings, bringing the vocals up at the expense of the instrumentation. Sterling described Lou's version of the album as the "closet mix," because it sounded like it had been recorded in a wardrobe: more intimate, less balanced. Lou's unilateral decision to make these changes is sometimes cited as an example of his high-handedness, though Doug and Moe also sang lead vocals on the record and their voices were enhanced in his closet mix. In any event, it was this version of the record that was released in the USA in March 1969, on the MGM label rather than Verve, with a cover photo of the band sitting on the couch at Andy's studio. The more conventional studio mix, by engineer Val Valentin, was released in Europe. Few listeners were aware of the difference at the time.

The LP was greeted with the first really good reviews the Velvets had enjoyed, including a laudatory notice in *Rolling Stone* by Lester Bangs, who emerged as one of Lou's most attentive and perceptive critics. Bangs observed that the musical journey between "Heroin" and "Jesus" demonstrated that the Velvets "have one of the broadest ranges of any group extant" and found brilliance in the album. Although he failed to appreciate "Pale Blue Eyes," his review was good enough to be quoted in adverts for the LP, printed together with a photograph of the Velvets looking like any other fashionable young band of the late 1960s, with scarves draped feyly around their necks. There were also excellent reviews in *Crawdaddy, Creem* and *Planet*. The Velvets were finally being recognized for the quality of their musicianship and Lou's songs, rather than their association with Warhol. Yet *The Velvet Underground* sold even fewer copies than its predecessors, failing to dent the *Billboard* Top 200. At this point, MGM seems to have abandoned all hope in the band.

The Velvets went into the Record Plant in New York in May 1969 to record songs for a fourth album, which they owed MGM, to fulfill their contract, though it was becoming clear that they would soon be leaving the label, and the company had no intention of releasing another album. "We did that to shut MGM up at the time," reveals Moe. "We had to finish the contract. I don't mean that we didn't do our best. It was *leave us alone*. . . . We didn't expect those [songs to come out]." In the circumstances, it is remarkable that the songs recorded at the Record Plant were so strong, including "Andy's Chest" (inspired by Andy's shooting), "Foggy Notion," "Ocean," "Sad Song," "We're Gonna Have a Real Good Time Together" and "I Can't Stand It," in which Lou implored Shelley by name to come back to him. ("That hurt. That was sad," says Shelley, who was shocked when she heard it many years later.) Lou also persuaded Moe to sing once again on "I'm Sticking with You," which had the charming quality of a nursery rhyme.

It was years before these songs enjoyed official release. Some started to appear in rerecorded, often inferior versions on Lou's solo albums in the 1970s, while others had to wait until the Velvets' back catalogue was reissued with archive material in the 1980s, by which time the importance of the Velvet Underground was more widely appreciated. What is most impressive is how prolific Lou was in the late 1960s. Like many top-flight songwriters, he was able to tune into an almost continuous stream of original ideas. "I have a radio in my head that's playing unrecorded things for me constantly." He just had to note down what he heard. This wasn't invariably true. There would be lean years when Radio Lou wasn't broadcasting. But, for now, he had more ideas than he could use. He was writing a lot of songs, good and varied songs, from the whimsical "I'm

Sticking with You" to the existential angst of "Ocean." Range is a
hallmark quality of the best songwriters, as true of Dylan and Lennon & McCartney as it was of Reed.

In many ways, 1969 was a golden year. Doug fitted in well, as
their live tapes and studio recordings show, helping to create a new
version of the band that was arguably as strong as that of the Cale
era (though different), and Lou seemed to be enjoying his work,
despite the loneliness and anxiety he suffered in his private life.
He sounded positively joyous recording "Foggy Notion" at the Record Plant. Nevertheless, their audience remained stubbornly small.
The Velvets mostly played clubs and dance halls in the northeastern states and in California, places like the Boston Tea Party, the
Second Fret in Philadelphia, La Cave in Cleveland and the Whisky
a Go Go in LA. It was rare that they drew more than a couple of
hundred people, and often their audiences were even smaller. In
the week of the Woodstock Festival, in August 1969, when 400,000
people gathered at Max Yasgur's farm in upstate New York to listen
to the most notable rock acts of the day, the Velvet Underground
were playing the obscure Woodrose Ballroom in Deerfield, Massachusetts. Sometimes they performed in coffeehouses, like a band
starting out. For context, the Doors, who released their debut album the same month as the Velvets released the Banana Album
in 1967, were playing Madison Square Garden by this time, while
the Velvets could only gaze in awe at the phenomenal worldwide
success of the Beatles and the Rolling Stones. Moe recalls being
as starstruck as a fan when Keith Richards visited Andy's studio.
"Wow, it's Keith!" The Stones weren't too big to borrow from the
Velvets, though. "I mean, even we've been influenced by the Velvet Underground," Mick Jagger admitted. "I'll tell you exactly what
we pinched from him [Lou]. Y'know, 'Stray Cat Blues'? The whole
sound and the way it's paced, we pinched from the very first Velvet Underground album. Y'know, the sound on 'Heroin.' Honest to
God, we did!"

While the Velvets were becoming slightly better known abroad, they didn't tour outside North America, so they failed to exploit a growing cult following in the United Kingdom and elsewhere, which was a mistake. It later became apparent that their principal audience was in Europe. And while they played a lot of shows in the USA in 1969–70, they only ever performed in sixteen US states, ignoring most of the country.

The band visited Texas for the first time in October 1969 to play six club shows. "Good evening. We're the Velvet Underground . . . glad you could all make it," Lou greeted the audience at the End of Cole Avenue in Dallas on October 19. "This is our last night here. Glad to see that you all showed up. Um, do you people have a curfew, or anything like that?"

"No," replied a young man in the audience.

"Does it matter what time you go home tonight? Do you have school tomorrow?"

"No!"

"Nobody here has school tomorrow?"

"Yeah," said a girl.

"Yeah. See. Because we could do either one long set, or we could do two sets, whichever made it easier for you."

"One long one."

"One long one? OK, then this is going to go on for a while. So we should get used to each other. Settle back. Pull up your cushions. Whatever else you have with you . . . that makes life bearable in Texas [laughter]. . . . This is a song called 'I'm Waiting for My [sic] Man.'" Lou's words were recorded and later used as the introduction to the live album, *1969 Velvet Underground Live with Lou Reed*, released five years later in 1974 on the back of his subsequent solo career. Aside from being a terrific album full of interesting cuts, *1969* demonstrates what a tiny audience the Velvets catered to. A mere handful of students gathered at the End of Cole Avenue to hear the band, the light smattering of applause on the recording revealing how few they were, as well as the striking fact that Lou consulted them personally about what time the gig should end.

Four songs were recorded in Dallas for the *1969* album, the other thirteen tracks being taken from shows at the Matrix in San Francisco, a quintessential hippie venue, where they also played to a minuscule audience. "There were a few nights when they started the first set with only four or five people in the club!" recalled Robert Quine, a twenty-seven-year-old law student who had begun to follow and record the Velvets for his own pleasure. An intense and depressive person, Quine later became Lou's lead guitarist, but their association started with him turning up at gigs with a tape recorder. "They didn't have a lot of fans in San Francisco and when they saw me there every night they became friendly, got me into the club for free, bought me drinks, and let me hang around backstage." Even on a good night, they never played to more than a hundred people at the Matrix. "I'm sure [the Velvets] were disappointed when they saw the size of the club," said co-owner Peter Abram. "The band was probably playing for $100 a night." The music, however, was exceptional. Lou was still writing prolifically and trying out new songs live, songs like "Sweet Bonnie Brown" and "New Age," which Doug believes he wrote about Shelley. (Shelley struggles to see herself in the lyrics. "This doesn't ring any bells for me, other than lines like 'I'll come running . . . ,' versions of which he used to say regularly.") The most important new song was "Sweet Jane." As performed at the Matrix and heard on *1969*, recorded the very day Lou wrote it, the prototype was a simple, regretful record of a love affair. "I can remember it starting out as a soft song," says Doug, adding, "It was very common to perform songs with little rehearsal that had been written very recently." It would change radically, becoming Lou's power-chord signature tune.

Doug Yule (left) began to rival Lou for leadership of the band. Sterling Morrison is seen third from left, Moe Tucker on the end.

The beginning of the end for Lou as a member of the Velvet Underground can be charted to the spring of 1970, when the band left MGM and signed with Atlantic Records. At the same time, Steve Sesnick began to promote Doug as their new front man. "Sesnick was in it for the money—he never said that to me, but that is my thinking now, and I don't think any less of him for it," says Moe, blaming Doug for falling for Sesnick's flattery. "I think he filled Doug's head a little too much, because Doug was handsome, cute, young—great smile. His head got filled with maybe Sesnick saying [things] like, 'If Lou leaves, you could do it.' [So] he started to get a real swell head and I didn't like him for a while." Doug maintains that he was a team player. "I loved being part of the band when Lou was there because the thing I enjoy most in music is singing harmony and being part of an ensemble, as opposed to being a leader and front man." Lou was a hard man to work with, however. Ever since they met, he had been telling Doug what to do, dominating him to the extent that Doug daren't smoke a joint if Lou didn't partake as well. Though apparently modest, Doug wasn't immune to flattery, and he started to see a bigger role for himself in the group. It was unfortunate that Moe, a moderating influence, stepped back from the band at this stage to have her first child.

The Velvets returned to New York to record their debut album for Atlantic, at the company's studio near Columbus Circle. With Moe too heavily pregnant to play drums, four people took turns with the sticks: studio engineer Adrian Barber, session musician Tommy Castanaro, Doug Yule and his teenage brother Billy. Their playing served to highlight what a vital contribution Moe had made. Without her unsophisticated but unique percussion, the Velvets sounded disappointingly ordinary on what would prove to be their most conventional album. Sterling also felt isolated, because Lou and Doug were making most of the musical decisions. "Things were not happy," comments Martha Morrison. "I remember sitting outside Atlantic [in Central Park with Sterling] when they were making that album. He was grousing and grumpy. It was hard to listen to." Martha encouraged Sterling to think ahead to life after the band, so he enrolled at City College to study English literature, paving the way for his own exit.

Unlike in the past, when the Velvets recorded everything live in a few days, they took months over the new album, which they titled *Loaded* because Lou believed it was loaded with hits, as well as having the connotation of inebriation. Starting work in April 1970, they also recorded a lot of songs, one of the first being "Satellite of Love," which didn't see the light of day until Lou resurrected it in 1972 for his solo album *Transformer*. Other strong songs that were tried but not used at the time included new versions of "Ocean" and "I'm Sticking with You." Many were ruled out because Lou and Doug were searching for a Top 40 hit. "Who Loves the Sun," eventually chosen as the opening track and a single, was typical of the new material, in that it was a relatively straightforward, upbeat pop song, good in its way but lacking the otherness that had characterized the Velvet Underground. It failed to become a hit. "Cool It Down," "Head Held High," "Lonesome Cowboy Bill," "I Found a Reason" and "Oh! Sweet Nothin'" were likewise all mildly diverting songs but bland by the band's standards. Three tracks stood out as being of greater interest: "New Age," "Rock 'n' Roll" (which celebrated the excitement of discovering pop music on the radio) and a swaggering new version of "Sweet Jane."

Like most artists, Lou was primarily invested in whatever he was doing in the present, rather than music he had made in the past, and he was enthusiastic about *Loaded* while the band was making the album. "It's just fantastic, because we've never really made a record before. All our records we made in one or two days, you know, and we kept the tape running, sort of cut them live," he told *Third Ear* magazine at the time. "You know, all our [previous] albums sound like basement tapes.[3] So it's a new experience and it's fantastic, it's really fantastic. . . . This is the closest that the reality ever came to matching the concept, because what we're hearing in our heads is finally coming out on record . . ." Lou distanced himself from the Cale era, saying that he didn't like "esoteric stuff," and predicted that the group would finally enjoy a commercial breakthrough with shorter, simpler songs. Lou may have had commercial concerns in mind when he chose to downplay the importance of drugs in their past. "We [have a reputation] for supposedly being a drug group. We're not representing drug culture; we're just a rock 'n' roll group." Asked if there was a time when he had to get high to perform, he replied, "No, when you're wrecked you play bad." He conceded that some people came to see them because of their druggy reputation, shouting out for "Heroin," which he was reluctant to perform at this stage. "I'd hate to think that was really totally where I was at," he

---

3   Referring to Bob Dylan's *Basement Tapes,* low-fi home recordings that were bootlegged at this time but later given official release.

said. "Same thing with 'Sister Ray'; if that's the way we were, there wouldn't have been a third album."

The *Third Ear* interview was also notable for critical remarks Lou made about more famous contemporary artists. He sneered at Jefferson Airplane and the Grateful Dead for making music on drugs for people on drugs, and said "Dylan gets on my nerves." This was mild compared to what he had to say about Frank Zappa, who had enjoyed more success than the Velvets since they started out together on MGM. Lou rubbished Zappa as a "low life . . . two-bit, pretentious, academic, and he can't play . . ." He failed to see the humor in *We're Only in It for the Money*, Zappa's parody of *Sgt. Pepper*. "Like, you know, make fun of the Beatles—try to do a song, try to do a really pretty song they did. . . . He can't do that, 'cause he's a loser. And that's why he dresses up funny. He's not happy with himself and I think he's right." Although Lou burst into laughter at this point in the interview, his remarks were crass and unnecessary. The impression given in this and many subsequent interviews was of a prickly man who was jealous of his contemporaries.

Toward the end of the Atlantic sessions, the Velvets began a residency upstairs at Max's Kansas City, their first significant shows in New York for three years. One explanation of why they had avoided the city for so long is that Sesnick wanted to build their reputation around the country before returning to the metropolis. Doug doesn't believe this to be true. "I've heard that strategy put forward, but it always sounded like hindsight. My sense at the time was that Sesnick was having difficulty getting gigs and took whatever he could find," he says. "The Max's gig certainly wasn't a triumphant return of the prodigal band. It felt more like a fill-in . . ."

They opened at Max's on June 24, 1970, playing two shows a night on the mezzanine, a small space that was less than ideal for gigs. The mezzanine was lined with tiles, which made the acoustics poor, the sight lines were obstructed and there was constant background noise: people coming and going on the stairs, chatting to friends and using the toilet. Lou found it a depressing experience to be playing such a small room four years on from their sensational run at the Dom with the Exploding Plastic Inevitable.

"We once did an album with a pop painter," he reminded the audience on opening night.

"You're doing better without him!" somebody retorted. But it wasn't true.

With Moe out of action, seventeen-year-old Billy Yule played drums with the band at Max's. He did so with an amateurish enthusiasm that made them sound even more like a bar band. Lou's depression deepened. "I hated it," he later said. "I couldn't do the songs I wanted to do, and I was under a lot of pressure to do things I didn't want to [do]. It made me sick." This was despite the fact that he had friends in the audience most nights, old friends, including Brigid Berlin and Danny Fields, and new friends like the young Patti Smith, who got up to dance. "The critic Donald Lyons was shocked that I had never seen them, and escorted me upstairs for the second set of their first night," she reminisced. "I loved to dance, and you could dance for hours to the music of the Velvet Underground." Bettye also looked in. Lou performed a new song at Max's on June 26, "Wild Child," about an actress named Betty [sic] who suffered with nerves. Bettye, who was doing some acting at the time, says it was about her, "Because I didn't like the audition process." She was part of a theater troupe who performed at a Manhattan restaurant where the deal was that they would also wait tables at lunch. It was this work that later caused Lou to refer to her as a "cocktail waitress," which his friends repeated as a put-down. "It's just a nasty, stupid story and it's totally untrue," she says, making a distinction between being a cocktail waitress and the kind of waitressing she briefly did.

When Moe came to see the show after the birth of her daughter, on June 27, she found Lou in low spirits. "Three or four weeks after Kerry was born, I went to see them at Max's. . . . Lou said, 'Come on,' and we sat on the stairs, and he told me that he was going to be leaving [the band]. Even though we were like brother and sister, I didn't say, 'What's the matter, why are you leaving?'" Moe had never been one for personal questions, but she saw that Lou was upset. "He was not happy that it had come to that. He needed to get out." It is a measure of how bad relations had become between Lou, Doug and Sterling that the others had no idea he was thinking of quitting. Sterling's focus was on his English course at City College. He brought his books into Max's each evening so he could study between sets. Although he was barely speaking to Lou—"I was mad at him for something"—he shared his misgivings about the residency. "Lou may have felt that we'd done too much to wind up just sort of playing a club in Manhattan, which I felt too. . . . I was against it," he told Ignacio Julia, author of *Feedback*, adding that playing at Max's at night tired Lou's voice, which affected his vocals in the studio, where they were still working on *Loaded* during the day. "I'm sure I said something like, 'This is stupid,' and probably got the reply from Sesnick, something like, 'Don't be negative, just go and read your books and mind your own business.'"

Lou decided that Sunday, August 23, 1970, would be his last show with the band. Doug remained oblivious. "That particular night was no different than most of them, since we had no idea that it was Lou's last." To witness his final performance, Lou invited some special guests. Sterling was sitting in a booth eating a cheeseburger and reading Thackeray's *Vanity Fair* when Lou came over and introduced a smartly dressed, middle-aged couple. "Sterling, I'd like you to meet my parents," he said. Sterling was astounded. "Lou always had an extremely troubled relationship with his parents. . . . So I was thinking, 'What in the world can this portend?'"

Lou chatted with the audience between songs that night, sounding relaxed. Indeed, he seemed to be having a good time with his parents and girlfriend in the room. "It's really fun to be able to play these for you," he said during the introduction to "Sunday Morning."

After the second and last show of the evening, Lou and Sterling had a fierce argument, according to Brigid Berlin, who was sitting a few feet away with the writer Jim Carroll, a mutual friend who later wrote *The Basketball Diaries*. "Sterling Morrison had a big fight with Lou, and that seemed to be the end of it." This must have been when Lou told Sterling that he was leaving.

The news went around Max's in a flash. Danny Fields went over to Brigid, who had a tape recorder on her table; it was a time when Factory people were habitually taping everything. He told her that Lou had quit the band and asked her if she had recorded his last show. "I said, 'Did you get that?' 'Let's see.' She [wound the tape]

THE VELVET UNDERGROUND LIVE AT MAX'S KANSAS CITY
Featuring: Lou Reed, Doug Yule, Billy Yule, Sterling Morrison

back. 'Yeah.'" The next morning they took the tape to the Velvets' record company, where Danny happened to work. "I knew they owed them another album. That was perfect for everybody. I think we got $10,000 on the spot, turned over the [tape] and it became the album [*Live at Max's Kansas City*]." The record was eventually released in 1972.

Doug Yule was the last person to know what was happening and came to blame Steve Sesnick for pushing Lou out of the band. "The circumstances around his departure were between him and Sesnick. I only heard about it the following week from Sesnick, who was spinning it his own way, as if Lou had quit unexpectedly rather than being forced out by Sesnick, as I heard later."

The Velvets completed their residency without Lou, and staggered on under Doug's leadership until 1973, though the band was a shadow of itself. Donald Lyons summed up the situation with a *bon mot*. When Danny Fields told him that Lou had left the band, he quipped: "I guess we have to call them the Velveteen Underground now."

VII

SOLO IN THE
SEVENTIES

• 1970–73 •

L EAVING THE VELVET UNDERGROUND had a profound effect
on Lou's mental health, triggering a second nervous breakdown,
as can now be revealed. "Yes, that was another breakdown, when
he returned home after the breakup of the Velvet Underground,"
confirms his sister. As with his first breakdown, Lou withdrew to his
parents' house in Freeport, giving up his apartment in New York,
which he could no longer afford, storing his precious guitars and his
collection of Velvet Underground concert posters in his bedroom. It
was little enough to show for five years as the guiding light of one of
the most innovative and ultimately influential bands of the 1960s.

When he felt able to work again, Lou was employed as a typist
in his father's office. The duties were light, allowing him time to
write creatively. He wrote poetry for *Fusion* magazine, the editor
of which also commissioned him to contribute to a book, *No One
Waved Good-bye*, on the topic of the casualties of rock 'n' roll culture, several young stars having died drug-related deaths in recent
months. Lou took the opportunity to reflect on his experiences as

a performer, revealing some ambivalence about his career. "At the age when identity is a problem some people join rock 'n' roll bands and perform for other people who share the same difficulties. The age difference between performer and beholder is not large. But, unfortunately, those in the fourth tier assume those on stage know something they do not. Which is not true," he wrote in his essay, "Fallen Knights and Fallen Angels," adding revealingly: "The singer has a soul but feels he isn't loved off stage." He referred to the drug use endemic in the music industry, as if this disappointed him, as did the fickleness of the public: "As my analyst put it, don't depend on anyone . . ."

On the weekends he took his dog, Seymour, for long, thoughtful walks along the South Shore. Meanwhile, the Velvet Underground continued without him. Lou contacted Sterling to ask if he would work with him in a new band, but Sterling declined. "I thought he had gone insane; gone insane in a very dull way," he explained. "He suddenly went home to Freeport and decided to become reconciled with his parents. . . . Lou was unstable in such a tedious way. It wasn't that he was running around crazy in the streets; at times he was incommunicative and remote and content to stay with his parents."

When *Loaded* was released in September 1970, Lou was dismayed to see his songs attributed to the band, while the photo on the back cover showed Doug alone in the studio, as if he were the mastermind of the project. Lou responded by registering the songs in his own name, ultimately going to law to establish copyright, which he did successfully. This was a battle between Lou and Sesnick, primarily. He was doubly disappointed by the fact that the tracks weren't sequenced as he wished, while "New Age" and "Sweet Jane" were truncated, the latter missing some words. "They took a song that I'd worked on for a year and ruined it." Despite the amount of time spent in the studio, the sound was also poor. Yet *Loaded* became the favorite Velvet Underground album for many

people, a record of catchy, commercial songs that fellow artists, including Mitch Ryder and Mott the Hoople, would cover, and more
were influenced by. "It changed my life as a songwriter," says Elliott
Murphy, whose own recording career Lou later mentored. "When
he had a strong guitar player working with him, like he did with
Doug Yule, I think he [flourished]. By the time of *Loaded*, Lou's
songwriting had just flowered."

Reviews were excellent. Writing in *Creem*, Lester Bangs praised
the album to the sky but deplored the way that Lou's contribution
was downplayed by the record company. "Doug Yule is probably a
very nice guy. . . . But honest to God, this is the most outrageous
misrepresentation and spit in the face of a great artist that I've ever
seen on an album jacket. They don't come right out and *say* that this
is a Doug Yule Production, they know they can't get away with that,
but the implication is clear." Lester called Lou to ask what was going
on, having heard rumors that he had "flipped out." Lou told him: "I
just walked out because we didn't have any money, I didn't want to
tour again—I can't get any writing done on tour, and the grind is
terrible—and like some other members of the band I've wondered
for a long time if we were *ever* going to be accepted on a scale large
enough to make us a 'success.'"

Barbara Hodes kept in touch by phone during this difficult period, but she didn't see much of Lou. "He told me he had a nervous
breakdown. I think he was completely overwhelmed with how the
Velvets had [ended] . . . he needed to get out of Dodge, so to speak."
The woman he saw most of was Bettye Kronstad, who got into the
habit of coming out to Freeport for the weekend, sleeping on the
sofa in the den. She got along well with Lou's family. "They were
very happy with me, I guess, because I was a girl," she laughs, noting
that Sid and Toby did everything they could to keep their sensitive
son in a good mood. "I think they were worried that he was peculiar, that he was different, that he was nervous, that he did have
a nervous breakdown. It was [like] china plates around Lou. Let's

just make sure that nothing happens . . ." Lou sometimes took Bettye to the Hayloft, but their weekends on Long Island were mostly
spent in conventional middle-class pursuits. They went swimming
at Sid's country club, where Lou tried to teach Bettye to play tennis. In return she took him horse-riding. Unfortunately, he failed to
persuade staff at the stables that he was competent to take a horse
out. "That didn't make him very happy." Nevertheless, Bettye recalls
this as a good time in their relationship, the period when she fell in
love with Lou. Away from New York, she found him to be a nicer,
gentler person. "The man I fell in love with wasn't a tough guy, he
was a teddy bear. He was a sweet, sensitive writer . . . a gentleman
and a scholar. He drank too much, but you know . . ."

Lou couldn't stay away from the city for long. In March 1971 he
took part in a poetry reading at St Mark's-in-the-Bowery with Allen
Ginsberg and Jim Carroll. It was his first public appearance since
leaving the Velvets. He recited some of his lyrics, together with poems
about Bettye and poems with a gay theme that elicited a cheer from
Danny Fields. Lou would give further readings over the years; they
reaffirmed his belief in himself as a writer, which is how Bettye liked
to see him, though she worried about Lou in New York. "The people
he had been hanging out with—the Warhol crowd—they didn't understand what he was going through. He was no longer the crazy Lou.
He was quiet and reflective, contemplative. He wasn't that character
anymore." Perhaps it was she who didn't understand Lou, who hadn't
changed as much as she liked to believe, while many of his friends
didn't understand her. "We made fun of her," chuckles Danny. "We
just called her the cocktail waitress. We couldn't believe he was [with
her]. Where did she come from?" Bettye sensed their condescension
and was irritated. She felt she was treated like she was no one of importance. Lou tried to integrate her into his circle by introducing her
to hip friends like Brigid Berlin. "I think that what he wanted Brigid
to do was Max's Kansas City-me or Warhol-me. . . . Let's Warholize
Bettye. So I went over there several times and we had evenings of

talking. My impression was that at the end of our sessions Brigid probably went back to Lou and said, 'I don't see anything wrong with her, I think she's fine the way she is.'" Others remained unconvinced. "I go away and I come back and Bettye's with him!" exclaims Barbara Hodes, who was also struck by the physical change in Lou since his second breakdown. "When he came back he was fat and he was drinking a bottle of Scotch a day."

He started to spend alternate weekends in New York with Bettye while he plotted his return to the music business with the help of friends. His chief advisers were Danny Fields, who was working at Atlantic Records, and Richard and Lisa Robinson. Lisa was a music writer, while Richard was an A&R (Artists and Repertoire) man for RCA. They all held Lou in high esteem. The Robinsons hosted soirees for him at their Upper West Side apartment, to introduce him to people who might be helpful in launching a solo career. "Lisa would invite me and Lou over to her house and all these people, the intelligentsia or whatever, rock 'n' roll people, and people in the music industry, would hang out and all sit around in a circle and listen to Lou pontificate," says Bettye. "I never had anything to say. We just all sat around and gazed adoringly at Lou, which was kind of boring for me."

There was a reunion with Nico at the Robinsons' apartment. Since leaving the Velvets three and a half years earlier, Nico had dyed her hair black, developed a heroin habit and put on weight. She scratched a living performing an eccentric solo act in clubs, singing gloomy songs, accompanying herself on harmonium. Enough time had passed for Lou and Nico to forget their problems and contemplate doing a show together again. "The Factory was then a 'thing of the past' (although, of course, it could never be that actually) as far as their careers/futures were concerned, and so they could regard each other differently at that point," explains Danny, who was present on April 29, 1971, when Lou and Nico rehearsed at the Robinsons'. Although Nico struggled to remember the words to their songs, Lou remained patient, encouraging her, and they conversed with the ease of old friends—moreover, old lovers—making each other laugh. She called him Lewis, teasingly. He confessed that he was hung over. "I'm so tired. I got drunk last night. Ah, I've got a headache!" Lisa hovered in the background, offering refreshments. At the end of the evening, Lou walked Nico to the subway. It had been a pleasant reunion, but no show resulted in the short term.

As Lou was still under contract to Atlantic, Danny tried to persuade his bosses to let his talented friend make a solo album for the company. "I was trying a lot to get them to think of him as an important songwriter, rather than a member of a band [for] which they'd never cared very much in the first place." Atlantic wasn't interested. So Danny became Lou's manager, trying to find him another record deal. It proved an onerous job. "I was his manager for two weeks. I couldn't take it. I could not have a personal relationship and a professional relationship with him simultaneously," he says. "Once you are working for him, and there are things that he wants, and it's about his career, he was relentless. 'Did you hear from them yet? What do you think?' Pinning me down, pinning me down. 'No, Lou, I told you. . . . Not just yet. . . . We're waiting. . . . Yes, I did. . . . No, not yet. . . . But we need you to . . .' It was enveloping. It was *horrible*—it was losing a friend in order to get a client."

It became apparent that Lou's best hope lay with RCA. Known as the Washing-machine Company, because the parent company manufactured household appliances, RCA Records had one huge artist in Elvis Presley and a mainstream star in John Denver, who had the first of his big hits in 1971 with "Take Me Home, Country Roads," but little presence in the burgeoning rock market. There was a new vice president of contemporary music, however, an ambitious thirty-year-old lawyer named Dennis Katz, elder brother of Blood, Sweat and Tears guitarist Steve Katz, who wanted to sign rock talent to RCA. When Richard Robinson suggested bringing Lou to the label, Katz was cautiously receptive. Lou was a first-class songwriter, but he was difficult to deal with and the Velvet Underground had never been commercially successful. He was also still under contract to Atlantic, which complicated matters. Luckily for Lou, he had another persuasive champion.

By the age of twenty-four, David Bowie had released three albums in his native United Kingdom, none of which had done spectacularly well, though he scored a hit single with "Space Oddity" in 1969 and showed a genius for self-publicity. Despite being married with a young child, Bowie had created an androgynous persona for himself that caught the attention of the press and public in Britain, and now he and his manager, Tony Defries, wanted to break America. They had struck a deal with RCA and were coming to New York in September 1971 to sign their contract. The Washing-machine Company got Bowie cheap, paying a modest $37,500 advance for his new album, *Hunky Dory*, which he had already recorded in London. The songs were clever and catchy, but nobody knew whether the album would take off. "David wasn't that famous. He wasn't famous *at all*," says his friend Tony Zanetta, who had recently starred in the Warhol stage show *Pork*. Bowie was fascinated with the Warhol scene, so much so that he had recorded a song about Andy on his album. He had also recorded a tribute to the Velvet Underground, the song "Queen Bitch," showing how much inspiration he had taken from their music, and Lou's attitude. His trip to New York presented an opportunity to meet his hero.

Lou met David at a dinner RCA arranged at the Ginger Man restaurant in Manhattan to welcome the Englishman to America. Lou was flattered to meet an up-and-coming artist who held him in high regard, while Bowie went out of his way to charm Lou. "David always went after the people he admired, that he thought he could learn something from," says his then wife, Angie Bowie. "They were whispering, kind of conspiratorial," adds Tony Zanetta, who also attended the dinner. "This was a thrill for him to meet Lou." There were two further meetings that week, at the Warwick Hotel, where the Bowies were staying, and at the Robinsons' apartment, where Lou and David locked themselves in a room to talk privately while Angie banged on the door to be let in. David was a handsome young man and there was a hint of sexual attraction between him and Lou. "I think there might have been something going on. I don't know. Lou probably went after him; I believe that," says Bettye who, like Angie, felt left out. "Lou did kind of fall in love with him a little bit. He would fall in love with anybody that was really crazy about him."

The respect David showed Lou helped persuade Dennis Katz to sign him to RCA. The deal was done directly after Bowie's visit to New York, on October 1. "I did sign him when nobody else was interested in signing him, and I got the release from Atlantic Records. They let him go without any overrides, without any payments or anything," boasts Katz, who subsequently became an important person in Lou's career. "Nobody else was interested in him. He was working for his father on Long Island when I signed him to RCA. There wouldn't be any Lou Reed, and you wouldn't be writing this book, if it weren't for me." If RCA got Bowie cheap, Lou was for peanuts. The company advanced $6,600 for his debut solo album, approximately $38,000 in today's money, adjusted for inflation, the price of a new car. "He didn't have any history in terms of being able to sell records. His claim to fame was being in the Velvets, that was it," says Bob Ringe, a member of the A&R team at RCA who worked with both Reed and Bowie. "At least Bowie had sold some records previously." It was nevertheless a break. On the strength of the deal, Lou moved back to Manhattan, renting a small apartment at East 78th Street. "It was a studio, pull-out [bed]. His grandmother's rocking chair was about the only chair in there," says Bettye, with whom he split the rent.

LOU WAS AN UNUSUAL artist in that he had two distinct careers: firstly as a member of the arty Velvet Underground between 1965 and

1970, a period when he had to subsume his personality to some degree to work in a team; then, he started all over again as a much more commercial solo artist in 1972. For most members of the public who were largely unaware of his first career, because the Velvets achieved so little success, Lou emerged almost from nowhere in the 1970s. In fact, he was a battle-scarred veteran of the music business. The experience of leading the Velvets to so little avail for five years had left him cynical, even bitter. And he was no longer in the first flush of youth, being almost thirty years old. This was the man who flew to London a few days after Christmas 1971 with Richard and Lisa Robinson to record his debut album for RCA. He was desperate to make it work, and willing to make whatever compromises were necessary.

The Americans checked into the Inn on the Park at Hyde Park Corner. Lou soon missed Bettye, so she flew over to join him. It was in London that she started to understand what it meant to be a rock musician's girlfriend at the start of the 1970s, and she didn't like it. "We were not treated with any kind of real respect," she says. "You could feel that the only reason anybody was talking to you was because you were Lou Reed's girlfriend, or Lou Reed's fiancée, or Lou Reed's wife. You didn't actually have any identity. You were an appendage."

Lou came to London to record his album, because London still enjoyed a cachet as the creative heart of popular music, thanks to the enormous success of bands like the Beatles. London was also known for the quality of its recording studios, and the expertise of its engineers. Lou recorded at Morgan Studios in north London, where Paul McCartney had recently finished his first solo album, with Richard Robinson producing. A couple of weeks into the project Lou met music journalists at his hotel to discuss the record. Unlike most members of the general public, these journalists knew all about his career with the Velvet Underground and were eager to ask him about it. Lou made it clear that he wanted to start afresh, distancing himself from his past. "It's been a process of elimination from the start. First no more Andy, then no more Nico, then no more John, then no more Velvet Underground. Suddenly, I'm Lou Reed," he said, rather pompously. "This [album] is the closest realization to what I hear in my head that I've ever done. It's a real rock 'n' roll album . . . I think that the general audience will find it more accessible." He claimed that there would be no "Velvet remnants" on the album, but the opposite was true. Seven of the ten songs were Velvet Underground leftovers, including "I Can't Stand It," "Walk and Talk It," "Lisa Says" and "Ocean." Of the rest, the only song of note was "Berlin," a vignette of life in the German city (which Lou had never visited), between the two world wars. It seemed to be inspired by the popular new movie *Cabaret*.

To accompany Lou, Richard Robinson hired British session musicians, including Steve Howe and Rick Wakeman of the progressive rock band Yes. "A message came through to the office from Lou's camp asking if myself and Steve Howe would play on his new album," recalls Wakeman, who was much in demand for session work at the time, and had played on Bowie's *Hunky Dory*. He received little guidance as to what Lou wanted. "Hardly got to speak to him, to be honest. There was a quick hello. Then he played the tracks, as they were at the time. I added my piano. He said thank you, and that was it really!" In the circumstances, Wakeman's cabaret club intro to "Berlin" worked surprisingly well.

The problem with this hands-off method was highlighted by the recording of "Ocean," a majestic number when the Velvets played it live, as can be heard on the *1969* album, with Moe using her cymbals to create a plangent percussive sound that echoes the emotion of the song, about a man struggling with insanity. To record "Ocean" in London, Lou used Clem Cattini, a veteran of British beat bands and countless studio sessions, and, despite Cattini being an excellent musician, the result was awkward, even crude. "There was a number I played timpani on, a thing called 'The Sea' [sic]. We finished it, and he said, 'That was great. I could see that you were getting into it, thinking of, like, the ocean . . .'" says Cattini. "To be honest, I wasn't really."

Considering Lou's tactless comments to the press about his former colleagues, it was surprising that he traveled to Paris to perform with Cale and Nico on January 29, 1972. A thousand people came to Le Bataclan, a club in the 11th arrondissement, to hear the trio play new and old songs, a fantastic show, subtle, focused and powerful, which was filmed and recorded, eventually emerging as the CD *Lou Reed, John Cale & Nico*, a far better album than the one Lou was making in London. The gig went so well that he suggested they work together further, but Cale wasn't interested.

There was more disappointment in May, when his solo album, simply titled *Lou Reed*, was released. The American critic Robert Christgau, who marked albums in the *Village Voice* as if they were school essays, awarded it a B+, but Nick Kent of the *New Musical Express* spoke for many when he observed that *Lou Reed* was "one of the more disappointing releases of 1972." It wasn't so much that the songs were bad as that they were badly produced, sounding like they were recorded in a shed, despite the use of a top-flight London studio, with Lou's voice sounding weak and uncertain. He took the reviews to heart. "Anything negative that anybody said about Lou he took very seriously, even if he didn't act like it," says Bettye. "He read it all." And he was doubly crushed by very poor sales.

Despite this critical and commercial failure, Dennis Katz gave Lou the go-ahead to make a second LP for RCA. The initial plan was for Richard to produce again, and by the terms of Lou's contract he would receive an enhanced advance of $15,000. It was enough for Lou to move to a nicer apartment at East 74th Street, and to ask Bettye to marry him. It seemed that the time was right. Lou was thirty. His ex, Shelley Albin, had just had a baby with her husband, which made it clear that she was never going to come back to him, and Lou desperately wanted *someone* to look after him. "He depended upon [women]," says Bettye. "They took care of him. A mother figure. A nurse. A cop. That's what they were." Nevertheless, they became engaged. To make it official, he bought Bettye a ring from Tiffany's, and a silver locket, in which she kept a picture of Lou and herself. He also gave her $500 to buy furniture for the apartment, directing her to a budget store in the neighborhood. "He was always very careful about money. *Very* careful."

The following months were relatively harmonious. Lou was writing songs for what became the *Transformer* album. He acquired a new manager in Fred Heller, on the recommendation of Dennis Katz. Bettye went horseriding in Central Park when the weather was fine. One day after her ride she met Lou in the park for lunch. They drank sangria in a cafe and then went to a movie. Lou was inspired to write "Perfect Day," his most famous love song. "The important lines about that, of course, are 'You [just] keep me hanging on.' That's what the song is about," says Bettye. "That's what he is saying to me: you keep me hanging on." She dismisses the urban legend that the song was actually about a couple of junkies. "Yeah, I read that. It's pure bullshit."

Other songs Lou wrote at this time included "Vicious," after Andy Warhol, whom he continued to see socially, suggested he write a song around the word.

"What kind of vicious?" asked Lou.

"Oh, vicious, you hit me with a flower," Andy replied camply.

Hitherto, Lou had addressed homosexuality in his songs in a matter-of-fact way, like his writer heroes William Burroughs, John Rechy and Hubert Selby Jr. By 1972, however, Bowie had created a new vogue for camp in pop music, whereby male stars dressed ostentatiously and wore makeup. Bowie went further than most. "I'm gay, and always have been," he told *Melody Maker* in 1972 as he promoted *Hunky Dory*, a statement so startling at the time that it put him on the cover of the music weekly. At this stage in his life, Lou was an unremarkable-looking man. Slightly chubby, with bushy hair, he mooched about in jeans and T-shirts. Seeing the success Bowie had achieved with his theatrical, androgynous image,

Lou decided to copy him. This can be seen as an act of desperation. If he didn't have a hit with *Transformer*, his career would be over.

He and David had stayed in touch by phone since their initial meeting in New York. When David recorded *The Rise and Fall of Ziggy Stardust and the Spiders from Mars*, he sent Lou an advance copy of the record with a bunch of roses. "I remember a great night at one of Lou's apartments when he played me the *Ziggy Stardust* album and told me about Bowie," says Erin Clermont, who continued to hang out with Lou, despite his impending marriage. "Bowie had sent Lou a couple dozen yellow roses, along with a can of red spray paint in case he wanted them another color." Shelley also recalls Lou raving about Bowie. "He would come to my studio—I used to work in a pottery studio—and he would give me what I call the David Bowie philosophy: you've got to do something really outrageous [to make it], you've got to figure out something to do [that's] never been done before, so people will talk about it, and it will be ahead of its time. Paint your fingernails black, dye your hair, be gay even if you're not gay, and wear sparkly stuff like Ziggy Stardust. All this stuff. And then you will make it."

The transformation began when he and Bettye returned to London in the summer of 1972 to record *Transformer*. Angie found the couple a place to stay, a townhouse at Cedar Court in Wimbledon, an odd choice of digs, being way out in the suburbs, and introduced Lou to Freddie Burretti, the tailor who made David's stage costumes. Lou bought a paisley jumpsuit, accessorized with a pink scarf and gold shoes with hearts embossed on the toes. He also experimented with pancake makeup, eyeliner and black nail varnish. "He and David put that together. Sometimes I put his eye makeup on," says Bettye. Unfortunately, Lou didn't carry this look with the same aplomb as Bowie, lacking the younger man's fashion-model physique.

David was on the road with the Spiders from Mars band, featuring guitarist Mick Ronson, performing songs from *Ziggy Stardust*. It was the hottest ticket in pop. He brought the show to the Royal

Festival Hall in London on July 8, inviting Lou to join him onstage. For the first time in his career, Lou appeared before an audience in glam gear: a black velvet suit decorated with sequins, worn with his new gold shoes. He and David performed three Velvet Underground classics, to the delight of the crowd. "On Saturday the magic was boosted by an unadvertised appearance of Lou Reed," wrote Ray Coleman in the *Melody Maker*, adding that "an electrifying heat came across that stage as David and Lou roared into 'White Light,' 'I'm Waiting for My [sic] Man' and 'Sweet Jane.' Their obvious admiration for each other's style was great to watch." Elated, Lou got wasted at the after-show party. "There were a lot of parties," sighs Bettye, "drinking ad nauseam."

The following night he appeared with an American pickup band called the Tots at the King's Cross Cinema in north London, a grubby little venue also known as the Scala. "That was the first time I had seen Lou perform," says Tony Zanetta, recalling that his two sets on the night were very different. "One he was absolutely brilliant, and the [other] he was absolutely awful. That was Lou—very erratic." Photographer Mick Rock took pictures of him onstage. One shot, a flattering image of Lou looking wistfully into the middle distance over his guitar, became the iconic image of the artist when it was chosen for the cover of *Transformer*. It was one of the few pictures taken that night in which he didn't look fat. In truth, the picture looked very little like him.

While Richard Robinson was packing his bag to join Lou in London to produce the new album, he was told that he wasn't required. It had been arranged with RCA that Bowie was going to produce *Transformer*. "We learned this news literally the day before Richard was set to fly to London," notes Lisa Robinson, who was "royally pissed off" on her husband's behalf. As he was to prove time and again, Lou was not a loyal friend.

The fact that Lou and David were on the same record label made the production deal possible, while Bowie knew that Lou's debut had been a failure and wanted to help his friend, no doubt thinking that it would benefit his reputation to be associated with a successful Reed record in America. As Angie says, "They did use each other pretty effectively." The album had to be made fast, however, in a break in Bowie's schedule that August, and he wanted to do it in London at Trident, the Soho studio where he and Ronson had made *Hunky Dory* and *Ziggy Stardust*. They had a good relationship with the resident engineer, Ken Scott, who had also worked for the Beatles. This was an experienced, successful team, but Bowie was nervous. "I was petrified that he said, yes, he would like to work with me in the producer capacity, because [I] felt so intimidated by my knowledge of the work he had already done. Even though there was only [a small amount of] time between us[4] it seemed like Lou had this great legacy of work, which indeed he did have . . . I really wanted it to work for him, and be a memorable album that people wouldn't forget."

Transformer turned out to be a dream of a record. In the first place, Lou had some great songs, including three Velvet Underground leftovers: "Andy's Chest," "Satellite of Love" and "Goodnight Ladies," all of which had interesting, witty lyrics. Unlike his debut solo album, the songs were skilfully arranged, performed and recorded. Lou didn't try to sing but rather spoke the words, in the manner of a world-weary *flâneur*. British session musicians were once again employed to create the music, but Bowie and Ronson gave them direction. "We went into the control room to hear what David Bowie wanted. I don't remember Lou Reed even coming out from behind the screens. . . . He just sort of sat there in the studio all the time," says John Halsey, one of three drummers on the album. "It was very much David Bowie driving the whole thing." Engineer Ken Scott says Lou wasn't even compos mentis. "He was stoned the entire time, so that creates problems." This gave Bowie freedom. "I

---

4 Bowie was almost five years younger than Lou.

think it probably made it a hell of a lot easier, because that allowed David to take more control . . ."

The eight new songs on the album included "Vicious," "Perfect Day," and "Make Up," the lyrics of which were borrowed from the new Gay Liberation movement. When Lou drawled ". . . we're coming out/Out of our closets" he was repeating a slogan used on marches and protests in New York and elsewhere, though he did so without any sense of political passion or personal commitment, and didn't identify himself explicitly as gay, though many listeners would assume he was.

The most important song was of course "Walk on the Wild Side." Lou had written "Wild Side," as he liked to call his most famous song, while recovering from his second breakdown, having been approached by producers who wanted to adapt Nelson Algren's 1956 novel, A Walk on the Wild Side, about the adventures of a drifter in the Depression, for Broadway. Lou was asked to write songs for the show, which fell through. "When they dropped the project, I took my song and changed the book's characters into people I knew from Warhol's Factory. I don't like to waste things."

"Walk on the Wild Side" was an unusual song in many ways, including the fact that each verse dealt with a different character, and these were all real people. Three of the verses concerned a trio of New York trans preformers—Jackie Curtis, Candy Darling and Holly Woodlawn—who hung out on the fringe of the Warhol crowd. Holly, the subject of the first verse, was an exotic creature of complicated background, a Puerto Rican who grew up in Miami with a Polish stepfather, to whom he owed his legal name (Harold Ajzenberg). He came to New York as a teenager in 1962, slept rough ("in the gutter") and got mixed up in drugs and prostitution before he took to dressing as a woman. Holly then came to the attention of Paul Morrissey, who cast him in Trash. When the movie came out, he was in jail, serving time for impersonating a French diplomat's wife in order to fraudulently cash a check at the United

Nations bank, a stunt he pulled off with an atrocious French accent
(*"Bonjour,* everybody!"). He had never met Lou, but Lou had heard
enough about Holly's wild life to describe how he came to New York
in the song. "It is accurate," says Holly, "for the most part."

When he sang in the second verse about Candy Darling giving
head in public toilets, Lou was writing about an old friend, maybe
from experience. He also knew Jackie Curtis, a speed freak with a
James Dean fixation. Inspiration for Little Joe, the character in the
third verse, was Joe Dallesandro, an actor in several Paul Morrissey
films.

The song was transformed in the studio. "If you had heard the song
when he wrote it, the way he wrote it, it was a little ditty," says Bettye.
"And it was turned into this incredible production that Bowie made.
Just incredible! That's why he and I were so incredibly surprised, because we both knew it was just a little ditty. But by the time Bowie
got done with it, holy cow!" In his more honest moments, Lou gave
Bowie and Ronson their due. "Odds are that if Bowie and Ronson
hadn't produced it, it wouldn't have been a hit!" he conceded in 1996.
"My way, there wouldn't have been a string part, especially since it's a
string part I didn't write." Credit must also go to multi-instrumentalist
Herbie Flowers, who played double bass on the track, overdubbing his
electric bass ten notes higher to create the song's jazzy gait. Flowers
also had a big hand in creating the Dixieland band arrangement of
"Goodnight Ladies," playing tuba on the recording. Notwithstanding
Lou's love of jazz, it should be noted that "Walk on the Wild Side"
sounds nothing like anything else he ever recorded. The lush strings,
the groovy bass part and the famous sax solo at the end created a se-
ductively slick, lounge lizard pop song that was entirely untypical of
his work. Even Lou's vocal sounded as if somebody else was singing.

It was Lou's idea to add a "doo da doo" refrain, in the style of
African-American girl groups. "Oh my God, who arranged for us
to do this session in the *morning*?" he said, coming into Trident.
"I can't possibly work until I've had some coffee." While he drank

his coffee Lou was introduced to the vocal group Thunder Thighs: a young Irishwoman named Casey Synge (pronounced sing) and her three American girlfriends: Karen Friedman, Jackie Hardin and Dari Lallou. "We are all white," clarifies Casey. "Everybody thinks we are black."

"I like the color of your nails," Lou told Karen, comparing nail varnish while he finished his coffee. "What do you think of mine?"

That made the girls laugh. "So we go into the booth to do 'Walk on the Wild Side' first," says Casey. Lou had already recorded his vocal. They misheard the fifth verse as "Jackie comes from LA," and laughed some more, because Jackie Hardin was from Los Angeles. "He was happy that we were amused by his song," says Casey. Lou then told them what to sing. When it was done, they moved on to other tracks. "All the rest we did was improvised. The only thing he knew he wanted was the doo da doos," says Casey, who had the idea of singing "spoke spoke" on another track, "Wagon Wheel," which brought some humor to a song about kicking a girl in the head. "Then the three hours were up and that was the end of the session. He was very nice. He said it was a pleasure working with us 'real girls.'"

Thunder Thighs left the studio in high spirits. It had been fun working with Lou, and "Walk on the Wild Side" was a terrific song. The reference to oral sex in the lyrics meant that it would never be heard on the radio, of course. "I remember being in the cab with Karen and Casey and discussing it," says Dari Lallou. "'What a drag, it's such a great song, and it's never going to get airplay.'"

Mick Ronson was in the producer's chair when Thunder Thighs sang their parts; there was no sign of Bowie, who had at least one row with Lou during the making of *Transformer*. Angie recalls Lou storming out of the studio, before coming back and making up with David. "It was something foolish. You know, [Lou] was tired. I don't think he wanted to sing [the song] again and then afterwards they were, you know, kissing each other, 'Oh yes, yes, yes, of course I would have done it again . . .'" When Barbara Hodes visited Lou in London, he told her that he'd had a major falling-out with the Englishman. "Lou told me the story about David either sabotaging or losing the master of 'Walk on the Wild Side' and they had [to do it again]."

The fact that Bowie was a bigger star than Lou, and getting bigger all the time, created tension. In September 1972, David returned to New York to play Carnegie Hall. He performed "I'm Waiting for the Man" and "White Light/White Heat" as part of his set, and received a standing ovation. Meanwhile, the author of these songs was trundling around the UK with the Tots playing student unions. The £450 he received for his trouble at Glasgow University on October 7 was typical of the money he was earning for small gigs at this time. It was irritating to be acknowledged as a major songwriter by one's peers and yet enjoy so little public recognition.

Returning to London to oversee the creation of the cover art for *Transformer*, Lou was reunited with his college friend Karl Stoecker, who was working as a commercial photographer in the capital. Mick Rock's stage photo of Lou was used on the front of *Transformer*, but Karl was commissioned to take the studio photographs for the back: a picture of Lou's friend and occasional road manager Ernie Thormahlen tipping his cap at an androgynous model. The conspicuous bulge in Ernie's jeans was created by a plastic banana. A rumor went about that the girl was a man in drag—a story perpetuated by Lou, who sometimes claimed that he dressed in drag for the photo. The girl was actually fashion model Gala Mitchell. "I guess it was the transformer idea—he was a she, she as a he," explains Karl. "The guy was supposed to be looking in the mirror, and the girl was in the mirror."

The album's gay overtones put off some American critics when *Transformer* was released in November 1972. Writing in *Rolling Stone*, Nick Tosches expressed disdain for "Make Up" in particular. "It isn't decadent—it isn't perverse, it isn't rock 'n' roll, it's just a stereotypical image of the faggot-as-sissy traipsing around and lisping about effeminacy," he sniped, describing "Perfect Day" as the worst song on the album before concluding that Lou "should forget this artsy-fartsy kind of homo stuff . . ." The *New York Times* was similarly scathing. "The public has never discovered him and unfortunately *Transformer* will not help his cause . . . a flaccid piece of work." In retrospect, these reviews seem misjudged, even a tad homophobic. *Transformer* was a strong album of clever, catchy songs, faultlessly produced by Bowie and Ronson, that showcased Lou as a distinctive and original singer-songwriter. RCA described him in press releases as "The Phantom of Rock," an inept attempt to sell an artist they didn't understand to a public who knew little or nothing about him. This was a false image he accepted and hid behind, to his regret. "I allowed it, and it was kind of a convenient thing to duck behind and use as a shield against just about everything," he later said. "The trouble was, I ducked behind the image for so long that after a while there was a real danger of it just becoming a parody thing, where even if I was trying to be serious you didn't know whether to take it seriously or not." The charm and wit of Lou's songs caught the ear of the public, nevertheless, and the record sold strongly. *Transformer* made Lou's career, though he struggled for years to match the quality of both the songs and the production.

DESPITE THEIR ENGAGEMENT, HIS relationship with Bettye remained volatile. One night after what she calls "a blow-out fight," she left the apartment. Lou immediately called Erin Clermont to tell her that they had split up. "And then he used the line that melted me: 'I'm lonely.'" Erin said she would be right over. "We went to bed, and a few hours later someone entered the apartment. It was Bettye . . . who just sat in a chair and stared at us. She didn't move, didn't speak. Have to say she did that well. I skulked out of bed, got my clothes and left." Ungallantly, Lou told Bettye that Erin was just a girl he'd picked up in a bar. Remarkably enough, both women forgave him.

Bettye knew that Lou was attracted to men as well as women, though he didn't tend to talk about this side of his life with his girlfriends. "There are some people that are bi or gay because they kind of really are. And then there are others who go to a certain lifestyle because it's safer for them than a lifestyle that is a little bit more threatening. And I believe that Lou falls in the latter category," she says, arguing that Lou found women more congenial as long-term partners. "I am just giving you my experiences as a girlfriend. . . . That is how I felt." On this shaky basis, they decided to go ahead and marry. Bettye's parents were aghast. Her mother told her that Lou was using her, while her father couldn't understand why she wanted to marry a man who wore makeup. "When I asked him to come to the wedding, the only thing he knew about Lou was the cover of that album, and he didn't come." More surprisingly, considering that Lou had been living at home recently, and he and Bettye had just attended Bunny's wedding, Lou didn't invite his parents or his sister. Bunny was upset. "He told me about the wedding but did not invite me to attend. I cried for two weeks."

The ceremony was conducted at Lou's apartment on East 74th Street on January 9, 1973. Bettye was a Presbyterian. Lou was Jewish. Perversely, they were married by a Catholic priest. "[Lou] thought it was funny." The only guests were Lou's manager, Fred Heller, and his wife. Lou and Bettye wore white. Afterwards, they attended a dinner hosted by RCA. Lou was drunk by the end. "He was always drunk, but he was dead drunk. What does Lou do when he is drunk? He goes home, goes to bed, and falls asleep." This was not the wedding night of a girl's dreams, but it was often the way their evenings ended. "That's an interesting [situation] for a twenty-two-year-old pretty woman to find herself in. . . . And he's coming across as the great sex figure of all time. Huh!"

They went through the motions of married life. Bettye took Lou's surname, and they went on their honeymoon to Jamaica. They discussed children. "I think he probably would have wanted to have them with me." But Bettye didn't have children with Lou. She declines to say whether she got pregnant and had a termination, as girlfriends had in the past, but says that she doesn't think that Lou would have made a good father. In truth, there wasn't much opportunity to get pregnant. "He wasn't terribly interested in sex."

Lou's attitude to his wife was changeable and ambiguous. He talked to friends about her in romantic terms, only to trash her in the next breath. "He said she was a 'princess,' and he was in love

Lou and Bettye on their wedding day, 1973.

with a 'fairy-tale princess.' You know, he would get drunk and he would get sort of maudlin when he spoke about her. Then the next thing you know he would be saying that 'some of the people who are dearest to me are the scum of the earth,'" recalls Ed McCormack, a journalist who was sent to interview Lou for *Rolling Stone* around this time and struck up a friendship with him. "It was a schizo kind of [relationship]."

Bettye was at Lou's side when he appeared onstage in New York on January 27, 1973, for an important concert. *Transformer* was selling. RCA was running print adverts to maintain momentum. A US tour was lined up. The idea was to get Lou off to a good start with two prestige shows at Alice Tully Hall, a venue within Lincoln Center associated with classical music. RCA top brass were present, together with Lou's manager and friends. His parents, sister and brother-in-law also attended, though Lou hadn't seen fit to invite them to his wedding. And the press came. "There was an enormous amount of pressure for that show. That was his New York solo debut. That was going to push *Transformer*. It was his comeback. The album *Lou Reed* wasn't received well. But this has Bowie behind it and it was brilliant, so it was now or never. This was the make or break, and Alice Tully was the debut. It was really important," says Bettye.

The first show went badly. "I think the reason why the first show didn't go well was because he was drunk," says Bettye. "In fact, I know that's why it didn't go well. He would drink almost all the time anyway. But he would especially drink when he was nervous and upset." Backstage, Lou sank into a funk of depression. Thankfully, there was enough time to get him sober for the second show. When he went on again at 11 p.m. he did better. It was this late show that John Rockwell reviewed for the *New York Times*. "His voice is limited and insecure; his manner tense and shy. But his music in its basic, repetitive way, makes a powerful impact, and his songs have a reality to them that transcends easy moralism," wrote Rockwell, who proved a sympathetic and astute observer of Lou's solo career. "His voice was so personal. Not only was it limited, it was a little shaky in pitch. But, boy, could he sell one of his songs. It was just wonderful."

There was a party afterwards at the Sherry-Netherland. Lincoln Swados hobbled into the hotel lobby with Lou and Bettye, eager to join the fun. It was appropriate that Lincoln was there. He had known Lou longer than most people and had brought Lou and Bettye together. "Lincoln was with us, and we were walking up to the hotel room and Lincoln was down the hall, and it took him a little bit longer to walk than you and me, he had the cane, and I said, 'Let's wait for Lincoln,'" says Bettye. Lou scowled and walked ahead. "He wasn't good-looking enough anymore, he was just weird-looking now, so he didn't want him in his circle. He cut him out of his life."

Lou embarked on a US college tour after Alice Tully Hall. As he traveled the country, "Walk on the Wild Side" started to get airplay on both sides of the Atlantic. Executives at RCA were as delighted as they were surprised by the success of the song. A&R man Bob Ringe notes that few among them had expressed much faith in the single in advance: "Everybody said radio would never play [it]. People thought we were out of our fucking minds. . . . Either people didn't catch [the oral sex reference], or they didn't know what it meant, or what he was saying, but it got on the fucking radio! I remember kids walking down the street doing, 'doo da doo . . .'"

Holly Woodlawn was home in New York when he first heard "Walk on the Wild Side" on the radio, having received no warning that Lou had written about him. "A friend of mine calls me up and said, 'Turn on the radio.' I turned on the radio and [heard] 'Holly came from Miami, FLA.' When I finally met [Lou] I asked him, 'How did you know I came from Miami?' He said, 'Honey, you have told the world already. I didn't have to do much research.'" Holly considered the song useful publicity for his career. Joe Dallesandro, on the other hand, was not pleased to hear Lou telling everybody he was a hustler. "He never knew me, didn't know me, never met me. He went, under Paul Morrissey's direction, to look at some of our movies, and wrote the song about the character in the movies," he grumbles. "He never knew the person." But Joe liked the tune. Everybody did.

The album followed the single up the charts. Considering the fact that RCA had only paid Lou an advance of $15,000, the company was already turning a profit. His college tour was enlarged to a tour of concert halls. Then he fired Fred Heller. Lou later claimed in court that he was "afraid" of his manager, "afraid he'd become physically abusive," an intriguing statement, which he didn't enlarge upon. He further complained that he hadn't received proper accounting for his first UK tour, adding, "I just didn't get along with him [Fred]," a surprising remark in light of the fact that the Hellers had been the only guests at his recent wedding. Lou also said that he was told by his advisers that there would be "no problem" if he wanted to fire his manager, but firing Heller was a serious blunder—he sued Lou for breach of contract.

After Heller was dismissed, Dennis Katz, who had recently left RCA, became Lou's new manager and lawyer, which proved to be a poisoned chalice. Ever since he started working with Paul Morrissey and Andy Warhol, Lou had had difficult relationships with managers, usually ending in mutual recrimination. He soon fell out with Morrissey and Warhol, and their replacement, Steve Sesnick. Danny Fields resigned after two weeks. Fred Heller lasted eight months. Dennis would serve two and a half years before he and Lou parted on poisonous terms. The pattern would be repeated into the future. "Lou always seemed to be falling out with somebody that mattered to him," says former RCA executive Bruce Somerfield. "Lou was not an easily managed person."

For the time being, however, the future looked bright. With *Transformer* and "Walk on the Wild Side" selling fast, Dennis was able to negotiate lucrative deals for his client: obtaining a $130,000 advance from RCA, and a $200,000 advance on a publishing deal between Lou's new company, Oakfield Avenue Music (surprisingly, he named his company after his parents' home address), and Dunbar Music, a subsidiary of RCA. Lou would get $50,000 up front, plus $12,500 a month until 1976. Suddenly, big money was flowing in.

Transformer entered the *Billboard* Top Forty on March 24, 1973, ultimately reaching number twenty-nine. Despite its reputation, the single "Walk on the Wild Side" wasn't a number one, or anything like it. It peaked at sixteen in the US. It did, however, spend two months in the US Top Forty, and it sold around the world, reaching number ten in the UK, where it spent nine weeks in the charts. While this wasn't a monster hit by the standards of most artists, in a year when "Tie a Yellow Ribbon round the Ole Oak Tree" was the dominant international number one, it was the biggest record of Lou's career by far, enough to make him an international star—at last. Was he happy? No. "He didn't want to be known for a pop song. He wanted to be known for serious music," says Bettye. "He got sick of it on tour. All they wanted to hear was *Transformer*. All they wanted to hear was 'Walk on the Wild Side.'"

VIII

SELF-PARODY

S O FAT THAT HIS belly hung over his leather trousers, his pancake makeup slick with sweat, Lou lurched around the stage, stooping now and again to swig from a bottle of Scotch, which he kept stashed behind a monitor. Commercial success had been a long time coming, but when it arrived in the summer of 1973 he was unable to cope.

Bettye was with her husband as he toured the United States to promote *Transformer*. She was his lighting and stage director now, having asked Lou to give her a job to do, rather than just being his "appendage." She still had to look after him, helping him on-stage, drunk, and putting him to bed after the show—dead drunk. Lou was drinking every day, starting around 3 p.m., mostly Scotch whisky, as well as ingesting a variety of drugs, and he treated Bettye roughly when he was under the influence. "We were on the road, and he was really drunk, and he would, like, pin you up against a wall and tussle you, like rough you up a little. Shove you around. Throw you up against a wall. Tussle you. Hit you . . . shake you," she says, becoming upset as she recalls. "And then one time he actually gave me a black eye, and that was when I said, 'All right, this is it. I'm not taking this anymore.'" So she hit him back. "I'm not going to let anybody do that to me, and it was pretty clear to me that the only way he would ever stop doing that was if I did it to him, so he'd have to walk onstage with a black eye." Yet Lou continued to shove his wife around.

Bettye found herself caught between Lou's demons and the men who had a financial interest in his career. They expected Bettye to keep him sober so he could work. "I was trying to physically stop him from taking all the goddamn drugs, and taking all the goddamn booze, and I would get between him and a bottle. And then he'd come after me physically. That's what was going on. . . . That's what you had to do in order to stop him, to stop him from drinking. You put yourself between him and the bottle. 'No! You can't have any more . . . No! No, you can't!'" The drink was making Lou heavy, which was another concern. Rock stars aren't supposed to be fat. "Everybody had a word with me about Lou's weight," sighs Bettye. "He got into really bad shape with all the drinking, and he didn't care. . . . It was pretty gross."

This unhappy tour wound up in Miami on June 1, 1973. The local sheriff's department was notoriously conservative, being the people who arrested Jim Morrison for allegedly exposing himself during a Doors concert in 1969, and they were waiting for Lou. When he sang about oral sex, the cops stopped the show, escorted him offstage and put him in handcuffs. "Dennis [Katz] and I and a couple of other people from the entourage followed the car to the jail. Dennis was a lawyer, so he got him out," says Bettye. "It was actually really frightening, but Lou thought it was funny because he was getting more publicity."

Apart from the problems that came with touring, Lou was under pressure to record a new album for RCA to build on the success of *Transformer*. Although he had been a prolific songwriter in the past, he was struggling to write new material with so much going on in his life, and the drinking didn't help. It was at this stage that Dennis introduced him to Bob Ezrin, a twenty-four-year-old Canadian producer who had been making a series of hugely successful records with Alice Cooper, including *School's Out*, one of the biggest hits of 1972. They met in Ezrin's hometown of Toronto, where they decided to reuse "Berlin" as the start of a song cycle of the same name, permeated with the sleazy atmosphere of interwar Germany, part Christopher Isherwood, part *Cabaret*, part *Threepenny Opera*. "His writing was so evocative—I could see, smell and feel the record. It reminded me of Brecht and Weill," explained Ezrin, who also saw the project in cinematic terms. *Berlin* would be promoted grandiosely as "a film for the ear." "We came up with a concept and he went and wrote it." In fact, Lou wrote very little for *Berlin*. Apart from the title song, which was old, he adapted four Velvet Underground tunes: "Oh, Jim," "Men of Good Fortune," "Sad Song" and "Stephanie Says," which became "Caroline Says" parts I and II. Still, he didn't have enough material.

Then Bettye received a call to inform her that her mother had cancer. The news prompted her to tell Lou the full story of her unhappy childhood, including the custody battle her parents fought over her, during which her father accused her mother of being promiscuous, alleging that she picked up servicemen in bars and was therefore unfit to look after a child. When Bettye went to bed that night, Lou sat up, drinking and writing. The next morning he told his wife that he had written the songs to complete *Berlin*. He sang them to Bettye, who was surprised to hear the story she had told Lou regurgitated, particularly in "The Kids," which described how a mother lost custody of her daughter after being accused of sleeping around with, among others, a serviceman. Bettye recognized specific details as statements she had made to Lou about her mother, mixed up with things he'd invented. "There is the whole thing with my mother and my father and me, 'They're taking her children away,' that stuff." Lou had also based aspects of the character of Caroline on his wife. "Yes, there's poetry on the shelf. That's mine," she says referring to a line in the song "The Bed." "Did I try to kill myself? [another line]. No. And that's how writers write. And he was desperate. He needed the material." She didn't like the way Lou had used her life for his work, but didn't feel able to stop him. "They were waiting for [an] album. He finally got an album. What am I going to do about that, say you can't use that album? I can't say that. Of course I was hurt. I was devastated. But I wasn't going to let him see that."

The Reeds returned to London to make the new record, staying once again at the Inn on the Park, while Lou worked with Ezrin and a cast of superstar musicians, including Jack Bruce and Steve Winwood, at Morgan Studios. *Berlin* would be the most expensive and highly produced album of Lou's career, with choirs, strings, horns and multiple overdubs, much of which he had nothing to do with. Ezrin wrote the arrangements. It was as much his record as Lou's, and Lou often seemed to be in the way. "Bob gave me directions: 'Keep him out of the studio,'" says Dinky Dawson, who was working with Lou at the time. "So me and Bettye would keep him out of the studio until it was his turn to come in."

The *Berlin* songs delineated a disastrous relationship between the characters of Caroline and Jim. Caroline accused Jim of being sexually inadequate ("Caroline Says I"). He accused her of being a "slut" who slept around and abused drugs ("The Kids"), and beat her. No less than three of the songs described domestic violence, including "Oh, Jim," in which Lou sang, "Beat her black and blue and get it straight." Caroline was also beaten in "Caroline Says II," while the last line of the last song, "Sad Song," had Lou singing that anyone else would have broken her arms. Did any of this reflect his own feelings or behavior?

As we have seen, Lou's friend Allan Hyman recalls him hitting a girlfriend, while Bettye is one of several sources to describe Lou as a misogynist. She also says that Lou hit her, which, indeed, he admitted to. "I needed a sycophant who I could bounce around and she fit the bill . . . but she called it love, ha!" he said of his relationship with his first wife in 1978, looking back on the marriage. In another interview he went so far as to suggest that women liked being *bounced* around. "I'm a chauvinist down to my toes," he told *Creem* in 1979. "I think women admire force all the more for not having it—nobody admires strength more than a weak person. It's axiomatic that a woman is all the more impressed that you could kill her. A straight guy might have something to learn from his gay friends, in that a woman can get turned off if you're appreciative of her when what she really wants is to be smacked across the mouth. I know this is a terrible, chauvinist point of view—this will be very unfavorable towards me . . ." Such comments were clearly meant to be outrageous, and project an image. But the evidence suggests that he may have meant it.

The sordid nature of *Berlin* affected those involved. "It was an emotionally hyper-charged atmosphere in that studio at that time," says Ezrin, who reveals that there was a lot of drug abuse in the making of the album. "I can honestly say that all of us were messing around with things we shouldn't have been messing around with." Lou was partying at the time with David Bowie, whom Ezrin considered to be a distraction. The stars were photographed together at the Café Royal in July, appearing to kiss gingerly for the cameras. The smirk on Lou's face indicated that it was probably a publicity stunt. Bowie, a better actor, managed to keep a straight face. The same night, Lou was photographed kissing his wife full on the mouth, though that picture didn't make the newspapers.

Bettye became very unhappy in London. Lou later claimed that she became so depressed that she attempted suicide in their hotel suite. "Like, during the recording session, my old lady—who was an asshole, but I needed to have an asshole around to bolster me up," he said in 1978, looking back on the marriage, ". . . anyway, my old lady, during a recording session, tried to commit suicide in the bathtub in the hotel. . . . Cut her wrists . . ." Bettye denies this. "I did not cut my wrists. . . . At that point in our relationship he probably would have liked me to have committed suicide—an easier way to get rid of me." It was nevertheless clear that their marriage was not going to last, and the end came soon enough.

The Reeds were at a party when Bettye caught Lou in a bathroom with another woman, shooting up. "It was heroin," she says. "The next day I said, 'I want a divorce.' He thought I was kidding, and I wasn't." Bettye told Dennis that she didn't want any money, over and above her wages for her lighting work, she just wanted to be free. Papers were drawn up for her to sign. Then she took a flight to the Dominican Republic, where she was granted a quickie divorce after just seven months of marriage. Strangely, she went back to living with Lou in New York as a divorcee within a fortnight.

Bettye has a vague memory of Lou being hospitalized around this time, late summer 1973, possibly once again with hepatitis, shortly after which he had to return to Europe for a tour. Even though they were now divorced, she agreed to go with him to keep him out of trouble. "Now I was just the nursemaid . . ."

To capitalize on the success of *Transformer*, and to promote *Berlin*, a new band of top-notch musicians were hired for the tour, led by Dick Wagner, a guitar ace from Detroit, partnered by another virtuoso guitarist named Steve Hunter, both of whom had played on *Berlin*. "They're great players, no question about it. Steve came from Mitch Ryder's band. Musically, you don't get any better than that," says Ray Colcord, who played keyboards in the band. "My job was quite clear. I was to provide a solid background so the guitar players could go nuts." Completing the band were Pentti "Whitey" Glan on drums, and Peter Walsh was on bass. During rehearsals at the Music Inn in Massachusetts, Lou was told that he wouldn't be required to play guitar in the show. Although Lou rated himself highly as a guitarist, few professional musicians agreed with him. "He thought he was like Jimi Hendrix. He used to brag about it—I never saw any evidence of that. In truth, the only thing I ever saw him do was strum a guitar," says Dick Wagner. "He played enough guitar to write the songs he wrote, and they are the most important part of the whole thing. He wrote some very simple, but really brilliant songs . . . I took what we had recorded with *Berlin*, and the other songs, and tried to make them into coliseum-size songs—the songs are mostly my arrangements—so we could be on the road and be majestic. Take the brilliance of his songs and take them to a new level."

They flew to London in September 1973, checking into Blake's Hotel in South Kensington, which Lou patronized for the rest of his career. He stayed initially in a small basement room, forming a friendship with the night porter. Bowie sent flowers to welcome him back to town. The band then flew to Germany for a festival on the 9th, for which Lou received $15,000, three times as much as he had been earning for a show during his recent US tour. This was the start of a new phase in his career, during which he played much bigger gigs, for which the new band was designed. The show began with a guitar duel between Hunter and Wagner, an instrumental they'd worked up in rehearsals as an introduction to "Vicious," later adapting it as the introduction to "Sweet Jane." When they segued into the familiar power chords, Lou strode on to an ovation. "What a great way to bring on the show!" says Peter Walsh. "When it finally got to the intro to 'Sweet Jane,' the crowd would get to their feet and go nuts because they would recognize 'Sweet Jane' right away." Without his guitar to occupy him, Lou was forced to be more theatrical onstage, making hand gestures and tossing his microphone around like Roger Daltrey. "The best thing to do with Lou was stand him there, let him do little things with his arms and his microphone, and let the expression on his face—that was why it was painted with white face—come through," says Dinky Dawson, "except he did get excited now and again, and swing the mic stand on to monitors, and trash [equipment] for the heck of it."

While the show proved popular, critics reserved most of their praise for the band. "Lou Reed, looking like a panda in ill-fitting leathers, lurched on in something akin to a swagger and a stagger minus that old Gerry & the Pacemakers guitar previously designed to hide his paunch, and grabbed the mic stand," Nick Kent wrote in the *New Musical Express*, reviewing an outdoor show at London's Crystal Palace on September 15. "From then on we were treated to Reed's clumsy but earnest attempts to carry himself off as a lead singer . . . but the band itself bristles with potential, showcasing as it does blisteringly fine guitarists in Steve Hunter and Dick Wagner." Lou was enraged by such coverage, accusing his guitarists of upstaging him. "I'm fed up with them," he told Dawson. "If they don't calm down, send them home." He insisted on traveling separately from the band, and ignored his musicians when they were offstage. "He wouldn't talk to me at all," Hunter complained. "In Europe, all the newspaper reviews talked about the band and kind of belittled him as being seemingly out of it, and he was. He was doing a lot of speed at that time. He was pretty drugged up," adds Wagner. "The band had most of the reviews, and I know Lou didn't like that."

Lou spent most of his time sequestered in his hotel suite with Bettye; his bodyguard, Bernie Gelb; and stage manager, Jim Jacobs, who didn't form a good opinion of his boss. "Lou wasn't a nice person," says Jacobs. "I don't say that with any malice, we had a perfectly good relationship, but he wasn't a nice person. No one could ever accuse Lou of being a nice guy, whatever his [widow] says. . . . It was 'Walk on the Wild Side' that made Lou, and that's David, but Lou didn't give a shit what anybody did for him. He didn't care. He was a dick. . . . It is [also] important to understand that Lou was a stone junkie. That had a lot to do with his personality. He loved to shoot up."

After a short period when he had sworn off drugs, Lou was dabbling again. "He was just mixing everything up, drinking and speed," says Pentti Glan. "I know he did dabble with heroin, too.

If he was [using on tour] it didn't [become obvious], but cocaine and amphetamine and drinking, that was primarily what [he was using]." Lou's minders Bernie Gelb and Jim Jacobs tried their best to keep him sober. "When we started rehearsals for Europe, I had an understanding with Lou that he wasn't going to drink on the tour, and he was good about it [initially]. He did other recreational drugs, but he was in control," says Bernie. "I would literally tuck him into bed every night. My room, or Jim's room, would be the room next to his. Once I got him into bed, I was reasonably sure he [wouldn't stray]. If he needed something, he would call me on the phone."

When they got to Paris, Lou and Bettye checked into the luxurious Hotel Bristol, a sign of how much money Lou was now making. Bettye tried to persuade Lou to take her sightseeing, but he wasn't interested in doing anything of the kind. "Lou did treat Bettye very poorly," says Steve Katz, Dennis's younger brother, who was traveling with the entourage. Lou and Bettye had a fight in their hotel before Lou's show on September 17. "We were sitting down, and he was incredibly obnoxious. It was the obnoxious Lou," Bettye recalls. "I got up from the table and said, 'I'm not taking this anymore.' He got up and shoved me. So I picked up a glass of milk—I was drinking milk—and threw it in his face, and said, 'I'm leaving you.'" This was somewhat after the event, in that they had already been divorced for a month. Nevertheless, Bettye ran out of the hotel in tears, and walked the streets alone while she faced up to life without Lou. Meanwhile, Lou did his gig at L'Olympia, which took an unexpected turn when a well-known Parisian trans person climbed onstage. Lou's minders threw the person off, but Lou called out for them to be brought back, having apparently taken a fancy to them. The next day Bettye flew home to New York. They never spoke again. She saw him one more time from a distance, when she sat in the audience at one of his shows. "He looked really angry with me. You don't leave Lou. He would just be angry with you for that—particularly me—it was an incredible betrayal as far as he was concerned."

With Bettye gone, Lou really started to misbehave. "We were in Amsterdam, and he hooked up with an old boyfriend, and this guy gave him speed after the show," says Bernie Gelb. "So when we picked him up in the morning he was already a little jangly. What I didn't know was that he still had some speed left over, which he did just before he went onstage in Brussels the next night, and had a huge health issue—a huge problem onstage." Lou was partway into his set when he bent over and split his leather pants. Bernie and Bob Ringe, now his European booking agent, ran on and wrapped Lou in gaffer tape to prevent him exposing himself. Lou continued to sing for a few minutes, then collapsed.

Bernie carried Lou to his dressing room. "What did you do?" he asked.

"I took some speed." Bernie was so angry that he felt like punching him. "Bernie, I can't go back onstage. Don't let anybody in here."

As the curtain came down, signaling that the show was over, the audience began to tear up the seats in anger. "Dennis comes running up with the promoter and says, 'You've got to get Lou back out there,'" recalls Gelb.

"Dennis, it's not happening."

"Let me in there to speak to him."

"Dennis, I can't. . . . Lou tells me he can't see anybody now, including you." They had an argument outside the dressing room. "He was really angry with me. The cops came and quelled the riot. I went back to Lou and stayed with him for about an hour until his heart rate came within a somewhat normal range, and I said, 'Lou, you can't do this to me again. Let's stick with our program. No more speed.' And he was good for the rest of the tour."

When Lou brought his band back to the United Kingdom, his dates were reported in the *New Musical Express* under the headline "RETURN OF THE PRINCE OF PONCE." Such irreverence didn't endear him to the British press, which tended to mock and applaud him in equal measure. More dismaying were the reviews of *Ber-*

lin, which were starting to appear on both sides of the Atlantic. In truth, the album received mixed reviews, including praise from John Rockwell in the *New York Times*, who thought *Berlin* "one of the strongest and most original rock records in years." The balance of opinion, though, was that *Berlin* was an overproduced record of mawkish songs that were depressing to listen to. Ezrin's decision to overdub a home recording of his son crying on to "The Kids" was the cherry on a sickly confection of misery. Writing in *Rolling Stone*, Stephen Davis slated *Berlin* as a "disaster . . . [Lou's] last shot at a once-promising career." Lou focused on the bad reviews, devastated by criticism of an album that, in his drunken, drug-addled hubris, he considered a masterpiece. Sales were respectable; Lou claimed 110,000 copies sold over the next two years. But this didn't meet the expectations of RCA, who had hoped to build on the success of *Transformer*, and *Berlin* henceforth carried the taint of failure. "The way that album was overlooked was probably the biggest disappointment I ever faced," Lou said in 1977, explaining that his distrust of journalists stemmed from this experience. It could be argued that he went into a career sulk after *Berlin* from which he never emerged. "I pulled the blinds *shut* at that point. And they've remained closed. . . . I don't care what people write about me anymore. I have no respect whatsoever for their opinions."

ALTHOUGH HE DIDN'T ENJOY commercial success with the Velvet Underground, Lou gained the respect of his peers, the critics and a select audience for the intelligence of his writing and the versatility of his music. He was one of the few songwriters of the 1960s who could legitimately be compared to the great Bob Dylan. His subsequent solo career started with a disappointment, then received a boost from the success of *Transformer*. After the perceived failure of *Berlin* he entered a much less impressive period when he squandered his reputation. There would be good work in the years ahead, but there would also be a lot of substandard tosh from an artist whose judgment was often clouded by alcohol and drugs and who relied increasingly on image. This did long-term damage to his career.

After his breakup with Bettye, Lou returned to Barbara Hodes, who had never understood his marriage. He also stepped up his amphetamine use, becoming a patient of an Upper East Side quack who dispensed legal shots of pharmaceutical amphetamine laced with vitamin supplements. Celebrities lined up for these legal highs. "Lou, this is going to kill you," Steve Katz warned Lou when he started to frequent the surgery.

"That's all right," he replied. "I'm enjoying myself."

That winter he went back on the road with a new bass guitarist in the band, Prakash John, whom Lou called "the Christian" because of his religious beliefs. The Christian had previously played with George Clinton's Parliament, and gave the band a funkier sound. They toured the northeastern United States during snowstorms that meant many venues were half empty. Lou's escalating use of amphetamines affected the pacing of the show. "One night he would want everything fast. Another night he would want everything slow," says Ray Colcord. He didn't always come in on time either. "Not now, Lou!" the musicians would yell when he started to sing in the wrong place, an echo of Lou's problems with Nico in the Velvet Underground. The tour culminated on December 21, 1973, with two celebrated shows at the Academy of Music in New York. The mood backstage on the night—a freezing cold evening—was tense. Lou had a tiff with Andy Warhol, who showed up unexpectedly, while Bernie Gelb argued money with the impresario Howard Stein, threatening to cancel the second show right up to the last minute unless Stein handed over more cash. "Howard Stein only wanted to pay for one show," says Gelb, who threatened to pull the plug on his artist unless he got another six thousand dollars. "I said, 'In two minutes Lou is going to walk out and grab the microphone, and no one is going to hear him, and it's going to be your fault.

You are the promoter.' He finally broke down, counted out the cash. I gave Dinky [Dawson] the signal just as Lou was walking on. I told the band to stretch the intro as long as they could, so I could get the money. . . . Literally, as Lou's about to walk onstage, we got the mic [switched] on. So that's the story behind the [long] intro." The concerts were recorded for a live album, *Rock 'n' Roll Animal*, produced by Steve Katz who, along with his brother, was trying to move Lou toward a mainstream audience by presenting classic Velvet Underground material alongside the best songs from *Berlin* and *Transformer* in an accessible rock setting. Lou was ambivalent about this. "I think they were trying to get him a little more mainstream, in terms of the American audience, and he was hesitant about going more mainstream," says his drummer Pentti Glan. "He wanted to be truer to himself."

Lou invited friends back to his apartment after the shows for what one guest, musician Alan Freedman, describes as some "serious and dangerous partying. . . . He was messing around with some very dangerous drugs." The binge continued for three days. On Christmas Eve, Lou was arrested while trying to buy more drugs on Long Island. "I got busted in Riverhead for trying to cash someone else's illegal [prescription]. I spent Christmas in the dangerous tier when it was discovered that someone with my name who was wanted for murder had escaped from jail in upstate New York," Lou later exaggerated the tale. Barbara Fulk, who worked at his new company, Transformer Enterprises, says that she bailed Lou out of jail the same day, "in a vintage white Cadillac limo . . . paid $500," meaning that he only spent a few hours in custody. Nevertheless, it was a foolish thing to do, especially as he could obtain as much speed as he liked legally from his Dr. Feelgood in New York. Lou probably simply ran out of drugs over the holidays. His stage manager, Jim Jacobs, was furious. "I was screaming at Lou, 'What the fuck are you doing? You are a star now, you can't do this shit.' He didn't care." Jacobs had had enough. "I was already on my way out at that point. I had a lot of commitments, and I didn't have time for Lou's shit anymore."

The album *Rock 'n' Roll Animal* consisted of just five songs, four Velvet Underground standards plus "Lady Day" from *Berlin*, the live arrangements of which were stretched out to a generous length. Chrissie Hynde, reviewing the album for the *New Musical Express* before her career as the leader of the Pretenders, wrote that Lou seemed to be putting on a cynical show for unhip people who'd missed the Velvets. She probably would have been even more disappointed had she known that the ecstatic audience applause on the record was overdubbed from a John Denver concert to add atmosphere. The irony was that this untypical Lou Reed album, with its swaggering arena-rock sound, proved a major success in what was the heyday of the live rock album (released in 1974, the same year as Dylan's *Before the Flood* and a year before *Frampton Comes Alive!*), selling much better than *Berlin*, reaching number forty-five in the US charts, twenty-six in the UK, and remaining to this day a favorite with many people who wouldn't normally buy a Reed record, let alone anything by the Velvet Underground. Considering it cost RCA next to nothing to make, this was a terrific result for the company. The record also expanded Lou's audience. But he hated it.

Lou and Barbara Hodes, at her apartment.

He was living with Barbara Hodes again, at her swanky apartment on Fifth Avenue. Despite the fact that this was the most successful period of his career, he let her pay the rent for all but one of
the months he stayed with her. He was a tightfisted boyfriend, and
not particularly romantic. "One Valentine's Day [1974] he brought
me a present—you tell me whether this is romantic—he went out
and bought me a snake, a garter snake called Edgar Allan Snake,"
Barbara says with a laugh. The couple kept Edgar in a terrarium and
fed him live fish. Lou wrote the songs for his next album in Barbara's bedroom. "I had a wonderful bedroom with the windows facing the Presbyterian church on Fifth Avenue, and you could see all
the way to New Jersey. Lou sat on the bed improvising 'Sally Can't
Dance.'" This was the title song of a studio album of the same name,
the first Lou Reed solo album of entirely new material. The sweet
melody belied a grim lyric, based on a real-life case of a girl who
frequented the clubs of New York and was raped and murdered by
men who stashed her body in the trunk of their car while they continued their night out. Lou sang about Sally's demise with amused
detachment, noting obscenely how she got raped "real good" before
she was killed. "And that's why Sally can't dance. They found her
in the trunk of a car," he explained. Here was another example of a
morbid preoccupation.

The most significant new song was "Kill Your Sons," in which he
addressed the topic of his electro-convulsive therapy. Despite the
implied criticism of Sid and Toby Reed, Lou remained in contact
with his parents. Sid even acted as a consultant in his son's business
affairs in 1973 when he looked over Lou's books and advised him to
settle the Fred Heller lawsuit: good advice, which his son ignored.
Lou introduced Barbara to his parents. Unlike most of his friends,
she took a dislike to Sid. "If you had met his father, you would understand why he was fucked up. The father was cold, nasty, withdrawn, grumpy. I felt sorry for his mother . . . I came away from that
just thinking it was a miracle that Lou didn't end up worse."

Sally Can't Dance was recorded at Electric Lady, the lavish studio Jimi Hendrix built in Greenwich Village, in the spring of 1974, with Steve Katz producing. "We had a hit album with *Rock 'n' Roll Animal* . . . and we wanted to back it up with something that was just as commercial," Steve explains the thinking behind the record, for which he made many of the key decisions. "Lou had to have certain aesthetic decisions made for him because of the drugs, actually. Although I loved him, it was very difficult working with him. And I don't think he had the ability to go in and do his own album alone." Dick Wagner and Steve Hunter had left the band, but Prakash and Pentti played on the record, together with guitarist Danny Weis and keyboardist Michael Fonfara, a moustachioed hedonist whom Lou called the Turk. Surprisingly, Doug Yule joined the band at this stage, following the expiration of the Velveteen Underground. Doug was a good musician, and enough time had passed for Lou to tolerate his presence again. Their former colleagues had left show business. Sterling was living with his wife in Austin, where he was a teaching assistant at the University of Texas, while Moe was living quietly with her family in California. Doug, Sterling, Moe and John Cale earned virtually nothing from their old VU recordings at this time. Lou did, however. In the spring of 1974, he received $40,000 from MGM.

In contrast to the cohesive sound and musical integrity of the Velvet Underground albums, *Sally Can't Dance* was a hodgepodge of fashionable musical styles. "I wanted to take Lou's songs, his newer songs, and sort of put them in a context of each song getting its own specific feel," says Steve Katz, explaining what he tried to achieve. In this way, "Kill Your Sons" was recorded as hard rock, sounding not unlike an Alice Cooper track; "Ennui" was a piano-driven ballad that wouldn't have been out of place on an Elton John album; while the predominant musical flavor was R&B. This was Lou's choice but reflected the ongoing influence of David Bowie, who was about to make his own white-soul album, *Young Americans*, which turned out to be a much better record, and advised Lou on his album. Barbara recalls Lou and David socializing together at this time, including one evening at her apartment when Bowie was so stoned that he was "crawling around on his hands and knees."

Lou called his sister, who was living on Long Island with her husband, Harold, to warn her about the album. "Bunny, I have to tell you something."

"What did you do now?"

"This song's coming out." Lou recited the lyrics of "Kill Your Sons," which, apart from touching on his ECT and making unflattering implications about their parents, described a sister who'd married a fat guy on Long Island who took the train to work and didn't have a brain.

"Are you serious?" asked Bunny. "You wipe out my lifestyle and my husband in four phrases?"

"Ah, I needed something to rhyme with train. So I had to take poetic license."

"Thank you very much, that's very sweet."

Bunny was always tolerant with Lou. "It was indeed written about Harold," she says now, sitting with her husband. "Harold found it enormously funny." Harold concurs with a chuckle: "He had one of the great senses of humor. . . . A lot of people didn't get it." This was perhaps the best way to deal with a brother-in-law like Lou Reed: laugh at his rudeness.

ONE SIDE EFFECT OF the amount of speed Lou was using was that he lost a lot of weight, going from pudgy to skeletal over the course of 1973–74. Barbara took a remarkable photo of Lou at her Fifth Avenue apartment in which he looks emaciated. His appearance became even more startling when he had a crew cut with Maltese crosses dyed in the sides in preparation for a spring tour of Europe. Then he had all his hair dyed blond.

Barbara Hodes photographed Lou looking emaciated.

Once again, Lou stayed at Blake's in London, where Prakash John witnessed a scrap with David Bowie. "I remember coming out of Blake's [and] seeing the limousine doors open and Lou and David Bowie falling out of the car in a cat fight . . . rolling around on the sidewalk outside Blake's Hotel. Who knows what they were fighting about. It looked to me like two women fighting over a guy . . . I thought, 'This is weird.'" Another night, Lou urinated on the floor of the hotel bar. "That grossed me out—that is unacceptable."

Lou found himself singing to tens of thousands of people as one of the main support acts for the Who at Charlton Athletic football ground in London on May 18, 1974, his biggest show yet. Other acts on the bill included Humble Pie and Bad Company. This huge open-air event was a far cry from Max's Kansas City, demonstrating how far Lou had come in four years. "The performance went well, except everybody was pretty drunk," says Michael Fonfara, who became Lou's new band leader at this time. He shared his boss's fondness for booze. It was one of the factors that drew them together over the next six years.

BACK IN NEW YORK, Lou moved out of Barbara's flat and rented a one-bedroom apartment on the ground floor of the Yorkgate building at 405 East 63rd Street. Considering that this was the high point of his career in terms of record sales, the Yorkgate was an un-

prepossessing address. Barbara—who had a key to the apartment—
could never understand why Lou chose to live in such dreary places.
He certainly lived less ostentatiously than many of his rock-star
contemporaries, in an era of conspicuous, often grotesque, overcon-
sumption. In contrast to the likes of Elton John and Rod Stewart,
who lived like movie stars, acquiring mansion homes and limousines, Lou didn't own property, or even a car. After a brief flirtation
with glam fashion, he also eschewed expensive bespoke clothing,
dressing in jeans, T-shirts and leather jackets. He had lost or given
away valuable artwork by Andy Warhol, as well as his Velvet Underground posters. So long as his rent was paid and he had a guitar, an
amp and a tape recorder, a bottle of Scotch, a carton of cigarettes, a
pint of coffee ice cream in the fridge and enough drugs to keep him
high while he wrote his songs, Lou seemed content living in low-
rent accommodation. He remained a true bohemian.

One day when she was visiting Lou's new apartment, Barbara noticed a pair of false eyelashes in the bathroom. "I asked Lou, 'What
are these false eyelashes doing here?' And he said, 'Oh, I met this
poor person at this club and I offered her a place to sleep.'" So Barbara met Rachel, a young trans woman (about ten years younger
than Lou) with an angelic face, long dark hair and plucked eyebrows. He was sleeping on the couch.

Rachel's real name was Richard, and he answered to Ricky. Lou's
friends believe that his surname was Humphreys, though the spell-
ing, like many of the facts of his background, remains uncertain and
somewhat mysterious. The consensus of opinion is that he was from
Philadelphia, where he once worked as a hairdresser. His childhood
had been tough. Rachel was streetwise in a way that Lou only pretended to be, and this was evidently part of the attraction. Rachel
was rough trade. They met one night at Club 82, an after-hours
bar in the East Village, when Lou was speeding. "I'd been up for
days, as usual, and everything was at that super-real, glowing stage.
I walked in, and there was this amazing person, this incredible head

kind of vibrating out of it all. I kept watching for ages. Rachel was wearing this amazing makeup and dress and was obviously in a different world to anyone else in the place. Eventually I spoke and she came home with me," he explained. "At the time I was living with a girl, a crazy blonde lady, and I kind of wanted us all three to live together." Barbara, who had until recently been living with Lou, confirms that he suggested a *menage à trois*. "I wasn't having any of that." Although Lou assured Barbara that Rachel liked her, Barbara was scared of Rachel, who, she says, carried a knife. "I didn't want my face slashed." So she left them to it, though she stayed friends with Lou. "Rachel was street trash, and I think that was the attraction to her."

Rachel's alternating persona was confusing. As a man who dressed as a woman but hadn't had a sex change, Rachel was a "he," though the feminine pronoun often seemed more appropriate, and many people used "she," or a mixture of the two. Journalists had fun with the dichotomy. Lester Bangs solved the problem in print by referring to Rachel as Thing, which was a little cruel, while journalist Ben Fong-Torres described Lou's new friend more elegantly as "a boyfriend named Rachel." It really came down to who Rachel wanted to be on any given day. If he wanted to be Rachel, he dressed in a feminine way, though rarely in full drag. "He wore one-pieces, very clingy, and literally just tucked himself under, and he didn't have boobs or anything, but he had long hair and a beautiful face and he wore makeup," recalls Liz Gilmore, who got to know the couple as the girlfriend of one of Lou's European promoters. "We were told, 'If he's dressed like a man, he's called Richard. If he's dressed like a woman, he's called Rachel.'" Lou and Rachel evidently enjoyed the confusion, and further muddied the water by wearing each other's clothes. "I would go there on different days and one thing Rachel wore the last time, Lou would be wearing [the next]," says Elliott Murphy, who was hanging out with Lou at his apartment, having written the liner notes for the *1969* album, which had only just been released, on the back of Lou's new celebrity. "They were always wearing Fiorucci jeans and things like that."

Rachel spoke quietly, with a lisp, and was subservient to Lou, though prone to melodrama, which made for two drama queens. Languid and effeminate, he could be ferocious in a fight—kicking, punching, wielding knives, even broken bottles. Lou claimed Rachel nearly blinded a guy in a fight in LA. While most of Lou's friends learned to rub along with Rachel, he was too strange for some. Prakash "the Christian" John says that his dog trembled when Rachel came into the studio. "I sensed the dog was terrified of Rachel. . . . When she walked out, I noticed the dog had defecated on the studio floor." But Lou found Rachel exciting, and they were together for a long time. "Rachel knows how to do it for me," he said, three years into the relationship. "No one else before ever did." Michael Fonfara, who worked with Lou throughout this period, has no doubts that theirs was a sexual relationship. "He was Lou's live-in lover." It wasn't, however, an exclusive relationship.

When it came time to design the cover for *Sally Can't Dance*, Lou met artist David Byrd at the Ninth Circle, a gay bar in Greenwich Village, to discuss the project. "Lou carried with him a shoebox full of SX-70 Polaroids (the camera of the day for cool art dudes). He told me the Polaroids were of his many 'girlfriends,' though being gay myself I could tell they were drag queens," recalls Byrd, who found Lou "quite magnetic and handsome in a kind of damaged way." Lou picked out Polaroids of a favorite "girlfriend," an androgynous creature with long hair, plucked eyebrows and a faint moustache who he wanted to represent Sally on the cover. Byrd used the picture as the basis of a portrait on the back of the sleeve. "I decided to do a blow-up of 'Sally' reflected in his mirrored glasses, smoking a fag and looking quite toasted." This was Rachel (credited in the sleeve notes under the absurd moniker René de la Bush), demonstrating how important he had already become to Lou. Byrd adds intriguingly that one of the Polaroids Lou showed him "was of René completely bound up in Saran Wrap [cling film]." We might imagine Lou and Rachel cocooned in plastic in their private moments.

Sally Can't Dance sold surprisingly strongly, reaching number ten in the US in the summer of 1974, the summer Richard Nixon resigned the presidency, making it the highest-charting album of Lou's entire career. He was bemused by this unexpected and undeserved success, considering that the album wasn't very good. "This is fantastic—the worse I am, the more it sells," he told Danny Fields. He said many other disobliging things about *Sally Can't Dance* over the years, to the annoyance of the musicians who played on the record. "I once said to him, 'Why don't you return your royalties, or share it with the rest of the band, if you hate it so much?' But I never got a good answer," says Prakash John. "You can't disparage your work when it has been successful for you. He did try to have commercial success. He pretends like he didn't."

When Prakash and Pentti Glan discovered that RCA was going to release a second album from the Academy of Music tapes—*Lou Reed Live*—without paying them any more money, they decided they'd had enough of Lou and quit the band. He carried on with replacement musicians, touring Australia that summer. Upon arrival in Sydney, he gave a memorable press conference that can be seen as an homage to Andy Warhol's style of dealing with journalists, as well as pandering to his image as deviant drug fiend. "Lou, you sing a lot about transvestites and sadomasochism. How would you describe yourself in light of these songs?" asked one bluff Aussie reporter at the airport.

"What does that have to do with me?" replied Lou, feyly.

"Could I put it bluntly, and pardon the question, are you a transvestite or a homosexual?"

"Sometimes."

"Which one?"

"I don't know. What's the difference?"

"Where do you spend your money?"

"On drugs."

It was what they wanted to hear.

He then went a step further and began to mime shooting up onstage during "Heroin." Gerard Malanga used the same routine during the Exploding Plastic Inevitable in 1966, only Gerard used a large prop syringe as a joke. Lou made it look real. First he wrapped his microphone cord around his left arm, which he extended toward the audience—palm up. Then he drew a real syringe from his jeans and appeared to mainline while the crowd howled with a mixture of disgust and excitement like the mob around the guillotine. Afterwards he passed his "used" syringe to the people in the front row. "What a tacky gesture," sniffed his former friend Lisa Robinson in a review of his October 9, 1974, show at the Felt Forum in New York. Of course, he intended to create shock and disgust. "Much of what Lou did was in bad taste. And that's one of the reasons people liked him," points out former RCA executive Bruce Somerfield. "He'd shoot his finger at good taste: I'm Lou Reed and fuck you! That was part of Lou's persona." It hadn't been part of his persona in the Velvet Underground, when he was a serious artist, but in order to reach and hold the attention of a broader rock audience in the mid-'70s he had become a parody of himself, against his ultimate better judgement. "Lou was being thrust into a commercial world, when really he wanted to be a poet," says Steve Katz, enlarging on the point. "Going commercial was like [becoming] a caricature of himself and, unfortunately, that's what he wanted to do."

Looking back on his career, Lou conceded that this was a bad period in his life, so bad that he felt like killing himself at times. "Back then, I thought I'd lost it and I did a bunch of things I was really unhappy with. And I did it all in public and on record and there it is," he confessed in 1989. "I just kind of blew it apart because my problem—amongst all the other problems that were going on, which you'd have to be deaf, dumb and blind to miss (i.e., the drugs)—was that I thought my ability had gone. I thought, 'It's gone,' and I got really upset about it. I thought it had deserted me, and it made me really crazy and suicidal, and I just did what a lot of people do about things like that, which was *more* drugs and I got more fucked up, to say the least." In fact, he had only begun his descent into drug addiction and chaos.

IX

HOWLING LIKE
THE DEVIL

• 1975–76 •

IN THE FIRST WEEK of 1975 Lou went back to Electric Lady to start work on the *Coney Island Baby* album, recording "Crazy Feeling," "She's My Best Friend," "Downtown Dirt" and the title song. Although these were all good songs, with hooky tunes and interesting lyrics, notably about Lou's love for Rachel and his childhood on Long Island, the vocals were sloppy and slurred, and his attitude to work was bad. "He was really sort of crazed at the time," says Steve Katz, who had recently caught Lou shooting up in the toilet. "He was impossible to work with. He was unreliable. . . . He just wasn't being a cooperative artist."

Lou had come to dislike the two records he had made with Steve, despite the fact that *Rock 'n' Roll Animal* and *Sally Can't Dance* had been so successful, and he now turned on his producer. "I give up! If you are gonna play these games, I *know* you're gonna outwit me," Steve told him after two miserable days in the studio. "I acknowledge that you're much smarter than I am." Lou claimed Steve walked out on the sessions at this stage; Steve says Lou left. Either way, work stopped. "I called Bruce Somerfield at RCA and I said, 'We have to call these sessions [off]. I don't have an artist here.'" Bruce came down to investigate. "I do not know [what] caused the massive blowup between Katz and Reed. . . . All I know is that [they] had a terrific falling-out at the January sessions," he later testified in a court case between artist and producer, whose relationship never recovered. "[Steve] told me that Reed had been abusive towards him and that he felt that he never again could have the same type of personal affection for Reed . . ."

In recent months Lou had also succeeded in alienating his band, most of whom had left to work for Alice Cooper. Only Michael Fonfara and Doug Yule remained. Lou belatedly realized that he needed a full band for a European tour starting in February. He rang around for suggestions and was referred to the Everyman Band, an obscure jazz-fusion group in upstate New York, with whom he would enjoy a surprisingly long association, the core members staying with him until 1980. "My name's Lou Reed, you probably haven't heard of me," he introduced himself over the phone to Larry Packer, who played violin and guitar with the group. The other members were saxophonist Marty Fogel, bass guitarist Bruce Yaw and Michael Suchorsky on drums. Lou invited them into the city for a jam session with himself, Fonfara and Yule. The Everyman Band were country boys with long hair and beards, who dressed in jeans, plaid shirts and work boots. Lou wore a transparent plastic suit the day they met in Manhattan, which was the first indication that they were not dealing with "a normal person," as Bruce Yaw observes. Still, they played well together. After the briefest of rehearsals, the musicians agreed to accompany Lou to Italy. It was to be a truly farcical tour, worthy of *Spinal Tap*, as if directed by Fellini.

They arrived at a chaotic Leonardo da Vinci airport during a baggage handlers' strike, part of a wider political malaise gripping the country, where the far left was pitted against the far right in a series of protests and riots that lent an element of anarchy to the tour.

Lou was driven into Rome with Rachel and his booking agent, Bob Ringe. "Let me see that," he said during the journey, taking Bob's tape recorder. Lou played with the machine, decided he didn't like it and tossed it out of the car window. "I'm looking at him like, 'What the fuck!' [But] I'm keeping my [cool]," says Bob. They were still in transit fifteen minutes later when Lou complained of a headache and asked to borrow his agent's sunglasses. "These suck," he said after trying on the shades. He threw them out the window, too. Now Bob was angry.

When they arrived at the Ambasciatori Palace Hotel, Lou wanted lunch. The kitchen had closed for the afternoon, but the manager arranged for a simple meal to be served in the dining room. "They bring out pasta and salad and bread," says Bob. "They put down this bowl of pasta. [Lou] takes one bite. He says, 'This fucking sucks.' He picks up the plate. He stands up and throws it against the fucking wall. And it splatters."

Bob lost it. "You motherfucker," he said, grabbing Lou. "I'm going to kill you!"

"Oh, Bob, I'm sorry," Lou apologized. When it came down to it, he was not a fighter. Bob told Rachel to take Lou upstairs while he said sorry to the manager.

Lou then phoned down to the front desk to say that he needed a doctor. He told the doctor who came to his room that he was depressed and needed amphetamines. The doctor prescribed pills, but not the pills Lou wanted. Lou pulled out a pharmacological reference book, which he now carried with him on tour, and pointed to the precise drug he required—a strong amphetamine. When the doctor demurred, Lou became belligerent and asked to see another doctor. This became his routine on tour in Europe. He would demand drugs from local doctors, whom he contacted via his hotel, bullying them until they gave him what he wanted. A prescription was important, because it allowed him to take his drugs across borders. Lou used the prescription medication to get high before going onstage. "It would throw him into a depression when he didn't have it, and it would make him a little bit overstimulated when he did. For the most part, it maintained him, except for the extremes that went both ways," explains Michael Fonfara, who became closer to Lou than anyone else in the band. "I didn't see it as being detrimental to his performances or his writing, which I thought was fairly brilliant. . . . He didn't seem to suffer." Others disagree, saying that Lou's behavior was obviously affected by his drug use.

Strike action in Rome meant that the first show of the Italian tour had to be postponed. So Lou went north to play Turin and Milan. The latter concert was cut short when the audience rioted, while the effect of prescribed medication on Lou was clear to at least one band member. Backstage before the gigs, Lou was like a zombie, says Larry Packer. "He would be on the side of the stage, and his jaw muscles would be involuntarily contracting. His jaw clenched. And he'd have his fists clenched. They would unroll his fingers and get the microphone in his hand, and let his fingers clench around the microphone . . . then they would more or less pick him up bodily and place him where the light would hit him, and the show would start." As the drugs kicked in, Lou became animated.

While they were in Turin, they were invited to a party hosted by the Agnelli family, the owners of Fiat. It was an extravagant affair in a mansion, reminiscent of the castle scene in *La Dolce Vita* featuring Lou's old friend Nico. During the evening he picked a fight with his fiddle player. "Lou Reed, all of a sudden, pulled a knife on me—a switchblade. This was outside the [Agnelli] house," says Larry. "He challenged me to this knife fight. I was unarmed. I looked at him and said, 'You fucking asshole!' and turned my back on him and walked away." This wasn't an isolated incident. During his relationship with Rachel, Lou became increasingly confrontational, threatening various people with knives, even guns. As a result he found himself in some dangerous situations. Larry claims that Lou drove one member of the tour entourage so crazy in Europe that he threatened to shoot the star. "Bruce [Yaw] and I talked him out of it."

After these difficult northern shows the tour party returned to Rome to play the Palazzo dello Sport, an indoor arena holding seven thousand people. There was a press conference beforehand, at which a reporter asked Lou why he had come to the eternal city. "I came to Rome because I want to fuck the pope," he replied, an outrageous statement that heightened tension around the gig, which turned into another full-blown riot. When Lou arrived at the Palazzo on February 15, 1975, a policeman emerged in body armor to welcome him. "*Buona sera!*" said the officer politely, having removed his helmet. "The crowd has already rushed to the stage and overturned the equipment of the support act." By the time Lou came on, the arena was in uproar. Gatecrashers had got in, claiming the show should be free, and they had commandeered the bar. Aside from Lou's remarks about the pope, there was a political dimension to the riot. Many of the gatecrashers identified themselves as communists, and they were opposed to the capitalist promoters, whom they characterized as fascists. The fact that Lou dressed in black, and was evidently in Italy to make money out of them, was enough for these radicals to condemn him as a fascist, too. He and the band were pelted with missiles as they began the opening number, "Sweet Jane." Larry was hit by a water bomb. "I looked around and there were one hundred fifty guys wearing bandanas throwing things at us." They fled the stage as the police let off tear gas, Bruce Yaw using his bass guitar as a club to clear a path to the dressing rooms. Rachel came into his own in the melee. "Rachel was a street guy. He was a really good street fighter. So he was a great guy to have around," says Bruce, who saw Rachel defend Lou with kicks and punches as they fought their way out of the hall.

Oddly, this chaotic show helped make Lou a big star in Italy. It created invaluable publicity, bringing his music to the attention of young people who might not otherwise have heard of him. Many were excited by his irreverent attitude to life, including religion. His louche, hedonistic image had enduring appeal in the Catholic nations of southern Europe, including Spain and Portugal, but particularly in Italy, where he remained a major draw for the rest of his career. "That concert that went really wrong gave him a lot of publicity and [attracted] people like me who didn't want to be classified as the reds or the blacks," explains Charlie Rapino, an Italian fan who later got to know Lou in the record business. "I think in Italy they like people who talk about sin, and they sin as well, being a Catholic country. And I think that appealed to us a lot [growing] up with a Catholic education."

Lou crashed from his amphetamine high after the riot. "[He] was doing so much amphetamine that he would go for days and days speeding, and then he would consume massive amounts of Valium, bottles of Valium, and alcohol, to come down," explains Bruce Yaw. Barbara Fulk, Lou's new road manager, confirms that she gave him Valium to calm him down.

Strike action and crowd trouble were making the Italian tour a nightmare, and a scheduled concert in Bologna was canceled. Instead, the party flew to Zurich, where Lou was due to perform on February 20. He checked into the local Novapark Hotel, complaining about the way the tour was being managed. Dennis Katz had not accompanied him to Europe. Deciding that he might need a new manager, Lou put in a call to New York to talk to Tony Defries, who until recently had managed David Bowie. Defries wanted to manage Lou. He was so excited to receive Lou's call that he caught the first plane to Switzerland, hoping to sign him. Barbara Fulk called Dennis to warn him that his rival was on his way, so Dennis also got on a plane.

Defries arrived in Zurich first, but Lou refused to meet him. "I had to go down to the lobby and tell him Lou decided he did not want to see him [after all]," says Barbara. Defries turned around and went back to America, washing his hands of Lou. Dennis arrived on the next plane from New York. He was admitted to Lou's hotel suite and emerged with his signature (typically loosely drawn with an egocentrically large "L" and "R") on a new management contract. Though Lou clearly thought he had been smart in playing Katz off against Defries, he would rue the day he signed this document, which extended his association with Katz for a further three years, during which time they fell out spectacularly.

That afternoon before his show, Lou asked to see a doctor. When the first doctor didn't give him the drugs he required, he asked to see another. Dr. Rudolf Breitenmoser came to the suite a couple of hours before Lou was due onstage. "Upon my arrival I was led to a darkened room (a luxury suite). I found four persons there," the doctor explained. Lou was sitting on the sofa, drumming his fingers nervously. "I approached him carefully and found the patient to be excited and stimulated. I immediately noted that the patient in question was someone whom I suspected to be addicted to amphetamines . . . I found out that another physician had already been called before me, but that he had left the scene immediately when he heard he was expected to prescribe amphetamine. As for myself, the question arose before me whether I would further help or harm the patient by prescribing amphetamines." The doctor took Lou's blood pressure and asked him how he was feeling. "The patient explained to me that he wanted to have me prescribe Dexedrine. To attain a maximum performance level, he was taking amphetamines before starting a concert." Despite concluding that Lou was addicted to amphetamines, and behaving irrationally, as well as being underweight, the doctor prescribed the drug Lou wanted, advising him to use as little as possible. This incident was later picked over in a court battle between Lou and Dennis Katz, during which Lou's lawyers argued that he had been "under extreme emotional stress" on tour, and thereby not in a fit state to understand what he was signing when he extended his contract with Dennis. They asked Dr. Breitenmoser to give a witness statement to help prove that he was in bad

The Velvets found a friend and mentor in Andy Warhol who is seen with members of the Exploding Plastic Inevitable at the Silver Factory in 1966. Clockwise from top: Warhol holding Nico's son, Ari; Lou; Nico; John Cale (with moustache); Moe Tucker in polka dots; Mary Woronov; Sterling Morrison and Gerard Malanga with his whip. The band record-ed the bulk of their first and greatest album, *The Velvet Underground & Nico*, in just two days at Scepter Records in New York in April 1966.

Nico is seen **left** singing in the studio with John and Lou. Nico toured with the band as part of the Exploding Plastic Inevitable in 1966–67 (**below**). She and John were then forced out of the group; John was replaced by Doug Yule who is seen in profile on tour with the Velvets in Massachusetts in 1969 (**far left**).

Lou is seen above (**bottom left of group picture**) with his road band the Tots, looking somewhat ridiculous in glam rock makeup, around the time of the release of *Transformer*. The hit single from the album, "Walk on the Wild Side," made Lou an international star, but he struggled to cope with success. By the time he played Amsterdam on September 20, 1973 (**below**), he was drinking heavily and using speed. He collapsed on stage the following night in Brussels.

By 1974, Lou's career had degenerated into self-parody. He resorted to pretending to inject drugs on stage (**right**) to excite audiences.

Lou's relationship with the transgender person known as Rachel was one of the most remarkable episodes in his personal life. When he wasn't dressed as a woman, Rachel answered to Richard or Ricky. He is seen (**below**) as a man, with Lou at CBGB in New York, in 1976. See page 207 for a picture of Rachel as a woman.

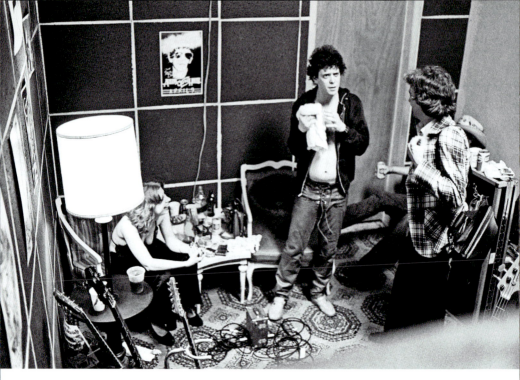

At the height of his drug mania in 1978, Lou was photographed looking pot-bellied and dishevelled backstage in Austin, Texas (**above**).

The extraordinary *Lou Reed Live, Take No Prisoners* was recorded at the Bottom Line in New York. Lou is seen (**below**) performing a song from *Berlin* at the club in 1979 with guitarist Chuck Hammer (**left**), Ellard 'Moose' Boles on bass (**middle**) and Michael Suchorsky on drums. He was drinking heavily again, and putting on weight.

Lou married his second wife Sylvia Morales on Valentine's Day, 1980. The newlyweds are seen (**right** and **below**) with their parents at Lou's apartment on Christopher St in Greenwich Village. His much maligned mother and father, Toby and Sid Reed, are on the left of the group pictures.

Guitarist Robert Quine challenged Lou to make more effort with his music during the early 1980s, but their personalities clashed. They are seen (**bottom**) on stage at the Beacon Theater, New York, in October 1984, promoting the *New Sensations* album.

Working with John Cale again on *Songs for Drella*, Lou did his best work since the Velvet Underground (**above left**).

Lou found love with his third wife, Laurie Anderson (**above right**).

Laurie tried to cheer up her grumpy husband along as they took part in the 2010 Coney Island Mermaid Parade (**below**) dressed as Queen Mermaid and King Neptune. Their dog Lolabelle sits between them.

Following his liver transplant, Lou was photographed walking with the aid of a stick near his Greenwich Village apartment in June 2013 (**right**). He died four months later.

shape, admitting that, "Reed's judgement was at that time . . . impaired by the habitual use of alcohol and certain medicinal drugs."

There was further drama as the tour continued through Germany, France, Denmark and Sweden. Lou fired Larry Packer after a show in Lund and faced a band revolt in Paris when the other musicians discovered that their salaries weren't being paid. There were also issues with Lou and Rachel. "I used to get calls from hotel managers that they would tear up these rooms," says Bob Ringe. "They were so fucking blitzed they would rip the carpet off the floor, the wallpaper off the walls. These rooms were trashed. . . . They were shooting speed, and the crash off of that is nasty. You didn't want to be around when he was coming off drugs—it got insane." The tour finished in London, where a waxwork of Lou had recently been erected at Madame Tussaud's, showing how famous he still was in Britain at this time.

BACK HOME, ON JUNE 1, 1975, a judge at the Supreme Court of New York ruled in favor of Lou's former manager, Fred Heller, ordering Lou to pay him $174,140 commission on his earnings for breach of contract. This was a major blow, putting Lou in what his lawyers described as "substantial financial jeopardy." He could have settled the case earlier, for as little as $30,000, and had been urged to do so by several advisers, including his accountant father, but he'd ignored their advice and now he faced a huge bill. Despite his success over the past few years, Lou simply didn't have the cash to pay Heller. It was probably for this reason that he promptly decamped to Toronto. Studio time was booked in the city, with the hope that Lou would resume work on *Coney Island Baby*, but he spent most of his stay hiding out with Rachel in the Continental Hyatt House. When he returned to New York later that month, Lou quietly moved apartments. A private detective named Arthur Moss called at the Yorkgate building on East 63rd Street on June 16 to serve Lou with a subpoena and restraining order in the Heller case. The building superintendent told him that Reed had moved to the building next door, the Royal York, adding that he had been seen coming and going "dressed in various wigs and in women's clothing." The superintendent may well have mistaken Rachel for Lou, but the possibility remains that he was wearing drag to avoid his creditor.

Now Lou's problems began to mount. At the same time that he was trying to deal with the Heller judgment, RCA was demanding a new album. Under the terms of his contract, Lou was obliged to deliver two albums a year, but he wasn't writing enough songs. Work on *Coney Island Baby* had stalled. RCA had just put out a live album, *Lou Reed Live*, but they still wanted a second LP for 1975. So Lou created one of the most extraordinary records ever made by a mainstream rock artist. Firstly, he asked Michael Fonfara to help him carry amplifiers and guitars up to his new, ninth-floor apartment. "I helped him carry the amplifiers up to that room, and made sure that they were all turned up to eleven [*sic*] and were feeding back—it was a pile of amplifiers all in one room that were strung up together, and one guitar to activate them with feedback. It was howling like the Devil. We had to leave the room and let the recording do the rest," says Fonfara. "RCA was invoking the contract, which stated they had to have a new record, and he wasn't ready, because he hadn't written enough songs yet. So he argued with them, and they were having a lot of fights. They said, 'We are going to demand by the terms of your contract that you produce a[nother] record for us this year.' I remember talking to him one night and he was saying, 'Fuck them. If they want to play hardball, I'll show them.' So he made an album of just nothing but feedback . . . RCA were aghast. . . . They didn't know what to do . . ." Fonfara was also bemused. "It was almost impossible for me to listen to. It was just noise, really."

Devoid of vocals, beat or melody, *Metal Machine Music* was four sides of squealing, howling feedback that created a feeling akin to a migraine (though some people claimed to like it). Lou insisted that each vinyl side should be precisely sixteen minutes long, except side four, which repeated until the needle was lifted out of the groove, a torturous detail he was especially proud of. Over the years, he spoke about this infamous work in conflicting terms, defending *Metal Machine Music* as a conceptual piece in the tradition of La Monte Young; other times stating that it was a joke; also admitting that drugs were a factor. "I was serious about it," he once said. "I was also really stoned." His manager didn't take it seriously. "I thought it was a joke, and so did Lou when he made it," scoffs Dennis Katz. "He liked playing mind games."

Metal Machine Music is perhaps best described as an artistic tantrum. Lou was prone to such behavior. "One of the things he would do, he would just blow up his career for a while," observes musician friend Scott Kempner. "How he had the courage to do that, I couldn't tell you." Surprisingly, RCA agreed to release this tantrum, showing a willingness to accommodate a difficult artist who had made money for them in the past. Lou wrote in the liner notes, "No one I know has listened to it all the way through, including myself. . . . Most of you won't like this, and I don't blame you at all. It is not meant for you . . . I love and adore it . . ." It was, he argued, an antidote to *Sally Can't Dance* and *Rock 'n' Roll Animal*, the success of which, ironically, made such self-indulgence possible. "This is not meant for the market," he stated haughtily, signing off with towering speed freak arrogance: "My week beats your year."

He was on tour when the record hit the shops in July 1975. Reviews ranged from bafflement to qualified praise. Writing in the *New York Times*, a sympathetic John Rockwell gave Lou credit for trying to do something different but wondered if he had "finally tripped over the line between outrageousness and sheer self-destructive indulgence." Lester Bangs was more forthright in *Creem*, writing that "what we are witnessing here is commercial suicide." Initial sales were modest—25,000 copies sold compared to 163,000 for *Lou Reed*

Live—but as *Metal Machine Music* cost next to nothing to make, this wasn't a calamity. "He made it in his bedroom and it probably cost nothing much to press a few copies and ship them," explains Bruce Somerfield. "It didn't make money, but I can't imagine it lost money." It is more difficult to evaluate the harm Lou did to his career in terms of alienating RCA and his audience. Members of the public who bought *Metal Machine Music* and found it unlistenable (many returned it to the store) were less likely to buy another Reed album, and Lou would not survive much longer as an RCA artist.

For the time being everything continued as normal. When he arrived in Tokyo on tour that summer, he was invited to the local RCA office for a party in celebration of the album, which was squealing in the background while the champagne was served. The Japanese executives bowed to Lou, and presented him with little electronic gifts, including the new pocket calculator, which pleased him, telling him how honored they were to meet him, and how brilliant *Metal Machine Music* was. "The head of RCA Japan was there, who really just knew exactly what Lou was trying to do in terms of manipulating [them] and getting toys and being a bad boy. Just handled Lou really, really well," recalls Bruce Yaw. "It was a great scene. This absurd [music] is going on and people are pretending, 'This is marvelous, fantastic art, the latest in electronic music . . .' sycophantic genuflecting." Lou was even persuaded that he might have a Japanese hit on his hands, which meant adapting his show. "Lou said, 'We're going to have to do it in the set,'" recalls Michael Fonfara. "So we set up a whole bunch of amplifiers and at one point he hit a guitar, and pounded it on the ground until it was just screaming, and set it down, and we'd all walk offstage while fifteen minutes of this went on. The audience were [rocking] their heads back and forth. I don't know what they liked in it."

The tour moved on to Australasia, where Lou discovered that he was broke. The first sign of trouble came when a check written on behalf of Transformer Enterprises bounced. Lou claimed that this is when he found out that he had lost the Heller case and was in contempt of court over his failure to pay Heller compensation. As we have seen, it seems that he had in fact known about the court judgment for some time, but it was in New Zealand that he was forced to confront his insolvency. Characteristically, he blamed his advisers for mismanaging his affairs rather than taking, or at least sharing, responsibility for the mess he found himself in. "I found out, in Australia [*sic*], on a tour, that every single royalty I'd ever gotten had been stolen!" he later said, with a good deal of hyperbole. "And that I hadn't had taxes reported for the past five years, that I was in contempt of court, there was a warrant out, I had no money in the bank, no apartment, and I had been taken for a ride by these people! And had about fifteen dollars in my pocket!"

Lou used one of the new pocket calculators he picked up in Japan to work out that, if he owed Heller $174,140 in commission for the period from June 1972 to October 1974, as the court had ruled, he must have grossed over a million dollars in that time. "Lou was astounded," says Bruce Yaw, who helped him do his sums. "Where did the money go? Because he didn't have it." The tour, which had been scheduled to continue in Europe, was canceled. Lou parted company with Barbara Fulk, in whom he lost confidence as an employee of Dennis Katz, and scraped together just enough cash to fly himself and his band home.

As soon as he got back to New York, he sacked Dennis. As he looked into his affairs more closely, Lou discovered that, in addition to the money he owed Heller, he owed $128,000 in taxes, bank charges and debts to sundry creditors, including hotels, credit-card companies and travel agents. American Express and the William Morris Agency were suing him, and his subscription to the Musicians' Union hadn't been paid. Lou identified what seemed to be a discrepancy between what he had earned over the past few years and what he had received in income, leading him to allege in court that Dennis and other advisers had misappropriated at least $500,000.

Dennis, who denied the allegations, felt equally aggrieved. "Dennis Katz felt betrayed by Lou," explains Elliott Murphy, who had become a client of Dennis's after Lou introduced them, at a time when Lou couldn't say enough good things about his manager. "He felt any damage to Lou's career had been done by himself, and Dennis felt he was the guy who got Lou back on his feet." So bitter did feelings run that Dennis rid himself of anything that reminded him of his former client, giving Elliott a proof copy of Andy Warhol's book *The Philosophy of Andy Warhol (From A to B and Back Again)*, with a handwritten inscription by the artist. "Dennis said, 'Do you want this? I don't want anything to do with Lou.' And he gave it to me."[5]

Lou was so broke that he had to leave his Upper East Side apartment and move into the Gramercy Park Hotel, a funky old joint on Lexington Avenue. He was in his room on September 30, 1975, when he was served with a court summons. Like Heller before him, Dennis Katz was suing him for breaking their management agreement—the one Lou had only recently extended—and depriving him of commission. He wanted $200,000, increasing Lou's liabilities to half a million. Faced with financial ruin, Lou struck an emergency deal with RCA that enabled him to keep working. He mortgaged his song catalogue (essentially getting a loan from RCA on the security of the copyright of his songs) to raise cash to pay his most pressing debts, including settling with Heller (but holding out against Dennis, whom he would fight in court). RCA further agreed to cover his bill at the Gramercy Park while he completed *Coney Island Baby.*

Although he agreed to resume work on the album, Lou refused to have anything further to do with Steve Katz, whom he officially fired as his producer on October 13, thereby breaking yet another contract, and decided to produce the album himself. Steve responded by suing Lou, meaning that he was now in litigation with both Katz brothers. Steve ripped into Lou in a sworn affidavit, claiming credit

---

5   Murphy later returned the book to Lou.

for rescuing his career after the "disaster" of *Berlin*. "Despite the success I brought him . . . Reed is now following a course destined to destroy his career completely," he said, describing *Metal Machine Music* as "a double album of the most obnoxious, unpleasant sounds imaginable." He addressed the issue of Lou's drug use with stunning frankness. "Lou Reed's recordings are an expression of his confusion, self-destruction and immersion in the drug culture. His whole being revolves around 'speed.' . . to which he is addicted . . ." He also characterized the artist as being as feckless with money. "Lou Reed is financially irresponsible. He spends his income quickly and recklessly, mostly on costly drugs. Notwithstanding the sums he has earned in the past, and whatever he might earn in the future, I know of no assets of value anywhere . . ."

In his defense, Lou said he had only agreed to work with Steve as a favor to his brother. He hated his production on *Sally Can't Dance,* and spoke up for *Metal Machine Music*. "Of course, as an electronic album, it would appeal to a limited audience. This was understood by both RCA and myself before its release. It is in the context of an experimental electronic music album that it must be evaluated. Obviously, it is not a rock 'n' roll album." He responded to allegations about his lifestyle by asking rhetorically: "If RCA felt I was as incompetent, drug crazed and irresponsible as Mr. Katz claims, one wonders why RCA would allow me to produce myself and to even get into the recording studio." This was a reference to his renewed work on *Coney Island Baby,* though he was in fact receiving professional help with the record, while the management of RCA was rapidly losing patience with Lou.

RECORD ENGINEER GODFREY DIAMOND was a type of person Lou gravitated to in his maturity: a young, good-looking man of talent but limited experience whom he thought he could control. The first phase of working with such a protégé—of which there were several—was bonding. When Lou first met Godfrey, a twenty-two-year-old staff engineer at Media Sound in New York, they hung out together, becoming friends. Lou visited Godfrey's family home and invited him over to Room 605 at the Gramercy Park Hotel, ostensibly to discuss his album, which is when Godfrey stepped through the looking glass into Louland.

"I went to the Gramercy. This was a trip, man. He had these people hanging around, and they were so strange to me, and I knew some weird people. These people were this beautiful array of homeless, degenerate-looking, brilliant, weird as shit [characters]. I walk in and he's got a camera on me right away, doing an Andy thing. He said, 'I'm recording everybody who comes in.' It's like a party. And I think I'm coming to [work]. They are drinking and doing blow. I start talking to these people. One guy is a taxi driver. He's known Lou for ten years, they are old friends and he writes books. One after another—characters. You had to be there to see these people—one step away from homeless on the street, half of them." Rachel was there, too. "Rachel was gorgeous, for a guy. Jesus! I guess he was a transvestite. God, he was just gorgeous looking . . . like a hot-looking chick. One of those guy-girl voices, very feminine, very sweet." The party went on all night. When Godfrey looked at his watch it was 6 a.m. He had to be at work at nine. He was exhausted. Lou offered him a line of crystal meth as a pick-me-up. "That was kind of a Lou thing. That was why he would go into the bathroom and disappear for long periods of time."

Lou and Godfrey also went clubbing together, frequenting hip joints like CBGB in the Bowery, where the up-and-coming acts of the American new wave were playing, bands like the Ramones (managed by Danny Fields) and Talking Heads. One night Lou introduced his engineer to Holly Woodlawn, with whom he had become friendly since "Walk on the Wild Side" made them both famous. Holly was singing Lou's songs in cabaret. When the bar closed he gave Holly and Godfrey a lift home by taxi. Godfrey had met a girl during the evening whom he wanted to bring along, but Lou became jealous. "I guess he had a possessive streak for the people that were close to him," says Godfrey. "I said, 'Lou, can I give her a ride?' It's like 4 a.m., we are all coming out of the club to go uptown . . . I didn't know what they were doing, but I knew where I was going. I was going to bring this chick home. She was really cute. So we are heading uptown. He drops Holly off and then he goes, 'She can get out here, too.'" Godfrey squeaked in protest, "Lou, that's not cool! I'm hanging with her." But Lou was adamant. They had to find another cab.

Godfrey and Lou recorded *Coney Island Baby* at Media Sound, starting all over again after the aborted Steve Katz sessions. Lou used his road band, swearing the musicians to secrecy for fear that Steve's lawyers would try for an injunction. Godfrey told Lou that he loved his new songs, and the way he played them as demos, strumming an electric guitar that wasn't plugged in. He wanted him to play guitar on the album. "Nobody else ever lets me play guitar on my records," said Lou in surprise. Throughout his solo career to date he'd relied on hired hands to play guitar, having been told that he wasn't a good enough musician.

"I have to have your guitar on the record. You are the spirit of these songs."

This was a turning point for Lou, who began to play much more guitar, both in the studio and onstage, becoming obsessive about it. Nevertheless, a more skilful guitarist, Bob Kulick, was brought in to put the finishing touches to *Coney Island Baby*. "He would explain to me what the song was about and then just send me [into the studio to do an overdub]," says Kulick, who saw that Lou's relationship with Rachel was the mainspring of the project. "I couldn't figure out what the motivation was until I heard a rough of 'Coney Island Baby' [where he sings], 'Man, I'd give it all up for you'—the end of the song, the plaintive line. That was for his mate—Ricky/Rachel, whatever it was on any given day . . . a guy who looked like a girl . . .

I remember how he would look me in the face and very seriously tell me about these songs [and] I finally figured out that this was all about this he/she person. That's what's going on here."

Lou was concerned that the dedication to Rachel sounded too sentimental, but Godfrey encouraged him to keep it. Other songs on the album can be interpreted as relating to Rachel, including "Charley's Girl" (sung to a "queen"), though Lou's friend Nelson Slater has another reading for at least part of the song. He says that the line in which Lou mentioned a girl named Sharon, saying he'd punch her in the face if he saw her again, referred to his brief relationship with Nelson's stepsister, Sharon, whose father was named Charley, and who "ran [Lou] around the block a few times." In any event, the lyric was another example of violence toward women. "Kicks" was yet another song about violence, from the point of view of a character who is turned on by watching a murder. The overdubbed voices were recorded at a studio party at Media Sound, Lou and his agent Bob Ringe being among those who can be heard chatting at the beginning and end of the track.

These were powerful songs sung with care, in comparison to the Katz sessions. Lou knew that his career was on the line, so he decided to behave. "Everybody told me, 'Watch out, he's going to drive you crazy in the studio. He's a nut. He's moody. He's going to not show up sometimes,'" says Godfrey. "Every day he was there on time and ready to go. I thought he was a dream." That wasn't to say that Lou behaved normally. During the mixing sessions Godfrey watched Lou draw tiny circles with a draftsman's pen in his notebook—classic speed-freak behavior. "And once in a while he'd write a little lyric. And then more circles—tiny, tiny circles."

Coney Island Baby divided opinion when it was released in January 1976. Dave Marsh of *Rolling Stone* described it as Lou's best solo album, which was too generous. It was less well received in the UK, where Lou had started to fall out of fashion with hip music writers, who were much more interested in new wave artists, and the nascent punk rock scene. In his *New Musical Express* review, Charles Shaar Murray charted a downward trajectory from the Velvet Underground, when Lou "produced his finest work," through the felicitous collaboration with David Bowie on *Transformer*, to the "useless and non-functional" *Coney Island Baby*. "The songs sound like sophomoric Reed pastiches." He concluded that the artist was all washed up. "Lou Reed's revolutionary days are long gone, and the years of his farthood lie heavy upon him. He's a walking antique. He's got nothing to offer but the remnants of a discarded attitude and the crumbs of what once seemed to be a major talent." As Marsh seemed overly kind, Murray was too harsh. The truth was in between. The public seemed to quite like the record, in as much as they went out and bought it in reasonable numbers. Lou telephoned Godfrey excitedly to tell him when they had entered the charts. "He called [and said], 'It's entering at sixty-five with a bullet!' He was so happy." The album peaked at forty-one in the US.

Encouraged by this modest success, Lou checked out of his hotel and rented a little apartment on East 52nd Street, which he shared with Rachel, as he began to think about his next move. He was writing poetry again, some of which was published. The American Literary Council of Little Magazines deemed his poem "The Slide," about homophobia, good enough for an award. He also began to show an interest in mentoring other artists. One such project was an album for Nelson Slater, who had signed with RCA. Lou asked Godfrey to help him record Nelson's debut, *Wild Angel*. "This is where it gets a little sad," says Godfrey. They had almost finished the LP when Godfrey mentioned that he had a vacation booked, so he couldn't stay to the end. "I could tell that he was pissed that I had to leave. He didn't want me to go with my girlfriend on vacation." This was the third and final stage of a typical Lou friendship with a young collaborator: when he discovered that his protégé had a mind of his own, he turned nasty. Lou remixed *Wild Angel* by himself, taking Godfrey's name off the record. "It didn't even have my name on it, and I did the entire record up to mixing half of the songs!" says Godfrey, who was so angry when he saw the result that he tossed his copy out of a window. "It was 'Fuck you!'" Nelson was no less disappointed, claiming that Lou ruined his album. In this way, Lou alienated two friends.

His friendship with singer-songwriter Elliott Murphy followed a similar trajectory. After Elliott wrote the liner notes for *1969*, Lou helped him move from Polydor to RCA and introduced him to his manager at the time, Dennis Katz. "Lou was going to produce my first album on RCA. That was the plan. But a couple of things happened that stopped that," explains Elliott. "I think he decided I was going to be his protégé. I think he wanted to do for me what David Bowie had done for him. He was so supportive, singing my praises to everyone. Without his support, I doubt I would have been signed to RCA, or Dennis Katz would have become involved. But he was into speed and he had a very hyper personality. I'll never forget I was at his house one night working to four or five in the morning on my songs for this album he was going to produce [*Lost Generation*]. I said, 'Lou, I've got to sleep a little bit.' I went home. Three hours later the phone rang. He said, 'Are you ready to start again?' I was not. And he didn't like that." Lou didn't produce *Lost Generation*, and the friendship cooled. They bumped into each other years later at the Rock 'n' Roll Hall of Fame annual dinner. "I was sitting there with Bruce [Springsteen] and his entourage. I noticed Lou was at another table. I went over to say hello and he was very cold."

By the summer of 1976, a new generation of artists was emerging on the New York club scene who looked up to Lou because of what he had achieved in the Velvet Underground, artists such as Talking Heads and Patti Smith, whom Lou was delighted to see performing his old VU song "We're Gonna Have a Real Good Time Together" at CBGB. A further connection was formed when John Cale produced Smith's debut album, *Horses*, and Lou appeared onstage with Cale, Smith and David Byrne at the Ocean Club. Lou was so enthused

Lou with Elliott Murphy, Lou's apartment on East 63rd St.

about Byrne's song "Psycho Killer," a song of alienation with a Ree-dian attitude, that he took a demo into RCA, offering to produce his band. RCA passed, and Talking Heads thought better of accepting Lou's patronage. "David Byrne calls me later," says Jonny Podell, who became Lou's new manager that year. "He says, 'Listen, this is awkward. It's great to meet you [and Lou, but] we don't want Lou to produce us. We don't know how to tell him.'"

Addicted to drugs, Lou had become a self-destructive artist who alienated friends and colleagues, including executives at RCA, where his contract was due to expire in 1976. *Metal Machine Music* had put a strain on the relationship between artist and label, while Lou was never the easiest person to work with. His record sales were in decline and he had little rapport with management. "I might have been the most highly ranked individual Lou would talk to at the label, and I wasn't very high up on the food chain," says Bruce Somerfield. "After Dennis left, the kind of people they brought in were not people that [understood Lou]." His erratic behavior didn't help him win new friends at the office. "When he was on his game, he had a good sense of humor. At other times, he was very bitter and difficult to get along with." The drugs had also taken a toll. Lou didn't look well. "If I would have picked up a newspaper at any point during the time I knew him and read that Lou Reed was found dead somewhere it wouldn't have been a surprise."

Luckily, another record company wanted him. Clive Davis was ten years older than Lou, a lawyer by background. He had a similar biography in other respects, being a fellow Jew from Brooklyn, and bisexual, though he didn't come to this realization about himself until late in life. He was also one of the biggest names in the American record business. By the mid-1960s, Clive was head of Columbia Records, where he gained a reputation for having "golden ears"—which is to say that he knew a hit when he heard it. A successful career was derailed in 1973 when he was fired by CBS for allegedly fiddling his expenses, the details of which he disputed, though he was found guilty on a related tax charge and had his license to practice law suspended. The scandal didn't finish him, however. He launched a new label, Arista Records, to which he signed singer-songwriters including Patti Smith and Ray Davies of the Kinks, and he began to court Lou as a prospective Arista artist, inviting him and Rachel to his apartment to watch the Macy's Thanksgiving Day Parade, and going on a bar crawl with the singer. "I accompanied him after midnight to three or four clubs . . . eye-opening."

Although Lou and RCA were no longer on the best of terms, Lou was still contracted to the company and its publishing subsidiary, Dunbar Music. Executives were willing to let him go and release him from the mortgage he had taken out on his song catalogue, on the condition that Dunbar retain all income from his RCA songs in North America, publishing and royalties, plus 20 percent of foreign income, until his advances were earned out. The terms of this "settlement agreement" show that RCA was as keen to get rid of Lou as he was to leave them. It was an amicable divorce on reasonable terms, though Lou had to relinquish income from his most famous songs, including "Walk on the Wild Side," to win his freedom. He signed the papers on August 19, 1976. Four days later, he signed a new five-album deal with Arista.

Clive Davis got Lou cheap. "There was nothing about that deal that was expensive, other than the recording [costs]. This was not a major money situation," explains the mogul, who says that he didn't sign Lou because he expected him to make big money for Arista, though of course he hoped he would, but because he was admired by up-and-coming artists whom he wanted to attract to the company. "He brought prestige to the label." So began a new chapter in a tumultuous career.

X

THE ARISTA YEARS

• 1976–80 •

THE FOUR YEARS THAT Lou spent as an Arista recording artist were subtly different to his previous years on RCA. He was an older man, thirty-four at the start of his new contract, and even less inclined to compromise. As a result his Arista albums were more personal. Yet there was a diminution. Past his commercial peak, he found himself on a smaller label with limited budgets, playing to a declining audience. His use of drugs and alcohol peaked at this time, with detrimental consequences for his work, which often sounded scrappy. His critics were harsh. And even when he pulled himself together to make better work, he found that few people were still listening.

Within days of signing the new deal, he took his band into the Record Plant to make *Rock 'n' Roll Heart*, his first Arista album and the first of three records he made with studio engineer Corky Stasiak, an affable Californian with a reputation for being patient with difficult artists. Few were more difficult than Lou. "He was hard to work with. A lot of artists are. You have to understand when you are working with an artist that this is their career on the line. What they do with you is what they present to the public, and it's very stressful," explains Corky, who watched Lou pass through three distinct personal phases over the next six years. "The first one was manic and drug-addicted."

Lou's chain-smoking, and the fact that his hands shook involuntarily, were outward signs of his debauched state of health by 1976. He was also more neurotic than ever, and extremely moody. "He put us through the twist—all of his sessions were emotional. He would be upset about something, and then if we got a great take he would be so happy [as if he was] bipolar," says Corky. Lou was told shortly after this that he did indeed have bipolar disorder, which would explain a lot of his behavior. "If one little thing went wrong it was, 'Uh-oh!'"

Lou needed a good album to relaunch his recording career, but he was struggling to write songs. So he reached back into the barrel of Velvet Underground leftovers. Unfortunately, the barrel was almost empty. He found two old songs for *Rock 'n' Roll Heart*, neither particularly strong: the mildly comical "A Sheltered Life" and "Follow the Leader," the new recording of which had the jittery quality of an amphetamine jag, punctuated by Marty Fogel's honking saxophone. Lou let his musicians follow their musical instincts on *Rock 'n' Roll Heart*, and their jazz roots showed on what was, ironically, one of his least rock 'n' roll albums. Most of the songs were lyrically slight. "I Believe in Love" and "Banging on My Drum" featured particularly banal words. One track, "Chooser and the Chosen One," was an instrumental, clearly to fill space. The whole album sounded careless and insubstantial, belying the fact that Lou was anxious about getting it right, phoning his engineer up to ten times a day with questions and suggestions. "I had to shut my phone off because he would call at eight o'clock in the morning and wake me up after we'd been [in the studio] to two or four in the morning. He had been up all night listening to the rough mixes." As soon as Corky reconnected his phone, it would ring.

"Corky, Lou."

"Hey, Lewis, how you doing?" replied his engineer as brightly as possible, copying Rachel's habit of addressing Lou by his given name (which Rachel pronounced with a lisp: "Oh, Lewith!").

"I was listening to the rough mixes, and it could use a little more bass."

So another difficult day began.

When it came time for playback, Lou disappeared into the bathroom to take speed. He emerged with eyes as big as saucers and yelled, "OK—play!" The songs sounded great to Lou, stoned, but *Rock 'n' Roll Heart* would be regarded as one of his weakest albums. The only song of substance was "Temporary Thing," while Clive Davis thought the title song had hit potential if Lou would develop it, but he rejected his advice. "I told Lou, 'You know, you could have a radio record here.' But he really felt the work was complete, and he was entitled to feel that." It was the start of a frustrating relationship.

To help launch the album, Lou hired Jonny Podell as his new manager. A hip guy who spoke and dressed like a rock star, Jonny represented Alice Cooper and the Allman Brothers, among other high-profile and highly profitable acts. He wasn't particularly into Lou's music, and he didn't buy into his image. "I don't think Lou was all real. He was [an] accountant's son, Jewish middle class from [Freeport] who decided to be a rock-star shock-style: I'm gay, I'm a junkie, I'm everything a rock star should be, and now I've got a boyfriend/girlfriend to keep everybody off balance at all times. I saw through the disguise." He was also aware that Lou had fallen out with his previous managers, some of whom he hated, which didn't bode well. "Lou could do hate. Drugs do that—drugs take resentment into hate."

It was drugs that they had common. "Lou, I guess, saw him in me; I, me in him: a drug addict." Jonny was a coke head at the time; Lou was a speed freak. "He would go into the bathroom and come out a *totally* different person, obviously on speed," says Jonny, who warned his client: "Lou, with all due respect, I love you, but you're going to kill yourself." Lou retorted that his drug was healthy. In his own twisted mind, he seemed to truly believe that amphetamine and methamphetamine really were healthy highs; he argued the point constantly. Jonny believes that drugs warped Lou's personality. "Once you get into drugs heavily, it does become you. Then you become the beast, as I did, and he did." While Lou had always been a contrarian, he became almost impossible to work with during the height of his drug use in the late 1970s, and was often unpleasant. Jonny found his client to be "generally unlikeable . . . not a charmer," citing two examples of his bad behavior. One evening, Jonny and his wife arranged to have dinner with Lou and Rachel. "Monica hated Lou, because Lou was the ultimate misogynist. . . . She resented the disrespect." Likewise, Lou loathed Monica. Before the dinner Jonny warned Lou that he had to be pleasant to his wife, or else. "We used terms like 'I'll stab you, and I'll throw you off a moving train.'" They met at Willy's Bar. "We are there fifteen minutes. Lou makes a crack that Monica has no tits. Monica goes into reactor mode." She told Lou exactly what she thought of him, got up and left. "I go to Lou, 'You did it. Go catch her and apologize. I'll kill you!' So there's Monica [crossing the road], Lou running after Monica, Rachel running after Lou, and I'm running after everybody. I wish I had that on film!" Another time, Jonny threw a party at his apartment, inviting Lou and the Allman Brothers. Lou promptly insulted the band, and a fight broke out. "Within fifteen minutes fists started swinging—a fistfight in the house!"

The music of the Allman Brothers may not have been to Lou's taste, but they sold millions of records in the 1970s. Lou's career had always been precarious, and his currency was falling as the decade wore on. "For me, it was a step down," says Jonny, whose first management decision was to get his client back on the road promoting *Rock 'n' Roll Heart*, having persuaded Arista to support a tour.

It was Lou's idea to decorate the stage with a bank of televisions on which he would play home movies, recorded on his latest toy, a Betamax video camera. The budget was limited, so Lou trawled the junk shops of Harlem for secondhand TVs, several of which failed to work in concert. "I thought he was nuts."

Guitarist Jeffrey Ross helped Lou carry the TVs home. Aged twenty-one, he was Lou's latest protégé. They wrote songs together, including "Such a Pretty Face," which became "Wait" on the *Street Hassle* album. Jeffrey was the inspiration. Flattering though this was, being Lou's golden boy was a mixed blessing. "In a very strange way, Lou adopted me," he says. "I was getting life lessons in *Oberführer* tones, or treated with casual disdain because I was clearly too young to have a grasp on anything . . . I think he felt he was mentoring me." Jeffrey found Rachel more simpatico. "Rachel was much more straightforward. Lou would say, 'I want this,' and Rachel would set about making it happen. Rachel was also the voice of reason. Rachel was compassionate."

Jeffrey hung out with the couple at their new apartment. It was a mark of Lou's drug-fueled paranoia that he'd moved to a building with a view of Jonny Podell's office, so he could spy on his manager. "It was a one-bedroom apartment—your typical Upper East Side professional apartment: parquet floor, store-bought furniture," says Jeffrey. "He was very fond of Tensor lamps with the really hot bulbs. . . . He would have a bottle of speed pills [under the lamp] melting down. He would go back into his room and spend a lot of time shooting speed. It's what he did. He would be creative for a while, then he would crash for hours, and I would sit at that apartment with Rachel, sit and play the guitar. Lou would eventually come out, and we would play together, or we wouldn't. That was the same in hotel rooms when we traveled. He did hide out a lot, like anyone with a drug issue." Lou and Rachel shared the apartment with two dachshunds, Duke and Baron. "He would sit there with those dogs and kiss them on the mouth," says Erin Clermont. "I

Lou and Rachel, about to cut their cake.

thought, 'He is more affectionate with those dogs than he is with people.'" Ross quips, "Lou kept us all as pets, man."

When Lou resumed touring in October 1976, after a fourteen-month layoff, Rachel was his new road manager. "On this tour, Rachel looked after the money, and kept me in shape, and watched over the road-crew, and it's been great. There's someone hustling around for me that I can totally trust," he said, explaining Rachel's role. He rewarded his boyfriend with jewelry, including two diamond rings, which, given what happened next, might be seen as engagement rings.

When the tour reached London in April 1977, the couple celebrated the fact that they had been together for three years with a remarkable party at the end of Lou's shows at the New Victoria Theatre. The party was held at Maunkberry's, a gay club in St James's. Rachel commissioned a three-tier cake for the occasion, a wedding cake by any other name, topped with a heart inscribed with the initials "L" and "R" and the words "One layer for each year. Hoping for many more." Wearing a skirt and high heels, Rachel towered over Lou as they cut the cake, the pair looking like a newly married couple. Then they kissed. "Basically, it was Lou and Rachel getting married," says Jeffrey Ross. "It's an affirmation of their relationship.

Whether or not they called it a marriage, I don't know. We weren't thinking of gay marriage at the time [but] in every respect they behaved like a married couple." Lou's band leader, Michael Fonfara, concurs. "She was his wife, for sure."

The relationship was tempestuous. It was noticed that Rachel's right wrist was bandaged on the evening of the party at Maunkberry's. "I've got a feeling [that] they used to have fights," says photographer Jill Furmanovsky, who took pictures of Lou and Rachel with the cake. "I don't know if she had cut herself, [or] whether she had got injured." Both enjoyed drama. "They adored each other, but they also had these terrible fallings-out," says Jill's friend Liz Gilmore, who traveled with the couple in Europe. "They argued, and they fell out, and they would have separate rooms, and then they would get back together again." Rachel was taken to the hospital in Amsterdam. "I went to hospital with him," says Liz, "and he sat up and winked at me like the whole thing had been faked. There was that kind of thing [going on]." Meanwhile, Lou was as capricious as a child, refusing to perform until the promoter bought him a leather jacket he wanted, and he was obviously stoned much of the time. He had discovered an ingenious new way of doping himself on tour—he had his drugs prescribed as eye drops. Excessive use of these narcotic drops made him irascible, even violent.

There are numerous examples of Lou threatening people during this period, often with knives, showing that violence was not just a theme in his songwriting. Jeffrey Ross says that Lou pulled a knife on an Arista representative in London. "He was playing with switchblades all the time. He had this fascination with knives. He pulled out a knife and held it to the neck of this guy." In addition, he threatened to stab at least two journalists. "If I wanted to get you, I'd go behind your back [and] stab you," he told writer Josh Alan Friedman in New York. Somewhat absurdly, he threatened another journalist with a butter knife during a breakfast interview in the Netherlands. This was the behavior of an angry and unstable person. "Lou was in a constant breakdown," opines Jeffrey Ross. "I think Lou had severe emotional stuff going on, and mood swings. Some of that was amphetamines. Some of that was maybe living with a transvestite, and not being sure where his sexuality [was]."

Lou had no compunction about stabbing people in the back, metaphorically. Shortly after Jonny Podell introduced him to a lawyer named Eric Kronfeld, Lou hired Kronfeld as his new manager, leaving Jonny out in the cold. "He totally did the scumbag move." Kronfeld worked with Lou into the 1980s, during which time he helped stabilize his finances. On his advice, Lou settled the lawsuit with Steve Katz, who was paid compensation. The court battle with his brother Dennis intensified, however, with Lou counter-suing his former manager, together with the lawyer and accountant who had advised him at the time, ultimately asking for punitive damages of $2 million. Both sides filed allegations, and Lou spent several days giving evidence in the case at the Supreme Court of New York. He was a rational and courteous witness but like many performers he showed a limited knowledge of his financial affairs.

Lou was much more interested in technology. Throughout his life, he delighted in gadgetry and gear, being an early adopter of everything from Betamax to CompuServe. He wasn't necessarily skillful at using technology, but he loved it. "He was an enthusiast," says Tom Sarig, who managed Lou at the end of his career. "When he got into something, he went full bore. The instruction booklet with print *this* small, and a thousand pages, he'd read the whole thing." In this spirit, Lou became enthused with Binaural Sound in the late 1970s, an eccentric new recording system developed by a German engineer named Manfred Schunke, who put microphones in polystyrene heads (like hat-shop dummies) that were positioned around a recording studio, or concert venue, to record music in the round, as human ears would hear it. Lou started to record his German concerts using this peculiar system, creating tapes that he used as the basis of his next, and arguably his best, Arista album, *Street Hassle*.

There were two guitarists in the band on tour in Europe in 1977, Stuart Heinrich and Jeffrey Ross. By the time Lou brought the Binaural concert tapes back to the United States, he had fallen out with Ross. "He took my name off the record," complains Jeffrey. "Off two songs he had promised me co-writer credit." Then bass player Bruce Yaw fell foul of the boss. Lou wanted Bruce to come into Manhattan to redub his parts on the live tapes but refused to pay for a hotel, suggesting that Bruce stay with his mother. "I said, 'I'm not going to do that. I'm a professional and I would be glad to play with you, but you have to pay me.' That was not something he wanted to hear from me. So he re-dubbed the bass parts himself. . . . That was the ending of my relationship with him."

Another contributor to *Street Hassle* whose name didn't appear on the finished album was guitarist Ritchie Fliegler, who has the distinction of being one of only a handful of musicians outside the Velvet Underground to have worked with both Lou and John Cale, enabling him to make a comparison of their strengths and weaknesses. "John is probably the greatest musician I ever met," he concludes. "[Lou] was a serviceable guitar player, but it was the tool he used for expression. It wasn't music for music's sake. . . . John was in service to the music. Lou was in service to the message of the story. I truly believe that if it weren't for the two of them, you wouldn't have heard from either of them." Like others, Ritchie found working with Lou on *Street Hassle* to be a tiresome experience. "Lou was an easy person to despise. He was the biggest prick I ever met, or ever worked for, but he sure wrote some great songs."

Hiring and firing musicians with such rapidity, erasing the contributions of those who fell out of favor and overdubbing new parts to cover the gaps, gave *Street Hassle* a muddy sound, while some of the songs—"Wait" and "Leave Me Alone"—were weak. Nevertheless, *Street Hassle* had a vitality that lifted it above Lou's other Arista albums, while sharing similarities with the punk-rock movement. Lou found himself described as the "godfather of punk" at this time, a title he didn't care for, and indeed he was generally disobliging about punk musicians. As provocative and irreverent outsiders, however, they shared a common attitude, and he played up to this on his new album. In the song "Dirt," for example, an update of "Downtown Dirt," he sang about someone who would eat shit and say he liked the taste if there was money to be made. "I was specifically referring to my manager-lawyer," he explained, apparently referring back to Dennis Katz. Like many of Lou's songs, "Dirt" had been gestating for some time, and his antagonism to Dennis was stronger than ever as they fought each other in court.

Another track, "I Wanna Be Black," was an outrageous parody of the preconceptions some white people have about African-Americans. Lou sang that he wanted to have a stable of whores (as if that's what black men typically did) and would welcome being assassinated like Martin Luther King Jr., or Malcolm X, if only he could be black. Christine Wiltshire, an African-American singer who sang backing vocals on "I Wanna Be Black," says that she wasn't offended. "I didn't take it as a personal opinion of his." At times, though, Lou tried so hard to be controversial that he sounded like a bigot. "I don't like niggers like Donna Summer," he said in one interview that year, referring in another interview to "nigger music" (by which he meant disco, Summer's "I Feel Love" being one of the biggest hits of 1977). He evidently thought this sort of language was amusing, making him seem edgy and streetwise. If he had said such things thirty years later it might have ended his career. Like many people of his generation, he was guilty of a good deal of casual racism. He even indulged in anti-Semitic rhetoric. "He hated Dylan. I once said to Lou, 'You know, Dylan's the only genius in your field,'" recalls his journalist friend Ed McCormack. "He said, 'You mean you actually like that pretentious kike?' He's Jewish himself. It was a typical Lou thing to say."

The centerpiece of *Street Hassle* was a three-part, eleven-minute song cycle of the same name, set to a simple phrase in A and E, arranged for strings and guitar, in which Lou described a murder and sang a lament for a lost love, with a preface voiced by Bruce Springsteen, who happened to be making his fourth album, *Darkness on the Edge of Town*, in the next studio. Lou stressed in an interview that the characters in "Street Hassle" were gay. "They're not heterosexual concerns running through that song," he told *Rolling Stone*, identifying himself as gay in passing, a subject we shall return to in a moment. "I don't make a [big] deal of it, but when I mention a pronoun, its gender is all-important. It's just that my gay people don't lisp. They're not any more affected than the straight world. They just *are*. That's important to me. I'm one of them, and I'm right there, just like anybody else." He was particularly proud of the lyrics to the middle section: a disinterested observation of the violence in everyday urban life, concluding that murder, at a time when the murder rate in New York was extremely high, was often simply a matter of "bad luck."

Time described *Street Hassle* as "one of his very best, bitterest and most adventurous records" when it was released in February 1978, comparing Lou's writing to the scabrous novels of Celine. Others were less impressed. Nick Kent pointed out in the *New Musical Express* that "at least half the record was shoddy," which was true, while Robert Christgau was troubled by some of the language. "I don't think the racism of 'I Wanna Be Black' is mitigated by 'irony,'" he wrote, giving the record a B in the *Village Voice*. The public showed little interest. After a period of relative popularity, Lou's sales were in long-term decline. Although many new-wave artists honored his name as one of the originators of what might be termed outsider rock, few young record buyers cared. They had their own heroes. The success of the Ramones, Blondie, Talking Heads, U2 and the Pretenders would eclipse Lou over the next few years. *Street Hassle* charted low in the USA, and not at all in the UK. "*Street Hassle* got great reviews [but] you learn very few albums sell off of reviews. There are examples, but very few," says Clive Davis, who blamed the lack of a hit single. "I think it did nicely for an album that did not have a hit single in it, but it certainly did not do sales commensurate with the reviews." Lou felt crushed. Despite its flaws, he knew that the record represented his best work for some time.

As in the past, he reacted to failure by becoming surly and confrontational, which was his demeanor on tour that spring, a tour during which his relationship with Rachel began to fray. In April 1978 he invited Erin Clermont to accompany him to Philadelphia, where he gave a show in front of invited journalists to promote *Street Hassle*. They spent the night together. During the evening Erin asked Lou about Rachel, who didn't seem to be around. Erin had long wondered what the attraction was. Lou told her bluntly, "She's more beautiful than any fucking woman," which was hardly a compliment to Erin. The next morning, to Erin's great surprise, Rachel joined them for the limousine ride back to New York. He had evidently been in Philadelphia all along. "It was so weird," says Erin. "We were in the car together and I had spent the whole night in the room with [Lou], in this hotel. I didn't even know where she was, and then she turns up in the car." Theirs had evidently become an open relationship.

The following month, Lou played the Bottom Line, an intimate new club in Greenwich Village that held just 450 people, a tenth of the audience he could draw any night in Europe even at this stage in his career. "Lou was accepted in Europe a lot better, and he made more money there. He always did. For some reason, Europeans are more open to anything a little different," notes the singer Genya Ravan, who guested on *Street Hassle* and appeared onstage with Lou at the Bottom Line. While he sometimes grumbled about his relative lack of popularity in his native land, Lou enjoyed the intimate atmosphere of the New York club, which he played many times over the next few years, while friends often dropped in to catch his act. "I was *proud* of him. For once, finally, he's himself, he's not copying anybody. Finally, he's got his own style," Andy Warhol noted in his diary after seeing Lou at the Bottom Line in March. "Because when John Cale and Lou were the Velvets, they really had a style, but when Lou went solo he got bad and was copying people . . ." This was well observed.

Another residency at the Bottom Line two months later was recorded in Binaural Sound for a remarkable live album, *Lou Reed Live, Take No Prisoners*, the most extraordinary aspect of which was that Lou talked to his audience as much as he sang. Like a camp Lenny Bruce, he repeatedly interrupted the songs to tell rambling anecdotes about his life, or anything else that was on his mind, his comments sprinkled with so many expletives that the album was issued with a sticker warning that the content was "offensive." He also took the opportunity to insult his critics, picking on John Rockwell and Robert Christgau. "You know how heavy it is if you get reviewed by Rockwell [in the *New York Times*], and he says you are intelligent?" he asked the audience. "Fuck you! I don't need you to tell me that I'm good." Rockwell took the jibe in good humor. "I thought it was kind of fun that Bob [Christgau] and I, who are friends, would be singled out by him. The key line was that he didn't need critics to tell him how good he was, but the subtext to that is that both Bob and I had told him how good he was. It wasn't like we were enemies." Christgau was less amused to hear Lou mock his grading system and call him a moron. "I wasn't offended. Was I pleased? No, I wasn't pleased either. The guy's a jerk," he says irritably. "He hated critics, hated them more than most musicians."

Some of Lou's stage patter was funny, though hardly original ("If you write as good as you talk, nobody reads ya!"). His reference to "niggers" was offensive, while his monologues often dribbled away into mumbled non sequiturs. He sounded drunk a lot of the time, and often was. "I do remember the Bottom Line performances being completely drunken and drug-ridden," says Michael Fonfara, who continued to play keyboards in the band. Backing singer Chrissy Faith didn't enjoy the shows at all, finding Lou hard to work with.

"I was fairly intimidated, because he was not really approachable, and as a woman when you are dealing with somebody who is not very centered in their sexuality there is another element there. So [I'm] trying to learn how to relate to this guy. And there were a lot of drugs, so you never knew what you were going to get." She was amazed that Arista proposed to issue a live double album of the shows. It was Lou's idea, and Clive Davis let him do what he wanted. This was fortunate, because, despite its flaws, *Take No Prisoners* is the most entertaining of the six live albums Lou released as a solo artist, giving a visceral sense of what it was like to hear him in a club. And when he let his band play, on "Berlin," "Pale Blue Eyes" and "Satellite of Love," the music was powerful and nuanced.

LOU WAS BACK LIVING in Greenwich Village, not far from the Bottom Line, in a dingy apartment above the old Stonewall Inn on Christopher Street. This was the scene of the eponymous 1969 riot that started the modern gay rights movement in America, which had gathered considerable momentum by 1978. The fact that Lou chose to live in the heart of the Village's gay scene, above what had been an iconic gay bar (a deli in 1978), made a statement, at a time when he was also in a long-term relationship with a man. Indeed, it was at this stage that Lou chose to identify himself in public as gay.

Having skirted around the subject of his sexuality for years, presenting a camp image and insinuating at times that he was gay or bisexual but never defining his sexuality, Lou made his position clear in two interviews he gave to promote *Take No Prisoners*. "I have such a heavy resentment thing because of all the prejudices against me being gay," he told Stephen Demorest of *Creem* magazine over lunch at the Russian Tea Room. He spoke about witnessing a recent demonstration about laws that discriminated against homosexuals in New York. As a result, for the first time in his life, he felt politically engaged. "[A] girl got up and talked about seeing a rabbi on TV who said 'Homosexuality is an abomination.' And I realized this guy was calling me—Lou Reed—an abomination, too." It was in this same *Creem* interview, published in March 1979, that Lou suggested he was given ECT as a teenager because of his "homosexual feelings," and that he had forced himself to have heterosexual relationships in college, only accepting his homosexuality in his twenties. "I just wouldn't want listeners to be under a false impression," he said. "I want them to know, if they're liking a man, that it's a gay one—from top to bottom." This statement, together with the aforementioned comments he made about the characters in "Street Hassle" to *Rolling Stone*, which published its interview in the same month, appeared to show Lou coming out. But he seems to have soon regretted discussing his sexuality in this way. Perhaps he concluded that it was bad for his image to be classified as gay. Perhaps he thought it was less than the whole story. He had female lovers, too, after all. Erin was still part of his life, while Barbara Hodes had also continued to see Lou until recently. Maybe he thought his sex life was nobody's business but his own. In any event, he never described himself as gay in public again.

Lou furnished the Christopher Street apartment thriftily, acquiring a secondhand leather sofa from a classified ad in the *Village Voice*. The seller was surprised when Lou turned up in person to collect the couch. He kept the apartment for several years, improving it over time. He had skylights put in to brighten the dark rooms, had bookshelves built and purchased a big TV and a huge stainless-steel bath. Unlike his previous apartments, Christopher Street became a real home, but he didn't own it. As his finances improved, Lou decided the time was right to buy a place.

His choice of property was unexpected: an old hunting lodge next to the Kittatinny Mountains, outside the village of Blairstown, New Jersey. The house was only fifty-eight miles from Manhattan by limousine, but Lou felt himself in the middle of nowhere when he arrived. There were no neighbors in sight, and he could walk for hours in the woods without seeing a soul. He found the place restful after the hubbub of Manhattan. "Even if you wanted to do something, there's nothing to do there. It's appalling how much sleep I get. You know, Andy used to say you can't see the stars in New York City because they're all on the ground [a phrase Lou later quoted in *Songs for Drella*]. Well, out there the stars are in the sky." He came to own 138 acres in the country, including a two-acre pond next to the lodge—a small stone building with an oversized porch made of boulders. The horror movie *Friday the 13th* was filmed at the neighboring summer camp soon after he bought the place.

He brought friends out to Blairstown. "The house was about half a mile off the road. And we're driving in this big black limousine through potholes. . . . It looks like a Gingerbread house from the Brothers Grimm. We parked the car. You had to go over a little bridge to the house [built] from stone and logs. It was like a log cabin, very rustic," recalls Ellard Boles, Lou's new bass guitarist.

Lou's country home, New Jersey.

Erin Clermont.

Nicknamed Moose for his size, the musician also became his roommate at Christopher Street, which Lou continued to rent and live in
part of the time, and where they played endless games of Mastermind. "I would kick his butt on this game. It would drive him crazy.
I mean, *crazy.*" At night, Lou slept with Baron the dachshund in the
master bedroom, while Moose slept with Duke in the spare room.
What about Rachel? "Rachel was kind of in and out," says Moose.
"Rachel wasn't there all the time."

Erin lived nearby in the Village and, when Lou wanted female
company, he would ring and ask if he could "pop by," no matter how
late. If Erin was out when he called, he would call back repeatedly
until she answered. She once came home to find that Lou had called
and hung up twenty-one times. "He had this need to talk to people.
He needed to have this contact. . . . In his drug years it was this
neurotic neediness." Lou and Erin went through a phase of visiting
sex clubs together: peep shows on 42nd Street; the new swingers'
club, Plato's Retreat; and the Eulenspiegel Society, a bondage and

S&M group. "It was on a voyeuristic basis. He had an intense interest in sex. I did, too. Also, exploring the variations of sex." Lou was more interested in watching than participating. "I knew I was safe with him because he didn't want to get involved in anything dangerous—no way!" Lou did, however, have adventures on the road during this time, and they were primarily gay.

"He did have the odd tryst on the road, but never anyone that got to hang around long. [They] were kicked out before morning," says Michael Fonfara. "Young men . . . he did prefer pretty boys." Moose recalls Lou sleeping with one guy in Buffalo. The next day on the bus, as the band members were discussing what a good time they'd had in town, Lou, who was eating an ice cream, gave his lolly a lascivious lick and said he'd had a wonderful time, too.

One night, Michael Fonfara spotted an attractive woman in the audience. "She was making eyes at me. . . . She was very demure in the way that she dressed. But I loved her exotic face. That's why I told the roadie to bring her backstage. I thought she had a good-looking figure. Not a really tall girl—about five [foot] five, maybe. Medium build, semi-voluptuous." They went back to the hotel. "We were going up in the elevator, and she looked over at me and said, 'Michael, I like you a lot, but I really, really just wanted to meet Lou. That's why I'm here with you.'" Michael called Lou to tell him about the girl, not expecting him to be interested. "He didn't want any girls back to his room—ever." Michael spoke up for her, however. "I'll babysit with her to make sure nothing happens and take her away again."

"OK, you got five minutes."

He took her to Lou's suite, where they made an instant connection. "After about two minutes they were sitting there with their heads together, and he looked up at me and said, 'Get lost!'"

The girl, Sylvia Morales, was born in England in 1956 when her US serviceman father, Pedro Morales, was stationed at an air force base in Cambridgeshire. She was currently living in New York

City, where she was studying and taking part in the downtown arts scene. Like Lou, she sometimes hung out at CBGB. According to biographer Victor Bockris, she also attended the Eulenspiegel Society and performed in a burlesque show. She already knew John Cale, who claims to have had a fling with her before she met Lou. "I picked Sylvia up one day in a club, went over to her apartment and that was it—a one-night stand." It all pointed to an intense interest in Lou Reed's world. Lou, fourteen years her senior, was intrigued by Sylvia, who quickly established herself as his new companion. Sylvia and Rachel were both on the scene for a while, which was problematic. "I know there was some effort to keep the two of them separate," says band member Chrissy Faith. "'Oh my God, Sylvia *and* Rachel are here!'"

Michael Fonfara was surprised to see Lou in a relationship with what he would have called "a real woman." "The entire time I knew him until he met Sylvia he was gay," he says. Indeed, Lou had only just come out in the press, which was awkward timing. Moose Boles saw Lou more as bisexual, and says that Sylvia accepted this. "She was at peace with who he was, and she loved him for who he was. That was the thing between them. She really took care of Lou on the road."

Rachel didn't disappear overnight, but he was seen less frequently in Lou's company, until one day at rehearsals in New York in early 1979. Lou was onstage with the band, Sylvia watching them play, when Rachel appeared in the room carrying a leather bag. When Lou finished playing he beckoned Rachel to come forward and took the bag from him. He was evidently returning his property. Then he left, disappearing back into the twilight world from which he emerged in 1974. "No one ever knew her real name, her full name, or what happened to her," says Erin. "He never mentioned her again."

UNUSUALLY, LOU CO-WROTE MUCH of his next album, *The Bells*. He co-wrote the song "Families" with Moose during the Thanksgiving vacation of 1978, which the men spent together at Christopher Street. The lyrics addressed what it felt like to be a disappointment to one's parents, with obvious autobiographical connotations. Lou co-wrote the title song, informed by the Edgar Allan Poe poem of the same name, with his long-serving saxophonist Marty Fogel. The lyrics were created extemporaneously in the studio, and Lou considered it one of his best. Other songs were written with guitarist Nils Lofgren and the jazz musician Don Cherry, who played trumpet on the album, which was recorded in Germany in Binaural Sound. The music was a strange hybrid of frenetic disco (a type of music Lou had previously professed to hate but which was in fashion) and jazz rock, with some intriguing lyrics. As ever, the critics were divided as to whether it was any good. Lester Bangs raved about it in *Rolling Stone*, while the *Los Angeles Times* dismissed it as a "dismal, turgid effort." It didn't chime with British critics. "*The Bells* is a delusion disguised as an album," wrote Charles Shaar Murray. "I'm not entirely sure whether Reed is attempting to delude his listeners or whether he is himself deluded." The public showed virtually no interest in the record, which Lou came to think of as one of his most underrated albums, and indeed he may have been right. "I think it sold two copies," he reflected, "and probably both to me."

When he went on tour to support the album, Lou had a new whizz-kid guitarist in his band. Chuck Hammer admired Lou's songs so much that he wrote and told him so. "I just said I loved his music, and I know *Berlin* is a masterpiece, and I'd love to work with him, and I'm the best unknown guitarist in America." Lou invited Chuck to an audition at his apartment. "These are the ground rules," he said, as controlling as ever. The guitarist was to come to Christopher Street promptly at 5 p.m. "I'll set you up in a room to play. I'm not going to stay in the room. I'll go into a different room. You play for twenty minutes. If at the end of twenty minutes I don't like what I hear, you just pack up and leave."

Chuck knocked at Lou's front door as arranged. Lou opened the door himself, unshaven and clearly disoriented. "What time is it?" he asked.

"Five o'clock."

"Day or night?"

After he passed the audition, Chuck was given a Roland Guitar Synthesizer to learn to play, a difficult instrument he likens to "wrestling with a gorilla." After a few days, Lou invited him out to Blairstown to hear how he was getting on. Chuck traveled out to the country by Greyhound bus, arranging to meet Lou in town. "Get off the bus, Lou is there in his Jeep with the top down." After years when he hadn't driven at all, Lou started to drive again in the country, acquiring a variety of vehicles, including the Jeep, a Mercedes 450SL sports car, a snowmobile and several motorcycles. "Lou takes the guitar, flings it in the back of the Jeep, says, 'Get in.' Drives thirty feet. Slams on the brakes. . . . There was a little bar . . . Lou takes me into the bar. He orders four Scotches for him, and four Scotches for me, and a beer each. I don't drink. [Four Scotches] lined up. He downs his and I have, like, one. He finished mine as well. Lou is now driving his Jeep, drunk out of his freaking mind, I'm in the passenger seat, and we are driving towards his house from town."

Lou treated Chuck as he had former protégés, bonding with him while also seeking to control him, and signaling that the good times wouldn't last. "Never cross me," he warned. He was trying to wean himself off methamphetamine by drinking more, and traveled on tour with a case of Johnny Walker Black Label. "He was drinking two bottles every three days on his own. Straight up," says Chuck, who counted the empties. Lou also liked to drink in bars on tour, routinely sending drinks back, saying they weren't mixed strong enough. "He *constantly* did that, and constantly abused waiters and waitresses." Tour days often started with a champagne breakfast at the hotel. "There would be jeroboams of champagne, and guys squeezing oranges, and we'd start before we even did the sound check for the gig. Everybody would be pie-faced, just flattened. And Lou would say, 'Tell them to put the rest of that bottle in the car, we're taking it to the rehearsal,'" says Michael Fonfara. "It was just a constant flow of booze. I guess that's rock 'n' roll." Lou started to get heavy again with so much drinking, so he and Michael went to the gym. Afterwards, Lou would sometimes treat himself to a shot of meth. "We used to go to the gym together in New York and work out, and then we'd get back to his place and he'd say, 'OK, you tie me off [apply a tourniquet to his arm so he could inject speed].' Oh Jesus!"

They were in the middle of a gig at the Stadthalle in Offenbach, Germany, on April 6, 1979, playing to an audience largely composed of American servicemen, when a heckler interrupted Lou's concentration. He stopped the show and ordered the lights to be turned on the audience to identify the culprit. "People started yelling," says Marty Fogel, "and Lou really got agitated and started yelling back." A woman climbed onstage. When she came toward Lou, he sidestepped, she stumbled and he grabbed her. "Lou proceeds to drag her off the stage by her hair, and pushes her off the stage. She fell fifteen feet—at least," says Chuck Hammer, "at which stage a full-blown riot breaks out—chairs start to fly—an incredible riot ensues." Lou was cowering backstage when the German police came to arrest him. Lou handed Sylvia his leather bag—evidently, something precious was in it—before they took him away. He spent the night in custody, where blood and urine samples were taken for drug tests. The fact that he passed is probably because he was now primarily drinking on tour. As soon as Lou was released, they all flew to Switzerland. "We had to leave the country," says Chuck, who recalls that a further German show was canceled.

A couple of days later, Lou arrived in London, where he asked to meet Charles Levison, Managing Director of Arista UK. Lou was increasingly unhappy about his low record sales, which he blamed on a lack of label promotion. Levison emerged shaken from their meeting, as Arista publicist Howard Harding recalls: "Charles, looking very agitated, said to me, 'You didn't tell me he was going to pull a gun on me!' 'What?' Apparently, Lou was so incensed he actually took out a firearm and threatened Charles Levison with it." Lou was fortunate that Levison didn't call the police.

That same week, Lou was onstage at the Hammersmith Odeon when he looked over and saw David Bowie sitting cross-legged on a flight case in the wings watching the show. Lou was so excited that he turned to his band and yelled, "Play! Play! Play! Play!" He was eager to impress the Englishman, who had become one of the great figures of rock 'n' roll in the few years since they had worked together on *Transformer*, releasing a series of varied, distinctive and ultimately classic albums that arguably placed him above Lou in the pantheon of rock. He was also commercially far more successful. When he came offstage, Lou hugged and kissed Bowie, who accompanied Lou and his band to the Chelsea Rendezvous for a reunion meal. "Isn't David great? Don't you just love David?" Lou kept saying. The stars sat together at the head of a table. Dom Perignon was served. After the meal, Lou switched to Irish coffee. He became drunk and loud, while Bowie remained subdued. Mindful of the success they had enjoyed in the past, badly needing another hit and emboldened with alcohol, Lou asked David if he would produce him again.

"Yes, if you clean up your act."

Shocked by the reply, Lou slapped Bowie. "Don't you ever say that to me!" he shouted. He slapped him again. "Don't ever fucking say that to *me*."

The musicians intervened, persuading Lou to move to another table, where he sat glowering at David for a few minutes. Then they made up. "They start talking again. It's like nothing's happened," says Marty Fogel. "But then it happens *again*. He stands up and starts slapping [David] around." Lou pulled David out of his chair.

"I told you never to say that!" he screamed, slapping his face. This time his band took him back to his hotel. They went to his room, where he normally liked to sit up late with the musicians, listening to a tape of the show they had just played.

There was a knock at the door.

"Who is it?"

"David Bowie."

Bowie had come to the hotel to fight Lou. "Come out and fight like a man!" Bowie challenged, marching up and down the hotel corridor while Lou snored. His band wasn't sure whether he was sleeping, or pretending.

There was further unpleasantness when Clive Davis came to see Lou at the Bottom Line in New York on June 4, 1979. Lou, who was now bloated with drink, his belly big and his face puffy, berated his label boss from the stage, asking, "Where is the money, Clive?" and "How come I don't hear my album on the radio?" Davis was not amused to be shown up in public by an artist who didn't even make Arista much money. "I had always done my best, but I realized he was frustrated [with sales]," he says. "It was upsetting." The following day, Lou was obliged to issue a public apology. "Like most artists, Lou was a blamer," comments Jonny Podell. "It was Clive's fault, my fault. . . . That's intrinsic in the business."

Feeling the need for somebody at his side whom he could trust, Lou asked Sylvia Morales to marry him, and she accepted. He announced their engagement onstage at the Bottom Line in December, also singing a sappy new song, "Love Is Here to Stay." But first he had to make another album for Arista.

At the suggestion of Corky Stasiak, Lou recorded *Growing Up in Public* at George Martin's new AIR Studios on the Caribbean island of Montserrat, arriving there on January 5, 1980. As a Beatles fan, Lou was thrilled to meet Martin, and he found the setup at AIR congenial. Dire Straits, Paul McCartney and the Police would all record hit albums at the facility over the next few years. Lou,

his band and their partners stayed in villas within the studio com-
pound. Each evening there was a communal, catered meal, washed
down with copious amounts of alcohol. One evening, Lou and Michael Fonfara wrote a comical paean to inebriation they called "The
Power of Positive Drinking." They were, as Michael says, "drunk as
skunks."

Growing Up in Public marked a departure from the jazz-rock
sound Lou had hitherto pursued with the Everyman Band, which
had of course morphed into Lou's band over the past five years as
musicians left and were replaced. Only two originals remained,
saxophonist Marty Fogel and drummer Michael Suchorsky. Moose
Boles, Michael Fonfara, Chuck Hammer and Stuart Heinrich had
joined the band separately, but they had likewise shown the boss
considerable loyalty. The music on the new album, largely written
by Fonfara, who also produced the record, was basic barroom boo-
gie. Lou sang, rather than narrating his songs. His voice, which
had deepened with years of cigarette smoking (he was trying to
quit), sounded strained, while the lyrics were unusually wordy and
autobiographical. "So Alone," "Love Is Here to Stay" and "Think It
Over" all appeared to be about his new fiancée, Sylvia, while "Keep
Away" may have expressed aspects of his breakup with Rachel. Most
interesting was "My Old Man." Uniquely, Lou used his own name in
this song, toward the end of which the bullying father tells him to
"act like a man." Lou claimed that it wasn't autobiography, though
it sounded like that to most people, including his band. "That [song]
I think was pretty autobiographical," says guitarist Stuart Heinrich.
"It did seem like a retrospective of his own life, and his surround-
ings, as opposed to mirroring the lives of others." Michael Fonfara
has no doubt that Lou was writing about himself, and sees the whole
album as autobiography. "He was explaining how he was brought
up, and what are some of the reasons for [the] behavior he has, and
what he thinks about the world, and what he wants everyone else to
know . . . how things happen like this. He talks about his mother be-

ing 'a harridan mother.' Some other things in there [like] 'Standing On Ceremony,' all these things are based on his family. It's almost like telling a therapist, only he is doing it in song."

Recording on Montserrat went smoothly. "The buzz around the band was 'Sylvia's really good for him, she's a sweetheart, she's really taking care of him. He's not doing as much drugs. He is drinking,'" recalls Corky, who had last worked with Lou on *Rock 'n' Roll Heart* in 1976, when he was out of his mind on drugs. Four years on, drink was the problem.

At the end of January 1980 everybody returned to New York, where Michael Fonfara and Corky Stasiak mixed the album at Electric Lady under Lou's supervision. He drank so much in the studio while they worked that he passed out. "There were times he would nod out and we would have to wheel him in the chair outside the studio so we could finish the overdubs and stuff," says Corky. Lou's drinking was not merely excessive; it had become dangerous. He confided to Michael and Corky that his doctor had told him that his liver was damaged. "His doctor told him that if he did any more, his liver would explode and he would die," says Michael, who believes that this is why Lou chose to review his life in *Growing Up in Public*. "He was feeling his mortality." If he wanted to live into his forties, he would have to change his lifestyle. Perhaps Sylvia could save him from himself.

XI

SECOND MARRIAGE

• 1980–87 •

OU MARRIED SYLVIA AT his apartment in New York on St. Valentine's Day, 1980. Many people were invited, in contrast to his first wedding, including his new twenty-three-year-old road manager, Daryl Bornstein, who had recent experience of his

boss's gay side, despite the fact that he was about to embark upon matrimony with a woman once again. A few days before the wedding, Lou took Daryl for a drink. "Lou wanted to go out, so we went out and stopped at some club—it was a gay bar—and we walked in and he made some comment like, 'I bet you've never been to one of these.' And then he grabbed my ass. I said, 'Yes, Lou, I have. And don't grab my ass.'"

Wedding guests were surprised to see Lou's parents at the ceremony. In his new, as yet unreleased, album, *Growing Up in Public*, Lou insinuated in "How Do You Speak to An Angel" that his mother was a "harridan" and, in this and other songs, that his dad was worse. He described a "simpering" ("How Do You Speak to an Angel"), "bullying" man who "beat my mother" ("My Old Man"), while denying in interviews that this was literally true, which might be seen as having his cake and eating it. Nevertheless, Sid and Toby were at Christopher Street to watch their son, dressed conventionally in jacket and tie, link his lot with Sylvia, who wore an off-white silk dress for their big day. He was thirty-eight; she was twenty-three. As the couple posed for photographs with their parents, Sylvia burst into tears. The new Mrs. Reed had a tough side, however, as she would show over the course of the marriage, during which she took an increasingly prominent role in Lou's career, helping to design his album covers and organize his tours, ultimately becoming his personal manager. "She seemed to be the adult in the relationship," comments Daryl Bornstein. "Sylvia was certainly more practical."

The wedding party adjourned to a local restaurant, after which Lou took everybody to the Broadway Arcade, at Broadway and 52nd Street, where guests were given a bucket of quarters to play pinball. Lou had started to frequent the arcade while shooting scenes in the neighborhood for Paul Simon's movie *One-trick Pony* (1980), in which he played a producer. The picture flopped, but Lou developed a passion for pinball. "I would call him a Pinhead. He would spend an hour, two hours, playing in a night," says arcade owner Steve

Epstein, who struck up an unlikely friendship with the star. The men ate together at Little Charley's Clam House in the Bowery (one of Lou's favourite restaurants), played golf together (one of his less well-known recreations) and went to see the Mets play at Shea Stadium, catching the subway to the venue and sitting in the bleachers like everybody else. Steve proved to be a good listener. "If he was bitching and moaning, I was more than happy to listen." He didn't care for Sylvia, however, "a sour type of person," and adds to the evidence that Lou hadn't entirely forsaken his gay life. Boyfriends came by the Broadway Arcade looking for Lou, and Steve passed on their messages. "I realized he definitely was a bisexual man."

Polite conversation at the wedding was that the new album sounded great, and Clive Davis was pleased, but *Growing Up in Public* was a disappointment upon release in May 1980. Mikal Gilmore, writing in *Rolling Stone*, expressed lukewarm praise ("a polished package of bombastic rock 'n' roll"); the UK music paper *Sounds* rubbished the album, the British music press having written Lou off in the post-punk era as being hopelessly old hat. His diminishing number of anglophone fans mostly ignored the record. He had released too many patchy albums over the past few years, and had lost the respect and attention of all but his most loyal listeners. His biggest and most receptive audience continued to be in the Latin nations of southern Europe, where his iconoclastic image went down particularly well, and where he toured to promote the album in the summer of 1980 and, once again, ran into trouble. A concert in Madrid degenerated into a riot, during which fans torched the arena and a frustrated Lou slammed his fist into the air-conditioning unit on his tour bus. He was drinking heavily, so much so that he told his road manager he was too sick to perform in Oporto. At least he wasn't using drugs. "It must have been in Portugal when Lou had a doctor come [to his room, because he was so hung over], and the doctor wanted to give Lou a shot, and Lou said, 'No shots.' He didn't want to have anything to do with needles," says Daryl Bornstein.

The failure of *Growing Up in Public* brought his relationship with Arista to an end. "I always felt bad that the years with Arista were not more fertile. I would have loved to have enjoyed more commercial success with Lou," says Clive Davis, who had hoped that Lou's status as the "godfather of punk" would result in a career lift in the late 1970s. When this didn't materialize, he made no attempt to extend the contract. Taken together with the fact that Lou was facing a health problem, it was time to step back and think about what he wanted to do with his career. So he told his band that he wouldn't be working for a while, citing his health as the principal reason. "He had a medical condition at that point. They thought he was going to die of sclerosis, or something liver-orientated," says Michael Fonfara, adding that Lou was devastated to have to stop drinking. "He was almost in tears!" He didn't, however, stop completely.

Keeping the Christopher Street apartment as his city base, Lou retreated to his country home, where he worked to get fit and sober. He swam in the pond next to his cabin and hiked through the woods. He ate healthily and took up tai chi, the start of an interest in the martial art that lasted for the rest of his life. The quintessential city dweller found country living surprisingly congenial, though he made urbanite mistakes, like feeding the Canada Geese that alighted on his pond, with the result that he was inundated with birds, who covered the foreshore in guano. He also fed the bears, until one climbed on to his porch looking for food. The man in black also took fright when he found a snake in one of his outbuildings. "I had to go up and help get it away," says neighbor Rita Teel. "I just went and kind of pushed it away with a stick." Lou and Sylvia became friendly with Rita and her husband, Bob, who did odd jobs for the couple and kept an eye on their isolated property when they were away. "Lou was a little introverted," says Rita. "Other than that, I think he was one of the nicest guys we ever had as a neighbor." Others were less sure about the rock star who had moved into their quiet, conservative area. "Blairstown has changed a bit over the years," notes Sylvia. "But the town was and still is primarily fairly Republican-conservative, with quite a few shotguns and pickup types who dominated the area for a while." Some saw Lou as a freak. Neighbor Judy Cook recalls watching Lou walk down the country road that ran past their homes with a woman and a stick. "He had a stick, and he used to make her stay at a distance," she laughs. "He [was] so weird sometimes."

Lou became a keen motorcyclist in New Jersey. "Tramontin motorcycles, which is nearby Blairstown, was a haven for him during the years he was a Harley-Davidson enthusiast," says Sylvia. Lou acquired a series of powerful Harleys, including a Super Glide and a Fat Boy. "He liked to hang out in the service department and watch the technicians work; he was fascinated with anything mechanical," says dealer Bob Tramontin. Lou on his bike, dressed from head to toe in black leather, even in midsummer, became a familiar figure around town. When he pulled into Dominick's pizzeria on Route 94 for a snack, local kids would cheek him by chanting "doo da doo" as he walked by. His apparent dislike of being recognized caused him to keep his helmet on, even when he visited the Blairstown Inn for a drink. Although he gave the impression that he became clean and sober around 1981 and remained so, there is abundant evidence that this wasn't strictly true. He stopped using hard drugs, but he struggled with sobriety for most of the rest of his life. "I often would not serve him when he came with the motorcycle, because I felt he was under the influence already when he arrived," says Kellie Peterson, proprietor of the Blairstown Inn, who was struck by the oddity of Lou wearing his helmet in her bar. "If he wasn't supposed to be drinking, and he was off the wagon, he might not have wanted to be seen . . . I never had a real argument with him. It was simply, 'No, I think you've had enough for today, and I don't think it would be a good idea if I gave you a drink.'" Lou wasn't pleased to be refused. "But he did not make a scene."

There is further evidence that he continued to drink even after being warned by his doctors that he had damaged his liver. "I can remember bringing a bottle of wine out there when I was there with my wife and my kids and they invited us for dinner, and I'm pretty sure he drank some," recalls school friend Richard Sigal, who resumed his acquaintance with Lou at this time, often visiting him in Blairstown. "I think he was also smoking some dope." Lou's attempts to get sober were analogous to his half-hearted efforts to stop smoking cigarettes. "I consider I have slipped," he once said, looking at the Marlboro in his hand. "But I have not stopped trying to quit. As opposed to saying that I've failed and there's an end to it." Here was the doublespeak of therapy and the sophistry of self-help books, of which he was an avid reader.

In his struggle to conquer his bad habits, he became anxious and depressed and was diagnosed as suffering with bipolar disorder. On June 3, 1980, Lou visited Erin Clermont to tell her about the diagnosis, adding that he had already found a cure for his problem. "He came over, exhilarated. He'd found the answer—lithium. I remember him saying, 'It all boils down to taking this salt, a natural product!'" Lithium salts have been used since the nineteenth century as a treatment for depression and manic behavior, but overuse can result in nausea, lethargy and more serious side effects, and it seems that Lou was taking too much. From what Erin could see, lithium "completely fucked him up."

Work is often the best medicine, and it wasn't long before he started writing for a comeback album. His manager, Eric Kronfeld, had negotiated a new deal with RCA, surprisingly, considering their history. It was important that the first album was good. The songs he was writing addressed a variety of topics. In "My House" he listed the three principal blessings of his new country life as his writing, his motorcycle and his wife, in that order, which put Sylvia in her place. Casting his mind back to student days, he wrote about the day President Kennedy died, and his reflections on the bravery of the president's widow ("The Heroine"). At a time when Lou kept a handgun at home in the country, he wrote "The Gun," in which he imagined himself in the shoes of a psychopath who murders a woman. "'The Gun' is none of me," he clarified. "The guy in 'The Gun' is a vicious, stupid, mean so-and-so. But I know people like that, and I wanted to act it out . . ." He wrote realistically about alcoholism in "Underneath the Bottle," in contrast to the mendacious "Power of Positive Drinking" from *Growing Up in Public*, and expressed his mental turmoil in "Waves of Fear" and "The Blue Mask," for which his comeback album would be named. There was more thought, sincerity and art in these songs than Lou had marshaled for years.

His relationship with his old band ended before he went into the studio to make the new album. During his career hiatus, his musicians had taken on other projects, some choosing to work with the jazz star Don Cherry. When Lou wanted them to come back and work for him, they were unavailable, which caused him to wash his hands of the group. He had also fallen out with several individual members over the years. "Because he was an ex-junkie, he had ex-junkie behavior patterns. Loyalty was paramount and the tiniest infraction would make an end to [a] relationship, because he would feel he couldn't trust you," notes Daryl Bornstein. "With the guys in the band it would be one funny look and that would be it, which was crazy because prior to that they would have been best friends. And Lou didn't have a lot of close friends." Lou fell out with his guitarist, Chuck Hammer, for instance, over a solo album Hammer was making for RCA, his profile having been raised by his recent work on Bowie's 1980 hit "Ashes to Ashes," which showed Bowie still to be a vital artist with a popular, contemporary sound. Lou announced that he wanted to produce Chuck's album, but only if he fired everybody else he had been working with to date. Chuck refused. This resulted in the end of their relationship. "I was so pissed at Lou for putting me in that position. . . . If I saw him in a grocery store, I walked out."

So Lou assembled a new band. He began by hiring a sophisticated, experienced drummer named Doane Perry, who had played one gig with him in 1979. Lou mailed demo tapes and hand-typed lyric sheets to Doane in Los Angeles, spending hours discussing arrangements over the phone with him before they went into the studio to cut the new album. "I made my charts over his words in terms of bar lines or accents, 'cause there was nothing notated. . . . He wasn't that sort of [musician]. . . . For instance, on the song 'The Blue Mask,' I remember pointing out to him, 'Lou, this is in 9/4 [time].' He said, 'It is?' Because Lou was very much a [simple] 4/4, 3/4, 6/8 kind of guy. And he was quite surprised, and a little bit delighted. . . . It was just that he didn't think about that [sort of thing]."

The next recruit was Fernando Saunders, a virtuoso musician from Detroit who played fretless bass in a subtle, lyrical style. "He said, 'I want someone with fresh ears.' Not copying the past," says Fernando, who had previously worked with Jeff Beck and John McLaughlin. "We had good chemistry from the first note." Fernando would work with Lou, on and off, for most of the rest of his career. His longevity was partly due to his placid temperament. "I never saw Lou trying to rile up Fernando, because Fernando wouldn't have risen to that," explains Doane. "There was a very Zen-like presence to Fernando that was imperturbable."

The third and most important member of the band was Robert Quine, who had first met Lou as a fan in the 1960s, taping Velvet Underground gigs. He had subsequently achieved renown as a guitarist with Richard Hell and the Voidoids, one of the most influential new-wave bands of the mid- to late 1970s. Robert was nine months younger than Lou, but appeared older because of his bald head and formal manner of dress, usually wearing a starched shirt and sports jacket onstage. He also favored dark glasses, which made a serious person seem more austere. "He was very taciturn at times, never rude, very quiet and inward," says Doane, who recalls that Quine even wore his shades in the studio. The man did not invite conversation. "Occasionally, he would make a remark that was more often than not cryptic."

This lean four-piece convened at RCA's Studio A in Manhattan in October 1981, a vast room where Elvis and Sinatra had recorded. "All the lights were on. It was like working in a great big cafeteria," recalls Doane. "We were set up tight like a band onstage." Lou stood to the right of Doane's drums as they recorded live; Quine on his right, Fernando to his left. They tackled the songs with intensity, even ferocity. During the maelstrom of "The Blue Mask" Lou turned and urged them all to play harder. Doane and Fernando held the tempo, resisting Lou's inclination to speed up. They knew that tension was to be gained if the rhythm section held back slightly, which is part of the distinctive sound of the album. "At the end of some songs he would almost be shaking with the intensity of it," says Doane. Others noticed Lou's hands trembling. It may have been nerves, delirium tremens or a side effect of the lithium.

Lou told his band that he was clean and sober. "He was coming out of that at that period, doing that album," says Fernando. "He said, 'Fernando, I went to healers, I went to prayer places, I went everywhere.' He realized that no healer who would touch your arm, no acupuncture or prayer is going to help you to stop drinking. You just have to stop. And I guess it got to the point where—he would tell me things—it got to the point where the doctor said, 'If you keep drinking like this you will have no liver.' So he had pretty much quit [by] himself." Lou wouldn't tolerate people around him using drugs. He lost his temper with Quine early in the sessions when the mournful guitarist (who committed suicide by drug overdose in 2004) asked for some cash to buy lunch. Fernando believes that Lou may have suspected he wanted money for drugs. "He didn't trust people with his money. People had taken advantage of him [in the past]."

Despite this altercation, the sessions went well. In contrast to the Everyman Band, the sound was skeletal hard rock. They could play softly when required. The arrangement of "The Gun" was a subtle, jazzy sketch, an unlikely musical setting for such a menacing story. But the band's signature sound was closer to the second Velvet Underground album. Quine filled the role John Cale had once played. He was a similarly serious, demanding musician who didn't like to compromise. Every guitar lick he played was original, every take different, constantly challenging Lou to do better. There was a healthy creative tension between the men, though jealousy intruded. One version of "Average Guy," a song in which Lou poked fun at himself, was so catchy that his engineer and co-producer, Sean Fullan, thought it could be a single. He was disappointed when Lou rejected the take in favor of a version in which Quine's guitar part wasn't as strong. "Looking back, I think maybe Quine was just too fucking good [on that cut]. You know, guitar players get competitive with each other," explains Fullan. "Solo artists are always very much in control. It is their name, their project. They are narcissists, and they have to be that way to survive, unfortunately."

As with his last album, Lou revealed himself in these new songs. His image, the eponymous and metaphorical blue mask, was ripped aside, showing him to be a highly neurotic, sometimes angry man. Emotions were still raw when he went to see Erin at her apartment in the Village after recording was finished. "He came over late, scared, panicked. I'd never seen him like this. He feared he was losing his career, his life. He seemed on the verge of a total breakdown. He had started [taking] lithium a while before this, and now it wasn't working, and he was falling apart. He was ashamed that I was seeing him this way. Apologized. Which of course he did not have to do with me. We talked until 5 a.m.," she says, referring to her diary of December 6, 1981. She wondered if Sylvia knew where Lou was in the middle of the night. "He also said, 'I've been self-medicating myself for years.' Meaning both drugs and alcohol." When Erin next saw him, on December 20, he seemed better. "Two weeks later, Lou returned, vastly improved. I questioned the bipolar diagnosis, the prescribed treatment, and the bad after-effects. I believed that the drugs had done this to him. He was intrigued, really listened to me—which was often not the case!"

The Blue Mask has come to be regarded as one of Lou's best solo albums, but while it was better than what had come directly before, it wasn't an unalloyed success. The words to a couple of songs, including "Women," were weak. "I love women/We all love women" was a trite lyric that sounded bogus coming from a man who evidently loved men as well, and was also known for his misogyny. Perversely, he chose this as the single to launch the album and, in the new MTV age, he made a film to promote the song. "During the shoot of the video his hands were shaking so badly he went to restring a guitar and he couldn't. His hands were shaking incredibly," says Fred Maher, who replaced Doane Perry on drums at this stage. "He was in pretty bad shape."

When Lou met the press to discuss the album, he showed a reluctance to discuss his gay past. If journalists tried to tackle him on this subject, reasonably enough considering the comments he had made about his sexuality as recently as 1979 and the public nature of his relationship with Rachel, he became sullen. "My past is *my* past, and it's my business," he told the *New York Times*. He had drawn a veil over that part of his life, a veil that would remain closed. He didn't refer to himself as gay anymore (it would have been difficult to do so now that he was married), and he never, ever mentioned Rachel, though he may have had his former boyfriend in mind when he said that Sylvia had helped "[get] rid of certain things that were bad for me, certain people."

As he talked up *The Blue Mask*, he attempted to make further adjustments to his image. "Some people like to think I'm just this black-leather-clad person in sunglasses. And there's certainly that side to me; I wouldn't want to deny my heritage. But while I have my share of street smarts, I'm not a rat from the streets by any means. I always wanted to be a writer, and I went to college to prepare myself for it." He spoke of his interest in philosophy and literature, and his ambition to write lyrics of the highest literary merit. "I don't hear anybody trying to do a *Lear*, or a *Hamlet* soliloquy, in rock 'n' roll. Who says you can't do that? People say rock 'n' roll is constricting, but you can do anything you want, any way you want. And my goal has been to make an album that would speak to people the way Shakespeare speaks to me, the way Joyce speaks to me. Something with that kind of power: something with *bite* to it." He also referred to wanting to write to the same standard as Dostoyevsky, another literary hero. While it is healthy for a writer to have ambitions, and there is no reason why rock 'n' roll lyrics shouldn't have artistic value, such statements were easily misconstrued as pretentious. As his sister says, "Only my brother could compare himself to Shakespeare."

The Blue Mask came out ten years after Lou's first RCA album, in March 1982. He was forty now, looking back, as a reformed toper and born-again heterosexual, on an erratic solo career that had spanned the 1970s and left him exposed at the start of the 1980s to a new world with new sounds and new fashions. In Ronald Reagan's America, the public was listening to the catchy songs of Hall and Oates (who had supported Lou in concert only a few years earlier, but were now a much more popular act than he was) and British bands like the Human League. The packaging of the new album, reusing the Mick Rock iconic photograph from *Transformer*, printed in blue monochrome, emphasized the impression of mature review and self-examination, while reminding record buyers of his greatest commercial success. The British music press remained unimpressed, *Sounds* being particularly dismissive of "Women" and the "JFK adulation schtick." There were better reviews in the USA, notably in the *New York Times* and *Rolling Stone*, which described *The Blue Mask* as "the least ironic album Reed's ever made." A touch of irony may have improved "Heavenly Arms," during which Lou declared his love for Sylvia by singing histrionically, "Only a woman can love a man." Nevertheless, on balance, this was a strong album. It didn't sell. When Sean Fullan tried to recover his producer's royalties some years later, he was informed that the record still hadn't earned out. "Eric Kronfeld's pat answer was, 'The album never re-couped its costs.'" Part of the problem was that Lou's music was no longer fashionable. Apart from a brief period in the 1970s, between *Transformer* in 1972 and *Coney Island Baby* in 1976, he had in fact always operated outside of fashion, appealing to a discerning mi-nority of listeners of an artistic, literary bent. But his uneven output in recent years alienated many of those fans, as it turned off critics, while younger audiences were diverted by a wide variety of fresh new acts. Also, he didn't tour to promote his record. "Touring is just too hard on my body and my spirit," he said at the time. "I don't want to subject myself to that now." He had been drunk or stoned for virtually every tour he had done in his solo career. So he stayed home in the country, playing his Sharpshooter pinball machine and riding his motorbikes.

EIGHT MONTHS LATER HE returned to the RCA studio to make the *Legendary Hearts* album, which would be released in a sleeve adorned with pictures of himself in motorcycle gear. Fernando Saunders was back for duty. "I became the guy that he would look [to] for advice, and final decisions. I guess you could call it band leader, but it was a little bit more than that. . . . My thing was keep-ing the band and Lou in peace." Peacekeeping on *Legendary Hearts* mostly concerned intervening between Lou and Robert Quine, who clashed over the guitar sound on two songs in particular, "Rooftop Garden" and "Betrayed," culminating in an argument in the stu-dio on November 29–30, 1982. Afterwards, Quine was sidelined. "Quine is not part of the mix now," engineer Corky Stasiak noted in his diary on December 8. Lou had his guitar erased from "Be-trayed." When Quine received a tape of the album he was so angry that he smashed it up with a hammer.

One of the better new songs was "The Last Shot," in which Lou addressed the issue of quitting drugs, giving a graphic description of a junkie's life: shooting up at the kitchen sink, splashing blood over the dishes. These were vivid images that certainly didn't glamorize drug use. Opinions vary as to whether Lou had sworn off the booze as well. Fernando Saunders says that Lou had "pretty much" stopped drinking by 1982, but most reformed drinkers agree that total abstinence is the only solution. He seemed out of sorts in the studio as he struggled with the vocal on another song, "Home of the Brave," in which he referred to Lincoln Swados's suicide attempt. Corky wondered what the problem was. "'I ask him if he is nervous. [He] takes offense and calls *me* obsessive.' Oh boy!" says Corky, referring again to his studio diary. Despite such problems, the engineer reports that Lou was relatively stable during the making of *Legendary Hearts,* in comparison to the drug fiend he'd encountered on *Rock 'n' Roll Heart* and the drunkard who fell asleep during *Growing Up in Public.* But the result was lackluster. "I didn't think it was a strong album."

He returned tentatively to live work to promote *Legendary Hearts,* playing the Bottom Line during a snowstorm in March 1983 and doing a gig at Studio 54. In the summer he undertook a short Italian tour at the invitation of RCA Italy, who wanted a live album (*Live in Italy*). "He had set up what I would call a luxury tour. It was basically an Italian vacation for him and Sylvia," says Fred Maher, who played drums. A highlight was playing to fifteen thousand people at the Roman arena in Verona, the size of the venues demonstrating how popular Lou remained on the Continent. The set list included Velvet Underground songs such as "Sister Ray" and "Some Kinda Love" that he hadn't performed in years. The arrangements were faithful and muscular. "When Lou asked Quine to be in his band, Quine had a couple of stipulations, one of which was that Lou had to start playing guitar again, because Quine loved Lou's playing in the Velvets," explains Fred. "And I think the other thing Bob insisted on was that when we did live shows we did Velvet songs."

Although Fred Maher was close friends with Quine, he concedes that the guitarist had a difficult personality that didn't sit well with Lou at a time when he was trying to conquer his bad habits. "Lou couldn't handle Bob's dark personality, because that was a [time when] Lou was trying to be positive and sober and forward looking. I think Quine just didn't want to know about that. It wasn't that Quine wanted him to have a drink, or get high—nothing like that—I think it was just a personality clash. Lou was pissed at him because he was always so negative. Bob was just negative, negative, negative, negative. . . . You either learn to love it, or it pisses you off." A problem arose in the studio when Quine came up with a guitar riff that caught Lou's attention. "Lou says, 'Wow, what's that? That's great!'" recalls Fernando. "Quine shows Lou the guitar part. The next thing, we are in the studio and, in two seconds, Lou [is singing] 'I Love You, Suzanne.'" Unfortunately, Lou failed to give Quine a co-writing credit, which became an issue when the song was released as a single that enjoyed relative success. "I don't think Lou would on purpose take something . . . but to him the lyric is the song. He's not really thinking about the contribution of the musicians . . . I think honestly Lou thought he wrote 'Suzanne.' But Robert Quine wrote that guitar part," says Fernando, who identifies this as the principal reason for their growing estrangement. "Quine was talking about this all the time. 'He took my riff!'"

"I Love You, Suzanne" became the first track on the 1984 album, *New Sensations*, without any credit for Quine, who wasn't invited to play on the album, unlike his buddy and band mate Fred Maher, who says, "I felt very weird about that, and spoke to Bob about it, and he said, 'Go ahead, do it, I don't care. He's an asshole.'" *New Sensations* had the mainstream rock sound of the mid-1980s, embellished with synthesizers and horns. The title song was the highlight, with an engaging lyric in which Lou referred to his Christmas Eve arrest for buying speed (in 1973, not two years ago as he sang) as well as his new passion for motorbikes, describing a ride from

Blairstown to the Delaware Water Gap on his GPZ motorcycle. "I love that GPZ so much," he sang, "I could kiss her." It was the best line on the album, reminding listeners that he still had a nice sense of humor.

There were other autobiographical references. He wrote about his love of playing pinball and video games at Steve Epstein's Broadway Arcade in "Down at the Arcade," while his friendships with Martin Scorsese and actor-playwright Sam Shepard inspired "Doin' The Things That We Want To." Like most of the songs on *New Sensations,* the sentiment was upbeat, though Shepard, who had known Lou since the 1960s, says that his friend was dissatisfied with his work. "I sensed he was frustrated about not being able to nail what he [was working on]. He didn't have super confidence about what he was doing." Lou was right to be doubtful. Despite its strengths, *New Sensations,* like most of the albums he had been making since *Transformer,* fell well short of perfection. Some of the writing was flat. His voice didn't sound strong, and the arrangements were less than scintillating. Nevertheless, *New Sensations* reached fifty-six in the US charts, also charting in the UK. This was his best result since *Coney Island Baby.*

He toured extensively to promote the album. Robert Quine rejoined the band for the shows, but their relationship deteriorated on the road. Part of the problem was that Lou was playing more guitar now, leaving less for Quine to do, while the guitarist was brooding on the injustice of "I Love You, Suzanne," which he had to play live. He was also irritated by the ban on drink and drugs on tour (Lou had decreed that there would be no alcohol, even in the hotel minibars), mockingly referring to the *No* Sensations tour. By the time they reached Australia, in December 1984, Quine had had enough. "By the second concert in Australia I called my wife and said, 'I'm certainly never playing with him again, ever.'" Yet another successful musical partnership was thereby broken.

• • •

LOU'S PECUNIARY SITUATION IMPROVED in the mid-1980s. *New Sensations* had been a commercial success, and the world tour was lucrative. The eight-year lawsuit with Dennis Katz was finally resolved in 1984, after numerous claims and counter-claims. Around the same time, he started to receive North American royalties on his back catalogue, including "Walk on the Wild Side," after several years when this income went directly to Dunbar Music in accordance with the "termination agreement" he made with RCA in 1976. "For many years he didn't make money from 'Wild Side,'" says Fernando Saunders. "[Then] he finally got this huge amount of money."

IN ADDITION, THE VELVET Underground's business affairs were reorganized to the advantage of all the former members after John Cale told his lawyer that they weren't receiving any royalties. Part of the reason was that the first three Velvet Underground albums were no longer in print in the USA, amazingly, and what money had accrued from international sales—from Verve, MGM and Atlantic Records—was not flowing through to the band members. The Velvet Underground Partnership was formed to make it easier for Atlantic and Polygram (which had absorbed Verve and MGM) to distribute royalties on an equitable percentage to Lou, John, Sterling and Moe, as well as Nico and Doug Yule. "It's based on the albums they participated [in], and the sales at that time of those albums," explains Cale's lawyer Chris Whent, who set up the partnership and thereby came to represent the whole band. "It's relatively complicated. The principal beneficiaries were in fact Lou, Moe, Sterling and John, although John's percentage is a little less because he didn't participate in the latter albums."

In order to form the partnership, John and Lou had to talk to each other again, which was awkward. "Nobody actually came to blows, but the relationship between John and Lou was always a fraught one," admits Whent. "I was often a sort of buffer between them." When the agreement was finalized, Polygram released the money it had been holding and decided to reissue the first three Velvet Underground albums, plus an album of unreleased material. This new record, *VU,* including terrific archive songs such as "Foggy Notion" and "Temptation Inside Your Heart," which the band had recorded toward the end of their MGM contract, was a surprise success, charting on both sides of the Atlantic in 1985. A second album of unreleased material, the less essential *Another View,* followed a year later. Thus began a revival of interest in the band, and better days for its former members.

Unlike the others, Lou had been making money from the V U songs for years. "He had been collecting on publishing, and of course he rerecorded a number of these songs," explains Chris Whent. Now all the Velvets began to receive regular, six-monthly royalty checks. While this was not particularly significant to Lou, it was to John, Moe and Sterling. Since leaving the band, John had pursued a solo career to critical acclaim, and had enjoyed success as a producer, but he had not found a mainstream audience for his esoteric music. Like Lou, he had also struggled with drink and drug issues. At least he was still in the music business. After working for years as a teaching assistant at the University of Texas, in Austin, Sterling had become a tug-boat skipper in Houston. "Sterling almost right up to his death had to work on that tug boat to keep afloat. . . . He was really concerned about money," says Martha Morrison, confirming that the Velvet Underground income that started to flow through was modest, but welcome. "Nothing to change your life." Moe was now a single mother bringing up five children in the remote country town of Douglas, Georgia. She struggled to find work in rural Georgia initially, despite replying to almost every ad in the local newspaper.

She drew the line at one vacancy. "I said, 'What the hell's a chicken catcher?' You know those big chicken houses? When it's time to take [the chickens] to the slaughterhouse, they have to catch them—that's a chicken catcher." She eventually found work in administration at a Walmart distribution center, but the pay was dreadful. One year her Christmas bonus was five dollars. In such circumstances, Velvet Underground royalties were a lifeline.

After years when he had relatively little wealth, Lou was now quite well off, his earnings boosted by endorsement deals for American Express and Honda. When his landlord increased his rent at Christopher Street, Lou decided to move his city base. He bought an apartment in a high-rise on the Upper West Side, only the second property he had ever bought, after the house in Blairstown, which he still owned. There was some jealousy among his bohemian friends that he had finally attained a bourgeois level of comfort. "The apartment in New York, which seemed grand to me at the time, was actually just a two-bedroom on the Upper West Side, in a kind of newish building—beige wall-to-wall carpeting, not at all interesting, furniture you could get at Jensen-Lewis," says Tama Janowitz, author of the book *Slaves of New York*, who was dating Lou's friend from Factory days, Ronnie Cutrone, and was in contact with other Warholians. "He was getting enough to live better than the 'rest of us'— Ondine and René Ricard, people of his generation. . . . There was quite a lot of hostility towards him, because Lou was [now rich]."

One weekend, Tama and Ronnie went to stay with the Reeds in the country. Part of the reason for the invitation was that Lou and Ronnie were fellow members of Alcoholics Anonymous. They were in a group called Completely Sober, which catered to show-business types in New York. AA was fashionable in the 1980s. "In those days in New York everybody ended up in some meeting or another, whether AA or NA [Narcotics Anonymous]," says Tama. "It was as much social as anything else. 'Oh, I've been sober for three days. . . . Oops, I slipped!' 'Oh, you are going to do fine, call your sponsor. Go out for coffee.' Believe me, nobody was that bothered whether they were sober for three days, or three years." Tama says that, during the weekend in the country, Sylvia mentioned that she wanted to start a family with Lou, but he wasn't interested. This became an issue in the marriage. Tama didn't warm to Sylvia personally. "She seemed obsessed with him. . . . [It felt like] she just never shut up about him . . . like a groupie. 'My husband, my husband . . .' Nobody is responding. 'My husband, Lou Reed, my husband, *Lou Reed*.' Come on, lady, the rest of us exist, too! She had lovely, lovely qualities, but I don't give a damn that you are married to Lou Reed."

Another friend who received an invitation to Blairstown was the South American singer Rubén Blades. Lou and Rubén got to know each other when they lent their voices to the anti-apartheid song "Sun City" in 1985, protesting against the situation in South Africa, one of a series of 1980s projects whereby rock stars worked together on an issue. It was a rare example of Lou showing any interest in politics. "I think that Lou was always disgusted at the idea of becoming a tool of political positions. I don't think he was ever relaxed with that. So he would support something from his position, but not become involved," says Rubén, who was, by contrast, highly political, to the extent that he ultimately served in the Panamanian government. He believes that Lou saw apartheid as a special case. "It can be applied to people who are gay, or of a different religion. It was everything Lou despised." The men consolidated their friendship during an all-star 1986 charity tour to promote the causes of Amnesty International. Lou admired Rubén's voice ("He used to say that I had a radio voice"), they made each other laugh and they discovered that they could work together.

Rubén added vocals to Lou's 1986 album, *Mistrial*, the sound of which was partly determined by Fernando Saunders, who coproduced the record and used drum machines to give the songs a contemporary setting in the age of Madonna and Prince. "The *Mistrial* album was just to have fun. It was not to impress Lou Reed fans, or critics, or people like that. Sometimes you've got to do a detour to get to the next level," says Fernando, defending an album that, in the estimation of many people, was a contender for Lou's worst record. "It definitely was a more poppy, well-recorded, produced record. Lou Reed fans and critics wouldn't give it recognition, [but] it is the record that got him back in big theaters and the big tours. . . . It made new Lou Reed fans."

Although the sound was poppy, the lyrics addressed dark subjects that Lou had returned to repeatedly throughout his career, including street life and the abuse of women. "Don't Hurt a Woman" was a disturbing new take on this subject, a song in which Lou apologized in character for hitting his partner, explaining that he sometimes lost his temper, but would "try to remember/Don't hurt a woman." This sounded like an apology for domestic violence. The contemporary production of two other songs from *Mistrial*, released as singles, earned Lou regular airplay in the latter half of 1986, with the result that he played Radio City Music Hall in October. With a capacity audience of six thousand, this was the biggest show he had ever done in New York City. He was so proud that he invited his sister, parents and friends. Later that month he performed on *Saturday Night Live*. Bowie was at the party afterwards, which may well have been the first time they had been in the same room since Lou slapped him in 1979. "I had no idea they had a hostile relationship," says friend Steve Epstein, who was present and recalls a bad atmosphere between the stars. "They weren't talking to each other. They were looking at each other . . . I have never seen Lou that tense. It was very strange."

This brief spell of commercial success was capped when Lou recorded a cover of the Sam and Dave classic "Soul Man" with Sam Moore, for a movie soundtrack. The contrast between Moore's tuneful tenor and Lou's laconic vocals, with a hot band behind them, and a jokey MTV video to promote the song, made "Soul Man" a minor UK hit in January 1987.

The previous December, Lou and Sylvia had flown to Los Angeles to attend Rubén Blades's wedding. In the new year, Rubén and his wife, Lisa, accepted an invitation to stay with the Reeds in New Jersey. Snow was on the ground when they arrived in Blairstown. Lou took his friend out on his snowmobile to show him the property. In the evening they worked on songs in his music room. "I wanted to write a song about family, and we started to talk about family and we both started getting upset," says Rubén of one of these evening sessions. "I think we were touching areas that were sensitive, or so private, that they made us angry, and the conversation was getting very confrontational. This was in the night. We had been drinking also [further evidence that Lou had not quit alcohol]. When I saw him getting into this place where his eyes went somewhere else, his whole attitude was different, I could sense it and I thought, 'I'm gonna leave it alone.' I simply became quiet, and he would be quiet, and we both knew we are not going to talk about it anymore tonight. And I went to my bedroom, and left him there in that room with all his guitars and amplifiers."

Later in the night Rubén was woken by loud guitar music. "All of a sudden, at like three o'clock in the morning, I heard [Lou playing] this distorted, cranked-up-to-hell beautiful melody and I got up—I was lying in bed with my wife—I got up, grabbed my notebook, came and sat [on the steps] outside the [music] room. I didn't go in. And he played the same thing over and over, and there was an incredible intense anger, but also an intense love in the [music]. An electric guitar distorted to hell. . . . And it moved me so much that I sat down there and wrote the lyrics to 'The Calm Before the Storm' [co-written with Lou for Blades's 1988 album, *Nothing but the Truth*], about his mother and his father, and my mother and my father . . . I am moved when I remember that night . . . it was anger and love at the same time."

Tama Janowitz had a similarly intense conversation with Lou about family during her visit to Blairstown. "He would talk to me about going through the electro-shock stuff. [Soft voice]: 'My mom sent me in for electro-shock and then took care of me afterwards.' That was pretty weird. . . . It was obviously something seminal and crucial in his life." Here was the vulnerable, damaged Lewis Alan Reed, still struggling to make sense of his life as he moved into middle age.

XII

NEW INSPIRATION

• 1987-92 •

ANDY WARHOL'S DEATH WAS as sudden as it was unexpected. The artist was admitted to New York Hospital on Friday, February 20, 1987, to have his gallbladder removed. The operation was carried out successfully on Saturday, but he died of heart failure on Sunday, aged fifty-eight. The estate sued the hospital, claiming negligence (the case was settled out of court), while Lou was among those friends who expressed their surprise and anger in private. "He was livid that his friend could die in hospital [that way]," says Steve Epstein. "He was very upset for weeks."

The strength of Lou's reaction was surely due in part to the guilt he felt about his recent estrangement from his mentor. They had managed to stay friends, more or less, until Lou attempted to get clean and sober in the early 1980s. Although Andy never encouraged people to use drugs, Lou distanced himself at that time from everybody he associated with his old life, including Andy, whom he didn't invite to his wedding in 1980. Shortly afterwards, he and Sylvia were in a cab with the artist when Lou asked the driver to slow down. Andy remarked that he would never have said that in the old days, a harmless enough comment that offended his hyper-sensitive friend. "He was being evil, so I never spoke to him again," said Lou, who snubbed Andy at the MTV Awards in 1984. "Lou sat in my row but never even looked over. I don't understand Lou," Andy told Pat Hackett, who wrote up his diary entries. His office was trying to win commissions to produce pop videos at the time, and he felt that Lou should be giving them his business. "I hate Lou Reed more and more, I really do, because he's not giving us any video work," he complained to Pat on September 20, 1986, which was the last time Lou was mentioned in the diary. When Andy said he "hated" somebody he was not to be taken literally—Lou said Andy spoke like a child at such times—but the rift was real. "There were some things that, for personal kinds of reasons, I kept him at a discreet arm's length," he said after the artist's death, at which point he finally felt able to express his debt to Warhol.

Two thousand people attended the artist's memorial at St. Patrick's Cathedral on April Fool's Day, 1987. There were limousines around the block, and a crowd of photographers to capture the arrival of the likes of Richard Gere, Debbie Harry, David Hockney, Philip Johnson, Liza Minnelli, Yoko Ono and Tom Wolfe, plus survivors of the thrilling nightmare that had been the Silver Factory. Brigid Berlin, Gerard Malanga and Paul Morrissey were present, as were more peripheral figures such as Holly Woodlawn. As Lou looked around at the faces, he began to think of an elegiac new song, "Dime Store Mystery." It would form part of the first of a series of three albums recorded in the wake of Andy's death, all of which touched on loss.

After the service, mourners gathered at the Century Plaza Hotel, in a room specially decorated with silver walls and covers from Warhol's *Interview* magazine. Lou was talking with Billy Name, who was back in circulation after leaving the scene for several years, during which time he traveled across the country to live in San

Lou and Sylvia at the Century Plaza Hotel, following Andy Warhol's memorial.

Francisco, cutting himself off from his old friends at the Factory, when John Cale walked past. "I was standing there talking with Lou and I could see John coming by, and he was just going to walk past us and I grabbed him," recalls Billy.

"John, look, I have Lou here," he said. "You've got to say hello."

John stopped to shake hands. "And then they started talking to-gether, and then they started talking about Andy." Julian Schnabel joined the discussion, encouraging John and Lou to collaborate on a requiem for Warhol. Others agreed that this would be a fine idea. A few days later, they met to discuss what evolved, over the next two years, into *Songs for Drella*. Some people were surprised at this change in Lou's attitude to his old mentor. Tama Janowitz notes that she had tried to get Lou to have dinner with Andy in recent years, only to be rebuffed. "Then Andy dies and Lou is out there with *Songs for Drella,* capitalizing on his friendship with his be-loved Andy. 'F— you!'" she exclaims. "When Andy was alive, you wouldn't even come to dinner with him . . . I don't know why Lou hated Andy, but he hated Andy. He was nasty to him, [and] Drella was a completely derogatory name. . . . Nobody would ever say that in front of him. It was cruel." Nevertheless, *Songs for Drella* would be the best work John and Lou had done, together or apart, since the Velvet Underground.

MEANWHILE, LOU PURSUED HIS solo career, adding new members to his band, the composition of which changed frequently during the latter part of his career. One of the most notable and long-serving new recruits was Mike Rathke, a twenty-four-year-old music stu-dent whose surname, and possibly his rodent-like dentition, earned him the nickname Rat. He met Lou in 1984 when he was dating Sylvia's sister, Julie Morales, whom Mike married and divorced in the 1990s, making him briefly Lou's brother-in-law. He became his lead guitarist and right-hand man in the spring of 1987, a position he held for twenty-two years. Like other musicians who worked for Lou for a long time, Mike had a patient, pliant nature. "I've been accused of being a yes-man, and this and that, but that is hardly true," he says in his defense. "We had our share of rubs, but it al-ways turned the corner." Their first gig was a club show in Chicago in May 1987. Fernando Saunders had temporarily left Lou's employ following *Mistrial*, which Lou now considered a mistake, so a new bass player joined them in Chicago: a young Israeli named Yossi Fine whose playing was singled out for praise in a local review of the show. "That's not good, Yossi," Lou growled at breakfast the next day, showing him the newspaper. He didn't want anybody upstaging him.

The Chicago gig was a warm-up for a series of major European events, including stadium concerts supporting U2, now one of the biggest bands in the world. Playing Wembley Stadium in London in front of 72,000 people was a challenge for the less experienced band members. Mike Rathke was so nervous that he almost threw up. "None of us had played for such a big audience," says Yossi, who recalls that they were pelted with plastic bottles. Bono, who was a fan, told Lou that the fact people were throwing things at him meant that they actually *liked* him, insisting that he go back and perform "Walk on the Wild Side" as an encore. Bono had sung a snatch of the song as part of U2's Live Aid set at Wembley two years earlier, and it had gone down well with the audience, who sang along with the doo da doos. Lou took his advice, also agreeing to his suggestion that he simplify some of his songs for audiences who didn't know his catalogue well. "I'll give you an example," he explained. "Bono loves 'Street Hassle.' And after we did it one night he told me, 'You know, if you sang "sha-la-la-la" more, the audience would sing along with it. That's the fun part of the song; I love it when you sing that. Stay with it—they'll love it.' Next time out I did that—changed the words around and did the 'sha-la-la-la' more. Sure enough, they really liked it. Funnily enough, I liked it, too."

Bono's encouraging words aside, many of the people Lou was playing to on the U2 tour had little idea who he was. "The people who went to see U2 shows, very few came to see Lou Reed," notes Yossi. "He was not an MTV [star]. He was not that famous . . . it was all about U2 [and] Lou felt he was passé at that point." He certainly wasn't selling many records. When his second contract with RCA expired, it wasn't renewed. Then Lou fell out with his manager, Eric Kronfeld. "He didn't like Eric," says Yossi. "He called him 'super pig.'" Friends say the feeling was mutual. "Nobody could really put up with him for very long. Eric Kronfeld *hated* him," says Lou's old friend Allan Hyman, who had become a successful attorney and happened to know Kronfeld in business. "He was never satisfied with anybody who represented him. He was always sure that everybody was stealing money from him." After they parted company, Lou began to manage himself, with the help of his wife, who ran the family business from home initially. Unlike a normal manager, Sylvia Reed had the great advantage of always being available to him.

Luckily, he still had admirers in the industry, people like Bill Bentley, who ran publicity at Seymour Stein's Sire label, which now offered him a contract. "My recollection is that Bill Bentley had talked Seymour into it. Bill really wanted him badly, and Seymour went along with it. Now Seymour may also have been excited, but Bill was really behind it," says Howie Klein, then general manager of Sire, a boutique label that operated under the Warner Brothers umbrella. Lou wasn't an expensive signing for the company, which had an impressive roster of artists, including Madonna and Talking Heads. He was paid modest advances in accordance with his sales. "It costs something else," chuckles Howie, who says that Lou was considered "a very difficult artist . . . he was never difficult with me all the time I knew him. He was a nice, sweet, wonderful guy, and there was not so much as a ripple, but everyone I knew, journalists and people in the industry, said, 'He's difficult.' That was the word people used about Lou Reed, and I never experienced it—ever." This was because Howie left Lou to his own devices, starting with his first Sire album.

As with *The Blue Mask*, Lou spent a lot of time preparing for *New York*, writing and rewriting the lyrics on his latest toy, a personal computer (and flying into a panic one day when he thought he'd accidentally erased everything). Despite the album title, and the predominantly metropolitan concerns of the songs, much of the preparation was done at his country home. Mike and Yossi came out to Blairstown to work on the arrangements, which proved to be a grind. "He would play the same two chords from ten o'clock in the morning till eight o'clock in the evening, E and A, E and A," sighs Yossi. "I did not have that type of patience after a while." When Yossi encouraged Lou to try something new, suggesting that he play bass on the record in the style of the hip heavy-metal band Metallica, Lou laid down the law. "Yossi, you are going to play with whatever bass I tell you to play, and whatever amp I tell you to work on," Lou lectured. "You think rock 'n' roll is Metallica, but let me tell you something—Metallica is shit." Yossi was reminded of this when Lou recorded with Metallica in 2011.

In the short time he had been in the band, Yossi had come to see that Lou had a pattern of behavior with employees. After a honeymoon period, during which he was super friendly, he became increasingly controlling, before taking offense and turning nasty. A precious few, such as Rat and Fernando, were able to ride his moods for a time, but Lou fell out with almost everybody in the end. "The thing about Lou was that at [a certain] point Lou did not like one person in particular. Every time it was somebody else's turn," says Yossi. "One time it was his [guitar] tech, another time it was the sound guy. He would pick someone. He always had an enemy in mind." When Yossi started to feel that he was next on Lou's shit list he became too depressed to work. "He called me, 'Why aren't you at rehearsal?' I just couldn't tell him [so I said], 'Look, man, I'm sick, I can't.' It never happened to me [before] or since. That's completely out of my character. But my body told me, this is not the right thing for you to do. I never went back. He was like, 'Well, you're going to regret it.' Whatever. I listened to my body. He could drain your energy."

So devalued was Lou's currency by 1988, as an unfashionable and erratic artist who was difficult to work with, that he struggled to find a producer for *New York*. Lou eventually asked his drummer Fred Maher for advice. "I started saying the usual names, the big names of that time . . . and absolutely nobody was interested in working with him," says Fred, who suggested that he might produce the record himself.

"What the fuck do you know about recording guitars? All you know is synth-pop crap," Lou said rudely, referring to the fact that Fred had recently enjoyed transatlantic success as a member of Scritti Politti.

Fred persuaded Lou to let him record one song as a test. They chose "Romeo Had Juliette," which, like several of his new songs, highlighted social problems in New York. Lou was particularly pleased with the opening lines:

Caught between the twisted stars the plotted lines the
     faulty map
That brought Columbus to New York . . .

While there was poetry in these images, there was also poetic license; Columbus never went near what is now New York. Nevertheless, the words served as a fitting introduction to an album about the city. Taking inspiration from Leonard Cohen's then recent album *I'm Your Man*, Fred recorded the song with Lou's vocal to the fore and persuaded him to speak the lyrics. "That's the key for Lou to be Lou. Lou doesn't really sing. I had been through two recording sessions with him—*Legendary Hearts* and *New Sensations*—when the producers and everybody was [saying], 'Lou, you've got to sing, man. Sing that song.' On those records he wasn't being Lou." In his youth, Lou had more voice. "There are Velvets tracks where he is singing, but some vocalists completely lose that voice as they get older, as I believe Lou did. Lou lost it. He could not sing like he could in the Velvets. That voice had gone. . . . So when we did 'Romeo Had Juliette' he went to the speaking voice." Lou was delighted with the result. "I sound like Lou Reed for the first time in years," he said, giving Fred the go-ahead to produce the whole album.

"Romeo Had Juliette" came easily. "He pumped that out like he was taking dictation," says Mike Rathke. In contrast, he labored over other tracks, including "Dirty Boulevard," though the result was ultimately just as successful. The lyrics told the story of an immigrant to New York in mordant language, referring to the "Statue of Bigotry," a neat pun, and an exploitative landlord who laughed until he wet himself at the rents he was able to charge. The authentic Lou Reed was heard in these epigrammatic lines. It had been a long time since he had sounded so good. "He was so happy to be in the studio. And his wit was sharp—a Lou that I had previously not known," says Fred, noting that Lou was also relaxed enough to joke about his alcoholism, exclaiming, "Hmmm, vodka!" as he glugged from a bottle of mineral water. When he came to record "Dirty Boulevard," Lou invited another famous New Yorker to add backing vocals. Dion DiMucci had been a star when Lou was a student, with hits like "The Wanderer." Both were reformed drug users, and survivors in a fickle industry. But it was the Big Apple that they had in common above all else. "New York is different," says Dion, who had known Lou since they met backstage at the Bottom Line in the 1970s. "By osmosis, you download it into your spirit. That was his experience [too]. He wasn't talking about roses and lilies. He was talking about the streets and garbage cans and rooftops and what was happening in the Village. The subculture."

There was one bucolic song, "Last Great American Whale," an attack on thoughtless people who dumped refuse on Lou's property in New Jersey. As the Reagan presidency passed to his vice president, George H. W. Bush, from a liberal, anti-Republican point of view, it was also one of a number of songs with an overt political dimension, which was a departure for Lou. Some of these songs worked better than others. Topical references to the controversial Austrian president, Kurt Waldheim ("Good Evening Mr. Waldheim"), and other prominent public figures on the right dated as quickly as their names fell out of the headlines. "Hold On," inspired by civil disturbances in New York in the summer of 1988, also soon lost its relevance. Far better was "Halloween Parade," in which Lou observed the annual Halloween Parade in Greenwich Village and reflected on friends who had disappeared from the city's gay scene, some of whom had died of AIDS. Here was a timely and meaningful song about a topic of lasting significance:

In the back of my mind I was afraid it might be true
In the back of my mind I was afraid that they meant you

Lou probably had several individuals in mind when he sang these tender words. Was Rachel among them? One day around this time, Jeffrey Ross, who'd played guitar in the band in the 1970s, heard someone call his name and turned around. "It's Rachel, who looks pretty much the same except very gaunt . . . a very gaunt transvestite, and embarrassingly she told me she was [living] under the [West Side] Highway and homeless at the time. We chatted for a minute. We had a hug. I headed off, being very sad." Others who also saw Rachel in a poor state on the streets believe that he died shortly thereafter. He would have been in his early forties, at most. Like so much about his life, it is impossible to be sure.

Nico was another former lover who came to a bad end at this time. Lou said nothing about her passing in public, as he said nothing about Rachel, though he undoubtedly knew about their fates. For years, Nico had been a heroin addict, playing clubs to support her habit, a shadow of her once-glamorous self, and beyond the pale as far as fashionable rock society was concerned (being as snobbish as any sort of high society). Recently, she had tried to conquer her habit with methadone. Nico was on vacation in Ibiza in July 1988 when, on a blazing-hot day, she decided to cycle into town to buy marijuana. She was found by a passing taxi driver slumped by the side of the road, dying the following day in a local hospital of a cerebral hemorrhage, aged forty-nine.

It was the death of Andy Warhol, above all, that remained the biggest loss for Lou. Andy had been Lou's second and most influential mentor, a towering figure in his career whose reputation overshadowed his own and grew posthumously. As touched upon, he was the inspiration for "Dime Store Mystery," the last song on *New York*, in which Lou used alliteration and assonance to excellent effect. This was a carefully crafted work of poetry, showing Lou not only to have found new inspiration but striving to express something meaningful, rather than just being out to shock, as he had been for too long.

I was sitting drumming, thinking, thumping, pondering
The mysteries of life
Outside the city shrieking screaming whispering
The mysteries of life.
There's a funeral tomorrow at St. Patrick's
The bells will ring for you . . .

Moreover, Andy's death seemed to inspire Lou to work harder, after years of uneven and often disappointing releases, as the artist had always urged him to. The *New York* album was the beginning of a sustained resurgence in his songwriting. Critics noted the difference and greeted *New York* with warm reviews in January 1989. Writing in the *Times*, Bryan Appleyard described the record as "a complete return to form." There was some criticism. "It reads worse than it sounds," wrote Tom Carson in the *Village Voice*, highlighting the weaker lyrics. While not perfect, *New York* was a great deal better than one had come to expect from Lou, who was rewarded with his first *Rolling Stone* cover. He admitted in the interview to making a mess of much of his solo career. "Most of the major mistakes were in public, and I put them on record to boot." He also acknowledged that he was a temperamental artist, who had been "really difficult in the past," describing himself as a cult figure who didn't sell many records. But this time he got lucky. *New York* sold better than any of his albums since *Sally Can't Dance,* reaching number fourteen in the UK charts, forty in the US. Lou's champion at Sire, Bill Bentley, got a gold disc to hang on his wall.

One of the many interesting aspects of the record was that Moe Tucker, who had recently started to record and tour on a small scale in her own right, played percussion on two tracks. John Cale was also invited to participate. "I don't know what he was going to play—probably viola," says Fred Maher, who, in addition to producing the album, played drums on all the songs save those that Moe was on. "So Lou had reached out to Cale, and Cale had said yes. Cale called the studio one day, asked for me, I said, 'Hi, John, it's nice to meet you on the phone. . . . We are thinking about this date, and we've got Moe coming in on so and so date.' He's like, 'What? Is this some kind of fucking Velvet Underground reunion?' 'I . . . er . . . no. I don't know.' Apparently, that pissed him off. So he never came in, and he never did play on the record, which was unfortunate. But I guess Lou never told him Moe was playing on the record." Here was an insight into how touchy Lou and John still were around each other, even at a time when they were collaborating on *Songs for Drella.* "They didn't see eye to eye all the time, but God, when they started playing together it was amazing," says Mike Rathke, who assisted Lou during *Drella* (and, like many friends interviewed for this book, continued to talk about him in the present tense in the months after he died). "It's funny that they don't get along, because they understand each other on this [musical] level. They understand, they can anticipate, they can react in ways most musicians can't. . . . You'd think they'd be really good friends. But there's the other side of music—the business." And Lou had to be the boss. "He wants to be in control. For sure. Period. Last word."

Lou and John first performed their requiem as a duo at the Brooklyn Academy of Music (BAM) over four nights in the winter of 1989, with images from Andy's career projected on to a screen behind them. A youthful-looking John sat at a grand piano. Wearing hexagonal spectacles, which lent him the appearance of "an intimidatingly intelligent monkey," as the music writer Mat Snow observed nicely, Lou sat opposite at a music stand, reading his lyrics as he played electric guitar, stumbling over his words at first, which made John frown. They began with "Small Town," the first of fourteen songs that told Andy's story in sequence, from his childhood in Pittsburgh, from the artist's point of view. The result was a sublime biography in words and music. If *New York* was Lou's finest album since *Transformer, Songs for Drella* was his best work since the Velvet Underground, and it is surely no coincidence that he had to collaborate with Cale to reach that standard again. He was usually at his best when he worked with a gifted partner. As ever, Lou wrote the lyrics, but he allowed Cale to be part of the editing process, which evidently made a big difference. "For him to let me be a part of going through all the lyrics and correcting was very difficult," Cale said. "We sat there and bandied them around. It's difficult for him to collaborate on that level. It's difficult for him to collaborate—period—and he admits it."

The highlight of the requiem was "A Dream," an eerie prose elegy written by Lou and narrated by John that evoked Andy's dream thoughts toward the end of his life. It was a melancholy piece, giving insight into what had been a lonely private life. Billy Name, who was mentioned in the song, thought it "a masterpiece, just terrific." There were also critical references to John and Lou, based on Andy's recently published and much publicized diaries. To Lou's credit, he included Andy's complaints about how he had snubbed him, and his final comment about why he hated him. It was as if Warhol himself were speaking.

Moe Tucker joined John and Lou onstage at BAM on their last night for an encore of "Pale Blue Eyes," capping one of the triumphs of Lou's career. Yet he and John were still not reconciled. "John loved Lou, even in the worst of times, because of what they went through together, and he respected his talent, of course. And I'm sure that Lou had great feeling for John. They just could not get along," says Moe. "'Let's do *Drella!*' The next thing you know they wanted to kill each other."

Sire's recording of *Songs for Drella* was a masterwork, one of the half-dozen or so essential albums of Lou's career. Unfortunately, that didn't translate into sales. The album sold respectably in the United Kingdom but didn't chart in the USA. It was perhaps too esoteric for the mainstream American public. "It wasn't a big album," says Howie Klein. "It didn't matter to me. It mattered because I wanted Lou to be happy and successful. That album was a masterpiece. I loved [it] so much. On a personal level, I loved listening to it. As a record company executive, I loved the fact that my label put out this really wonderful piece of art. It wasn't a failure. It didn't lose money, but it didn't sell the numbers in the United States that we needed for it to be a big runaway hit. So there were people who looked at it as a waste of time, but I didn't care. I loved it."

EACH YEAR, LOU SPENT part of the summer working in Europe, where momentous changes were taking place as the Soviet Union crumbled and its client states overturned their tyrannical leaders. Poland was first to break free, in 1989. Then the Berlin Wall fell in November 1989, and the Romanian dictator Ceauşescu was toppled in December. In what was termed the Velvet Revolution, because it was peaceful (not after the Velvet Underground, as is sometimes claimed by fans of the band), totalitarian rule was also overthrown in Czechoslovakia, where the playwright and activist Vaclav Havel, a founder member of Charter 77, became president. Havel was an admirer of Lou's music. On a visit to New York in the 1960s, he bought *White Light/White Heat* and smuggled it back into Czechoslovakia, where Western pop music was copied and distributed illicitly. In April 1990, as the democratically elected president of the free Czech and Slovak Federal Republic, Havel agreed to meet Lou. It was the start of a remarkable new friendship.

The initial meeting at Prague Castle was brief. The president was a busy man, but he wanted to tell Lou how important his music had been to himself and his dissident friends in the Soviet era. He explained that when a Czech band, the Plastic People of the Universe, played music in the style of the Velvet Underground in the 1970s, the musicians were arrested. Havel helped rally international support to free them. "And it seemed to us that this community that originated in this way shouldn't just dissolve after this but should go on in some more stable form, and that's how the Charter 77 human rights movement originated," he explained. He asked Lou if he would play for his friends that evening in a local club. Lou was initially reluctant, saying he was "a very private person" and that playing at short notice would make him nervous. But he couldn't refuse a head of state, moreover a man of such charm and integrity.

That evening he got onstage with veterans of the Plastic People of the Universe to perform Velvet Underground songs. "Any song I called they knew. It was as if Moe, John and Sterl were right there behind me, and it was a glorious feeling." "Did you enjoy yourself?" the president asked afterwards. Lou said he had. "[Havel] then introduced me to an astonishing array of people, all dissidents, all of whom had been jailed. Some had been jailed for playing my music," Lou reported in an article he wrote about his Czech adventure, beginning to realize that the songs he had created in semi-obscurity in the 1960s had affected people in far-flung places he didn't know, and in circumstances he had never imagined. Finally, Havel gave him a gift. "These are your lyrics, hand-printed and translated into Czechoslovakian," he explained, handing him a book inscribed with tiny handwriting. "There are only two hundred of them. They were very dangerous to have. People went to jail, and now you have one." It was a humbling experience.

Two months later, Lou was back in Europe for the Andy Warhol Exposition, a celebration of the artist's life and work staged by the Cartier Foundation at Jouy-en-Josas, near Paris. Cartier had flown some of Andy's closest associates over from the USA for the event, including Lou and John Cale, who had agreed to perform together. Moe and Sterling were also present. All four former Velvets attended a luncheon on June 15, 1990, with family and friends, everybody dressed up for what was a rare and special occasion. It was an enjoyable lunch, with issues. Sterling hadn't been on speaking terms with Lou for years. "Sterling had this bug up his ass that Lou was a crook. He kept saying, 'I don't want to see Lou, he's a crook. He took my money from the records and he never gave me anything,'" says Billy Name, who acted as mediator between the men. Still, tensions remained. When the Velvets posed for a group photo, Moe sat between Lou and Sterling to keep the peace. "It was uncomfortable," she says. The band's lawyer, Chris Whent, also present, identifies another raw issue, dating back to 1968: "Sterling and Moe always bore with them the [guilt] that when Lou said, 'Either John goes or I go,' they went with Lou. There was always a sense of betrayal there."

That afternoon, John and Lou performed a short set of *Drella* songs on an open-air stage, Lou wearing black leather and shades. He had recently let his hair grow long at the back in the unfortunate mullet style. After playing five songs to a small but appreciative audience, he and John exchanged a glance, and John went backstage to ask Moe if she had her drum mallets ready, and Sterling to strap on a guitar. That was when the others knew for sure that they were all going to play together again. Lou smoked a cigarette while he waited, telling the audience laconically that they had "a little surprise."

Playing together for the first time in twenty-two years, the classic lineup of the band gave a rusty rendition of "Heroin" in Jouy-en-Josas.

Moe and Sterling were evidently nervous, but they all enjoyed themselves. "It was so nice to look over and see them," says Moe. Martha was astonished to behold her husband onstage with Lou again. "I had to sit down, I was so surprised." Afterwards, Sterling seemed to forget his animosity toward Lou, and put an arm around his old band mate. Suddenly everybody relaxed. The Velvets spent the next few days together in Paris, seeing the sights and going out for dinner. "Sylvia said to me, 'I've never seen Lou in such a great mood.' I said, 'I have to say the same [about Sterling],'" says Martha. "Our men had made up and dropped that negativ[ity], so everybody was relieved."

The Cartier event seemed to bode well for further collaborations, and indeed John and Lou performed *Songs for Drella* in Tokyo that summer. Then Lou refused to tour with the show. "The two of us could have done a world tour and made a decent amount of money, but no," John complained. "Because of Lou, we never performed *Drella* again."

Lou had his own career to consider, and a new project. In recent years, he had become friendly with Doc Pomus, who wrote the lyrics for many classic songs, including "Save the Last Dance for Me" and "Lonely Avenue," as well as twenty numbers recorded by Elvis Presley. Crippled by polio, using crutches and later a wheelchair to get around, Doc was a popular figure on the New York music scene until his death from lung cancer in March 1991. Lou was a fan. "I grew up listening to so many songs written by Doc Pomus, so it was a pleasure to know him. He was a great spirit," he explained in a 1998 television documentary, during which he became uncharacteristically emotional. "Doc died from cancer. I was interested in some kind of magic, some kind of transcendence, that would take one away from everything. And I wrote [the album] *Magic and Loss* because there had been loss to temper any magic, and . . . there didn't seem to be any . . ." Lou struggled to express and compose himself ". . . anything that I knew of that helped you with this particular subject matter."

The first song written for the album was "What's Good." As he progressed with his meditation on death, he drew inspiration not only from the loss of Doc but other friends, too. *Magic and Loss* would be dedicated "to Doc and especially to Rita." Lou didn't specify who Rita was, though it was assumed that he was referring to his old Factory buddy Kenneth Rapp, known as Rotten Rita, who had died shortly before. He may also have been thinking of his New Jersey neighbors Bob and Rita Teel. Bob died of cancer in 1987, and Lou remained friendly with his widow, who recalls him saying that he had written a song about her. "He [Lou] was a very soft-hearted man, but because of the image he had, people didn't know it," says Rita, noting that Lou offered her children his snowmobile after Bob died. "Lou was always good to us."

Lou had another friend in mind when he wrote "Harry's Circumcision," in which the character attempts suicide. This was inspired by the death of his college roommate Lincoln Swados, whose emaciated body was found in the Lower East Side trash nest he called home in 1989. The autopsy revealed that he had multiple health issues, including lung cancer. In the years before he died, Lincoln had sung his heart out on street corners, rolling himself about on a skateboard, becoming one of New York's familiar, if slightly alarming, street people. The spirits of Andy, Nico and Rachel also seemed to flit between the tombstone tracks.

Magic and Loss was the third of what can be seen as a trio of albums recorded after Warhol's death, united by the fact that the writing was of higher quality than Lou had achieved in years, and the fact that loss was a running theme. While death has always been one of the principal subjects of classical music, it is seldom addressed with much seriousness in popular music, which has traditionally been the domain of the young. By middle age, however, the end of life starts to be as compelling as the beginning, and Lou, forty-nine years old when he made *Magic and Loss*, went deep into the subject, even describing a cremation in "Gassed and Stoked." "He was an amazing lyricist [about] subjects no one else wanted to touch," observes Rob Wasserman, who played upright bass on *Magic and Loss* and *New York* and toured with Lou extensively in latter years. As with *New York* and *Songs for Drella*, this was an ambitious work, realized with a clarity of thought that would have been beyond Lou when he was abusing drink and drugs. "Giving up those things has made it possible to do works of larger scope. Because my concentration now lasts for more than a minute," he said. "Also, I used to have to rely on my handwriting and I couldn't read what I wrote." He now referred to the old days as "when I was a lunatic."

On tour, he performed *Magic and Loss* in its entirety in the first part of his show: fourteen consecutive songs about death, none familiar to the audience. He had likewise insisted in the liner notes to *New York* that the album should be listened to straight through in one sitting, "as though it were a book or a movie." This asked a lot of audiences with only a casual interest in his music, and put some people off. "[*Magic and Loss*] is probably the best concept album, detailing reactions to the suffering and death of friends afflicted by terminal illness, released so far this year," Ben Thompson wrote in the *Independent on Sunday*, reviewing a show in Birmingham in March 1992. "But live entertainment it is not." Lou glared at audience members who called out requests for more familiar songs in concerts, telling them to get a refund if they didn't like it, though he rewarded those who stayed with some of his classics in the second half of the evening.

Lou was never the most engaging or gracious performer, and he got even grumpier as he got older, yet he retained a loyal following. "He had his fans who would love anything he did. If he farted into a paper bag they would go, 'It's the most brilliant thing ever!' He didn't particularly like that kind of person," says Struan Oglanby, a Canadian guitar technician who started to work for Lou on the *Magic and Loss* tour and got to know him well. "It was an odd thing. He wanted attention, but he didn't want the kind of people who gave

him that attention." Struan bonded with his boss over a mutual interest in technology. "At the heart of everything, Lou loves his gear,"
says Struan, referring to what had become a full-blown obsession
with guitars, microphones and recording techniques. One of Lou's
frustrations was that audiences didn't appreciate the nuances of
sound that he heard. "Usually, what he wanted to think about was
his gear, and his guitar sound. We would spend hours upon hours
doing the most minute tests of microphones and amps and things
. . . he would play like just an A chord [until six in the morning], so
it would be a test. There was a lot of pseudo-science going on with
these tests. And so he would play the same A chord and we would
have the microphone three inches from the [guitar], and have a pro-
tractor out to measure the distance and angle, and we would keep
charts on these things. . . . There's a fine line between fascination
and obsession and a disorder."

Sylvia had a lot to put up with, living with such a demanding
man, and twelve years into the marriage Lou was no longer as lovey-
dovey as he had been with his second wife, who now had the additional burden of managing his career. "There was always bickering,
lots and lots of bickering," comments Struan. "She was playing a
role which she wasn't necessarily either suited for, or trained for,
and he would put expectations on her that somebody much more
experienced [would be used to], and she dealt with him the best
she could. I don't know if she wanted to be in that position. I know
she enjoyed the perks of that position. I know that she loved being
associated with him. I think she did it for that. . . . There was some
shouting that went on, but it was more her having enough of it, and
being rubbed raw. And there were pleasant times, too. She did a lot
of sitting back, letting him be him."

Was Lou done with his gay life in this second marriage (or third,
if one counts Rachel)? Not according to the elderly jazz singer Little
Jimmy Scott, whose womanly contralto and diminutive size was
caused by a hormone deficiency. Scott enjoyed a successful record-

ing career in the 1940s and '50s before falling into obscurity, only to have his career revived in old age partly thanks to Lou, who heard him sing at Doc Pomus's funeral and invited him to add backing vocals to *Magic and Loss*, before joining him on tour as a guest artist. All went well until March 1992, when Lou and Jimmy had an altercation backstage in Europe.

Jimmy claimed Lou tried to kiss him. "Jimmy got pissed off and put him in a headlock," says his wife. "I don't know if Lou thought Jimmy was bisexual like himself, but he was not. Jimmy never was. He was just small in build, and whatever. Jimmy got angry. 'I don't go that way—back off.'" As Jeanie Scott related the story in 2014, Jimmy added corroboration from his deathbed (he died a few weeks later). He may have misconstrued Lou's attempt to be friendly. Either that, or one has to believe that Lou really did fancy this little old man.

It may have been this odd incident that caused Lou to hire a bodyguard, his first since the early 1970s. He hadn't really been successful enough, or famous enough, in the intervening years to warrant one. Joe Doyle, a genial former New York City cop, joined the *Magic and Loss* tour in Denver in May 1992. Apart from preventing the likes of Jimmy Scott from strangling Lou, part of the job was saving Lou from himself. "I wasn't hired for that. I made it part of my job." Such a situation occurred during that summer's festival season.

In June, Lou played Glastonbury in England. The following month, he appeared at the Leysin festival in Switzerland. There was a party one night in the Swiss hotel bar with members of his road crew performing his songs for fun. "We did some Lou covers [including] 'Vicious,'" says Struan Oglanby, who was part of the bar band. Lou was watching, evidently enjoying himself. "Then I noticed that he had a drink in front of him. Oh shit! Who gave him that?" The bodyguard Joe Doyle also saw the bottle, and took it away. "He didn't need people taking a picture with that in his hand, with everybody knowing that he was trying to stay clean." Struan says Lou drank enough to wake up the next day with a hangover. After this lapse, he says that Lou "didn't drink much at all," but there were "times he had a few drinks and was tipsy." Doyle's reaction indicates that such lapses were covered up as much as possible, preserving the image of Lou as a reformed boozer, for the sake of his pride as much as anything, having declared himself clean and sober, rather than somebody who still struggled with sobriety.

A couple of drinks actually seemed to improve his mood. "It never brought out his meanness; it was the opposite. He seemed to be a jolly [drinker]," says Struan, which was also the impression of Sire executive Howie Klein. "I remember one night we were in New York, there was snow on the ground, it was freezing, way after midnight, we were walking around, and he was high on something—I don't know if he was drunk or what it was," says Howie. "I found that it was great, because it totally loosened [Lou] up, to the point that he went into some of his deepest, innermost thoughts that he had never discussed with me before. . . . That is the only time I recall him being [high]."

Lou was among the stars who appeared at a concert at Madison Square Garden in New York in October 1992 to celebrate Bob Dylan's first thirty years in the music business. He performed an obscure song from the end of Dylan's born-again phase, "Foot of Pride," which proved a highlight. His very presence at the event was surprising, considering the fact that he often made jealous, disparaging comments about Dylan in private. "What the fuck has Bob Dylan ever done that I haven't done?" he asked Struan one day. "[I] knew him well enough [by then] to let him carry on, rather than say, 'Here's a long list of things that Bob Dylan has done that you haven't done.' That would have been the wrong approach. He couldn't stand [Dylan]. Dylan's best album wasn't a Bowie album." It was impolitic at this stage to mention that Bowie had played any part in Lou's career.

Back in Europe the following month, Lou met the most significant person in the last quarter of his life. Born into a religious, wealthy family in Chicago in June 1947, making her five years Lou's junior, Laurie Anderson was an androgynous little woman with short, spiky hair and the mischievous smile of a naughty schoolboy. Interested in art and music from a young age, she played violin well enough to perform with the Chicago Youth Symphony Orchestra and, in 1965, traveled to Europe with Talented Teens USA. The following year, she moved to New York, where she became part of the downtown art scene, forming friendships with some of the most notable composers of the day, before emerging in her own right as one of the foremost performance artists of the 1970s, combining observational writing, minimalist music (she played keyboards and electric violin) and cutting-edge lighting effects. Her speciality was the semi-autobiographical shaggy-dog story, usually surreal and unsettling, and often very funny, delivered in a confidential, wry tone of voice. Her sense of humor saved her from seeming pretentious, unlike some of her contemporaries, all of whom she eclipsed in terms of fame when her recording "O Superman (For Massenet)" became a surprise European hit in 1981. The robotic "ha-ha-ha-ha" backing track had a catchy quality not unlike the "doo da doos" in "Walk on the Wild Side." "You know, people come up to me and go 'doo da doo, doo da doo,'" Lou once remarked, "and they come up to her and go 'ha-ha-ha-ha.'"

"I met Lou in Munich," Laurie recalled in an article she wrote for *Rolling Stone* after his death. "It was 1992, and we were both playing in John Zorn's Kristallnacht festival commemorating the Night of Broken Glass in 1938, which marked the beginning of the Holocaust." Lou asked her to perform with his band. He complimented her warmly afterwards, and she decided that she liked him. The feeling was mutual. Lou suggested they meet up again when they got back to New York, where they both lived and worked, Laurie in a magnificent downtown loft. They had a lot in common. As well as a love for the city, they were both outsiders with a strong intellect and a leaning toward the avant-garde, serious artists who'd had one flukey hit for which they were best known, both cigarette smokers and "gear heads" with a fascination for equipment, while Laurie's boyish looks appealed to bisexual Lou. This didn't bode well for his marriage.

XIII

RETURN TO THE VELVET UNDERGROUND

• 1992–96 •

HE FOUR ORIGINAL MEMBERS of the Velvet Underground had a band meeting at the Paramount Hotel in New York at the end of 1992 to discuss a box set of their music, *Peel Slowly and See*, which was eventually released in 1995. During lunch, they talked about working together again. The Cartier event had been enjoyable, so why not play more shows on a bigger scale and make some money? For once, everybody seemed to think that this was a good idea. In the run-up to Christmas, they jammed together at Big Mike's rehearsal space, and Lou joined John and Sterling onstage at New York University to see if they could still tolerate each other in concert. Having decided that they could, the decision was made to re-form for a European tour in the summer of 1993, choosing to tour Europe rather than the United States because 80 percent of their record sales were in Europe.

John Cale appeared with Sterling on the *Tonight Show* in January, telling Jay Leno that the Velvets were getting back together for the money, though he later downplayed the pecuniary incentive, emphasizing instead their artistic aims. John said that he wanted the Velvets to make new music, "[to] demonstrate that whatever the four of us did before was not immured in 1969." Time was set aside for him and Lou to write together with a view to recording a new Velvet Underground studio album, as well as performing new songs in concert. Not everybody shared Cale's enthusiasm for new material. Moe simply wanted to play the old songs for their fans, as authentically as possible, and she was honest enough to admit that the money was important. It meant that she might be able to buy a new car, or even her first home, after a lifetime of renting.

The money increased when U2—whose members held the Velvets in high regard—invited the band to support them on their summer tour of Europe. While the money meant less to Lou than the others, he was not so rich that it didn't matter. *New York* had been a hit, but his last two albums sold poorly, and a successful reunion tour might boost his career. He also wanted to help Moe, who had always been his best friend in the band. Lou was intrigued by the quiet life she led in Georgia. "So does everybody in town know who you are?" he asked when they met in New York.

"Are you kidding me? They never heard of the Velvet Underground."

Lou was only prepared to work with the others again on his terms. Importantly, Sylvia Reed was put in charge of the tour, ensuring that "my artist," as she called her husband during meetings, received prima donna treatment. Sylvia became "the buffer" between Lou and John and Sterling, says Moe, which was important "because he could piss people off." Little thanks Sylvia got. "If the slightest thing went wrong, he would be yelling at her." To make sure that Lou had everything his way, his guitar technician, Struan Oglanby, was appointed stage manager, while his brother-in-law Mike Rathke was tasked with mixing and producing recordings of the shows for a live album, which would be released by Lou's record company. "I was Lou's guy, so I didn't really develop any closeness with anybody else," admits Sire boss Howie Klein.

Lou conducted band rehearsals in New York like an impatient teacher dealing with slow children. He was playing custom-built headless guitars these days—a guitar lacking a traditional head-stock. Having heard that the ideal material for a guitar neck was Hawaiian koa wood, he'd persuaded a New York guitar maker to handcraft his guitar necks in this obscure material. "He had a way—even though he wasn't a significant volume purchaser, and wasn't really selling that many records—of convincing people that he was their prime client and they had to pay lots and lots of attention to him, and field all his calls, no matter what time of night, and how preposterous the idea was," notes Struan. "So he made poor Ned [Steinberger] find a way to bond koa wood to this carbon compos-ite [guitar neck], which required extensive testing of glues; it was a nightmare to go through. He used these things, and then he'd ditch them a couple of months later because he didn't like them, and go on to the next thing. That was very much what he did with people . . . he had all these guitars and he dropped them and never used them again."

Lou played his headless guitars through his Big Rig, a special-effects box as tall as a refrigerator and so heavy it took six roadies to move it. The Big Rig had been custom-made at a cost of £10,649 by an English engineer named Pete Cornish, whom Lou had ini-tially asked to cure a hum in his stage equipment. When Cornish eliminated the hum, he became beloved and trusted by Lou, as an animal dotes upon a person who extracts a thorn from its paw. The Big Rig became a symbol of his dominance in the re-formed band: he had the biggest, loudest and most expensive equipment, *ergo* he was in charge.

The fun the Velvets had in France drained away. "It was like being with a group of grumpy old people—bitching about things," Struan says of rehearsals. The musicians weren't that old. The men turned fifty-one during the reunion year, while Moe was forty-eight. But they were old enough to be set in their ways, and Moe and Sterling were out of practice. "Sterling finally figured out his amp, 'What does this thing do?' Sterling was a tug-boat captain at that point [so] he was rusty. Moe was definitely rusty. And then John and Lou went right back to being John and Lou. . . . That whole reunion was bitchy . . . I had to be everybody's guy, but Lou wanted to be sure the deck was stacked in his favor. He said, 'Always be sure my stuff is taken care of first.' He always wanted to make sure Moe was taken care of, too, because he loved her. She had no equipment, so we got her equipment, and made her special kick-drum pedals and things. Rehearsals were a laborious process of remembering chords and settings on guitars, and then Lou trying to tell everybody else how to set up their equipment, because he was the expert on these things. So that led to tension."

Lou would say, "We've got to do this," and "John, I think you should have this."

"Lou!" Cale barked back. "Don't tell me what to do."

The original plan of writing enough songs for a new album was scaled down to creating just a few new songs, most of which sounded like sketchy ideas rather than fully realized works, and the most significant of which, "Coyote," sounded more than anything like an outtake from one of Lou's recent albums. The band nevertheless decided to incorporate "Coyote" in the show. Then it was time to fly to Europe.

Lou traveled first class in the bubble of the 747 that took them all to London, the others sitting in cheaper seats. Their own glum faces greeted them from the newsstands at Heathrow airport, glowering back from the covers of the music monthlies. "So Happy to be Back" was the splendidly sarcastic headline on the cover of *Vox*, under a picture of four scowling middle-aged musicians, the Velvets having invited the press to their rehearsals in New York to try to drum up interest in the tour. Ticket sales were slow in places. There were further rehearsals in London, where Lou took time out to hit golf balls with Joe Doyle in Hyde Park. The fact that he was the only

The Velvets reunited, 1993.

band member to have a bodyguard was something else that set him apart from the others.

The first show, on June 1, 1993, was at the Edinburgh Playhouse in Scotland, a medium-sized venue holding just over three thousand people, where they were playing two nights. For Europeans who had been listening to the Velvet Underground since their teens, never having a chance to enjoy them live, because the classic lineup never toured outside North America, a ticket to see the band in

1993 was almost as unexpected as seeing the resurrected Elvis, and just as exciting for a certain sort of person. As Pat Kane observed in his *Guardian* review, Velvet Underground aficionados were of a type. "I have no problem defining the exact nature of the Edinburgh audience . . . 'I've never seen so many books in so many bags,' said the mumsy bag-search security lady. 'Where do you find time to read them all?'. . . Where do they find time? They're *middle class, missus!*"

The Velvets had always appealed to arty middle-class intellectuals, many of whom discovered their records as students. These fans presented themselves in Edinburgh as affluent professional people in early middle age. So large did the Velvet Underground loom in their imagination that it was almost enough to *see* Lou, John, Moe and Sterling together. But what did they sound like?

Opening with "We're Gonna Have a Real Good Time Together," the band played a long and well-constructed set, including classics like "Heroin" and "Venus in Furs," with Cale's frenzied viola greeted with cheers like an old friend, as well as less familiar material such as "Hey Mr. Rain" and "The Gift." There were differences from the recordings. Performed live in 1993 with state-of-the-art equipment, the songs sounded brighter and cleaner than on the original albums, which had an appropriately grungy, underground sound. More worryingly, Lou chose to sing rather than speak his lyrics, which was a stretch for his voice, and he forced the tempos. "Everything was too fast—everything. Every night I was [grinding my teeth]," laments Moe. "The best example is maybe 'Waiting for the Man.' It's a whole different thing if it's too fast. The tempo it was played at originally was perfect."

"Hello, we haven't seen you in a while, but it seems like yesterday," Lou greeted the audience, whereupon someone yelled, "Nico!"

"That will take some doing."

Almost as unlikely as Nico's appearance was the moment when Moe walked to the front to sing "After Hours," with an endearing modesty that contrasted with Lou's rock-star posturing. Cale's voice was also heard on several songs, including "I'm Waiting for the Man," which was a welcome surprise. Sterling seemed least comfortable, playing his Fender in a timorous and not always timely way. Lou glared when he fluffed his break in "Rock 'n' Roll." At the end, all four stood awkwardly together, accepting the applause, which was, of course, meant to convey respect for what they had achieved in the past as much as appreciation for the show. For those who had always loved the band, love was reaffirmed. "'What were they like?' people wanted to know the next day," Allan Jones wrote dreamily in the *Melody Maker*. "Like nothing else at all apart from themselves."

The tour moved on to London, where the Velvets played a small show at the Forum in Kentish Town and a big concert at Wembley Arena. "That was the most thrilled I ever was to be with the band, to be at [Wembley] and to have people screaming for Sterling," says Martha Morrison. But her husband wasn't happy. He struggled to master his parts and seemed overwhelmed by the experience of playing to large audiences. Lou showed little sympathy, berating his colleague backstage in a way the others found embarrassing. Even Moe is moved to criticism. "Lou made it rough on everybody. He really did. I love him to death, and have no hard feelings, but, as John said, he need[ed] to join the band. We [were] not Lou's backup band, this [was] the Velvets. We are all [equal]. He was treating Sterl pretty [badly]. I remember after one show I was thinking, 'Sterl, punch him!' I don't know what Sterl had done, or not done, but it was no big deal whatever the hell it was, and certainly nothing to be reprimanded [about]. And by who—Lou? We are equals in this. Wake up! This isn't your Lou tour. I walked by, I didn't stop and listen, but as I walked by I could hear a sentence or two and I thought, 'Sterl, punch him in the mouth!'" Instead, Sterling drowned his sorrows in the hotel bar, telling everybody what an asshole Lou was.

Despite the historic nature of the tour, Wembley wasn't a sellout. The band traveled to the Netherlands next, where they played a club show and another arena that was 63 percent full. Ticket sales for the rest of the tour were around 90 percent. Nevertheless, Lou insisted that they stay in deluxe hotels. Thrifty Moe was shocked at the money they spent on tour. "[Lou] lived well and it didn't worry him to go and have a $70 dinner, and maybe that doesn't sound like much, but I'll be damned if I ever do that." She thought money was wasted on expenses. She did, however, get an advance so she could fly her mother and children over to see the band in Prague, after which they all met Vaclav Havel. "My mother was so thrilled to be meeting an actual history person," says Moe, who felt she was paying Mom back for her first drum kit.

By the time they reached Paris, Lou and Sterling were barely speaking. "The whole vibe between Lou and Sterling was completely foul at that point," says Struan Oglanby. Because the shows at L'Olympia were to be filmed and recorded, Lou insisted on an exhaustive sound check. "Seven hours!" exclaims Moe. "That didn't go over well with Cale. They were all ridiculous, but this was the topper. God!" He was vindicated, however, by the quality of the shows. "All Tomorrow's Parties" and a pounding version of "Some Kinda Love" were particularly effective, as were Moe's two songs, "After Hours" and "I'm Sticking with You." The audience cheered and clapped along to this diffident little woman who cupped a hand over her right ear as she sang, better to hear herself. "She is very shy and modest, and getting up there is a big deal for her," says her daughter Kate Mikulka, who together with her siblings held up a banner with Moe's name on it. "I had tears in my eyes."

After Paris they played Berlin. Then they joined U2's mammoth Zooropa tour as a support act. They played three stadium shows with the band in France and Switzerland, to audiences of sixty thousand a night. They also did two huge festivals, including Glastonbury. The Velvets played to far more people during these few shows than they had in total during the entire 1960s, and the U2 dates helped keep the reunion in the black, but the gigs weren't enjoyable for the band. Moe decries the lack of interaction with their audience at events where most people could only see them on screens. Sterling was depressed, and Lou and John were increasingly tetchy with each other, so much so that Lou chose to be driven to one gig rather than fly with the rest of the band. They finished up with a few smaller shows in Italy, where Lou remained popular, but by this stage his relationship with John was dreadful. "One night in Italy, I think it was in Bologna, I was doing 'Waiting for the Man' with a huge orchestral introduction, and I was trying to give them the tempo from the piano, but I was too far off," Cale recalled. "Lou went and told my tech to turn the piano off. At that point I was ready to knock his teeth down his throat." The last show was in Naples, on July 9. Then they flew home to the USA for a break, and began to ponder what, if anything, they wanted to do together next.

There would be a live album and video of the European tour. That much was decided. In addition, they had offers to do a North American tour, as well as dates in Japan and Australia. Having got this far, it made economic sense to play more shows. "You know, they didn't make that much money [in Europe]," says tour manager Mike "Coach" Sexton. "They made money, but they didn't make a lot of money. . . . It didn't make them all rich." The original idea of recording a new studio album had fallen by the wayside, but the band was keen on an offer to make a live acoustic album in the popular *MTV Unplugged* series, which had been a shot in the arm for Eric Clapton's career the previous year. "We were going to do *MTV Unplugged*. They wanted us to do that, and we all liked the idea. We were thinking about percussion things I could [use]. It got to that point," confirms Moe. "I was thinking we could play 'Sister Ray' acoustically. This could be something! 'Heroin' acoustic. A lot of the songs would transpose fine." If they made the *Unplugged* record, they would tour the US to support it, but who would produce the album?

John Cale was spending the summer on Long Island when Lou came out to see him to discuss the issue. "I'm the only one who can produce the VU," Lou said, a ridiculous statement to make, considering the fact that it was Cale who had experience and success as a record producer. He suggested that they use an independent producer whom they both trusted, but Lou wouldn't hear of it. "I must produce," he insisted.

"Absolutely not."

The argument continued by fax, in what was the era of the fax machine. Lou had recently established an office for his company, Sister Ray Enterprises, on the sixth floor of a building at 584 Broadway in SoHo, which was run by Sylvia. He kept his archive of concert tapes and career memorabilia there, together with a fancy sound system. Journalists came to the office to interview Lou, many leaving in frustration after he had lectured, insulted and dismissed them. There was also a good deal of sitting around wasting time. "A lot of time was spent listening to his $10,000 speakers, and waiting for the phone to ring," says Struan, who ran the office briefly. "That [involved] taking care of things he needed. We had an assistant, Josh. Lou would call me at the office and say, 'Tell Josh to bring me a hard-boiled egg.' . . . So Josh would leave the [office] on Broadway, go purchase a hard-boiled egg for Lou and deliver it to [his] apartment. Then come back to the office."

One day that summer, Lou told Struan to send Cale a fax. "He wrote down on a piece of paper, 'I am going to be the only producer on this album, or there is going to be no album, and if you don't like it you can go and fuck yourself.' That was the gist of the message. He said, 'Send that to John now.' I put the [paper in the] fax [machine]. I had my finger on the button." Before he pressed the button, Struan asked Lou: "Are you sure you want me to send this?"

"Yes."

"Are you really sure? Because there is only going to be one result."

"Yes."

The fax was sent and, of course, it ended the reunion. There was no *MTV Unplugged*, no more shows. "I think it was more important to him to have things done his way than anything else. That was an absolute in his life," says Struan, adding that Lou didn't seem to care that he had wrecked the reunion. "There was no discussion after that. The Velvet Underground was dropped, the same way guitars and people were dropped . . . I think it was something that was way in the past for him [anyway], on the other side of a lot of haze."

Sire issued a tour album recorded in Paris, *Live MCMXCIII*, together with a complementary concert video. It was good to see and hear the classic lineup together onstage, well recorded, with Cale playing and singing as he had in their heyday. Nevertheless, *MCMXCIII* was a souvenir of an event out of time, lacking the intrinsic interest of their original live albums, of which the second, *1969*, was one of the best records they ever made. And *MCMXCIII* didn't sell well.

The reunion had one happy outcome, however. Moe was able to buy a house.

THAT OCTOBER, TWO MIDDLE-AGED people could be seen wandering between the stands at the Audio Engineering Society convention in New York. Eleven months had passed since Lou had met Laurie Anderson in Germany. During that time they had spoken on the telephone, arranging to meet at the microphones stand. "I had no idea this was meant to be a date," she later wrote, "but when we went for coffee after that, he said, 'Would you like to see a movie?' 'Sure.' 'And then after that, dinner?' 'OK.' 'And then we can take a walk?' 'Um . . .' From then on, we were never really apart."

As Lou and Laurie became better acquainted, Lou and Sylvia separated. The fact that she wanted a family and he didn't, a subject touched upon in the song "Beginning of a Great Adventure," had become a problem. "He told me she wanted children and he never wanted children," says Erin Clermont. "He is not a fatherly type." The days when Lou sang of his love for Sylvia were over. He now spoke to her like she worked for him, which she did. "One thing that was very hard to take was the way he talked to Sylvia. I did see a brutal side to him. He was just cruel to her. I thought she was so sweet. She was a very sweet woman, but he was done with her, and he was not nice to her," says singer Victoria Williams, who appeared with Lou on an MTV special the week after the AES convention in October 1993. "I heard him talk to her roughly, and he didn't use loving terms."

Sylvia moved out of their apartment on West End Avenue but continued to manage her husband's career from the Sister Ray office. Effectively single again, Lou returned to familiar habits. He played golf with Steve Epstein at Twin Brooks Country Club in New Jersey, showing up with a young man, whom Steve took to be his latest boyfriend. He also had a romantic reunion with Erin. "I was walking home with this pack on my back, and we ran into each other and had a nice chat. He had this dog with him. Then he wrote me a really nice email [Lou and Erin were early adopters of the internet] that said how much he missed me, and we got together again."

Shortly afterwards, Lou called Erin. "I have to tell you something," he said. "I'm involved with someone."

"Oh, who?"

"Laurie Anderson."

Erin was surprised, partly because she had assumed that Laurie was gay. Then she began to wonder if the dog Lou was walking the day they met was Laurie's rat terrier, Lolabelle, and became cross. "I thought he was treating me rather shabbily, actually. I never got to say that to him. I thought he treated me shabbily that he did not let me know [earlier that] Laurie was in the picture."

Lou and Laurie began to appear together in public, at events such as the November 1993 premiere of *The Black Rider*, a stage work by Robert Wilson. They were also together in Toronto in February 1994. Sylvia filed for divorce on March 17. One of the first things

Lou did when he received the papers was tell Struan to change the locks at Sister Ray. "It was that sort of panic." Although the divorce had an inevitability about it, friends say that both parties were upset, though Sylvia had suffered the most. She only filed for divorce after he left her publicly for another woman, who happened to be famous, which made the situation even more humiliating. "She [was] inordinately angry that Lou left her. He dumped her for Laurie—Lou traded up—that's tough," comments Daryl Bornstein. Lou still found reason to complain. He bitched about Sylvia to Steve Epstein, always a sympathetic listener, yet when Steve went through a crisis in his own life soon afterwards and tried to talk to Lou about it, Lou said he couldn't deal with his "negative energy." Steve was left wondering what sort of friend Lou was. "A true friendship would have been, 'Let me help you through this.' That wasn't what he was about."

Many people were surprised by Lou's relationship with Laurie, "the next one in his list of astonishing women," as Danny Fields remarks. It soon became clear that this wasn't a fling; it was love. "When Laurie came along, that was the first time in those years that there was any sort of sign of him spending time with anybody, and it was very much a romantic thing," says Struan, who had hitherto considered Lou to be asexual. "There was obviously love there, and it was a romantic relationship from the beginning." Lou seemed changed. "I did see a *twinge* of happiness when he got together with Laurie," remarks Sam Shepard. "I was glad of that." Others noted a dramatic improvement. "Lou changed in a very big way, and I attributed that to his relationship with Laurie," says Howie Klein, who found Lou to be "a gentler, happier, more easygoing person." The couple held hands in the studio as they worked on Laurie's 1994 album, *Bright Red*. Lou let his hair grow long and curly, like it was in his youth, apparently to please her. He so cherished the sound of her voice—a warm, attractive voice—that he kept all the messages she left on his answering machine. Photographer Bob Gruen took a picture of the couple at a function and sent prints to Lou as a gift, because he looked so happy. "He sent me back a very sweet letter saying he gave the pictures to his mother, and his mother put them on the wall, and that made his mother happy, and that makes him happy. It was such a shock, because Lou was not known as a sweet guy," says Gruen. "I thought, 'If she can tolerate him, they'll be great.'"

The divorce was finalized on April 26, 1995. Lou lost the New Jersey property in the settlement, together with the vehicles he kept in the country, but he seemed most upset about the fact that Sylvia kept their latest dog, Champion Mr. Sox. "He was devastated by the loss of Mr. Sox," says Struan, who briefly took over the running of Sister Ray. In doing so, he came to appreciate what Sylvia had had to put up with. "It was a constant barrage. And the idea that if you weren't fulfilling that list of needs you were somehow disloyal, or against him in some way; everything from 'I need a pack of gum' to 'We need a better record contract.' It was anything that came into his head."

Despite the cost of the divorce, Lou was in good financial shape. Indeed, he started to live really well at this point. He moved to a grand apartment building at 45 Christopher Street, a few doors from where he had lived in the 1970s, but a much better address. The old place had been cramped. His new penthouse apartment had a terrace with superb views across Manhattan, and room for a rooftop studio, which he had insulated with lead curtains so he could play his guitar as loudly as wanted. He had the Big Rig broken up into sections so it could be hauled up to this eyrie, and he hired interior decorators to make the place look beautiful. "He was buying like art furniture. . . . He started paying people to do all sorts of things for him," says Erin, who had never known Lou to spend so much cash. "He really pampered himself. He had a masseuse who came by, and all sorts of creature comforts at a high level."

Lou asked Struan to install an Apple PowerBook in each room in the penthouse, all linked and connected with the internet. Late one night, not long after the job was done, Lou rang his technician at home. "What's up?" asked Struan, looking at the clock. It was 3 a.m.

"Let me talk to your wife."

Struan was surprised. "He had never expressed any interest whatsoever in meeting my wife, talking to my wife, never enquired about my home life. He wasn't interested in anyone's life, past what they were doing with him at that moment." He asked Lou why he wanted to talk to his wife. "She's sleeping." There was a pause, during which Lou could be heard breathing hard down the phone like Darth Vader, a favorite telephone technique when he was pissed off. Then he yelled: "These computers you put in are total fucking shit!" After letting him rant and rave, Struan tried to divine the problem. "You had to be really careful with him. You couldn't say, 'Calm down.' It was always a circuitous route to get to where you wanted to be."

"Everything seemed to work fine—is the network going down?"

"No."

"So what is it?"

"It's total shit."

"Let's get specific, what is it technically that's not working?"

"The dictionary sucks."

Struan had installed a digital version of the *Oxford English Dictionary*. "What does my wife have to do with the dictionary?"

"I'm trying to look up something, and it's not in there."

"What are you trying to look up?" asked Struan, careful not to imply that he might know a word Lou didn't know. "You couldn't insult his intelligence—that was the worst possible thing you could probably do."

"The word 'simmer' is not in here."

Simmer?

"I'm pretty sure that is in there. Why are you trying to look that up?"

"I'm trying to make a can of soup, and it says 'to simmer.' What exactly does that mean?"

Struan was dumbfounded. "So he wanted to talk to my wife about cooking—some good old-fashioned sexism." This absurd exchange was not untypical of Lou in the latter part of his life, when, despite the humanizing influence of Laurie Anderson, his obsessive nature reached almost autistic levels. Age, wealth and fame meant he had little reason to check his bad behavior.

LIKE MR. TOAD, LOU had always hurtled from one enthusiasm to another, soon tiring of his toys. Headless guitars became as passe as Binaural Sound, his koa-wood axes shut away in his storage locker with Manfred Schunke's white plastic heads and other curios. He was also done with pinball, and motorbikes. Lou's new vehicular enthusiasm was for bicycles. "We went down to this bicycle shop in Greenwich Village and we went through twelve to fifteen different bicycles, and he rode each one around the block," recalls Struan. "Then he had me ride them around the block. . . . And then we'd discuss the merits of these bicycles. We spent hours at this shop. He wanted to make sure he got the best thing. He was this way with everything. We finally picked the bicycle and the accessories for it. 'Is this the best pump, the best saddle bag?' Then he wobbled off in traffic back home."

Laurie rode a bike, and her influence was strong. The couple was becoming united in everything, from bicycling to Buddhism. Most significantly, Lou started to make art music again, as he had in the 1960s, and like his girlfriend. "He looked up to her work in a big way, and he wanted his work to be that good," says Howie Klein. Lou's collaboration with Robert Wilson on *Time Rocker*, an avant-garde rock opera inspired by H. G. Wells's *The Time Machine*, was a case in point. Born in Texas in 1941, Wilson had established himself as one of the most innovative figures in modern theater by the 1990s, combining words, music and artwork in his shows. "I was preparing an exhibition for London celebrating the hundredth anniversary of *The Time Machine* by H. G. Wells and had thought to also make a stage work based on the same material . . . I had asked Lou if he would be interested in working with me, and he said yes," explains Wilson, who, like Lou, was better known in Europe than in his native United States. "I had just directed *The Black Rider* with Tom Waits at the Thalia Theatre in Hamburg, and the producers there were asking for me to create another work. *Time Rocker* was discussed, and we all agreed it would be a perfect complement to follow the Waits work. We started [with] a workshop in Hamburg in which I made drawings and staged the work visually without text. After a while I started to sketch in existing music of Lou's to get a sense of the structure and pace of the work. Lou was very excited and said it reminded him a little bit of Warhol, and it was easy for him to relate to it because it was so visual. . . . This was the time where I really started to appreciate Lou, and especially the loudness of his work."

Lou wrote fifteen songs for *Time Rocker*, which he worked on with Wilson throughout 1995 and the first half of 1996, the show opening in Germany in June. It was a work of high art—far removed from mainstream rock—that relatively few people saw, but this was the direction in which his career was headed. As ever, Lou found writing to order easy and enjoyable, and writing for a professional cast was particularly liberating. "I'm not writing for me, and I'm using melodies and writing for voices that aren't my own. And also, they can sing melodies I can't sing, which is really great."

He began to work with other, similar people in the art world, in music, theater and cinema. During his marriage to Sylvia, Lou had recorded music for mainstream Hollywood films, including *Get Crazy* (1983), *Perfect* (1985) and *Permanent Record* (1988). Such work was easy, lucrative and enjoyable for a songwriter who liked the challenge of writing to order. He also did a little acting, playing a rock star in *Get Crazy*. He was not much of an actor, though, and these films were among the lamest examples of mainstream Amer-

Acting in *Blue in the Face.*

ican cinema. Lou described the comedy *Get Crazy* as "the worst movie I've ever, ever seen in my life." During his relationship with Laurie, he showed more interest in working with art-house film-makers on smaller pictures, with better results.

He spent one blisteringly hot day in the summer of 1994 being filmed leaning over the counter of a cigar store set in Garrison, New York, talking extemporaneously about his relationship with New York City for an experimental movie called *Blue in the Face.* Filmmakers Paul Auster and Wayne Wang used the footage to link scenes in the picture. Nobody thought the filming had gone partic-ularly well at the time, but Lou stole the movie. His lethargic, ap-parently autobiographical and unscripted monologue, touching on his childhood in Brooklyn ("I couldn't have been unhappier"), his teenage years on Long Island ("infinitely worse . . . at least in Brook-lyn you could walk around") and smoking ("while I am smoking cigarettes, I am not downing a bottle of Scotch in fifteen minutes. So, looked at from that point of view, it's a health tool"), was funny and revealing. The film did well on an art-house level, and Lou and Paul Auster became friends. "I remember we spent some very pleas-ant afternoons together smoking cigars on the roof of his building on Christopher Street," says Auster, who is best known as one of America's foremost literary novelists. Lou told Paul that he wanted to write a crime novel. He often quoted from Raymond Chandler's novels as exemplars of good style. "He told me, 'I want to write a novel. I'm really going to do it.' And I said, 'Well, good luck.' And then about six months later he said, 'You know it's so hard, it's so beyond what I'm capable of that I have to give up . . . I admire you for being able to do it.' He said he certainly couldn't. I told him, 'Well, I can't write songs . . .' Everyone has his talent, and his gifts. It was touching to see him admit failure."

Paul Auster and his wife, the novelist Siri Hustvedt, became part of a circle of intellectual friends with whom Lou and Laurie Anderson increasingly socialized. Philip Glass, Salman Rushdie, Julian Schnabel, Wim Wenders, Hal Willner and Robert Wilson were also part of this clique, people with whom Lou and Laurie ate dinner in the smartest Manhattan restaurants, partied with, collaborated with and supported by attending each other's events. It was a civilized, privileged milieu, removed from everyday life, and it became Lou's world in the latter part of his life. He kept in touch with relatively few people from his bohemian past.

When John, Sterling and Moe agreed to perform together at the new Andy Warhol Museum in Pittsburgh in November 1994, Lou decided not to join them. Moe and John were in the lobby of their Pittsburgh hotel before the event, when Sterling arrived from Houston, where he was still working on a tug boat. The recent reunion tour hadn't changed his finances that much. He was changed in another way, however. "When Sterl walked in, we were both shocked at how sick he looked," says Moe. "He just looked awful." Sterling thought he'd pulled a muscle, but it became obvious that something much more serious was wrong. "We were there five or six days, and each day it became more evident that he was really sick." At the end of the week, Martha Morrison, who was living with the children in upstate New York, begged her husband not to go back to work in

Texas. "I said, 'Please come home with me.' He said no. . . . And then he came home in a wheelchair."

Sterling had non-Hodgkin's lymphoma. Despite a bone-marrow transplant, it became apparent that he was dying. He spent his last days in bed at Martha's house in Poughkeepsie, where Lou, John and Moe came to say goodbye to their band mate. Lou took the train up from New York on a day when Moe was also visiting. He went upstairs to see Sterling with Moe and Martha. Then the women left the men alone. Lou found his friend emaciated, and bald. "Sterl lay in bed, seeming to drift off, and I wondered if I should leave," Lou later wrote in the *New York Times*. But Sterling roused himself and asked Lou to help him sit up. They sat together for a while, with Lou holding his hand. In these quiet moments Lou felt that they resolved their differences. It was a powerful and moving experience. "I missed the train back to New York and sat on the cement pavement waiting for another. I very badly wanted a cigarette and a drink. My God, I thought, We'll never play guitar together again. No more Nico. No more Andy. No more Sterl."

Sterling died on August 30, 1995, the day after his fifty-third birthday. The following January, Lou, John, Moe and Martha stood together onstage at the Waldorf Astoria in New York as the band was inducted into the Rock 'n' Roll Hall of Fame. Lou would be posthumously inducted in his own right in 2015. The important contribution of Nico and Doug Yule to their history was officially ignored and would have gone unremarked save for John mentioning Nico's name in his speech. Finally, Lou, John and Moe performed a eulogy for Sterling, "Last Night I Said Goodbye to My Friend." It was the last performance by the Velvet Underground.

XIV

LOVE, LOU

• 1996–2008 •

OU EXPRESSED HIS LOVE for Laurie Anderson in songs including "Adventurer," which mentioned her recent trekking expedition to the Himalayas, where she got altitude sickness and almost died. Laurie was prone to weird mishaps; she also came to grief when she stepped out of a cab in New York and fell down a manhole. In "Trade In," he sang about wanting to marry again, having met a special woman, while "Hookywooky" was an unusually frisky song in which he described a rooftop party at Laurie's building on Canal Street. Many friends were there, including ex-boyfriends with whom she still got along, in contrast to Lou, who noted that none of his exes spoke to him. He felt like shoving the men off the roof. Then he wanted to "hookywooky" with his beloved, the meaning of which was clear.

He recorded these songs for the album *Set the Twilight Reeling* in his home studio on the roof of his new penthouse. One afternoon while he was working with his band in the studio, there was a big storm. "We had done a song called 'Riptide' on that album. It had so

Lou and Laurie Anderson, 1996.

much energy that when we finished the downbeat of the track there was an immediate thunderstorm and lightning outside in New York, and it started blowing things around," says Tony "Thunder" Smith, who became Lou's drummer at this time. It seemed almost like the music triggered the storm. The musicians ran out on to the terrace to rescue Lou's plants, as he barked orders like Captain Ahab on the deck of the *Pequod*.

Smith had been hired after Lou's previous drummer, Danny Frankel, took time off to be with his dying father. Lou wasn't particularly sympathetic. "Lou said he couldn't wait. He had to get the record going," says Frankel. "It's funny that musicians treat other musicians like they complain record companies mistreat them."

Lou's recording career was once again in jeopardy. Following a corporate upheaval at Warner Brothers, he was one of several Sire artists who were shunted across to the main Warner label. As a result, he lost the protection of the executives who had looked after him at Sire and became exposed to the harsh realities of the modern record industry. As he went out on tour to promote *Set the Twilight Reeling* in 1996, he became dissatisfied with the low level of promotion the company was giving his record and was generally grumpy. "He was getting nasty," notes his technician Struan Oglanby. "The shows weren't selling out. The album was tanking. As I would joke, the album went wood." Lou had developed a quasi-paternal relationship with Struan over the past few years, as he tended to do with young employees. "He had no kids, and my dad fucked off when I was nine. There was definitely a bond there that way with us. It was never expressed that way, but there was a familial thing." But Lou's affections were inconstant, and now he seemed to want to pick a fight with his favorite. If any little thing went wrong, if his hairdryer didn't work backstage, or his amp setting was off by the slightest degree, Lou flew into a rage. It became too much for Struan on March 14, 1996. "You know, I don't have to put up with this shit," he told Lou after he snapped at him during sound check at the Bronco Bowl in Dallas. Lou screamed at Struan to get back to his work station. "I was on a plane the next day, and went to work for the Smashing Pumpkins. . . . Never heard from him again."

When *Set the Twilight Reeling* failed to chart in the USA (it did better in Europe), Lou had a crisis meeting with the chairman of Warner Brothers, during which he complained about promotion for his album and other matters. "[He] wasn't happy he wasn't selling more, and this and that, but he really wanted to make sure I cared about his [girlfriend]," recalls Danny Goldberg. Laurie was also a Warner Brothers artist, and Lou spent a good part of the meeting talking about her, as if he thought the label didn't appreciate her either. "I think he was maybe just frustrated that his last few albums had been taken for granted, that they were treated as prestige items rather than albums that were supposed to be marketed, and he wanted more enthusiastic, focused marketing." Goldberg had bigger problems. He was trying to restructure Warners and re-sign major artists like REM, at a time when new technology was threatening their business model. "So in that context Lou Reed was a relatively minor responsibility." In fact, the company decided to drop him; Lou was too much trouble. Howie Klein intervened before this became public. "I was always very concerned about his career and tried to be as supportive as I could without interfering with the other company," says Howie, who'd recently been appointed head of the Reprise label within the Warner group, "but as it turned out Lou didn't get along with one of the top executives there. They had one of those classic Lou things. It wasn't working out, and they decided to drop him. I don't know if I'm talking out of school here, and if anyone ever knew this, because we made it very, very smooth. Instead of Lou being in any way embarrassed, or humiliated, that he was being dropped, instead it was a celebration of me being able to say to Lou, 'I've got great news, I've talked Warner Brothers into letting you be on Reprise.'" So Lou moved to his sixth and last record label.

As he entered his final years, Lou found himself working in a contracting record industry run by young people who had little or no emotional attachment to older niche artists like himself who didn't make hits. At the same time, Lou was drifting further away from the mainstream. That summer he was in Hamburg for the premiere of his collaboration with Robert Wilson, the stage show *Time Rocker*, in which the Wellsian time machine was represented by a skeletal fish. The show, a highbrow rock opera with stylized sets and costumes, appealed to a discerning European theater audience who relished Wilson's original and vivid work. There was more skepticism when the show transferred to New York. The *Village Voice* condemned it as a "schlocky musical," while the *New York Times* concluded that Wilson's visuals were better than Lou's music.

After *Time Rocker*, Lou resumed his usual summer touring schedule, which typically included a string of European dates. That year he kept a tour diary for the *New Yorker* as he crisscrossed the Continent, creating a fascinating record of a middle-aged rock star on the road at the end of the twentieth century, flitting from one country to another, staying in deluxe hotels and meeting up with famous friends along the way, yet not immune from the discomforts of international travel.

He found himself in Austria on July 7, 1996, playing in a medieval castle near Linz. Lou observed that audiences were much the same wherever he went in Europe. "The audience here is the same as the audience in Budapest—or Udine, for that matter. People have mastered the jutting neck and sliding head-and-shoulder movements associated with rock-moves," he noted, grumbling that he couldn't do these moves himself, as a creaky middle-aged man, because he'd put his back out exercising with a StairMaster. After Linz, he traveled to Rome to play the EUR complex. Then he flew to Barcelona for a festival. David Bowie, who was also on the bill, watched Lou's helicopter land at their luxury hotel, "to see if we crashed, I suppose," Lou noted lugubriously. Bowie was with his second wife, Iman. Seeing them together reminded Lou of Laurie, who was touring the United States. He felt lonely and hoped the hotel's internet connection was working so they could hook up later online.

Iggy Pop was another old friend on the festival bill in Spain, still performing stripped to the waist despite the fact he was about to turn fifty, and displaying a remarkable physique for a man of his age. "How does he stay in such great shape?" Lou wondered, reflecting on his own struggle to stay fit. "I was doing crunches every day, but that's how I threw my back out."

He noted that the hotel rooms he was given on tour were often bigger than his New York apartment, ruing his failure to play the Manhattan property market to his advantage over the years. "I still rent, which is pretty much how I started out." He vowed to do something about it, and indeed he moved home not long after this, buying a new apartment in Greenwich Village: a large duplex at the corner of West 11th Street and the West Side Highway. This was the biggest, fanciest apartment he had ever had, and it was his last home in the city. To make the place comfortable he had bookshelves built and a new home studio installed, decorating the walls of the apartment with original artwork by famous friends, including Julian Schnabel, who lived in a huge faux-palazzo on the other side of West 11th Street. Also on display was an antique door from Tibet and ceremonial swords Lou used for tai chi practice. The view from the terrace was across the Hudson River to the New Jersey shore. As friends observed, looking across the water to Jersey, "America starts over there," meaning the continental hump of workaday America, which chic Manhattanites like themselves had little in common with. Traffic roared night and day on the broad highway beneath Lou's windows, but between the highway and the river was a pleasant landscaped strip of land where he and Laurie walked their dog, Lolabelle, who was like a child to them. It was a two-mile walk south along the river to Laurie's home studio on Canal Street, which she maintained as an independent base throughout their relationship.

Back on tour in Europe, Sunday, July 14, 1996, found Lou in a fancy hotel in Antibes, watching the boats on the water. On Wednesday he was in Prague, hanging out with his pal Vaclav Havel. "We drink and smoke . . ." Lou wrote in his diary, a casual admission that he was back on the sauce. Then he suffered a problem any traveler may face. "Shampoo exploded in my suitcase and freeze-dried breakfast mineral powder leaked across everything," he noted on July 18. He tried to mop up the mess with a damp cloth, only to create a lather. Two days later, en route to Belgium—"Travel time: six and a half hours. Playing time: one hour"—his luggage was lost. This was the grumpy rock star seen shuffling through airports, ignoring fans who asked for autographs, his back aching, his carry-on luggage full of suds, worrying about his weight and missing his girlfriend and his dog. "An interviewer asks me why don't I smile much."

As his diary revealed, Lou was on speaking terms with David Bowie again. Indeed, when Bowie celebrated his fiftieth birthday with a concert at Madison Square Garden in January 1997, Lou was among the guest artists. Introduced to the audience by the English superstar as "the King of New York," he performed four songs with Bowie, including a compelling "I'm Waiting for the Man." It was the first time they had worked together since *Transformer*, and while Lou didn't look overjoyed to be onstage with his former producer, he didn't hit him.

The consensus was that Lou was mellowing, thanks partly to Laurie's influence and also to the fact he wasn't drinking manically anymore. "Everybody says I am really nice now," he told the *Sunday Telegraph* in advance of the 1997 Meltdown Festival in London, which Laurie was curating and at which he was performing. He had become enthused about playing acoustic guitar recently, having found an electronic gizmo that eliminated feedback, lending his instrument what he called "the sound of diamonds." The Meltdown show was recorded for release as the CD *Perfect Night*. "I myself don't notice a difference at all," he said of his supposed good mood, "but I have been told." Few journalists would agree.

"What do you regard as the lowest depth of misery?" Lou was once asked.

"Being interviewed by an English journalist."

There were several reasons for his notorious loathing of the British press. It is generally true that the press in the United Kingdom is more irreverent than in the USA, and while Lou had always commanded attention and respect in the UK, he was also sharply criticized and sometimes mocked. Although he didn't admit that this was the principal cause of his problem, he brooded on his bad reviews. His insistence on only talking about his current work in interviews, without reference to the past, or his private life, frustrated journalists who weren't content just to report what he wanted to tell them in order to sell his latest record. When they probed for more interesting material, he became irritable. Over time, he became so defensive that it was almost impossible to talk to him about anything other than his new record, or recording technology, a deadly dull subject, which he found fascinating. "His paranoia sucks the life out of you," groaned a writer for the *Times* after a typically frustrating encounter in 2012. More generally, Lou had no patience for journalists who were inadequately briefed, or asked him questions he felt he had been asked too often before, though most celebrities learn to cope with this as part of their job. His crustiness was, to some extent, the carapace of an insecure, emotionally fragile man who was seldom at ease with journalists, distrusting their motives. "I get nervous about interviews," he once admitted. He was never a great rock 'n' roll interviewee like John Lennon or Bob Dylan, whose best interviews were highly entertaining as well as intellectually stimulating. A file of Lou's late interviews, in particular, makes for tedious reading, as a succession of journalists tried to engage him in conversation, only to be rebuffed by a suspicious, surly old man. This was not in fact an issue peculiar to his dealings with the British. Lou had run-ins with journalists of all nations over the years, as he had a habit of falling out with people generally. As we have seen, his biography is littered with quarrels. To some extent, he was simply disagreeable.

His particular problem with British journalists, a feud he played up in his last years, as if it amused him, was compounded and made ridiculous by the fact that he had to engage with them every time he released a record. Despite being the so-called King of New York, Lou's main market was Europe, where he still sold albums in reasonable numbers, where he played his biggest shows and where he had admirers in high places. A prime example of his enduring status in the UK in particular came in 1997, when the BBC collaborated with him in a remix of "Perfect Day," featuring guest artists including Bono, David Bowie, Lesley Garrett and Elton John, all filmed for a sumptuous complementary video to promote the corporation. When the recording was subsequently issued in aid of charity, it went to number one.

HOME AFTER HIS TRAVELS, Lou was mooching around the Gagosian Gallery in Chelsea one weekend when he recognized a colleague. "We are there looking at art and somebody comes up behind me and picks me up and holds me tight and says, 'Guess who?' 'I don't know—put me down!' It's Lou," recalls Godfrey Diamond, Lou's producer on *Coney Island Baby*, one of many working relationships that had gone bad. Enough time had passed for Lou to forget the details. He invited Godfrey back to his apartment to listen to some new songs. "He played me a couple of songs, and I'm listening. There was some good stuff there. I said, 'Lou, all I want you to do is give me another "Sweet Jane." You're the master of writing songs about people. I don't know anybody else who can write about a person the way you can.' He looks at me and goes, 'Godfrey, I try to write "Sweet Jane" every day,' in this deep, awful, mean, aggravated, upset voice. Clearly, that wasn't the thing to say."

Godfrey's comment about wanting Lou to record another "Sweet Jane" embodied an existential problem facing "legacy" artists whose audience was more interested in old songs than new work. Lou's interests were precisely opposite, and he made some of his boldest, most interesting music at the end of his career, though few people were paying attention. His late album *Ecstasy*, songs from which he played for Godfrey, was rich in powerful, hooky songs like "The Rock Minuet" and "Baton Rouge," related in his best world-weary speaking voice. "I remember thinking, 'Ah, this is the Lou Reed that I remember!' Him telling a story. . . . Also that thing he had of bringing in a sense of humor," notes Jane Scarpantoni, who, having listened to Lou's music for years, was thrilled to play cello on *Ecstasy*. She went on to work with Lou extensively at the tail end of his career. "To me, if you listen to 'Baton Rouge,' that's a song about

divorce if ever I've heard one . . . I don't know if it's about Sylvia."
Other new songs seemed to relate to Lou's life. Infidelity was the
subject of "Mad": a man cheated on his partner when she was out
of town. She threw a coffee cup at him and called him scum, and
dumb, "dumb as my thumb," a simple but telling rhyme, articulated with such feeling that it was tempting to think that this was
something that had happened. Ultimately, it didn't matter, as Jane
observes. "Whether that truth is him, or someone else, or a totally
fabricated [story], you know that the emotion is for real and he's not
fooling around."

In comparison to the upbeat lovers of *Set the Twilight Reeling*, the
characters in *Ecstasy* were in agony. Lou drew on the Oedipus story
to create "The Rock Minuet," described by Paul Zollo, editor of *Performing Songwriter*, as "maybe the most graphically violent song
ever written in waltz-time." In this remarkable work he presented
a series of violent vignettes, including scenes of drug abuse, rough
and transgressive sex, torture and murder. He delivered his lines in
a matter-of-fact tone that made the imagery more disturbing, pushing boundaries again. Even Lou hadn't written so explicitly before
about the links between abuse, violence and eroticism, describing
scenes where two men tied up a victim and sewed up his eyes for
kicks; another where the protagonist picked up a guy by the water-
front "and thought of his father as he cut his windpipe."

A package arrived from London while Lou was recording. "I
made this [guitar] pedal that sounded to me like an amplifier when
it's just about to explode, or it's very ill," explains engineer Pete Cornish. "I made this pedal and sent it to Lou, saying, 'This simulates
imminent amp death.' He immediately called it the Death Pedal."
Lou used the Death Pedal on another terrific new song, "Like a Possum," becoming so excited by the crunching tone the guitar pedal
gave his instrument that he kept playing, repeating the lyrics of the
song until they became a semi-abstract collage on top of the churning music, creating a track that was reminiscent of "Sister Ray."

Here again were themes of drug taking and casual sex, all to fill
an inner emptiness. This had been a theme of his writing throughout his career, as it was an issue in his life. The recording was very
long, at over eighteen minutes. "The question came up—why edit
it?" asks drummer Tony Smith. "Lou hadn't done something like
this in many years—a never-ending piece that grows and builds. . . .
Lou said, 'I want it exactly like it is.'"

Like most of his songs, "Like a Possum" was surely a mixture
of experience, observation and imagination, but it was nonetheless
the authentic expression of a man who knew what it felt like to indulge himself, as he sang, until it hurt. He told *Newsday* that the
fact listeners reacted strongly to the material was a sign of quality.
"It's like watching a movie, a really good one. You know it isn't real.
But at a certain point, if it's really done well, you're there. That's
what I try to do on the record." Still, the American public showed
little appetite for an album about "violent death and violent sex,"
as *Newsday* wrote in 2000. Lou's record company relied on foreign
sales to earn back the modest amounts they advanced him to make
his albums. "So even if a record was a little iffy in the United States,
which it usually was, he would do really well in France, for sure; in
Scandinavia he was very big; Italy; Germany. So even though those
weren't gigantic numbers, they added up," explains Howie Klein.
By the start of the new century, however, Lou's sales were in decline
all over the world, as were the sales of most artists in the internet
age. The fact that he was making such challenging new music didn't
help broaden his audience, and he followed *Ecstasy* with a work that
most people found completely indigestible. Nevertheless, *The Raven*
was another fascinating album.

Lou had always felt drawn to the work of Edgar Allan Poe, a
man described by one contemporary as "intelligent, wayward and
willful," which also described Lou. They had a lot in common. Both
were American outsiders who wrote sensational stories of the outré
and morbid. They dressed in black, dosed themselves with alcohol

and opium and lived in Greenwich Village. As he walked the dog, Lou traversed the same streets Poe walked in the nineteenth century. Robert Wilson first suggested that that they collaborate on a theater piece inspired by Poe's work, as a result of which *POEtry*, another stylized rock opera based on literary source material, debuted at the Thalia Theatre in Hamburg in 2000. Lou then decided to independently record a studio album based on Poe's writing, a grandiose concept album that would make *Berlin* seem modest. Over the course of three years, *The Raven* grew into a sprawling double album featuring numerous guest artists of distinction, including his jazz hero Ornette Coleman, the vocal group the Blind Boys of Alabama and David Bowie, presumably as payback for Lou appearing at his fiftieth birthday show. Lou also mentored the British singer Antony Hegarty, a large, sorrowful young man who added his tremulous falsetto to the project. Prose passages were narrated by actors Steve Buscemi, Willem Dafoe and Amanda Plummer.

The Raven included theatrical set pieces, sound effects, old songs ("Perfect Day" and "The Bed") mixed up with new songs based on Poe's work. Lou felt free to rewrite anything that took his fancy, including Poe's epic poem "The Raven," which gave the record its name, as well as short stories and essays such as "The Imp of the Perverse," which addressed a dilemma that spoke to him personally. "Why am I drawn to do what I should not? I have wrestled with this thought innumerable times: the impulse of destructive desire—the desire for self-mortification," Lou explained. "Why do we do what we should not? Why do we love what we cannot have? Why do we have a passion for exactly the wrong thing? What do we mean by 'wrong'?" He worked on this ambitious album in New York through September 2001, when the Twin Towers of the World Trade Center, which he could see from his apartment, were hit by passenger planes, caught fire and fell. "Fire Music" on *The Raven* was his response to the disaster.

Reprise hated the record. "It was a bad time," recalls Fernando Saunders. "I spoke to Lou. He said, 'The record company doesn't want to put it out.'" *The Raven* was eventually granted a delayed, low-key release in 2003, when it received muted reviews. *Rolling Stone* found much to admire but predicted that the unconventional aspects would "bewilder the rock & roll animals among Reed's following." Yet he was often at his best when he eschewed the mainstream. For those that liked him to be bold, as he had been with the Velvet Underground, here was a record to stimulate the imagination. "I think so. The public didn't judge it that way," says Howie Klein, whose policy had always been to leave Lou alone as much as possible. "My job was to be supportive of him, and to be protective of him, give him an environment where he felt he had everything he needed to be creative." But the accountants had had enough.

Time was catching up with Lou. He turned sixty in 2002. He used an autocue onstage to help him remember his lyrics. Years of hard living and cigarette smoking had given his face the texture of an ancient, deflated leather football, with an underlying redness that indicated health issues. He was diagnosed as diabetic, as a result of which he became increasingly finicky about food. He learned how to tell waiters "no butter . . . no sugar" in almost every European language, which was important, because he spent a lot of time on the road in Europe in his last decade. "Lou got discouraged about making albums," explains Fernando. "Lou said, 'Why make the records? Nobody buys them.'" So he concentrated on his live show, mixing up the set to keep himself interested and pushing his musicians to do their very best. "When you were onstage you had to give it everything you got," notes Rob Wasserman, who, along with Fernando, played bass for Lou in later years, sometimes together onstage, unusually.

Lou enjoyed experimenting with unorthodox band formations. In 2003 he invited Antony Hegarty, cellist Jane Scarpantoni and his tai chi teacher, a Chinese-born man who had recently immigrated to the US named Master Ren Guang-Yi, to tour with him, along with Fernando and Mike Rathke. Lou and Ren met up a couple of times a week when he was in New York to practice tai chi on the roof of his apartment, to the amusement of his neighbors, moving indoors if the weather was inclement. Lou's interest in tai chi went back to the 1980s, but he became evangelical about the health benefits of the martial art in his latter years, and invited Ren to tour with him to spread the message. "He asked me 2003 to go together on tour. We did 150 shows together—Europe, Asia, Japan, USA—we go a lot of place," explains Master Ren in stilted English. "He wanted more people to know tai chi. . . . A lot of people do tai chi [now] from [seeing] Lou and our show. This is amazing." Ren appeared onstage with the band dressed in what looked like silk pajamas, making graceful and occasionally dramatic tai chi moves under Lou's fond gaze as the band played rock 'n' roll.

This was the weird but good show Lou brought to the Wiltern Theater in Los Angeles in June 2003. When it was discovered that he still owed Reprise an album, his few remaining friends at Warners persuaded management to release enough money to make one last record. The resulting live album, *Animal Serenade*, is valuable partly as a record of Antony Hegarty's sublime vocals on "Candy Says." Lou, who had got into the habit of referring to record-company executives contemptuously as "music-industry baboons," put a photo of a baboon on the cover of the CD, which was released in 2004. Sales were poor, and Reprise dropped him. Despite having written some of the most original music of the rock era, Lou ended his career without a mainstream record deal, though he would make one more significant album as a guest artist.

IT WAS THE TIME of endings. Sid Reed died in January 2005, never having responded publicly to what his son said about him, or insinuated in songs like "Kill Your Sons" and "My Old Man." One would never guess he was such a brute, judging by his obituary in the *New York Times*. "Devoted father of Bunny and Lou," it read, "a man of integrity and dignity for ninety-one years."

There was a paternal aspect to Lou's relationship with his last manager, Tom Sarig, who started to work with him at this time. "He was kind of like my dad and my son at the same time," says Sarig, who was born in 1966, making him thirty-nine when he started working with Lou. Like a lot of rock stars, Lou was immature in many ways—wilful, demanding, petulant and egocentric. He required a lot of looking after, but paradoxically he also insisted on being in charge. They got into the habit of meeting once a week for breakfast in a restaurant near Lou's apartment to talk over his issues, and ideas for new projects. One topic of discussion was his recording career. Lou had signed with an independent label, Sanctuary, after being dropped by Warners, but the company had run into financial trouble before they'd made a record with him. One of the first things Sarig did was to get Lou out of this deal. Lou had plenty of ideas about new projects, but his experience with *The Raven* had put him off songwriting. "He wasn't feeling like writing a lot of new material, because of that. 'I just did the best thing I could and fucking Warners didn't do anything with it,' you know. So we started looking for other things to do, other ideas he had."

Photography had become a favorite hobby, and a first volume of Lou's pictures was published in 2003 under the title *Emotion in Action*. The way the images were sequenced was intended "to tell a story of sorts, a dream," as he explained in his introduction. With that in mind, the selected images—of ice, sky, water; numerous views of New York, often from the terraces of his various apartments; also pictures taken abroad, including images of wild animals on safari—succeeded in mimicking the sensations of a nightmare, though, individually, the images were less interesting. What was most remarkable about this and two subsequent books of photos, *Lou Reed's New York* and *Romanticism*, was the lack of human beings in the pictures, or anything personal. Laurie was glimpsed just twice over the course of three books, once apparently by accident. The impression was of the photographer, solitary and cold-hearted as a raptor, watching the world through a predatory lens-eye. In this sense, the books were a true autobiography.

Another project was an album of electronic meditation music, without lyrics or tunes, a beige version of *Metal Machine Music*. Although Lou had lost his enthusiasm for writing new songs, he recorded this ambient meditation music in his home studio, and he flattered himself that other people might like to hear it. "Lou Reed does meditation music. It was odd, but Lou was one of a kind," says Sarig of *Hudson River Meditations*, which was released on an independent label in 2007. Lou took the cover photo, of the Hudson River, from his terrace. "He was thrilled that I found a buyer to put it out."

While Lou employed Sarig to develop his career, he also had a succession of personal assistants running errands for him, young people such as Zeljko McMullen, who found himself working at Sister Ray Enterprises after replying to a job advertisement on the website Craigslist. "[It said], 'New York-based musician photographer seeks office intern.' It didn't say anything about who it was. It was $12 an hour." Initially, there was also a female assistant. "She was so stressed out by him that she was not having her period . . ." Zeljko took over, cataloguing Lou's books, photos and tapes, manning the phone and taking care of whatever the boss needed. "He wanted someone to order him car services, make appointments for massages, all of that frou-frou stuff . . ." When Lou and Laurie went on tour, Zeljko stayed at Lou's apartment to look after the dog and to learn to use his home studio. He also worked briefly with the star onstage. Once again, there was an intense period of bonding. "It almost turned into a weird father-son relationship. He never had kids. My father died when I was very young. . . . He would tell people he was trying to adopt me. It was a joke." Then Lou overloaded his assistant with responsibilities, demands and complaints until he snapped. When he texted to complain about the seat he'd been assigned on a flight to Colorado in September 2006, grumbling, "You know I like window seats," Zeljko quit.

Significantly, Lou was asked to revive *Berlin* onstage at St Anne's Warehouse in Brooklyn that year. "Our agent didn't want us to do it because there was no money in it, and it was one of these artsy-fartsy not-for-profit [projects]," says Tom Sarig. Lou was also skeptical at first, partly because he wasn't inclined to look back. "On that basis, he was tentative about *Berlin*, but with the people involved it became an exciting thing, and when he actually did it he said it was the best thing he ever did." Lou worked with Bob Ezrin again on the show, employing his regular band plus additional sidemen and guest vocalists like Antony Hegarty; also a choir, horn and string section. "Lou was like the king with thirty people onstage," says Sarig. Steve Hunter came back to play with Lou after more than thirty years, even though Lou ignored him on tour in 1973. "He [Steve] played on the original record and a lot of stuff back in the day, and had gone, to all intents and purposes, blind. He was teaching guitar in a blind school. And they pulled him back to do this tour, and completely rejuvenated his career," explains Rupert Christie, who played keyboards in the show, though he didn't rate the original album. "It's all slightly awkward and the subject matter is ridiculous."

Julian Schnabel created film sequences for the show, made the backdrop and filmed the opening night on December 14, 2006. Lou's sister, Bunny, and his frail, widowed mother, Toby, were in the audience. "We were flying by the seat of our pants," says Christie, noting that there hadn't been time to rehearse properly. *Berlin* was performed in its entirety. As it was a relatively short work, Lou played some of his better-known songs at the end, rewarding the audience with what the conductor Sir Thomas Beecham would have referred to as a lollipop. The *New York Times* noted that *Berlin* live in 2006 was an improvement on the original LP. "In its time, *Berlin* carried Mr. Reed's music to an ornate extreme, but now its trappings are secondary. What comes through is the way it feels."

The following February, he took the show to Australia for the Sydney Festival. The more gigs they played, the better *Berlin* sounded. By the time Lou toured Europe in the summer of 2007, the band was tight and the sound excellent (something he cared about intensely). "We were rocking it by then," says Christie. Audiences responded enthusiastically. Jonathan Ross and David Walliams were among the celebrity fans who came backstage after the show in London to pay their respects, not that Lou was grateful. They interrupted him just as he was getting undressed for his massage. "He had done an interview once for Ross, who thought they were best mates. It was all just about to kick off and Lou was angry. He hated anybody going into his dressing room after a gig because he would get a massage," explains Rupert Christie, who says that Lou had no idea who Ross and Walliams were. "I explained who everybody was: 'This is David Walliams, a very big comedian in the UK. This is Jonathan, he is a radio deejay and chat-show host.' He said, 'These are your fucking friends?'. . . He wasn't too pleased." Songs that had been reviled were acclaimed and, unwelcome celebrity visitors aside, Lou had seldom looked happier. "He was in great shape," says Tom Sarig. "He was in great voice. He had perfected the *Berlin* character. He never got tired of it."

Lou started to think about songwriting again, and maybe making another album. During the London run of *Berlin* he met with an executive from Decca to discuss a possible deal. "Lou at the beginning could be a cautious, distant person," says Charlie Rapino, vice president of A&R at Decca, who admits that Lou seemed only half interested in his proposition. "Lou knew he was probably making more money performing *Berlin* live [at that point]. He was a highly intelligent man. A record at that point wouldn't really matter. He wouldn't make money on it." However, he had started to write songs again, including "Power of the Heart," which he wanted people to hear. As they discussed the options over dinner in an Italian restaurant in Hammersmith, Lou asked for some white wine and a glass filled with ice. He poured the wine over the ice, to dilute it. A bottle of soave was consumed. "We drank a whole bottle. It was me, him and Hal Willner," recalls Rapino, a modest amount for three with food, but more than most recovering alcoholics would consider wise. No record deal resulted.

Lou wound up touring *Berlin* in Europe in 2007 and 2008, happy tours, during which he seemed at peace with himself. "Lou was very intense," says band member Rob Wasserman. "I didn't see him as a grumpy guy at all. He was a very humorous person . . . he was moody, but he was a fun person to be around for me. I think he really enjoyed playing live." Musicians like Rob became friends, and Lou's late tours were social and convivial. To keep costs down, he flew business class, but he insisted on deluxe hotel accommodation for everybody, and he liked his band to come out for dinner with him in the evening, usually to a gourmet restaurant. After decades of touring Europe, he knew the best places to go in every major city, and his manager kept lists of favorite restaurants, annotated and updated with the names of dishes Lou liked. He had become an extremely picky eater, partly because of his health, also as an extension of his general cussedness. "He was going through a stage of eating particular color salads," recalls Rupert Christie. "'Tonight I'll have a red salad.' 'What's in that?' 'Tomatoes, peppers, can't be anything green in it!' The next night would be a green salad. If there was anything red in it, he would get really angry." He drank diluted white wine with his meal. "He didn't drink a lot, but he would always have a spritzer."

When his tour coincided with Laurie's dates, the couple met up for a few days' rest and relaxation. "He was always looking forward to seeing her, and when they were together they were like children, they were so happy to be together," says Jane Scarpantoni, who spent time with the couple during a tour break in Sardinia. "I thought, 'Ah! He is head over heels for her. And vice versa.'"

When they were apart, they emailed and spoke by phone. Laurie was performing in Los Angeles in April 2008, talking to Lou on her mobile phone, when she began to list the things she hadn't done in life and might not do now that she was almost sixty-one. "Like what?" asked Lou, who was sixty-six.

"You know," she said, in her singsong voice. "I never learned German, I never studied physics, I never got married . . ."

"Why don't we get married?" He'd had this in mind for some time. Lou was a man who liked to be married, despite his bisexuality; he liked to have a woman to look after him. He suggested they meet the next day in Boulder, Colorado, the next stop on Laurie's tour.

"Don't you think that's too soon?"

"No, I don't."

Lou flew to Boulder. They wrote their vows and were married at a friend's house in the city on Saturday, April 12. That evening Laurie did her show as scheduled at the Boulder Theater. Lou understood. It was third time lucky for a man who found himself well matched in his final marriage. A relationship that had already lasted nearly fifteen years deepened and achieved a new level of tenderness, quietening and enriching the last years of what had been a turbulent life. But there were more storms to come.

XV

NEVERMORE

• 2008–13 •

URING THE LAST FIVE years of his life Lou kept himself
busy with a wide range of projects, including books of his
photographs, films, speaking engagements, stage shows and
endorsement deals. "Between the branding, the photography stuff,
music, film, theater, he was working on, like, ten to twenty different
projects at a time," says his manager Tom Sarig, adding that Lou's
interest in a subject was more important than the fee. "Lou wouldn't
do *anything*; you couldn't get him to do anything that he wasn't
into." One of these late projects was *Lou Reed's New York Shuffle*,
a radio show that debuted on the SIRIUS network in the USA in
May 2008. Lou co-presented with his producer friend Hal Willner,
who acted as his music archivist and foil. The music played was an
eclectic mixture spanning jazz, electronica and doo-wop, the tone
of the conversation that of two old men kibitzing. The homemade
nature of the show was enhanced by the fact that Lou recorded it at
his apartment when he was in town. "It was something he enjoyed,"

says Sarig. "We would [also] take it on the road when Lou was on tour and do installments from the road."

Aside from his regular stage show, Lou toured with the musicians Ulrich Krieger and Sarth Calhorn in 2008–10 as Metal Machine Trio, performing what they called Deep Noise, electronica inspired by *Metal Machine Music*, which had developed a cult following over the years. "We did several shows in New York that were successful, and we booked two tours of Europe, and put out [two] live records of Metal Machine Trio, and that was a joy for him," says Sarig. "There was no pressure on him to sing. He would still [sing] a couple of things, so the fans didn't go crazy. But he just enjoyed this chaotic noise music."

Lou used some of this Deep Noise music as the soundtrack for *Red Shirley*, a short documentary film he made in 2009 about his ninety-nine-year-old aunt, Shulamit "Shirley" Rabinowitz. Lou was fond of his aunt, and he was kindly toward her during their on-screen interview, yet couldn't quite eradicate his habitual grudging tone. "You're joking?" he asked her, as she explained how she had left Poland for the New World at nineteen with two suitcases and no English, as if she, like the rest of mankind, was trying to deceive him. "Aw, come on. . . . You can't be serious. You're joking, right? . . . You're kidding?"

To his credit, Lou helped support Shirley in her old age. "Lou really took care of her for a long time, and paid for aid, and paid for her apartment," says his sister. Here was another side to the man, a kinder person who could be generous. There were other examples of his charity. Back in the old days at Max's Kansas City, Lou got to know a professional dancer named Mike Quashie, who, dressed in a loincloth and wielding a spear, danced the shango, the watusi and—his showstopper—the limbo on the New York stage, acquiring a degree of celebrity as the Limbo King. They remained friends. Lou invited Mike to a party to celebrate his 2008 marriage to Laurie Anderson. When Mike subsequently had a nervous breakdown and fell behind with the rent on his Greenwich Village apartment, Lou came to his aid. "When I was sick, he paid my rent for about six months," says Mike, who later moved into sheltered accommodation in the Bronx, where Lou visited him. "He was very kind to me. . . . He was a great friend."

At the same time, Lou was capable of turning his back on people who *thought* he was their friend. When Little Jimmy Scott broke his hip in 2007, his wife, Jeanie, asked Lou to take part in a fund-raising concert for the singer. "[Lou] would say to me, 'Whatever Jimmy needs at all, just call me.' [And] that was the only time we ever asked him for a favor, to be on the show, to sing one song, and he got really nasty about it. He didn't want to be bothered. . . . He says one thing and behaves the opposite way." So we see two sides to the man, apparently contradictory, but nevertheless part of his character.

IT HAD LONG BEEN an article of faith for Lou that Long Island was an irredeemable shit-hole. He left the suburbs for New York City in his twenties, and seemed determined never to return. "This is funny, this is ironic. He always told me, 'Dion, I have one fear and one fear only, and that's the suburbs,'" chuckles Dion DiMucci. "And he ended up living on Long Island at the end of his life. That is totally ironic." In 2009 Lou bought a summer home between the villages of Amagansett and Springs on the fashionable eastern extremity of Long Island, beyond the Hamptons. The area is very different to the lower-middle-class South Shore where Lou grew up. It is where the rich and famous vacation, including fellow entertainers. Sir Paul McCartney owns a holiday home nearby. But it is still Long Island.

For $1.5 million, Lou purchased a shingle-sided cottage on an acre and a half of land, with a sun deck and a lap pool, the house shaded by pine trees, between which he slung a hammock. It was a place where he and Laurie could relax as they moved into old age. They had friends locally, many of whom were fellow Manhattanites who also worked in show business, people like Jenni Muldaur, who sang in the *Berlin* show. Jenni was a neighbor both in Greenwich Village and on Long Island and, despite the age gap between them (she was born in 1965, the daughter of singer Maria Muldaur), they became close during these last years. "I would say he was one of my best friends. I saw him almost every day. . . . The guy was a very powerful force of nature, and for all the hardness on the outside there was just the most soft, beautiful inside," she says. "He was sort of like a father [and a] brother. . . . It had a lot of layers. And we were just pals. We did stuff together." Lou liked to walk and swim when he was in the country. "We did things like go to the beach with the dog, so all these mundane things." In New York, he enjoyed going to movies with Jenni. "We went to a ton of old movies at the Film Forum." He also liked to kick back at home in front of the TV to watch a boxing match, or *Mad Men.*

Lou's drinking had crept up again, and he made yet another attempt to stop. In May 2010 he was one of the guest stars at a Peter Gabriel concert in New York, where he ran into his former manager Jonny Podell, who'd also struggled with addiction. "He hugs me, whispers in my ear, 'Eighteen months, JP.' He was in AA. He was sober eighteen months." The following month, Lou and Laurie appeared in fancy dress as King Neptune and Queen Mermaid at the Coney Island Mermaid Parade. Lou looked glum as they rode through the crowd in a pedal car. Laurie smiled and waved, trying to jolly her husband along. Onlookers remarked on how old he looked, and somewhat strange. When he cracked a smile he revealed an extraordinary new set of white metal teeth, a radical look for a sexagenarian, more suitable for a rapper. "He thought it looked cool," says Tom Sarig, adding that Lou saw himself as more of a man of the streets than an intellectual at the end of his life. "I remember talking to him about it a few times specifically and he said, 'What is an intellectual exactly? It's a way a person thinks.' He said he didn't think that way, that he was a guy from the streets."

That summer, Lou toured with Damon Albarn's band Gorillaz, performing "Some Kind of Nature" as one of the headline acts at the Glastonbury Festival, where his movements were noticeably stiff and slow. This was followed by a collaboration with another hugely popular band, with whom he made his very last record, *Lulu*. Suitably for a transgressive artist who reveled in subverting expectations, it turned out to be one of the most controversial works of his whole career.

The story originated as two *fin-de-siècle* plays by the German dramatist Frank Wedekind, *Erdgeist* (*Earth Spirit*) and *Die Büchse der Pandora* (*Pandora's Box*), which followed the adventures of a libidinous good-time girl named Lulu (coincidentally, Lou's nickname at the Silver Factory) who took a string of lovers, most of whom met with disaster. She shot one man dead during a jealous argument, thus ending the first play. The second play tracked her descent into prostitution in London where she was ultimately murdered by Jack the Ripper. Bizarre and explicit, the plays were originally meant as a satire on the German bourgeoisie of the late nineteenth century, but the story resonated beyond its era. It was first adapted for the screen in 1929, and made into an opera by Alban Berg in the 1930s. When Robert Wilson decided to create a new stage version with the Berliner Ensemble for the twenty-first century, he turned once again to Lou. "For me, Lou was never someone who was very concerned about the commercial aspect of the rock industry. He was an inventor," Wilson explains. "It was with this music in mind that I asked him to work on Wedekind's *Lulu*!"

As Lou started work on this project he began to suffer liver problems again. Then his dog got sick. Lou and Laurie did everything they could to help Lolabelle, employing a form of musical therapy that involved the animal resting her paws on a keyboard, giving the impression that she was playing piano in return for treats (as can be seen on YouTube). Lou was almost as distraught as a bereaved parent when the dog died. "Lou was going through a very difficult time," says Wilson. "First, there was the issue of his health, and second, and even more problematic, was the long, slow death of his dog, Lolabelle. When we met, he could only speak about his love for his dog." When Lou delivered the music for *Lulu*, his first set of new songs since *The Raven*, a lament for a dead dog was mixed in.

This production of *Lulu* was initially staged in Germany in 2011, then in Venice and Paris. "It did quite well on an artsy European level," says Sarig. Events then took an unexpected turn. Despite disparaging Metallica in private in the past, Lou had recently performed with the heavy-metal band at Madison Square Garden to celebrate the twenty-fifth anniversary of the Rock 'n' Roll Hall of Fame. Lou and Metallica were an odd combination, and not everybody was impressed with their performance. "Those guys aren't at his level," sniffs Fernando Saunders. "Those guys can't hardly even play 'Sweet Jane' with him." But Lou enjoyed himself and started to talk about recording an album of his old songs with the band at their studio in Marin County, California. Then he changed his mind and said he would prefer to make an album of his new *Lulu* songs with Metallica, which they agreed to.

There were warning voices from the start. "I remember advising Lou against it," says Sarig, who sensed that an adaptation of an obscure European theater work wouldn't appeal to Metallica's conservative fans. It was going to be hard enough to get them to accept Lou singing with "their band." "I thought the commercial viability was much less than if we did Lou's greatest hits with Metallica. I remember Lou getting angry at me for that—quite angry. . . . At one of our breakfasts, as we were on the launch pad to go to Marin County, I said, 'I don't know if this is a great idea. We should stick to the first idea. That was a great idea—the greatest hits.' And he got so pissed off at me."

Metallica was used to working slowly on their records, and expected to spend a good amount of time with Lou in the studio before they attempted to record anything. They were taken aback when he took charge of the sessions and forced the pace to the extent that they recorded all ten basic tracks in as many days, during which time he virtually told them what to play. Lou became so tyrannical that guitarist Kirk Hammett had to negotiate to get a couple of solos on the album, while Lou challenged the band's leader to a fight. "One time, I had to point something out to him about how things were functioning in the outside world and he got hot and bothered," says Lars Ulrich. "He challenged me to a street fight . . ." This was a late display of machismo by a sick old man. Suddenly, Lou looked terrible, haggard and jaundiced, and no doubt his behavior was affected by the fact that he wasn't feeling well.

Eight of the ten songs he recorded with Metallica were directly inspired by Wedekind's plays. Shocking in its day, Lou made the story even more explicit. From the point of view of the eponymous heroine, he croaked in his ruined voice about being penetrated with knives, fists and cocks, pleading for the ultimate violation and gloating over the suicides of Lulu's lovers. To hear Lou playing the part of a depraved woman was itself disconcerting; he also sang from the point of view of the doctor who married her. The words came in a stream of consciousness, without verses or choruses. Some of the rhymes were clunky, while he took his preoccupation with transgressive sex and violence toward women to new extremes. "I'm a woman who likes men," he growled in "Mistress Dread," one of several songs on the album that touched on bondage. "I wish you'd tie me up and beat me . . . I beg you to degrade me . . . Please spit into my mouth." This was hard to listen to, while the underlying story was difficult to discern. As with *Berlin*, Lou was less interested in narrative than in emotion. Also like *Berlin*, he shoehorned in songs that were unrelated to the story. Unless one saw "Little Dog" as a metaphor for the heroine, it was hard to see what it had to do with anything other than his grief for Lolabelle, while the closing song, "Junior Dad," had been written years earlier, in collaboration with Rob Wasserman. Tom Sarig believes the lyrics related to Lou's relationship with his father. If so, the bogeyman of his life became the subject of the last song on his last album, ending a lifelong obsession.

This grisly melodrama was set to Metallica's thrash-metal music, as loud and repetitive as a great machine spinning out of control, alleviated with snatches of electronica. The band's front man, James Hetfield, essentially sang backing vocals to Lou, who pronounced himself delighted with the result. He told the press bombastically that *Lulu* was a record for a sophisticated adult audience who hadn't outgrown rock, adding that this was the future of serious music. "If you say, 'I want more rock, I want rock an adult can listen to, I want to still have the pleasure of rock, I don't want to have it dumbed down for me . . .' If you want to be able to continue to get that thrill that only rock can give you, then that's what this record is," he raved. "You know, this is the end of old European classical music. It's dead and buried once and for all. But this is the new breed, the new generation of classics—rock classic . . . Power." Dismissing classical music in this way was absurd, but Lou had always been prone to such statements, especially when stoned. Use of medication in his last years may account for his increased excitability.

Metallica's followers had expressed their misgivings about *Lulu* ever since news of the project emerged. One outraged fan adapted the subtitles of Oliver Hirschbiegel's film *Downfall*, so Hitler was seen to fly into a rage after being told that Metallica was working with Reed. Lou, to his credit, saw the funny side of the satire and posted a link to it on his new website. Despite the signs that fans weren't going to like what they heard, Metallica's record company, Vertigo, shipped *Lulu* in large quantities in the autumn of 2011, evidently anticipating success, while Lou and the band embarked on a promotional tour of TV studios.

The double CD that landed on reviewers' desks was a nasty object, illustrated with images of a dismembered female mannequin, the lettering scrawled in what looked like blood. Then there were the songs, a Blitzkrieg of head-banging rock combined with the most outrageous lyrics Lou had ever written, some of the words verging on the obscene, though one had to read the lyric sheet to make complete sense of what Lou said, in a voice that had become thin and quavery with illness. Many critics were revolted; others were baffled. A few, like Brad Nelson in the *Village Voice*, rated it highly. Offering the faintest praise, *Rolling Stone* reported that *Lulu* was "less ridiculous than you might expect." Print reviews meant little to Metallica's core audience, who spoke to each other online, where the consensus was that the album was "garbage," this being one of the more popular words used to denounce it on Amazon, where fans also complained that it was "the worst metal album of all time," awarding it the lowest rating. Lou's own, much smaller, audience was used to his eccentric projects. It was reassuring, in a way, that his last record turned out to be a wild one. As Mike Rathke notes, Lou never mellowed. "He never slowed down, and he never calmed down."

Despite ill health, Lou wanted to perform the *Lulu* songs live on tour with Metallica, but the band was spooked by the negative reaction of their fans and plans for a full-blown *Lulu* tour were scrapped. "Metallica's management got a little scared of pushing the envelope too far with this record," says Tom Sarig. "They've got a huge business. I can understand [it]." The CD was a flop by the band's standards, selling 32,000 copies in the USA over two years, less than a tenth of what they had hoped for, though this wasn't bad for a Lou record. In any event, it was the bitter end of a forty-four-year recording career.

BY THE TIME LOU turned seventy in March 2012, he was in poor health. "Lou was sick for the last couple of years [of his life]," Laurie Anderson noted after his death. To some extent, he had brought his problems on himself. He had abused drink and drugs since his teens. As a result, he had suffered bouts of hepatitis since his twenties, and was advised in his thirties that he had seriously damaged his liver. Although he curbed his drug taking at that time, he didn't stop drinking completely, and his liver problems became progressively more complicated in his final years. He was now obliged to submit to a course of interferon injections to treat his hepatitis C. The treatment made him feel lousy.

Things were serious enough for him to make his last will and testament in April. Laurie would be the principal beneficiary, but he set aside $500,000 for Bunny to help look after their mother, Toby, who now had dementia and was living in a care home on Long Island. He bequeathed his property to Laurie, together with Sister Ray Enterprises, his personal belongings and 75 percent of his "residuary estate," which included cash and investments and income from royalties and song publishing, as well as any posthumous business done in his name. The remaining quarter share would go to Bunny. His estate would be managed by trustees, who would make regular payments to Laurie and Bunny out of revenue.

Having settled his affairs, Lou went back to work. He continued to tour as long as possible and appeared to enjoy himself on the road. "Lou would do some amazing things. I remember on this last tour, 2012, he did 'Junior Dad.' And when he was singing that song there was a moment he thrilled everybody. He dropped down to his knees with his guitar behind his back [and] clutched the mic," recalls his drummer Tony "Thunder" Smith. "And you are looking at him and, Oh my God, it's like the divine light came through him. That energy. That gift as a singer, as a leader, as a front man, to be able to hold the audience. . . . You either have it or you don't, and Lou, God rest his soul, definitely had it."

This was the end of his career as a performer. He had been under the care of doctors for some time. Now he was diagnosed with liver cancer. Shows booked for 2013, starting with the Coachella Festival in California in April, were canceled. The band was told ten days beforehand that he wasn't going to play, but not the reason why.

Lou was at the Cleveland Clinic in Ohio. Unless he received a liver transplant, he would die. "When Lou first came, he was very sick, and before the transplant Lou had to come to Cleveland off and on to get certain therapies," explains Charles Miller, Director of Liver Transplantation at the Cleveland Clinic, and Lou's surgeon. "He was getting sicker and sicker, and a little crabbier as time rolled on. And one time he wanted to get back to New York really badly. He called me, he said, 'Charlie, let me out of here, I want to go home.' I said, 'Lou, I'll be there just as soon as I can. I'll walk over and I'll say goodbye.' On the way over I got a phone call. The liver had materialized, almost out of seemingly thin air, for Lou."

Dr. Miller walked into Lou's room. "Hi, Lou!" he said. "I know you want to go home. But I've got another idea. I think I have a liver for you."

"Are you shitting me?"

"No, I think I have a liver for you. As soon as it gets here, I'll have a look at it . . ."

"When can we do it? When can we do it?"

"A couple of hours."

Considering the reckless way he had abused his liver over the years, Lou might be considered very lucky indeed to have the opportunity of a transplant. Essentially, he was in a position to buy himself a second chance.

As the liver donor was taken off life support and died, Lou received new life. Dr. Miller sewed the donor liver into his body while listening to "Walk on the Wild Side." The operation went well. "They put it in immediately, and it started to work immediately. Every week it gets better," Laurie explained in a June 2013 interview with the *Times,* which broke the story. "I don't think he'll ever totally recover from this, but he'll certainly be back to doing [things] in a few months." Apparently displeased with his wife's prognosis, Lou posted a contrary message online: "I am a triumph of modern medicine, physics and chemistry. I am bigger and stronger than ever." A few days later he was photographed walking with a cane near his New York apartment. On June 14 he posted a picture of himself doing a tai chi kick in his living room.

His first public appearance after the transplant was as a guest speaker at a festival in France on June 20. His voice was shaky as he read from his adaptation of Poe's "The Raven," in which the eponymous bird can be interpreted as the personification of Death. "Quoth the Raven 'Nevermore.'" Lou spoke to reporters briefly, irascible and thoughtful by turn. "How could time go that quickly?" he asked rhetorically. "It never ceases to amaze me. The other day I was nineteen. I could fall down and get back up. Now if I fall down, you are talking about nine months of physical therapy."

He spent the rest of the summer with Laurie and their new dog, Willy, at their home on Long Island. He walked on the beach, swam in his pool and ate more than usual, relishing dessert in particular. Everything suddenly felt precious. "He would say, especially towards the end, 'I'm so lucky,'" says Jenni Muldaur. "He would say, 'Do you know how lucky we are?'" Lou received get-well messages from friends and colleagues and replied in more kindly terms than in the past. "Lou very much became a changed person," says Velvet Underground lawyer Chris Whent. "He was much easier to deal with, much mellower, more ready to share affection, and prouder than I can tell you of what the Velvets did." Lou took a close interest in the re-release of the band's MGM albums in deluxe new editions, and spoke by phone to John Cale in Los Angeles, where Cale was now based, about the possibility of working together on a new arrangement of *Songs for Drella*. One day, Moe Tucker received an unexpected gift of candy at home in Georgia with a note, "To Moesy with all love and respect, Lou." "I called him and said, 'Thank you, you made me feel special.' And he said, 'You are.' But he didn't say, 'I'm sick.' I think this package from nowhere had something to do with starting to say goodbye, because it was really unusual."

He went to London in September to help Mick Rock promote a book of photographs he had taken of Lou over the years. They met the press at Trident Studios in Soho, where Lou had recorded *Transformer*, after which the book was named. He also attended an awards ceremony at the Royal Opera House, where he spoke briefly about his debt to Warhol. Back in New York, he did an interview to promote a range of headphones. During the conversation, he spoke about his first guitar. "Your father gave you a guitar?" the interviewer asked. Lou snarled in reply: "My father didn't give me shit." Fernando Saunders was struck by the vehemence of this remark, believing that it went to the root of Lou's psychology. "Lou had a lot of bitterness," he says. "That interview when he said his father didn't do shit for him, I think that's the answer right there . . . I think that's where all that came from."

Lou's failing health was still more evident when he did a book signing with Mick Rock at the former premises of CBGB in New York in October. His energy level was down. He spoke softly, as if it took a lot of effort, and he looked awful. When people at the back of the room continued to talk over him, he lost his temper and yelled at them: "Hey! Shut up." At the end, photographer Bob Gruen stepped forward to say hello and shake Lou's hand, shocked by how he looked. "We all knew he was ill. He was yellow that day. It was obvious."

THE YELLOW TINGE TO his skin indicated that his new liver wasn't working. "We all agreed that we did everything we could," says Charles Miller, who met Lou at the Cleveland Clinic in October. Laurie took him home to New York, where he spent time with friends, including his neighbor Julian Schnabel. They watched Schnabel's film of the first night of their 2006 *Berlin* show. "[He] said, 'Does anybody know?' He never felt like people really got it. He always felt, in a way, unappreciated . . ." Then Lou left the city for the last time, returning the way he had come in life, past the old neighborhoods in Brooklyn where he played stick ball and stoop ball as a kid, past Freeport, and out into rural Long Island. It was fall and the trees were resplendent in autumn colors as the car turned off the Montauk Highway, bumped over the railway track and rolled down the lane to the little gray house in the woods.

On Friday, October 25, Lou was visited at home by a local doctor and his friends Jenni Muldaur and Hal Willner. They sat with him while Laurie made a quick trip into Manhattan. "He was in a lot of pain," says Jenni. Lou was most comfortable lying on the floor, so they lay down with him to watch David Cronenberg's *Crash* and to listen to a music compilation Hal had made. "We had the most peaceful night, and it was quite beautiful," says Jenni. "And then Laurie came back. She needed to do something [in] the city. She came back late at night."

Lou and Laurie stayed up through Saturday night, talking and practicing breathing exercises, Lou repeating his Buddhist mantra "*om ah hung.*" On the morning of Sunday, October 27, 2013, he asked his wife to take him into the light. She says that these were his last words. Buddhists seek the Clear Light of the Void at the time of death; it is analogous to a Christian seeing the light. More prosaically, Lou wanted to sit in the sunshine. When he was settled on the sun deck, he practiced a tai chi exercise with his hands. "I have never seen an expression as full of wonder as Lou's as he died," Laurie later wrote in a tender and moving obituary for *Rolling Stone*. "His hands were doing the water-flowing 21-form of tai chi. His eyes were wide open. I was holding in my arms the person I loved most in the world, and talking to him as he died. His heart stopped. He wasn't afraid. I had gotten to walk with him to the end of the world." It was 12:30 p.m. Cause of death was cardiopulmonary arrest, as a consequence of the cancer that had started in his liver and then spread. He was seventy-one. "It's good that he could die with her holding him," observes Lou's old playmate Billy Name. "He was able to die a graceful, elegant death, instead of being alone, and flopping out or something. She made his life beautiful."

Friends gathered at the house to sit and pray with Lou's body during Sunday night. The body was transported to the nearby town of Center Moriches on Monday, where it was cremated. The next morning, Bunny told their mother. She had to speak loudly to get through to her, and didn't know if Mom would fully understand, but Lou's death registered. Toby sat up and gabbled excitedly. "She said something like 'ton,'" says Bunny's husband. "She was trying to say 'son.'" Toby died nine days later.

DESPITE THE FACT THAT Lou had been a niche artist with relatively modest record sales, his death received considerable media attention. The CNN screen on Times Square flashed his picture with the inevitable cliché, used in countless headlines, "He walked on the wild side." Celebrity friends paid tribute on Twitter. "He was a master," wrote David Bowie, with little discernible warmth. Newspapers ran substantial obituaries. Lou's cerebral, literary brand of rock had always appealed to writers and editors, and the press coverage of his

death reflected this fact more than his popularity with the general public. While the tone of most obituaries was laudatory, Lou's antagonism toward journalists colored some articles. Writing in the *New Statesman*, Kate Mossman noted his "studied charmlessness," adding that he "could be one of the coldest, most humourless and—worse—boring characters rock 'n' roll has ever seen."

Posthumous publicity boosted sales of his music, increasing the value of his estate to over $30 million—a surprisingly large sum for a man who had been in a financial muddle for much of his career. Laurie and Bunny were rich women. Bunny considers it remarkable that Lou lived as long as he did, bearing in mind "the emotional issues that pursued him throughout his life." They had remained close, which was an achievement when one considers how tricky he was. "In his heart, my brother was a profoundly good, moral person," she concludes.

Although Lou had been raised in the Jewish faith, he and Laurie had developed an interest in Tibetan Buddhism, which teaches that there is an intermediate state between death and reincarnation as another human being, a period symbolically taken to last forty-nine days, known as the Bardo. Every Sunday for the seven weeks of the Bardo after he died, Laurie met with friends to talk about aspects of his life as he made his spiritual journey. In the final stage the deceased is believed to be judged. Good karma accumulated in life can send the deceased to Buddhist Heaven, before returning to Earth to start all over again, while bad karma can result in a period of torment and pain not unlike being in Hell before reincarnation; it is only the fortunate few who achieve Nirvana and escape the circle. The Bardo process is marked by prayers, ending, in Lou's case, on December 15, 2013. The next day, friends and colleagues gathered at the Apollo Theater in Harlem for a memorial concert.

Taking an overview of his career, Lou's biggest achievement was as a member of the Velvet Underground, and the two surviving members of the original band were among the artists invited to the memorial. Laurie asked Moe if she would sing one of Lou's songs. John Cale then contacted Moe to suggest that he accompany her onstage, but Moe was concerned that there wasn't enough time to rehearse, and she thought she might cry if she tried to sing. "I said, 'No, I don't think so.' And then [Cale] backed out . . . I think I gave him the excuse, I think that gave him [an] out, because he was so emotional about Lou dying."

John did not attend the memorial. Instead, Moe read a letter he had written for the occasion. "We got each other . . . he got me and I got him," it read in part. "Much will always be made of the band we formed together in my dingy little living-room apartment—I'll leave those remarks for others—I prefer to consider how much I gained from my friendship with Lou—the part the rest of the world is not privy to: the dreams, ideas and plans we shared and, to a degree, achieved." Privately, John, a reformed drinker, was disappointed that Lou had returned to the bottle in recent years. "It came as a shock," he later said of his death, "even though I was resigned to the fact that he was doing himself in. 'What the hell are you doing? It's all about the work, not drinking a bottle of wine.' I don't understand. He went out in blazing colors, I suppose."

Although many famous artists performed at the memorial, including Debbie Harry, Paul Simon and Patti Smith, the words spoken by Laurie were the most poignant part of the evening. "From the moment we met, Lou and I started to talk, and we talked nonstop about everything *conceivable* for twenty-one years," she told the audience, referring back to their 1992 meeting. She then offered a series of insights into the private life of the man she had known. She referred to his image as a black-clad tough guy, saying: "He had learned how not to be Lou Reed many years ago. And he could put Lou Reed on and take him off like one of his jackets." She noted his extraordinary facility for songwriting, how he would sometimes wake in the night and write ideas down, and how songs often came to him fully formed. "He never changed a word. First thought best thought." She described an emotional man, who often cried, though she noted that outsiders experienced his anger and frustration. "But in the last few years, each time he was angry it was followed by an apology until the anger and the apology got closer and closer, until they were almost on top of each other, and finally almost the same thing."

She spoke about their everyday life together as a couple in New York, where they often went out at night to see a show or attend an event, the home they built together on Long Island, and their travels. She described a mutual love affair that had lasted to death. "I never had a single doubt that we loved each other beyond anything else from the time we first met until the moment he died. Almost every day we said, 'And you, you are the love of my life.' . . . And even if I was angry and frustrated, I was never for one second bored." On a lighter note, she recalled her husband's "over-the-top *insane* laugh," mimicking his cackle, described his habit of showing how the hairs on his arms bristled when he heard music he liked, and how he often used to tell her when they went for pizza, "Like you always say, 'You can't lose money with bread and cheese.'" The audience laughed. This was like one of the funny stories in Anderson's shows, freighted with a deeper meaning about the way people misunderstand each other. "I don't remember ever saying that. Or actually anything about bread and cheese, but it had become something Lou loved to quote . . . I had said a lot of other things that I *hoped* would be memorable, maybe even quotable, but it was this one that he seemed to really have by heart . . ."

As the laughter subsided, she concluded: "Lou showed me so many things. And I got to show some things to him, too. During the last few months of his life Lou was so *dazzled* by nature, by the beauty of water and trees, and he often said, 'You always told me the trees were dancing, and now I see that they are. They're dancing.'"

This was a moving and insightful speech, while the memorial as a whole was a fitting send-off for a major artist. At his best, Lou

Reed captured aspects of urban life in songs that had an economy of language, a distinct, often witty point of view and a literary quality uncommon in rock 'n' roll. While he specialized in the underbelly of life, he didn't just write about drug users and trans people. He had range. Lou was a limited performer and a variable recording artist with a kamikaze streak, but he stands as one of the most distinctive American artists of the rock era. "In the pantheon sense, he's up there. Whether he's the greatest American rock performer, I'd give Dylan that, obviously, just thinking of the white guys," concludes the critic John Rockwell. "I'd put [Lou] up there, but one notch down, bearing in mind there are a lot of notches below."

For all those gathered at the Apollo Theater, many friends were absent. This was a memorial led by his third wife, attended by those who'd been in favor during the past few years, a time when Lou had mellowed and developed an elite new social circle. He had cut his ties with his rapscallion past, and people from that past. Absent friends had their own memories: more mixed, perhaps more realistic, no less profound. Erin Clermont was not among those invited to the memorial, despite being Lou's friend and lover over four decades, during which time he frequently called her late at night, when he was speeding, asking to pop around. Many nights he climbed the five flights of marble stairs to her small apartment in Greenwich Village. There is a cigarette burn on the side table in her lounge to remind her of his visits. "It's hard to think that the phone is not going to ring at three in the morning [and he's going to say], 'How are you doing?'" she says, impersonating his gruff voice. His death was the end of part of her life, too. "What a guy," she sighs. "What a guy!"

AUTHOR'S NOTE
AND ACKNOWLEDGMENTS

UNLIKE TOO MANY CELEBRITIES, Lou Reed didn't write an autobiography. "Why would I? Write about myself? Set the record straight? There's not a record to set straight. I am what I am. It is what it is, and fuck you," he told *Mojo* with characteristic acerbity in 2013. An artist's work is the most important part of his life, but for those of us who were fascinated by Reed's songs it is natural to want to know more about the man who wrote and sang them.

To paraphrase Frank Zappa, it is difficult to write about what it means to listen to music, beyond giving a basic description of the work, a suggestion of what the author gets from it, and what critics have said. The effect remains ethereal, and what makes for a good or bad song is very much a matter of taste. In writing about a songwriter, it is easier to discuss the ideas and images conveyed in lyrics, which is partly why so much attention is paid to lyrics in books of this kind. Also, writers are interested in the words of other writers; it is a subject they understand. Above all, however, this book is a portrait of a human being, of his personality and actions, and the trajectory of his career, which is to say, it is a biography.

As with any significant artist with a long career, there have been several biographies of Lou Reed, and there will be more. Of those published in his lifetime, Victor Bockris's book, first published in 1994 as *Lou Reed: The Biography* and recently updated as *Transformer:*

The Complete Lou Reed Story, was the best. It has its faults, as all books do. Bockris doesn't always get his facts right, and he has an unfortunate habit of quoting anonymous sources. But it is of interest. Two less impressive biographies were published quickly after Reed's death: *Lou Reed: The Life* by Mick Wall and *The Life and Music of Lou Reed* by Jeremy Reed, the latter being an updated book. There will be others. I hope that *Notes from the Velvet Underground* surpasses all these books in all vital aspects. A good biography should be entertaining, enlightening and convincing. It should be well constructed and clearly written with a nonjudgmental tone, conveying a sense of the subject's character and personality, his work, his relationships, and the times in which he lived. That is what I have always aimed for. It is of course for the reader to decide what they think of the result.

To explain a little more about my approach, *Notes from the Velvet Underground* covers Reed's whole life with a slight emphasis on his work with the Velvet Underground, upon which his reputation largely rests. The songs he wrote for the band in the 1960s were the mainstay of his act for the rest of his career, and he was always closely associated with underground culture: the underbelly of urban life and the excitement of the illicit. Reed was one of the most literary rock musicians, making his notes from underground and reporting back to us in song, hence this book's title, which also invokes Dostoyevsky's underground man, another damaged, hyperconscious outsider. Reed aspired to write as well as the Russian.

As a biographer, it is helpful to have a preexisting interest in and sympathy for the subject, and I have always felt drawn to outsiders. I developed my enthusiasm for Reed's songs at a young age, when music makes a strong and lasting impression, hooked by his second solo album, *Transformer,* then by the Velvet Underground. Buying his subsequent albums could be a frustrating business, and sometimes felt like a waste of money. He was an inconsistent artist who released some shoddy work, and I found him to be a stiff and awkward performer in concert. Nevertheless, I always liked the way he expressed himself, I was intrigued by his subject matter, and I enjoyed his intelligence and sense of humor. So I kept listening. As some readers may agree, his work started to get more interesting again in recent years, if not more popular, and I have made an effort to reflect that in this book, which I started directly after his death in October 2013.

This is my tenth biographical book, written over the course of twenty years. My debut was a book about the murderers Fred and Rosemary West, published in 1995. I have written one other true-crime book (about a misfit gang of robbers), two books about the American author Charles Bukowski (another outsider), a book about the leading figures in professional golf, a history of the arts in the 1970s, an investigation into the so-called 27 Club of rock musicians who died at that young age, and three biographies of popular musicians: Bob Dylan, Paul McCartney and now Lou Reed. These might seem like eclectic subjects, but all these books are essentially about remarkable and intriguing people. It is the psychology of the individual that attracts me.

All biographies are built on a foundation of knowledge laid down over the years by previous writers. The first job is to read and assimilate everything that is in the public domain—books, newspaper articles, magazine interviews—as well as listening to and watching everything pertinent. I then do extensive research of my own. I visit the places where the subject lived and worked; I locate as many documents as I can find, including court records and what Americans call vital records (births, deaths and marriages), allowing me to construct the factual skeleton of the story; and I communicate with everybody I am able to reach who played a part in the life, including friends, family members, lovers, spouses and colleagues, in this case interviewing approximately one hundred and forty people. The job is then to assemble all this information in a way that tells the story better than it has been told before, and moves the story on, correcting mistakes, adding detail, introducing new themes and nuances, creating a compelling and entertainingly fresh portrait.

The first person I contacted about this book was Reed's widow, Laurie Anderson. She chose not to participate. This is not unusual, and it isn't a calamity. One doesn't require anyone's permission to write biography, and the people closest to the subject often have their own agenda. There is, however, a prejudice that biographies are only valid if they are "authorized," a frequently misused term implying that there is an authority who ordains what is legitimate. There is not. In fact, with exceptions, so-called authorized biographies all too easily become vanity projects to promote an image of a public figure while burying or misrepresenting difficult truths. There are bad unauthorized biographies, of course. Writing a good book of any kind is hard. A particular challenge for the independent biographer is getting people to speak. Some won't cooperate, because they feel they aren't allowed to, whether or not there is interference. Others are brave enough to make up their own mind. If the biographer is sincere and persistent, they will get people to talk, while retaining the advantage of having the freedom to write a book that is not censored or influenced by interested parties.

Lives are messy, and Reed's was messier than most. He was a complex, difficult man. The whole truth must come out in a book of this kind, as much as one is able to find out about the truth. Most lives remain mysterious to some degree. Readers sometimes want to know if the author likes or dislikes his subject. I try to be neutral, though the shape and tone of the book is subjective. The aim is to assemble the best available evidence in a way that seems true and fair. I didn't know Reed personally, so I learned about him from people who did, and formulated a story partly based on their testimony, following the themes that emerged, while editing out what seemed to be bogus or irrelevant. Ultimately, it is up to readers to decide what they think about the subject, if they have to form a conclusion. To my mind, it isn't a question of liking or disliking someone like Lou Reed; it is enough that he is significant and interesting.

In writing biographies of popular musicians, my experience has been that some readers come to these books with a bias. They may have been listening to the artist's music for many years, during which time the songs have become part of their lives. They identify with the artist, have strong ideas about which records are best, and often believe they know the truth about them, though they haven't made a close study of the subject. If they then read what they take as criticism of their idol, though it may simply be somebody's opinion, they can become offended. It is better to keep an open mind, accepting that opinions differ, as interviewees often have contradictory memories of events (it is rare for two witnesses to remember an incident exactly the same way), that what you believe is not necessarily true, and that there is good and bad in most people.

I am grateful to everyone who assisted me during my research including, in alphabetical order: Shelley Albin, Paul Auster, Cornelius and Pat Bass, Brigid Berlin, Rubén Blades, Ellard "Moose" Boles, Daryl Bornstein, Randy Brecker, David Byrd, Felix Cavaliere, Robert Christgau, Rupert Christie, Erin Clermont, Ray Colcord, Pete Cornish, David Croland, Joe Dallesandro, Thomas Dargan, Clive Davis, Stuart "Dinky" Dawson, Godfrey Diamond, Dion DiMucci, Norman Dolph, Joe Doyle, Allen Edwards, Patti Elam, Steve Epstein, Chrissy Faith, Danny Fields, Yossi Fine, Ritchie Fliegler, Henry Flynt, Marty Fogel, Michael Fonfara, Danny Frankel, Alan Freedman, Vincent Fremont, Josh Alan Friedman, Barbara Fulk, Sean Fullan, Jill Furmanovsky, Bernie Gelb, Liz Gilmore, Pentti "Whitey" Glan, Danny Goldberg, Dr. James Gorney, Paula Gorney (née Swarzman), Bob Gruen, Pat Hackett, John Halsey, Chuck Hammer, Howard Harding, Stuart Heinrich, Catherine Hesketh (née Guinness), Barbara Hodes, Allan Hyman, Jerome Jackson, Elyse "Ellie" Jacobs, Jim Jacobs, Tama Janowitz, Prakash John, Dennis Katz, Steve Katz, Scott Kempner, Howie Klein, Professor Michael S. Kogan, Bettye Kronstad, Bob Kulick, Steve Labar, Dari Lallou, Gloria Lauden, Lisa Law, Jeffrey Lichtman, Fred Maher, Tom "Bones" Malone, Peter Maloney,

Ed McCormack, Zeljko Mcmullen, Kate Mikulka, Richard Mishkin, Paul Morrissey, Martha Morrison, Jenni Muldaur, Elliott Murphy, Billy Name, Mandy Newall, Judith November (née Titus), Richard Nusser, Struan Oglanby, Larry Packer, John Passalacqua, Doane Perry, Kellie Petersen, Terry Philips, Jonny Podell, Mike Quashie (the Limbo King), Charlie Rapino, Mike Rathke, Genya Ravan, Master Ren Guang-Yi, Bob Ringe, John Rockwell, Jeffrey Ross, Ed Sanders, Tom Sarig, Fernando Saunders, Jane Scarpantoni, Fred Schmidt, Jeanie and the late Jimmy Scott, Mike "Coach" Sexton, Sam Shepard, Jon Sholle, Richard Sigal, Tony "Thunder" Smith, Bruce Somerfeld, Pete Stampfel, Corky Stasiak, Chris Stein, Rosalind Stevenson, Karl Stoecker, Casey Synge, Rita Teel, Robert Tramontin, Moe Tucker, the late Dick Wagner, Rick Wakeman, Peter Walsh, Rob Wasserman, Merrill "Bunny" Weiner (née Reed) and her husband, Harold, Chris Whent, Victoria Williams, Robert Wilson, Christine Wiltshire, Holly Woodlawn, Mary Woronov, Bruce Yaw, Doug Yule and Tony Zanetta.

I drew on a handful of interviews conducted for some of my previous books. These include my interviews with the late Al Aronowitz for *Down the Highway*; with Clem Cattini and Herbie Flowers for *Fab*; and Angie Bowie and Ken Scott for *Seventies*.

I am grateful to staff at the Andy Warhol Museum, the British Library and New York University Registrar's Office; Bill Bentley in Los Angeles; Ken Lally and Ravi Romano in Blairstown; June Koffi and Ivy K. Marvel at Brooklyn Public Library; Rose Luna at Freeport High School; Consuelo Velez at Caroline G. Atkinson School in Freeport; Regina G. Feeney and Cynthia J. Krieg at Freeport Memorial Library; Corey E. Stewart at the National Personnel Records Center in St Louis; Diana Rahmaan at PS 92 in Brooklyn; Mary M. O'Brien at Syracuse University Archives; Edda Tasiemka at the Hans Tasiemka Archives in London; and Richie Unterberger in San Francisco.

Finally, thank you to Andrea Henry, Sheila Lee and Michelle Signore at Transworld; to copyeditor Sarah Day; to lawyer Lucy Moorman; and to my agent, Gordon Wise, at Curtis Brown.

SOURCE NOTES

Lou Reed is abbreviated in these notes to LR. Full details of court cases are given in the first instance, then abbreviated. I also abbreviate the titles of some newspapers, as will become apparent. For chart positions, I relied upon *Billboard* and the *Guinness Book of British Hit Singles* (ed. Roberts), in combination with *The Essential Rock Discography* (Strong). See the bibliography for full publication details.

I CONEY ISLAND BABY, 1942–59

p. 1–2   LA and the Eldorados at St Lawrence University, based on author's interviews with Richard Mishkin (quoted dialogue) and Nelson Slater.

p. 2   Physical description of LR, his draft record and author's interviews.

p. 2   LR birth and ancestry, vital records and US census.

p. 2   Louis Firbank: the otherwise excellent *Cambridge Biographical Encyclopaedia* (Cambridge, 1994), for example, has LR born Louis Firbank in 1944, which is wrong in every respect.

p. 3   Harold Weiner quoted from author's interview.

p. 3   Contemporaneous events with birth, *Brooklyn Eagle*.

p. 4   LR: "I know what . . .": Q, Feb. 1992.

p. 4   For Sid Reed's character and much else in this chapter I am grateful to Merrill "Bunny" Weiner for giving me (in 2014) a detailed written account of her family history, including her brother's first breakdown. I quote Mrs. Weiner from this document throughout this chapter, unless otherwise specified. I also refer to a later version of the document posted online at Cuepoint in 2015.

p. 4   Julian Schnabel: "He put his . . .": *Rolling Stone*, 11/21/13.

p. 4   "Shirley" Rabinowitz background, LR's 2010 film *Red Shirley*.

p. 4   Surname changes, census records and Merrill Weiner's family history.

p. 4–5   Toby Reed's background, census records, author's interview and correspondence with Merrill "Bunny" Weiner, plus her family history.

p. 5   Mysterious brother: Mick Wall writes in *Lou Reed: The Life*, "Lewis was the eldest children [sic] of three, with a younger sister, Elizabeth [sic], whom he was close to, and a younger brother . . ." Completely wrong.

p. 6   LR wrote in *Between Thought and Expression* that he wrote "My Old Man" for his father, but denied in a Sept. 1980 interview with *Creem* that Sid hit his mother.

p. 6   LR: "I see myself . . .": *GQ*, Sept. 1986.
p. 6   LR: "the armpit . . .": *Rolling Stone*, 3/6/03.
p. 7   LR: "My parents were . . .": *Melody Maker*, 12/18/76.
p. 7   First wife (Bettye Kronstad) quoted from author's interview.
p. 7–8   Allan Hyman quoted throughout from author's interview.
p. 8   Merrill "Bunny" Weiner: "We were Jewish . . .": correspondence with author.
p. 8   LR's education, thanks to Rose Luna at Freeport High School and Consuelo
            Velez at Caroline G. Atkinson Intermediate School in Freeport for school re-
            cords; also Regina G. Feeney and Cynthia J. Krieg at Freeport Memorial Library.
p. 8   Honor roll student, Freeport *Leader*, 6/26/52.
p. 8   LR's IQ/days off school, school records.
p. 8   Summer job at Jones Beach, author's interview with Richard Sigal
            (quoted throughout).
p. 8   Bullied at Junior High, 2015 version of Merrill "Bunny" Weiner's family history.
p. 9   Jerome Jackson quoted from author's interview.
p. 9   Phil Harris quoted from an interview with Olivier Landemaine, olivier.lander-
            maine.free.fr.
p. 11–13   Dating stories, author's interviews with Hyman and Sigal.
p. 12–13   Judy Titus quoted from author's interview.
p. 14   LR's year-book entry, 1959 Freeport High *Voyageur*.
p. 15–18   LR's first breakdown and treatment, sister's 2014 written history (quoted with
            reference to 2015 version) and author's interview with Hyman.
p. 15   Toby Reed: "The pediatrician . . .": recalled by daughter in 2015 version of the
            family history.
p. 16   ECT background, *New Encyclopaedia Britannica*.
p. 16   LR receives twenty-four shocks, *Between Thought and Expression* (Reed).
p. 17   Law on homosexuality, *How We Got Here* (Frum).
p. 17   Bockris writes that ECT was intended to cure LR of homosexuality and "mood
            swings," *Transformer: The Complete Lou Reed Story*.
p. 17   LR: "That's what was . . .": *Creem*, March 1979.

II ON TO THE DARKENED SEA, 1960–64

p. 19   Removed from New York University, NYU registrar.
p. 19   LR: "I was miserable . . . ": *Melody Maker*, 4/21/79.
p. 19   Merrill "Bunny" Weiner quoted from her written history, unless otherwise
            stated.
p. 20   Fraternity party, author's interview with Allan Hyman (quoted throughout from
            author's interview).
p. 20–21   LA and the Eldorados, author's interviews with Hyman, Richard Mishkin and
            Nelson Slater, all quoted from author's interviews.
p. 21–22   Cavaliere quoted from author's interview.
p. 22   Lincoln Swados background, *The Four of Us* (Swados), and author's interviews.
p. 22–23   Sigal quoted throughout from author's interview.
p. 23   Insomnia, LR mentions to Paul Zollo, *Performing Songwriter*, 2000.
p. 23   Maloney quoted from author's interview.
p. 23   Jim Tucker background, author's interview with Moe Tucker.
p. 23–24   Sterling Morrison meets LR, quoted from *Feed-back* (Julià).
            Morrison background, author's interview with his widow, Martha Morrison
            (quoted).
p. 24   Dismissed from ROTC, LR interview in *People*, 3/30/81.
p. 24–26   Shelley Albin quoted throughout from author's interviews. Also dialogue with
            LR.
p. 25   Quotes from *Junky* (Burroughs, p. 49) and *City of Night* (Rechy, p. 321).
p. 26   LR on Shelley: "Look, you couldn't . . .": author's interview with Erin Clermont.
p. 26   LR: "I remember that . . .": *Creem*, March 1979.

p. 29　　James and Paula Gorney quoted from author's interviews.

p. 30　　Stoecker quoted from author's interview.

p. 30　　Car accident, author's interviews with Stoecker, Barbara Hodes and correspondence with Merrill Weiner (quoted).

p. 30　　LR: "I liked Ornette . . .": *Creem,* Sept. 1980.

p. 30–32　*Lonely Woman Quarterly,* Syracuse University archives.

p. 31　　Kogan quarrel, author's interview with Professor Kogan (quoted).

p. 32–33　Schwartz background, *Delmore Schwartz* (Atlas), *Humboldt's Gift* (Bellow), and author's interviews with former students, including Clermont, Gorney and Rosalind Stevenson.

p. 34　　LR: "Once, drunk in . . .": *Sounds,* 5/6/78.

p. 35　　Reads *City of Night/poster* on wall, author's interviews with Clermont, quoted throughout from author's interviews.

p. 36　　Sex boasts, James Gorney interview.

p. 38　　LR: "I had recently . . .": his essay *Fallen Knights and Fallen Angels,* published in *No One Waved Good-bye* (Somma). Also *Between Thought and Expression* (Reed).

p. 39　　Ambition to write Great American Novel, LR in *Rolling Stone,* 11/5/87, for example.

p. 39–40　Lyrics quoted from "Heroin," Oakfield Avenue Music Ltd.

p. 40　　LR graduates, Syracuse University registrar service.

p. 40–41　LR: "because of various . . ." and "Jaw gave me . . .": *Fallen Knights and Fallen Angels* (Reed).

III HONEYBUN, BLACK JACK, STERL AND MOESY, 1964–65

p. 42–44　Terry Philips quoted throughout from author's interview.

p. 43　　LR: "hack shit": *Independent,* 4/26/03.

p. 43–44　LR on his "horrifying job," Q, May 2000.

p. 44　　LR wrote for Kiss, *Music from the Elder* (1981).

p. 45–47　Cale on meeting LR, etc., quoted from *What's Welsh for Zen* (unless otherwise specified).

p. 46　　La Monte Young background/downtown music scene, author's interviews and correspondence with Henry Flynt and Billy Name. Also *The Rest is Noise* (Ross).

p. 46　　MacLise background, *NY Times,* 5/5/11.

p. 46–47　Cale arrested/conversation with LR, *What's Welsh for Zen* (Cale).

p. 47–48　Background on the Primitives, *White Light/White Heat* (Unterberger).

p. 48　　Cale: "When I first . . .": *Option,* July 1990.

p. 48–49　LR medical, Selective Service records.

p. 49　　Flynt conversation with Cale, author's interview with Flynt.

p. 50　　Lyrics quoted from "I'm Waiting for the Man," Oakfield Avenue Music Ltd.

p. 50　　LR maxim, recalled by former road manager Daryl Bornstein in interview with author.

p. 51　　Lyrics quoted from "Black Angel's Death Song" by Reed and Cale, John Cale Music, Inc./Oakfield Avenue Music Ltd.

p. 51　　Cale: "I wasn't going . . .": *What's Welsh for Zen* (Cale).

p. 52　　Giving blood, posing for photos, etc., LR quoted ("And when my . . .") by Bockris in *Lou Reed.*

p. 52　　LR meets Morrison in NYC, recalled by Morrison in the *Austin Sun,* Oct. 1975.

p. 52–53　De Maria quoted from Smithsonian oral-history interview, 10/4/72.

p. 53　　The Warlocks at the Cinémathèque, *The Velvet Underground* (Kugelberg).

p. 53　　Morrison on working at Pickwick, *Austin Sun,* Oct. 1975.

p. 53–54　Morrison on band name, *Feed-back* (Julià).

p. 54　　1965 demo tape/dialogue, *Peel Slowly and See* box set (Polydor, 1995).

p. 54　　Aronowitz background, author's interview for *Down the Highway.*

p. 55　　Aronowitz on meeting the Velvets, his blog *The Blacklisted Journalist.*

p. 55   Martha Morrison quoted from author's interview.
p. 55–56   Moe Tucker quoted throughout from author's interview.
p. 56   Summit High gig, author's interviews with Martha Morrison and Moe Tucker; *Disc and Music Echo* (1/29/72); Norris quoted from *The Velvet Underground* (Kugelberg).
p. 57   Cale: "No chicks": author's interview with Tucker.
p. 57   Cale didn't bring pop clichés to the band, Morrison in *Lou Reed* (Bockris).
p. 58–59   Malanga on meeting the Velvets, *Up-tight* (Bockris) and *Feed-back* (Julià).
p. 59   Morrison: "Who is this lunatic?": *Austin Sun*, Oct. 1975.
p. 59   Paul Morrissey quoted throughout from author's interview, unless otherwise stated.
p. 60   Warhol quoted from *POPism* (Warhol).
p. 60–61   Inside the Silver Factory, author's interviews with Brigid Berlin, Danny Fields, Billy Name, Paul Morrissey and Mary Woronov. Background reading includes *POPism* (Warhol).
p. 62   Ondine injected himself in eye, interview with Woronov.
p. 62   Herko suicide, *POPism* (Warhol) and *Famous for Fifteen Minutes* (Ultra Violet).
p. 62   Told Slater he intended to use meth for the rest of his life, author's interview.
p. 62   Edie Sedgwick background, *Edie* (Stein).
p. 63   Heliczer film, *White Light/White Heat* (Unterberger).
p. 63   New Year's Eve revelry, author's interviews and *POPism* (Warhol).

IV THE EXPLODING PLASTIC INEVITABLE, 1966

p. 64–65   Psychiatrists' dinner, author's interview with Moe Tucker, Jonas Mekas's *Scenes from the Life of Andy Warhol*, coverage in the *NY Times* and *NY Herald Tribune*, 1/14/65 (quoted diners).
p. 64   Questions to diners, *POPism* (Warhol).
p. 65–66   Morrissey quoted throughout from author's interview, unless otherwise indicated.
p. 66   Nico on LR, documentary *Nico: Icon* (ZDF, 1995).
p. 66   Mishkin quoted throughout from author's interview.
p. 66   Cale on LR and Nico, *Nico: Icon* (ZDF, 1995).
p. 66   Woronov quoted throughout from author's interviews, unless otherwise indicated.
p. 68–67   Nico background, *Nico* (Witts); *Nico* (Young); and *Nico: Icon* (ZDF, 1995).
p. 67   Albin and Hodes on "I'll Be Your Mirror," author's interviews.
p. 67   Martha Morrison quoted throughout from author's interview.
p. 68   Billy Name quoted throughout from author's interview.
p. 68   LR on Warhol's work ethic, *The Autobiography and Sex Life of Andy Warhol* (Wilcock).
p. 69   Nico: "Lou wanted to . . .": *Nico* (Witts).
p. 69   Edie Sedgwick's death, *Edie* (Stein).
p. 69–71   Road trip, author's interviews, *POPism* (Warhol), *Up-tight* (Bockris) and *The Autobiography and Sex Life of Andy Warhol* (Wilcock), from which the hecklers are quoted.
p. 70   Warhol fondled LR, photograph published in *Andy Warhol: The Factory Years* (Finkelstein).
p. 70   Fields quoted throughout from author's interviews.
p. 71   Moe Tucker quoted throughout from author's interview.
p. 73   Morrissey: "It was packed . . .": *Up-tight* (Bockris).
p. 74   Woronov quoted from author's interviews, except "Dwarfed by Mario Montez's . . ." and dialogue with Ingrid Superstar (her book *Swimming Underground)*.
p. 74   Dancing at the Dom, author's interviews with Ellie Jacobs and Martha Morrison.
p. 75   Cale: "Lou had very . . ." and LR to Nico, "We know what *we're* doing, Nico": *Nico* (Witts).

p. 75   Norman Dolph records the Velvets, author's interview with Dolph (quoted throughout).

p. 76   Warhol's advice to LR in the studio, *Peel Slowly and See* booklet.

p. 75–78   Scepter Records sessions, author's interview with Dolph, Martha Morrison and Moe Tucker. Background, *The Velvet Underground & Nico* (Harvard).

p. 76   Cale: "Basically, Lou . . .": *Nico* (Witts).

p. 77   LR: "It's about a . . .": *Penthouse* interview, 1977 (vol. 12, no. 2). Lyric quoted from "There She Goes Again," Oakfield Avenue Music Ltd.

p. 78   Hyman quoted from author's interview.

p. 78   Nico: "I cannot make love . . .": recalled by Cale in *Nico* (Witts).

p. 78   Morrison on Nico crying, *Nico: Icon* (ZDF, 1995).

p. 78   Paid $5 a day each, Morrison in *Q*, July 1993.

p. 79   MGM deal, contracts including 7/19/66 letter of agreement; also *Up-tight* (Bockris).

p. 79–81   At the Castle, thanks to Lisa Law and Patti Elam (quoted).

p. 79–80   At the Trip, *LA Free Press*, 13/5/66 ("their drummer is . . .").

p. 80   The Trip closes, *Variety*, 5/17/66.

p. 80–81   At Venice Beach, author's interview with Woronov (quoted).

p. 81   Warhol and Morrissey meet Bill Graham, *POPism* (Warhol), including dialogue.

p. 81   Graham: "I hope . . .": recalled by Moe Tucker.

p. 81   Gleason review, *San Francisco Chronicle*, 5/30/66.

p. 82   LR: "Let's say we . . .": *Modern Hi-fi and Music*, 1975.

p. 82   Hospitalized with hepatitis, *Between Thought and Expression* (Reed); author's interview with Clermont.

p. 82   Schwartz dies, *Delmore Schwartz* (Atlas). Clermont quoted from author's interview.

p. 82   LR: "O Delmore . . .": quoted from his preface to the 2012 New Directions edition of *In Dreams Begin Responsibilities and Other Stories* (Schwartz).

p. 82   Merrill "Bunny" Weiner quoted from correspondence with the author.

p. 83   Grand Street apartment, author's interviews with Ellie Jacobs, Martha Morrison and Moe Tucker.

p. 83   West 3rd Street apartment and Stanley Amos, *POPism* (Warhol; Warhol and LR quoted).

p. 84   Friendship with transgender people, Fields interview.

p. 84   Cale on LR: "very full of . . .": *Nico* (Witts).

p. 84   LR on after-hours bars, *Between Thought and Expression* (Reed).

p. 84   Billy Name on bar-crawling with LR, author's interview.

p. 85   Shelley Albin quoted from author's interview. NB: LR indicated that "Pale Blue Eyes" was about Shelley in his book *Between Thought and Expression*.

p. 85–87   Barbara Hodes quoted throughout from author's interviews.

p. 88   *Village Voice* review: "zombie night . . .": 9/29/66.

p. 88   Mishkin and Flynt quoted from author's interview.

p. 88   LR: "So she photographs great!": *Up-tight* (Bockris).

p. 88–89   Morrissey: "Then Tom said . . ." and "He sang it! . . .": *Nico* (Witts).

p. 89   Stevenson quoted from author's interview.

p. 89   Malanga notes yellow eyes, *Up-tight* (Bockris).

p. 89–90   World's First Mod Wedding, author's interviews and *Detroit News*, 11/21/66.

p. 90–91   Philadelphia shows, *Philadelphia Daily News*, 11/12/66.

p. 91   Single releases, *White Light/White Heat* (Unterberger).

V LIGHT AND DARK, 1967–68

p. 92   Moe Tucker quoted throughout from author's interviews.

p. 92   LR: "We thought . . .": *Penthouse*, 1977 (vol. 12, no. 2).

p. 93   Emerson claim, Billy Name (quoted throughout from author's interview); *White Light/White Heat* (Unterberger). Emerson background, *NY Post* obituary, 6/4/75.

p. 93   *Village Voice* review of the Banana Album, 4/13/67.
p. 94   Morrissey quoted throughout from author's interview.
p. 94   Bowie quoted from *New York* magazine, 9/29/03.
p. 94–95   Chris Stein quoted from author's interview.
p. 95   Woronov quoted throughout from author's interviews.
p. 95   Brigid Berlin quoted throughout from author's interviews.
p. 96   LR discussion with Warhol: "It was the worst . . .": recalled by LR in *Rolling Stone*, 5/4/89.
p. 97   Cale: "Suddenly Lou . . .": *What's Welsh for Zen* (Cale).
p. 97   Philip Johnson party, *POPism* (Warhol) and Moe Tucker interview.
p. 97–98   Moves to fur district, thanks to Barbara Hodes (quoted from author's interview).
p. 99   "Sister Ray" named for a drag queen, *Rolling Stone*, 11/21/13.
p. 99   Phrase quoted from "Sister Ray," John Cale Music, Inc./Oakfield Avenue Music Ltd.
p. 100   LR: "I wrote the . . .": *Peel Slowly and See* booklet.
p. 101   McGuire review, *Crawdaddy* 17.
p. 101   Cumulative sales, thanks to Chris Whent.
p. 102   Cale: "there was heroin involved": *What's Welsh for Zen* (Cale).
p. 102   LR and Cale almost came to blows, *Lou Reed* (Bockris).
p. 103   Swados's suicide attempt, *The Four of Us* (Swados).
p. 103–5   Bettye Kronstad quoted throughout from author's interview, including dialogue with LR.
p. 105   Laurie Anderson involved in Columbia University demonstration, *Laurie Anderson* (Goldberg).
p. 105   Clermont quoted throughout from author's interview.
p. 106–7   Croland quoted from author's interview.
p. 106   Woronov on Max's Kansas City/Andrea Feldman's behavior, *Swimming Underground* (Woronov).
p. 107–8   Warhol shooting, *POPism* (Warhol), author's interview with Billy Name (quoted) and press coverage including *NY Post*, 6/4/68 (headline).
p. 108   Sesnick quoted from *Lou Reed* (Wrenn).
p. 109   Warhol: "Why didn't you visit . . .": recalled by LR in *Musician*, 4/1/89.
p. 109   Shelley Albin quoted from author's interview.
p. 109   Solanas sentenced, *The Times*, 6/11/69.
p. 109   Riviera Café coup, recalled by Sterling Morrison in *Up-tight* (Bockris).
p. 110–11   Doug Yule quoted from correspondence with the author, except dialogue with Sesnick and LR and "The next two days . . .," which are from Yule's essay *My First Days with the Velvet Underground*, published online at olivier.landemaine.free.fr.
p. 111   Cale on being fired, *Lou Reed* (Bockris).

VI A NEW VU, 1968–70

p. 112   Yule: "The sound was . . .," etc.: *My First Days with the Velvet Underground* (Yule).
p. 112   Moe Tucker quoted throughout from author's interview.
p. 113   Contracts VD, author's interview with Barbara Hodes.
p. 113   Candy Darling and tampons, *Swimming Underground* (Woronov).
p. 113   Lyric quoted from "Some Kinda Love," Oakfield Avenue Music Ltd.
p. 114   Kronstad quoted throughout from author's interview.
p. 115   Lyric quoted from "That's the Story of My Life," Oakfield Avenue Music Ltd.
p. 115   Billy Name quoted from author's interview.
p. 115   LR visits Billy, *POPism* (Warhol).
p. 115   LR: "It was supposed . . .": *Peel Slowly and See* booklet.
p. 115   Woronov quoted from author's interview.
p. 116   LR: "I couldn't sing . . .": *Peel Slowly and See* booklet.

p. 116   LR: "It's not just . . .": Nov. 1969 radio interview, reported in *White Light/White Heat* (Unterberger).

p. 116   Shelley Albin quoted throughout from author's interview.

p. 117   Yule: "I never saw . . .": correspondence with author.

p. 117   Norris quoted from an interview with *Kicks*, reported in *White Light/White Heat* (Unterberger).

p. 117   Closet mix, *Peel Slowly and See*.

p. 117   Bangs review, *Rolling Stone*, 5/17/69.

p. 118   LR: "I have a . . .": *Guardian*, 2/16/96.

p. 119   Jagger: "I mean, even . . .": *NME*, 10/15/77.

p. 120   LR at End of Cole Avenue, *1969 Velvet Underground Live with Lou Reed* (Mercury, 1974).

p. 121   Quine quoted from his liner notes to *The Velvet Underground, Bootleg Series Vol. 1*, save "They didn't have . . .," which is from an interview with *ZigZag*, April 1985.

p. 121   Abram quoted from the *San Francisco Chronicle*, Nov. 2001.

p. 121   The "prototype" of "Sweet Jane," *Pass Thru Fire* (Reed); LR to *NME*, 1/24/76.

p. 121   Yule: "I can remember . . ." etc., correspondence with author.

p. 123   Yule scared to smoke a joint, *White Light/White Heat* (Unterberger).

p. 123   Martha Morrison quoted from author's interview.

p. 124–25   LR interview with *Third Ear*, reprinted in *The Velvet Underground* (Kugelberg). NB: Kugelberg identifies the interview as taking place in 1968, but references in the interview date it to 1970.

p. 125   Yule: "I've heard that . . .": correspondence with the author.

p. 126   LR: "We once did . . ." etc.: *Village Voice*, 7/2/70.

p. 126   LR: "I hated it . . .": *White Light/White Heat* (Unterberger).

p. 126   Patti Smith quoted from the *New Yorker*, 11/11/13.

p. 127   Morrison: "I was mad . . ." etc.,: *Feed-back* (Julià).

p. 127   Yule: "That particular night . . ." etc.,: correspondence with author.

p. 127   LR introduces his parents to Morrison (quoted), *Up-tight* (Bockris).

p. 128   Berlin quoted from author's interview.

p. 128–29   Fields quoted from author's interview.

VII SOLO IN THE SEVENTIES, 1970–73

p. 130   Merrill "Bunny" Weiner quoted from correspondence with the author.

p. 130–31   LR on showbusiness, *No One Waved Good-bye* (Somma).

p. 131   Sterling Morrison quoted from the *Austin Sun*, Oct. 1975.

p. 131   LR: "They took a song . . .": *Melody Maker*, 1/22/72.

p. 132   Elliott Murphy quoted from author's interview.

p. 132   Lester Bangs's interview with LR, *Creem*, May 1971.

p. 132   Hodes quoted throughout from author's interviews.

p. 132–3   Kronstad quoted throughout from author's interview.

p. 133   Fields quoted throughout from author's interviews.

p. 134–35   LR's 4/29/71 meeting with Nico, tape recording of same (courtesy of Danny Fields).

p. 135–36   RCA background, thanks to Dennis Katz, Bob Ringe and Bruce Somerfield (all quoted from author's interviews).

p. 136   Zanetta quoted throughout from author's interview.

p. 136   Angie Bowie quoted throughout from author's interview.

p. 137   Dennis Katz quoted from author's interview.

p. 137   RCA deal, contract of 10/1/72.

p. 139   LR: "It's been a . . .": *Disc and Music Echo*, 1/29/72.

p. 139   Rick Wakeman quoted from correspondence with the author.

p. 139–40   Clem Cattini quoted from interview with the author.

p. 140   Cale declines to work further with LR, *Lou Reed* (Bockris).

p. 140   Christgau rating, www.robertchristgau.com.
p. 140   Kent: "one of the more . . .": *NME*, 6/9/72.
p. 140   Advance for *Transformer* 10/1/72 contract.
p. 141   Lyric quoted from "Perfect Day," Oakfield Avenue Music Ltd.
p. 141   LR and Warhol discuss "Vicious," LR to *NME*, 4/28/73.
p. 141   Bowie: "I'm gay . . .": *Melody Maker*, 1/22/72.
p. 142   Clermont quoted throughout from correspondence with author.
p. 142   Shelley Albin quoted from interview with author.
p. 142   LR's address in Wimbledon, thanks to Barbara Hodes.
p. 143   Coleman review, *Melody Maker*, 7/15/72.
p. 143   Background on King's Cross show, *NME*, 7/22/72.
p. 143   Richard Robinson replaced, *There Goes Gravity* (Lisa Robinson; quoted).
p. 144   Bowie on producing *Transformer*, *Lou Reed: Transformer*, Classic Albums documentary (Sister Ray Enterprises, 2001).
p. 144   Halsey quoted from author's interview.
p. 144–45   Scott quoted from author's interview.
p. 145   Lyric quoted from "Make Up," Oakfield Avenue Music Ltd.
p. 145   LR on the genesis of "Walk on the Wild Side," *Between Thought and Expression* (Reed).
p. 145–46   Holly Woodlawn background and all quotes, author's interviews.
p. 146   LR: "Odds are that . . .": *Mojo*, March 1996.
p. 147   Thunder Thighs, author's interviews with Lallou and Synge (both quoted).
p. 147   Phrase quoted from "Wagon Wheel," Oakfield Avenue Music Ltd.
p. 148   Paid £450 in Glasgow, financial records in *Dennis Katz vs Lou Reed, Transformer Enterprises Ltd and Oakfield Avenue Music Ltd*, Supreme Court of the State of New York, case 19748/75.
p. 148   Stoecker quoted from author's interview.
p. 149   Tosches review, *Rolling Stone*, 1/4/73.
p. 149   *NY Times* review, 12/17/72.
p. 149   LR: "I allowed it . . .": *Mojo*, March 1996.
p. 152   McCormack quoted from author's interview.
p. 152   Backstage at Alice Tully Hall, author's interviews with Kronstad (quoted), *Rolling Stone*, 3/1/73.
p. 152–3   Rockwell review, *NY Times*, 29/1/73, save for "His voice was . . ." (interview with author).
p. 153   Quotation from "Walk on the Wild Side," Oakfield Avenue Music Ltd.
p. 154   Dallesandro quoted from author's interview.
p. 154   LR sacks Heller, *Lou Reed vs Fred Heller*, Supreme Court of the State of New York, case 4692/1973.
p. 155   Deals done by Katz, *Dennis Katz vs Lou Reed*.

VIII SELF-PARODY, 1973–74

p. 156–57   Kronstad quoted throughout from author's interview.
p. 158   Ezrin: "His writing was . . .": *The Times*, 5/25/07. Additional background: Ezrin's 8/18/73 interview with *NME*; and *Circus*, Dec. 1973.
p. 158–59   Lyric quoted from "The Kids," Oakfield Avenue Music Ltd.
p. 159   Ezrin wrote arrangements, LR to *American Songwriter*, 1/2/09.
p. 159   Dawson quoted throughout from author's interview.
p. 159   Lyric quoted from "Oh, Jim," Oakfield Avenue Music Ltd.
p. 160   LR: "I needed a . . .": *Melody Maker*, 5/13/78.
p. 160   LR: "I'm a chauvinist . . .": *Creem*, March 1979.
p. 160   Ezrin: "It was an . . .": *Lou Reed: Rock 'n' Roll Heart* documentary (American Masters, 1998); also *The Times*, 5/25/07.
p. 160   LR kissing Bowie and wife at the Café Royal, as photographed by Mick Rock.
p. 160–61   LR: "Like, during the . . .": *Melody Maker*, 5/13/78.

p. 161–62   Colcord and Wagner quoted throughout from author's interviews.
p. 162   Thanks to Susie Curtois for Blake's Hotel background.
p. 162   Walsh quoted from author's interview.
p. 163   Kent review, *New Musical Express (NME)*, 9/29/73.
p. 163   LR: "I'm fed up . . .": recalled by Dawson to author.
p. 163   Hunter quoted from *NME*, 3/15/75.
p. 163   Jacobs quoted throughout from author's interview.
p. 163–64   Glan quoted throughout from author's interview.
p. 164   Gelb quoted throughout from author's interview. Also dialogue with LR.
p. 164   Steve Katz quoted throughout from author's interview.
p. 165   Thanks to Bob Ringe for background on Brussels show.
p. 165   "Return of the prince of ponce," *NME*, 9/22/73.
p. 166   Rockwell review of *Berlin*, *NY Times*, 12/9/73.
p. 166   *Rolling Stone* review, 12/20/73.
p. 166   Sales of *Berlin*, LR statement in *Steven Katz and Anxiety Productions Ltd vs Lou Reed and RCA*, Supreme Court of the State of New York, case 18712/75.
p. 166   LR: "The way that . . .": *Melody Maker*, 4/16/77.
p. 167   Returns to live with Barbara Hodes, author's interviews. Hodes quoted throughout from author's interviews.
p. 167   Prakash John joins the band, author's interview. John quoted throughout from author's interview.
p. 167   Academy of Music fee, payment schedule in *Dennis Katz vs Lou Reed*.
p. 168   Freedman quoted from author's interview.
p. 168   LR: "I got busted . . .": *Between Thought and Expression* (LR).
p. 168   Fulk quoted from correspondence with the author.
p. 169   Hynde review, *NME*, 3/2/14.
p. 170   "Sally Can't Dance" lyric, Oakfield Avenue Music Ltd.
p. 170   LR: "And that's why . . .": *NYC Man* liner notes (BMG, 2003).
p. 171   Sid Reed advises LR, *Steven Katz and Anxiety Productions Ltd vs Lou Reed and RCA*.
p. 171   Sterling Morrison teaching, author's interviews with Martha Morrison.
p. 171   Moe Tucker's life after 1973, author's interview.
p. 171   Velvet Underground income, *Lou Reed vs Fred Heller*.
p. 172   Merrill "Bunny" Weiner and Harold Weiner quoted from author's interview.
p. 172–73   LR emaciated photo, thanks to Barbara Hodes.
p. 173   Michael Fonfara quoted throughout from author's interview.
p. 174–76   Rachel background, thanks to various interviewees for their recollections, including Michael Fonfara, Liz Gilmore, Barbara Hodes, Prakash John and Jeffrey Ross.
p. 174   LR on Rachel: "I'd been up . . .": *Penthouse* interview, 1977 (vol. 12, no. 2).
p. 175   Bangs on Rachel, *Creem*, Feb. 1976; Fong-Torres, *GQ*, Sept. 1986.
p. 175   Gilmore quoted from author's interview.
p. 175–76   Murphy quoted from author's interview.
p. 176   Rachel and the police, LR to *Penthouse* (1977). Also, "Rachel knows how . . ."
p. 176–77   Byrd quoted from correspondence with the author.
p. 177   LR: "This is fantastic . . .": *Gig* 1974, quoted in the liner notes for the CD of *Sally Can't Dance*.
p. 177   Sydney press conference, 8/14/74, YouTube.
p. 178   Robinson review, *NME*, 19/10/74.
p. 178   Somerfield quoted from author's interview.
p. 178–79   LR: "Back then, I . . .": *Q*, Feb. 1989.

IX HOWLING LIKE THE DEVIL, 1975–76

p. 180   Steve Katz quoted throughout from author's interview, except "I give up . . .": *Lou Reed & The Velvet Underground* (Clapton).

p. 180–81 Conflicting claims over who walked out on the sessions, and Somerfield quote—"I do not know . . ."—court papers in *Steven Katz and Anxiety Productions Ltd vs Lou Reed*.

p. 181 Everyman Band background, thanks to Marty Fogel, Larry Packer and Bruce Yaw (the last two quoted throughout from author's interviews).

p. 182 Drive into Rome, author's interviews with Bob Ringe (quoted throughout).

p. 182 LR demands to see a doctor, thanks to Packer.

p. 183 Fonfara quoted throughout from author's interview.

p. 184 LR greeted by police, thanks to Packer. Background on Rome riot, *Chicago Tribune*, 2/17/75.

p. 185 Rapino quoted from author's interview.

p. 185 Fulk gives Valium/ Defries flies in, author's correspondence with Fulk.

p. 186–87 Dr. Breitenmoser's story, his 1/25/82 witness statement in *Dennis Katz vs Lou Reed, Transformer Enterprises Ltd*.

p. 186 LR "under extreme emotional distress," defense statement in *Dennis Katz vs Lou Reed*.

p. 186 Waxwork, *Record Mirror*, 8/3/75.

p. 187–88 Loses Heller case, *Lou Reed vs Fred Heller*.

p. 188 Toronto, and Arthur Moss's story (affidavit of 7/28/75), *Lou Reed vs Fred Heller*.

p. 189 LR: "I was serious . . .": *Lou Reed: Rock 'n' Roll Heart* documentary (American Masters, 1998).

p. 189 Dennis Katz quoted from conversation with author.

p. 189 Kempner quoted from author's interview.

p. 189 LR: "No one I . . .": liner notes to *Metal Machine Music* (RCA, 1975).

p. 189 Rockwell review of *Metal Machine Music (MMM)*, *NYTimes*, 6/20/75.

p. 189 Bangs review, *Creem*, Sept. 1975.

p. 189 Sales of *MMM*, quoted by LR and Steve Katz in *Steven Katz and Anxiety Productions Ltd vs Lou Reed*. Copies returned, LR to *NME*, 1/24/76.

p. 190 Somerfield quoted throughout from author's interview.

p. 190–92 Financial crisis, 6/1/75 judgment in *Lou Reed vs Fred Heller*, and related documents in this case and *Dennis Katz vs Lou Reed*.

p. 191 LR: "I found out . . .": *Dazed and Confused*, April 1996.

p. 191 Fulk leaves, correspondence with author.

p. 191–92 Additional debts of $128,000/LR accuses Dennis Katz and others of misappropriating funds, *Dennis Katz vs Lou Reed*.

p. 192 Murphy quoted throughout from author's interview.

p. 192 Summons served, *Dennis Katz vs Lou Reed*.

p. 192–93 LR mortgages song catalogue, legal documents in *Arista Music et al. vs Oakfield Avenue Music, Inc.*, Supreme Court of the State of New York, case 93024/83; *Reed vs Fred Heller*, and *Steven Katz and Anxiety Productions Ltd vs Lou Reed*.

p. 192–93 Steve Katz sues, *Steven Katz and Anxiety Productions Ltd vs Lou Reed*.

p. 194–98 Godfrey Diamond quoted from author's interview, including dialogue with LR.

p. 195–96 Kulick quoted from author's interview.

p. 196 Nelson Slater quoted from author's interview.

p. 196–97 Marsh reviews *Coney Island Baby*, *Rolling Stone*, Jan. 1976; Murray review, *NME* 1/24/76.

p. 197 Poetry award, *Between Thought and Expression* (Reed).

p. 197 Slater disappointed with *Wild Angel*, author's interview.

p. 198 LR sees Smith perform "We're Gonna Have a Real Good Time Together," *Lou Reed* (Bockris).

p. 199 Podell quoted from author's interview.

p. 200 Clive Davis quoted from author's interview. Background on his career, *The Soundtrack of My Life* (Davis).

p. 200–1 1976 "settlement agreement," copy of and related documents in *Arista Music et al. vs Oakfield Avenue Music, Inc.*

X THE ARISTA YEARS, 1976–80

p. 202–4 Corky Stasiak quoted throughout from author's interview, including dialogue with LR.

p. 204 Davis quoted throughout from author's interview.

p. 204–6 Podell quoted throughout from author's interview.

p. 206–7 Ross quoted throughout from author's interview.

p. 206–7 Clermont quoted throughout from author's interview.

p. 207 LR: "On this tour . . .": *Penthouse* interview, 1977 (vol. 12, no.2).

p. 207–8 Anniversary party, author's interviews with Michael Fonfara (quoted throughout from author's interviews), Jeffrey Ross and Liz Furmanovsky, who took pictures of the event, published in the *NME*, 5/7/77.

p. 208 Gilmore quoted from author's interview.

p. 208 Eye drops, author's interview with Ritchie Fliegler.

p. 208 Threatens Friedman, Friedman's article in *Soho Weekly News*, March 1978, and correspondence with author.

p. 208–9 Threatens journalist with butter knife, author's interview with Gilmore.

p. 209 Hires Kronfeld, author's interview with Podell.

p. 209 Settles with Steve Katz, court papers.

p. 209 Details of *LR vs Dennis Katz*, court papers (Supreme Court of the State of New York, case 19748/75).

p. 209 Sarig quoted from author's interview.

p. 210 Falls out with Bruce Yaw, author's interview with Yaw.

p. 210 Fliegler quoted from author's interview.

p. 211 LR: "I was specifically . . .": *Between Thought and Expression* (Reed).

p. 211 Wiltshire quoted from author's interview.

p. 211 LR: "I don't like niggers . . .": *Soho Weekly News*, March 1978.

p. 211 LR: "nigger music": *Creem*, Dec. 1976.

p. 211 McCormack quoted from author's interview.

p. 212 LR: "They're not heterosexual . . .": *Rolling Stone*, 3/22/79.

p. 212 Phrase quoted from "Street Hassle," Metal Machine Music, Inc.

p. 212 *Street Hassle* reviews: *Time*, 4/24/78; *NME*, 11/25/78; and *Village Voice*, 5/29/79.

p. 213 LR: "She's more beautiful . . .": recalled by Erin Clermont.

p. 213 Ravan quoted from author's interview.

p. 214 Warhol quoted from his *Diaries*.

p. 214 Rockwell and Christgau quoted from author's interviews.

p. 215 Faith quoted throughout from author's interview.

p. 215–16 LR: "I have such . . .": *Creem*, March 1979.

p. 216–18 Blairstown property, author's local enquiries, real-estate records and field notes. Thanks to Sylvia Ramos (Reed), Ravi Romano and Rita Teel.

p. 217 LR: "Even if you . . .": *Creem*, March 1979.

p. 218 Ellard "Moose" Boles quoted throughout from author's interview.

p. 219–20 Sylvia Morales's background, her UK birth certificate, author's interviews and *Lou Reed* (Bockris). Cale quoted from his book *What's Welsh for Zen*.

p. 221 LR creates the lyric for "The Bells" extemporaneously, *Lou Reed: Walk on the Wild Side* (Roberts).

p. 221 Reviews of *The Bells*: *Rolling Stone*, 6/14/79; *LA Times*, 1/24/79; and Murray in *NME*, 4/28/79.

p. 221 LR: "I think it . . .": *Mojo*, March 1996.

p. 221–22 Hammer quoted throughout from author's interview.

p. 223 Arrested in Germany, author's interviews with band members. Also LR's interview with William Burroughs, reported in *Transformer: The Complete Lou Reed Story* (Bockris).

p. 224 LR threatened Levison, author's interview with Howard Harding (quoted).

p. 224 LR: "Play! Play! . . .": recalled by Hammer.

p. 224   LR: "Isn't David great?" etc.: recalled by Marty Fogel.
p. 224–25   Fight with Bowie, author's interviews with Fogel and Hammer. Also *Melody Maker*, 4/21/79.
p. 225   LR: "Where is the money, Clive?": *The Soundtrack of My Life (Davis)*.
p. 225–27   Recording *Growing Up in Public*, author's interviews with Boles, Fogel, Fonfara, Hammer, Heinrich and Stasiak.
p. 226   Phrase quoted from "My Old Man," Metal Machine Music, Inc.

XI SECOND MARRIAGE, 1980–87

p. 229   Bornstein quoted throughout from author's interviews.
p. 229   Lyrics quoted from "How Do You Speak to An Angel" and "My Old Man," Metal Machine Music, Inc.
p. 229   Wedding, thanks in particular to Corky Stasiak for his diary notes and photographs.
p. 229–30   Epstein quoted throughout from author's interview.
p. 230   *Growing Up in Public* reviews, *Rolling Stone* (7/10/80); and *Sounds* (5/3/80).
p. 231   Davis quoted from author's interview.
p. 231   Fonfara quoted from author's interview.
p. 231–32   Country life, author's field notes and interviews. Thanks to Rita Teel (quoted from author's interview), Sylvia Ramos (formerly Reed; quoted from correspondence with the author), Judy Cook (quoted from author's interview), Bob Tramontin (quoted from author's correspondence), John Passalacqua at Dominick's pizzeria and Kellie Peterson (quoted from author's interview). Also thanks to Ken Lally and Ravi Romano.
p. 233   Sigal renews friendship, author's interview (quoted).
p. 233   LR: "I consider I . . .": *Times* magazine, 3/25/2000. LR mentioned self-help books in interviews, including Allen Carr's *Easy Way to Stop Smoking (Times*, 7/21/07).
p. 233   Clermont quoted throughout from author's interviews and correspondence, with thanks for consulting her diary.
p. 233   Lithium side effects, *Companion to Psychiatric Studies* (Johnstone).
p. 234   LR: "'The Gun' is none . . .": *NME*, 3/6/82.
p. 234   Hammer quoted from author's interview.
p. 235–36   Perry quoted from author's interview.
p. 235   Saunders quoted throughout from author's interview.
p. 235–36   Quine background, author's interviews with Sean Fullan, Fred Maher, Doane Perry and Fernando Saunders; also Quine's *Daily Telegraph* obituary, 6/14/04.
p. 237   Fullan quoted from author's interview.
p. 238   Lyric quoted from "Women," Metal Machine Music, Inc.
p. 238   Maher quoted throughout from author's interview.
p. 238   LR: "My past is . . .": *NY Times*, 3/10/82.
p. 239   Spoke of admiration for Dostoyevsky, to *NME*, for example, 4/21/79.
p. 239   Merrill "Bunny" Weiner quoted from author's interview.
p. 239   Reviews of *The Blue Mask*, *Sounds* (3/13/82), *NY Times* (3/10/82) and *Rolling Stone* (4/15/82).
p. 239–40   Lyric quoted from "Heavenly Arms," Metal Machine Music, Inc.
P. 240   LR: "Touring is just . . .": *NYTimes*, 3/10/82.
P. 240–41   Stasiak quoted from author's interview.
P. 240   Quine smashes tape, *Lou Reed* (Bockris).
P. 242–43   Background on *New Sensations*, thanks to horn players Randy Brecker and Tom "Bones" Malone.
P. 243   Lyric quoted from "New Sensations," Metal Machine Music, Inc.
P. 243   Shepard quoted from author's interview.
P. 243   Quine on the "No Sensations" tour, *Lou Reed* (Bockris).
P. 244   Katz case resolved, *Dennis Katz vs Lou Reed, Transformer Enterprises Ltd and Oakfield Avenue Music Ltd*; and Supreme Court of New York records office.

P. 244–45   Velvet Underground Partnership, thanks to Chris Whent (quoted from author's interview).
P. 245   Cale's drug and alcohol issues, *What's Welsh for Zen* (Cale) and *Week in Week Out* (BBC Wales, 2009).
P. 245   Martha Morrison quoted from author's interview.
P. 245–46   Moe Tucker quoted from author's interview.
P. 246   LR buys apartment on West End Avenue, thanks to Saunders.
P. 246   Janowitz quoted throughout from author's interview.
P. 246   LR attends Completely Sober, thanks to Tony Zanetta.
P. 248   Lyric quoted from "Don't Hurt a Woman," Metal Machine Music, Inc. (quoted). Also *What's Welsh for Zen* (Cale).
P. 249   Blades quoted from author's interview.

XII NEW INSPIRATION, 1987–92

p. 251   Death of Warhol, *Holy Terror* (Colacello) and *The Andy Warhol Diaries* (Warhol). Lawsuit, *NY Times,* 5 and 12/23/91. Epstein quoted from author's interview.
p. 252   LR: "He was being . . .": *Between Thought and Expression* (Reed).
p. 252   Warhol quoted from his *Diaries.* Thanks also to Pat Hackett.
p. 252   LR on Warhol's use of language, *Lou Reed* (Bockris).
p. 252   LR: "There were some . . .": *NME,* 10/6/89.
p. 252–54   Warhol's memorial service, author's interviews, *Holy Terror* (Colacello) and *NYTimes,* 4/2/87.
p. 252   Inspired to write "Dime Store Mystery," *Times,* 1/31/89.
p. 253–54   Meets Cale at wake, author's interview with Billy Name.
p. 254   Janowitz quoted from author's interview.
p. 254   Rathke joins the band, author's interview (quoted throughout).
p. 255–57   Fine quoted throughout from author's interview (including dialogue with LR).
p. 255   LR: "I'll give you . . .": *Rolling Stone,* 11/5/87.
p. 256   Hyman quoted from author's interview.
p. 256   Klein quoted throughout from author's interview.
p. 258–59   Maher quoted throughout from author's interview.
p. 258   Lyric quoted from "Romeo Had Juliette," Metal Machine Music, Inc.
p. 259   Lyric quoted from "Dirty Boulevard," Metal Machine Music, Inc.
p. 259   Dion DiMucci quoted from author's interview.
p. 260   Lyric quoted from "Halloween Parade," Metal Machine Music, Inc.
p. 260   Ross on Rachel's fate, quoted from author's interview. Thanks also to Bob Gruen.
p. 260–61   Nico's demise, *Nico* (Witts).
p. 261   Lyric quoted from "Dime Store Mystery," Metal Music, Inc.
p. 261   *New York* reviews: *The Times,* 1/21/89 and *Village Voice,* Jan. 1989.
p. 261–62   *Rolling Stone* cover interview (quoted), 5/4/89.
p. 263   BAM performance, film of same and author's interviews with Brigid Berlin, Billy Name (quoted) and Moe Tucker (quoted throughout from author's interview).
p. 263   Snow quoted from Q, July 1993.
p. 263   Cale: "For him to . . .": *Option,* July 1990.
p. 265–66   Meeting Havel, *Between Thought and Expression* (Reed).
p. 266   Cartier event, film of the performance and author's interviews with Martha Morrison, Billy Name, Moe Tucker and Chris Whent (all quoted).
p. 267   Cale: "The two of . . .": *What's Welsh for Zen* (Cale).
p. 267   LR on Pomus, *Rock 'n' Roll Heart* documentary (American Masters, 1998).
p. 268   Rita Teel quoted from author's interview.
p. 268   Swados's demise, his sister Elizabeth's book, *The Four of Us.* Inspires "Harry's Circumcision," LR quoted in *Lou Reed* (Bockris).
p. 268–69   Wasserman quoted from author's interview.
p. 269   LR: "Giving up those . . .": Q, Feb. 1992.
p. 269   LR: "as though it . . .": liner notes to *New York.*

p. 269 Thompson review, *Independent on Sunday*, 3/22/92.
p. 269–70 Oglanby quoted throughout from author's interview.
p. 271 Scott altercation, thanks to Jimmy and Jeanie Scott (quoted).
p. 271 Doyle quoted from author's interview.
p. 273 Anderson background, *Laurie Anderson* (Goldberg); *Guardian*, 5/13/95; author's research.
p. 273 LR: "You know, people . . .": *Q*, May 2000.
p. 273 Anderson quoted on meeting LR from the obituary she wrote for her husband for *Rolling Stone*, 11/21/13.

XIII RETURN TO THE VELVET UNDERGROUND, 1992–96

p. 275 Eighty percent of sales in Europe, author's interview with Moe Tucker.
p. 275 Cale on the *Tonight Show*, *What's Welsh for Zen* (Cale).
p. 276 Cale: "[to] demonstrate that . . .": *NME*, 6/5/93.
p. 276 Tucker's thoughts, conversation and quotes, author's interview.
p. 276 Sylvia: "my artist": recalled by Martha Morrison.
p. 276–77 Klein quoted throughout from author's interview.
p. 277–78 Oglanby quoted throughout from author's interview.
p. 277 Big Rig, author's interview with Pete Cornish.
p. 278 Rehearsal dialogue, recalled by Struan Oglanby.
p. 278 Travel arrangements, Martha Morrison.
p. 278 "So Happy to be Back," *Vox*, July 1993.
p. 278–79 Golfing in London, author's interview with Joe Doyle.
p. 280 Kane quoted from the *Guardian*, 6/4/93.
p. 280 Audience repartee, *Musician*, 8/1/93.
p. 281 Jones review, *Melody Maker*, 6/12/93.
p. 281 Martha Morrison quoted throughout from author's interview.
p. 282 Ticket sales, thanks to Mike "Coach' Sexton (quoted from author's interview).
p. 282 Mikulka quoted from author's interview.
p. 283 LR driven to show/argues with Cale, *What's Welsh for Zen* (Cale quoted).
p. 285 LR and Laurie Anderson at AES convention, her article in *Rolling Stone*, 11/21/13 (quoted).
p. 285 Clermont quoted throughout from author's interview.
p. 286 Williams quoted from author's interview.
p. 286–88 LR and Steve Epstein, author's interview with Epstein (quoted).
p. 287 Sylvia files for divorce, Supreme Court of New York records.
p. 287 Bornstein quoted from author's interview.
p. 287 Fields quoted from author's interview.
p. 287 Shepard quoted from author's interview.
p. 287 Holding hands in studio, author's interview with Fernando Saunders.
p. 288 Gruen quoted from author's interview.
p. 288 LR moves to 45 Christopher Street, thanks to Erin Clermont.
p. 289–90 Dialogue with Oglanby, recalled by Oglanby to the author.
p. 291 Robert Wilson quoted from correspondence with the author.
p. 291 LR: "I'm not writing . . .": *Observer*, 8/16/96.
p. 292 LR: "the worst movie . . .": *Creem*, Nov. 1984.
p. 292 LR film dialogue, *Blue in the Face* (Auster).
p. 293 Auster quoted from interview with the author.
p. 293–94 Morrison's terminal illness, thanks to Martha Morrison and Moe Tucker.
p. 294 LR: "Sterl lay in bed . . .": his obituary article in the *NY Times*, 12/31/95.

XIV LOVE, LOU, 1996–2008

p. 295 Anderson's mishaps, *Laurie Anderson* (Goldberg).

p. 295-96   Recording *Set the Twilight Reeling*, thanks to Struan Oglanby, Fernando Saun-
             ders and Tony Smith (all quoted throughout from author's interviews).
p. 296   Frankel quoted from author's interview.
p. 296-97   Background on Warner Brothers shake-up, *Billboard*, 4/29/95.
p. 297-98   Goldberg quoted from author's interview.
p. 298   Klein quoted throughout from author's interview.
p. 298   Reviews of *Time Rocker* in the US, *Village Voice* (11/25/97) and *NY Times*
             (11/23/97).
p. 299-300   Tour diary, *New Yorker*, 8/26/96.
p. 299-300   West 11th Street apartment, thanks to Godfrey Diamond, Zeljko McMullen and
             Jane Scarpantoni.
p. 300   America starts "over there," remark made to the author by LR's friend and neigh-
             bor Danny Fields.
p. 301   Bowie concert, videotape of Jan. 1997 show.
p. 301   LR: "Everybody says . . .": *Sunday Telegraph*, 1/29/97.
p. 301   LR: "the sound of diamonds": *Perfect Night* liner notes.
p. 301   LR on "the lowest depth of misery," *Vanity Fair*, Feb. 1996.
p. 302   "His paranoia . . ." Will Hodgkinson in *The Times*, 7/28/12.
p. 302   LR: "I get nervous . . .": *Pulse!*, Feb. 1992.
p. 303   Diamond quoted from author's interview.
p. 303-4   Scarpantoni quoted throughout from author's interview.
p. 304   Lyric quoted from "Mad,' Lou Reed Music.
p. 304   Zollo quoted from *Performing Songwriter*, 2000.
p. 304   Lyric quoted from "The Rock Minuet,' Lou Reed Music.
p. 304   Cornish quoted from author's interview.
p. 305   LR: "It's like watching . . .": *Newsday*, 3/29/2000.
p. 305   Poe "intelligent, wayward and willful": *Poe: A Life Cut Short* (Ackroyd).
p. 306   LR: "Why am I . . .": liner notes to *The Raven* (Reprise, 2003).
p. 306   The making of "Fire Music," LR in *Independent on Sunday*, 1/4/04.
p. 307   Diagnosed diabetic, thanks to Fernando Saunders; "no butter. . .," recalled by
             Jane Scarpantoni.
p. 308   Wasserman quoted throughout from author's interview.
p. 308   Master Ren quoted from author's interview.
p. 308   LR: "music-industry baboons": author's interview with Tom Sarig.
p. 308-9   Sid Reed dies, *NY Times* obit., 1/18/05.
p. 309-10   Sarig quoted throughout from author's interview.
p. 309   LR: "to tell a . . .": *Emotion in Action* (Reed).
p. 310-11   McMullen quoted from author's interview.
p. 311   Christie quoted throughout from author's interview.
p. 311-12   *NYTimes* review of *Berlin*, 12/16/06.
p. 312-13   Rapino quoted from author's interview.
p. 313-14   LR and Anderson decide to marry/dialogue, recalled by Anderson in *The Times*,
             6/1/13 and *Rolling Stone*, 11/21/13.

XV NEVERMORE, 2008-13

p. 315-16   Sarig quoted throughout from author's interview.
p. 316   LR quoted from *Red Shirley*, Sister Ray, 2010.
p. 316   Merrill "Bunny' Weiner quoted throughout from her correspondence and inter-
             view with the author, unless otherwise stated.
p. 317   Quashie quoted from author's interview.
p. 317   Jeanie Scott quoted from author's interview.
p. 317   Dion quoted from author's interview.
p. 317   LR buys home on Long Island, real-estate records and local enquiries.
p. 318   Muldaur quoted throughout from author's interview.

p. 318   Podell quoted from author's interview.
p. 318   Coney Island Mermaid Parade, video footage.
p. 319–20 Wilson quoted from correspondence with the author.
p. 320   Saunders quoted throughout from author's interview.
p. 321   Hammett and Ulrich on working with LR, 31/5/14 article on www.blabber-mouth.net.
p. 321   Lyric quoted from "Mistress Dread," Lou Reed Music.
p. 321   Writing "Junior Dad," thanks to Rob Wasserman.
p. 322   LR on *Lulu*, *Interview*, Nov. 2011.
p. 323   *Lulu* reviews, *Village Voice* (1/20/12), *Rolling Stone* (11/1/11) and postings on www.amazon.com.
p. 323   Rathke, quoted from author's interview.
p. 323   *Lulu* sales, *Billboard*, 27/10/13.
p. 323   Anderson: "Lou was sick . . .," given a course of interferon: her article for *Rolling Stone*, 11/21/13.
p. 324   LR's will, Surrogate Court of New York.
p. 324   Smith quoted from author's interview.
p. 324   Cancelled shows, thanks to Smith and Wasserman.
p. 325   Charles Miller quoted from his eulogy at LR's memorial, 12/16/13. Also dialogue with LR and details of the operation.
p. 325   Anderson: "I don't think . . .": *The Times*, 6/1/13.
p. 325–26 LR: "I am a triumph . . .": www.loureed.com.
p. 326   LR: "How could time . . .": the *Guardian*, 6/20/13.
p. 326   Whent quoted from author's interview. Also LR on the phone with Cale.
p. 326   Moe Tucker quoted throughout from author's interview.
p. 327   LR: "My father didn't . . .": Parrot Zik promotion, 9/21/13.
p. 327   NY book signing, videotape of 10/3/13 event at John Varvatos. Bob Gruen quoted from author's interview.
p. 327   Dr. Miller on Oct, 2013 meeting with LR, *NYTimes*, 10/27/13.
p. 327   Schnabel quoted from *Rolling Stone*, 11/21/13.
p. 328   LR's last moments, Anderson's article in *Rolling Stone*, 11/21/13. Also her 10/31/13 letter to *East Hampton Star* and 12/16/13 eulogy.
p. 328   Cause of death/cremation, death certificate.
p. 328   Billy Name quoted from author's interview.
p. 329   Telling Toby, thanks to Merrill (Bunny) and Harold Weiner (quoted).
p. 330   Mossman obituary, *New Statesman*, 11/1/13.
p. 330   Posthumous sales, *Billboard*, 11/9/13.
p. 330   Value of estate, *NY Post*, 8/30/14.
p. 330   Merrill Weiner—"the emotional issues . . ."—written statement to author; "In his heart . . .," interview with the author.
p. 331   Cale's letter, read at the memorial.
p. 331   Cale: "It came as . . .": *Financial Times*, 8/23/14.
p. 331–32 Anderson's eulogy, Apollo Theater, 12/16/14.
p. 333   Rockwell quoted from author's interview.
p. 333   Clermont quoted from author's interview.

BIBLIOGRAPHY

I found Richie Unterberger's *White Light/White Heat* to be the best history of the Velvet Underground, and *POPism* (ghostwritten for Andy Warhol by Pat Hackett) and Mary Woronov's *Swimming Underground* the most evocative books about the Silver Factory. Reed was an admirer of Woronov's memoir. "[My] friend Mary Woronov, who was at the Factory, has written a book called *Swimming Underground* that I think has the most accurate portrait of Andy Warhol that you will ever run into," he said. "It's hilarious and it'll give you a couple of chills." I second that. He was less keen on Victor Bockris's books about himself and his colleagues, but they are nonetheless all worthwhile.

Ackroyd, Peter, *Poe: A Life Cut Short*, London: Chatto and Windus, 2008.
Algren, Nelson, *A Walk on the Wild Side*, Edinburgh: Canongate, 2006 (1st ed., 1956).
Atlas, James, *Delmore Schwartz: The Life of an American Poet*, New York: Farrar, Straus and Giroux, 1977.
Auster, Paul, *Smoke and Blue in the Face*, London: Faber and Faber, 1995.
Barnes, Peter, *Lulu: A Sex Tragedy*, London: Methuen, 1971.
Bellow, Saul, *Humboldt's Gift*, Harmondsworth: Penguin, 1976.
Bockris, Victor, *Lou Reed: The Biography*, London: Hutchinson, 1994 (updated as *Transformer: The Complete Lou Reed Story*, London: HarperCollins, 2014).
Bockris, Victor, with Gerard Malanga, *Up-tight: The Velvet Underground Story*, London: Bloomsbury, 2002.
Burroughs, William S., *Junky*, Harmondsworth: Penguin, 1977.
Cale, John, with Victor Bockris, *What's Welsh for Zen*, London: Bloomsbury, 1999.
Clapton, Diana, *Lou Reed & The Velvet Underground*, London: Bobcat Books, 1987.
Colacello, Bob, *Holy Terror: Andy Warhol Close Up*, New York: HarperCollins, 1990.
Davis, Clive, with Anthony DeCurtis, *The Soundtrack of My Life*, New York: Simon and Schuster, 2013.
Doggett, Peter, *Lou Reed: Growing Up in Public*, London: Omnibus, 1991.
Evans-Wentz, W. Y., *The Tibetan Book of the Dead*, Oxford: Oxford University Press, 1960.

Finkelstein, Nat, *Andy Warhol: The Factory Years*, Edinburgh: Canongate, 1989.

Frum, David, *How We Got Here: The 70s: The Decade that Brought You Modern Life (For Better or Worse)*, New York: Basic Books, 2000.

Goldberg, RoseLee, *Laurie Anderson*, London: Thames and Hudson, 2000.

Harvard, Joe, *The Velvet Underground & Nico*, London: Bloomsbury, 2013.

Heylin, Clinton (ed.), *All Yesterday's Parties: The Velvet Underground in Print 1966-1971*, Cambridge, MA: Da Capo, 2005.

Johnstone, Eve C. et al. (eds.), *Companion to Psychiatric Studies*, Edinburgh: Churchill Livingstone, 2010.

Julia, Ignacio, *Feed-back, The Velvet Underground: Legend, Truth*, privately published in Catalonia, 2008.

Koch, Stephen, *Stargazer: The Life, World and Films of Andy Warhol*, New York: Marion Boyars, 2002.

Kugelberg, Johan, *The Velvet Underground*, New York: Rizzoli, 2009.

Larkin, Colin (ed.), *The Encyclopaedia of Popular Music*, London: Omnibus Press, 2007.

Leigh, Michael, *The Velvet Underground*, Wet Angel Books, 2011 (1st ed., 1963).

Manbeck, John B. (consulting ed.), *The Neighborhoods of Brooklyn*, New Haven, CT: Yale University Press, 1998.

The New Encyclopaedia Britannica, Chicago: Encyclopaedia Britannica Inc., 2005.

Newsday (eds.), *Long Island, Our Story*, Melville, NY: Newsday, 1998.

Newsday (eds.), *Home Town Long Island*, Melville, NY: Newsday, 1999.

Poe, Edgar Allan, *Poems and Prose*, New York: Everyman, 1995.

Rechy, John, *City of Night*, New York: Grove, 2013 (1st ed., 1963).

Reed, Jeremy, *The Life and Music of Lou Reed, Waiting for the Man*, London: Omnibus, 2014.

Reed, Lou, *Between Thought and Expression: Selected Lyrics of Lou Reed*, New York: Hyperion, 1991.

—, *Emotion in Action*, Gottingen: Steidl, 2003.

—, *Lou Reed's New York*, Gottingen: Steidl, 2006.

—, *Pass Thru Fire: The Collected Lyrics*, Cambridge, MA: Da Capo Press, 2008.

—, *Romanticism*, Gottingen: Steidl, 2009.

—, *Words and Music*, Secaucaus, NJ: Warner Bros. Publications, 1991.

Roberts, Chris, *Lou Reed: Walk on the Wild Side: The Stories behind the Songs*, London: Carlton Books, 2004.

Roberts, David (ed.), *The Guinness Book of British Hit Singles*, London: Guinness, 2002.

Robinson, Lisa, *There Goes Gravity: A Life in Rock 'n' Roll*, New York: Riverhead Books, 2013.

Ross, Alex, *The Rest is Noise*, London: Fourth Estate, 2008.

Schwartz, Delmore, *In Dreams Begin Responsibilities and Other Stories*, New York: New Directions, 2012.

Selby Jr., Hubert, *Last Exit to Brooklyn*, London: Bloomsbury, 2000 (1st ed. 1964).

Somma, Robert (ed.), *No One Waved Good-bye: A Casualty Report on Rock 'n' Roll*, New York: Outerbridge and Dienstfrey, 1971.

Sounes, Howard, *Down the Highway: The Life of Bob Dylan*, London: Doubleday, 2001.

—, *Seventies: The Sights, Sounds and Ideas of a Brilliant Decade*, London: Simon and Schuster, 2006.

Stein, Jean, and George Plimpton, *Edie*, New York: Knopf, 1982.

Strong, Martin C., *The Essential Rock Discography*, Edinburgh: Canongate, 2006.

Swados, Elizabeth, *The Four of Us: A Family Memoir*, New York: Farrar, Straus and Giroux, 1991.

Ultra Violet, *Famous for Fifteen Minutes: My Years with Andy Warhol*, Orlando: Harcourt Brace Jovanovich, 1988.

Unterberger, Richie, *White Light/White Heat: The Velvet Underground Day-by-Day*, London, Jawbone Press, 2009.

Von Sacher-Masoch, Leopold, *Venus in Furs*, New York: Blast Books, 1989 (1st ed., 1870).

Warhol, Andy, and Pat Hackett, *POPism*, Orlando: Harcourt, 1980.

Warhol, Andy, edited by Pat Hackett, *The Andy Warhol Diaries*, London: Simon and Schuster, 1989.

Whitburn, Joel, *Billboard Book of Top 40 Hits*, New York: Billboard, 1996.

Wilcock, John, and Christopher Trela, *The Autobiography and Sex Life of Andy Warhol*, New York: Trela Media, 2010.

Witts, Richard, *Nico: The Life and Lies of an Icon*, London: Virgin, 1993.

Woronov, Mary, *Swimming Underground: My Years in the Warhol Factory*, London: Serpent's Tail, 2000.

Wrenn, Michael, *Lou Reed: Between the Lines*, London: Plexus, 1993.

Young, James, *Nico: Songs They Never Play on the Radio*, London: Bloomsbury, 1999.

IMAGE CREDITS

Every effort has been made to trace copyright holders; any who have been overlooked are invited to get in touch with the publishers.

Pages 2–3

Velvet Undergound, Cambridge, Massachussetts, 1969: © Jeff Albertson/Corbis; Velvet Undergound in the studio, Scepter Records, April 1966: © Steve Schapiro/Corbis; Velvet Underground, c. 1967: © Pictorial Press Ltd/Alamy.

Pages 4–5

LR and his band in the Netherlands, c. 1972: © Retna/Photoshot; LR onstage, 1974: photo © Michael Zagaris/Handtint © Kristin Sundbom; LR and Rachel, CBGB, New York, August 1976: © Bob Gruen/ www. bobgruen.com; LR onstage, Amsterdam, September 20, 1973: Gijsbert Hanekroot/Redferns/Getty Images.

Pages 6–7

LR backstage at the Austin Opry House, April 9, 1978: copyright 1978 Scott Newton; LR marries Sylvia Morales, February 1980: photos all courtesy Corky Stasiak; LR and Robert Quine performing at the Beacon Theater, New York, October 18, 1984: Ebet Roberts/ Redferns/Getty Images; LR and his band onstage, the Bottom Line, New York, 1979: Chuck Hammer personal archive.

Page 8

John Cale and LR, Montana Studios, New York, December 1988: Marilyn K. Yee/New York Times Co/Getty Images; LR and Laurie Anderson, Turin, July 10, 2002: © Guido Harari/Contrasto/eyevine; LR, West Village, New York, June 6, 2013: © Tom Meinelt/Splash News/Corbis; Laurie Anderson and LR at the Mermaid Parade, Coney Island, New York, June 19, 2010: ©Wenn Ltd/Alamy.

INDEX

HOWARD SOUNES is known for writing detailed and revelatory biographies of the musicians Bob Dylan (*Down the Highway*) and Paul McCartney (*Fab*) as well as other extraordinary personalities: the murderers Fred and Rosemary West (*Fred & Rose*) and the American poet Charles Bukowski (*Locked in the Arms of a Crazy Life*). Each book is based on extensive original research. For more information visit www.howardsounes.com.